Endorsed by
University of Cambridge International Examinations

Complete
Biology
for IGCSE

Ron Pickering

D1567081

OXFORD
UNIVERSITY PRESS

OXFORD
UNIVERSITY PRESS

Great Clarendon Street Oxford OX2 6DP
Oxford University Press is a department of the University of Oxford.
It furthers the University's objective of excellence in research,
scholarship, and education by publishing worldwide in

Oxford   New York

Auckland   Cape Town   Dar es Salaam   Hong Kong   Karachi
Kuala Lumpur   Madrid   Melbourne   Mexico City   Nairobi
New Delhi   Shanghai   Taipei   Toronto

With offices in

Argentina   Austria   Brazil   Chile   Czech Republic   France   Greece
Guatemala   Hungary   Italy   Japan   Poland   Portugal   Singapore
South Korea   Switzerland   Thailand   Turkey   Ukraine   Vietnam

Oxford is a registered trade mark of Oxford University Press
in the UK and in certain other countries

British Library Cataloguing in Publication Data

Data available

ISBN: 978 0 19 915136 3

10 9 8 7 6 5 4

Printed in China by Printplus

Acknowledgements

We are grateful to our reviewers and project managers for getting *Complete Biology for IGCSE* from the
ideas stage to the finished product.

Thanks go to my wife Janet and our two sons Chris and Tom, for keeping me on the straight and
narrow, and to our badly behaved dog, Moth, for making certain I don't stick to it too religiously!
I should also like to acknowledge the part played by my Mum and Dad – reference to Section 3
will make it clear that I owe them a great deal!

Ron Pickering

The publisher would like to thank the following for their kind permission to reproduce photographs:

*13 Oxford Scientific Films, 19t,b Ron Pickering, 221,r Oxford Scientific Films, 301,r Oxford Scientific
Films, 341 Science Photo Library, 34r Art Directors &Trip, 40 no credit, 49 Art Directors &Trip, 50
Martyn F Chillmaid, 51 Anthony Blake Photo Library, 55t,b Still Pictures, 58 4- (montage - details to
come), 73 Holt Studios, 79 Geoscience, 86 Science -- Photo Library, 88 Oxford Scientific Films, 89 no
credit, 93 Biofotos/Heather Angel, 94t no credit, 94b Science Photo Library, 95 P234034-LM, 97t
George Blonsky/Alami, 97b National Medical - Slidebank, 98, 99, 100, 104, 105l,r Science Photo
Library, 109 Corbis UK Ltd, 110, 124 OUP, 127 Science Photo Library, 142 Getty Images, 153 no credit,
154 JLP/Jose Luis Pelaez/Zefa/Corbis, 158 Corbis Sygma, 159 Art Directors &Trip, 163t CC001678,
163b ist2-1504527, 171 Telegraph Colour Library, 172 Ron Pickering, 173 Science Photo Library, 180l
Telegraph Colour Library C John Birdsall R Associated Press, 183L Images of Africa R Courtesy
Guinness Book of Records, 185 Science Photo Library, 187 ist2-657155, 189, 190 Holt Studios, 193t
Science Photo Library, 193b, 194 Holt Studios, 200 Tony Stone/Getty Images, 201, 208, 209L Science
Photo Library, 209R National Medical Slidebank, 218 Tony Stone Images, 219ll Bridgeman Art Library,
219l ml, mr, lr, 222, 225, 226 Science Photo Library, 230, 231 OUP, 237 John Walmsley, 238 Ron
Pickering, 244 OUP, 254 42-15785175,26142-16884682, 263 OUP, 278 42-16677430ï*

The illustrations are by:
Barking Dog Art, Julian Baker, Jeff Edwards, Fakenham Photosetting, Ian Foulis and Associates,
Roger Gorringe, Nick Hawken, ODI, David Pattinson, Halli Marie Verrinder and Q2A.

Introduction

Biology is the study of life and living organisms. During the past few hundred years biology has changed from concentrating on the **structure** of living organisms (often by examining dead specimens!) to looking more at how they work or **function**. Over this time we have discovered much about health and disease, about the interactions of different organisms making up food chains, about the genes which control the activities of our bodies and how humans can control the lives of other organisms. These advances in biological knowledge raise new issues, however. We need to understand how our activities affect the environment, how humans can take responsibility for their own health and welfare and how we must be careful to make appropriate rules for the use of our genetic information.

In *Complete Biology for IGCSE* you will be studying a range of living organisms, the life processes they carry out, the effects that these life processes might have on our health, and the responsibilities which we have towards other organisms. This will help you to understand, and perhaps contribute to, the accelerating biological revolution which will increasingly affect the lives of all of us.

This book has been organised to help you to find information quickly and easily. It is written in two-page units or 'spreads'. Each unit is a topic which forms part of the IGCSE Biology Syllabus, and the 'spreads' are collected into the four major sections of the syllabus. Your teacher will be able to help you to relate the units to the sections of your syllabus.

Each person has their own way of working, but the following tips might help you to get the most from this book:

- Use the **contents** page – this will provide information on large topics, such as reflexes or water pollution.
- Use the **index** – this will allow you to use a single word such as 'neurone' or 'eutrophication' to direct you to pages where you can find out more about that word.
- Use the **questions** – this is the best way of checking whether you have learned and understood the material on each spread. Questions are to be found on most spreads and within or at the end of each section. Harder questions are identified by the icon ☐. The longer examination-style questions would be the equivalent of IGCSE standard.

I hope that you enjoy using this book, and that it helps you to understand the world of biology. You, like every other living organism, are a part of this world – perhaps one day you will find yourself working to help others to understand more about it.

Ron Pickering
June 2006

Contents

1·1 Biology is the study of life and living organisms

Objectives
- To understand that living things differ from non-living things
- To be able to list the characteristics of living things
- To understand that energy must be expended to maintain life

The dawn of life
Scientists believe that the Earth was formed from an enormous cloud of gases about 5 billion years ago. Atmospheric conditions were harsh (there was no molecular oxygen, for example), the environment was very unstable, and conditions were unsuitable for life as we know it.

Many scientists believe that the first and simplest living organisms appeared on Earth about 2.8 billion years ago. These organisms probably fed on molecules in a sort of 'soup' (called the **primordial soup**) which made up some of the shallow seas on the Earth at that time. A question that has always intrigued scientists, philosophers and religious leaders is:

> What distinguishes these first living organisms from the molecules in the primordial soup?

In other words, what is life?

Characteristics of living organisms
You know that a horse is alive, but a steel girder is not. However, it is not always so obvious whether something is alive or not – is a dried-out seed or a virus particle living or non-living? To try to answer questions like this, biologists use a list of characteristics that living organisms show.

Living organisms:
- **Respire**
- show **Irritability** (sensitivity to their environment) and **movement**
- **Nourish** themselves
- **Grow** and **develop**
- **Excrete**
- **Reproduce**.

The opposite page gives more detail of the characteristics of life.

You may see other similar lists of these characteristics using slightly different words. You can remember this particular list using the word **RINGER**. It gives **Ringer's solution** its name. This is a solution of ions and molecules that physiologists use to keep living tissues in – it keeps the cells alive.

As well as the characteristics in the 'ringer' list, living things have a **complex organisation** that is not found in the non-living world. A snowflake or a crystal of quartz is an organised collection of identical molecules, but even the simplest living cell contains many different complex substances arranged in very specific structures.

Living things also show **variation** – the offspring are often different from one another and from their parents. This is important in adaptation to the environment and in the process of **evolution**.

How the characteristics of life depend on each other
Each of the characteristics of life is linked to the others – for example, organisms can only grow if they are nourished. As they take nourishment from their environment, they may also produce waste materials which they must then excrete. To respond to the environment they must organise their cells and tissues to carry out actions. Because of the random nature of reproduction, they are likely to show variation from generation to generation.

Depending on energy
The organisation in living things and their ability to carry out their life processes depends on a supply of **energy**. Many biologists today define life as a set of processes that result from the organisation of matter and which depend on the expenditure of energy. In this book we shall see:
- how energy is liberated from food molecules and trapped in a usable form
- how molecules are organised into the structures of living organisms
- how living organisms use energy to drive their life processes.

Respiration is the process by which living cells release energy from organic molecules. The form of respiration that releases the most energy uses oxygen. Many organisms have **gaseous exchange** systems that supply their cells with oxygen from their environment.

Irritability (or **sensitivity**) is the ability to detect changes in the environment either inside or outside the organism, and to respond to them. These responses often involve movement.

Nutrition supplies an organism with the food it needs for respiration, growth, repair and reproduction. Plants make their foods using the process of photosynthesis, whilst animals obtain their foods 'ready-made' by eating them.

Growth and **development** are the processes by which an organism changes in size and in form. For example, as a young animal increases in size (as it grows), the relative sizes of its body parts change (it develops).

Excretion removes the waste products of processes such as respiration and nutrition from the organism's body.

Reproduction is the generation of offspring – new individuals. An organism may simply split into two, or reproduction may be a more complex process involving fertilisation. Reproduction makes new organisms of the same species as the parents. This depends on a set of chemical plans (the genetic information). contained within each living organism.

1 Approximately how many years passed between the formation of the Earth and the appearance of the first living organisms?

2 What sort of molecules do you think might have been present in the primordial soup?

3 **RINGER** is a word that helps people remember the characteristics of living organisms. Think of your own word to help you remember these characteristics.

4 Suggest *two* ways in which reproduction is essential to living organisms.

Characteristics and classification of living organisms

7

1·2 The variety of life

Objectives

- To appreciate why classification is necessary
- To understand the use of a key
- To be able to name the five kingdoms, and describe their distinguishing characteristics
- To understand the hierarchy of classification
- To know why a binomial system of nomenclature is valuable

put all living organisms into categories. The science of placing organisms into categories on the basis of their observable characteristics is called **classification**. There are so many different types of living organism (i.e. an enormous **variety of life**) that the study of these organisms would be impossible without an ordered way of describing them.

The need to classify living things

Variation and natural selection lead to evolution. Evolution, and the isolation of populations, leads to the development of new species (see page 220). Each species has different characteristics, and some of these characteristics can be inherited by successive generations of this species. Observing these inherited characteristics allows scientists to

Classification keys

Taxonomists (people who study classification) place organisms into groups by asking questions about their characteristics, such as 'Does the organism photosynthesise?' or 'Does the organism contain many cells?'. A series of questions like this is called a **classification key**. Examples of such keys are shown below.

This kind of key, with only two answers to each question (in this case, YES or NO), is called a dichotomous key ('dichotomous' means branching). It can be written as a branching or spider key, using the same questions:

The five kingdoms
Bacteria
Protoctistans
Plants
Fungi
Animals

Branching keys are easy to use, but take up a lot of space when fully drawn out. For this reason the listed form of a dichotomous key is usually used for identification of organisms outside the laboratory.

		YES	
1	Does the organism have cells with a definite nucleus?	YES	Go to question 2
		NO	It is a bacterium
2	Is the organism made up of many different cells?	YES	Go to question 3
		NO	It is a protoctistan
3	Is the organism a heterotroph?	YES	Go to question 4
		NO	It is a plant
4	Does the organism have cell walls and does it feed by external digestion?	YES	It is a fungus
		NO	It is an animal

A key may be used to place an organism in one of the five kingdoms.

Five Kingdoms

Using the key opposite, it is possible to place any living organism into one of five very large groups. These groups, distinguished from one another by major and obvious characteristics, are called the **five Kingdoms**. Each of these kingdoms contains an enormous number of different species, and keys can be used within a kingdom to place any individual species into further groups. The diagram below shows the names of these groups, and how the lion is classified within the Animal Kingdom. The sequence of kingdom, **phylum, class, order, family, genus** and **species** is called a **hierarchy of classification**.

Notice that each classification group is given a name. Lions belong to the class Mammalia and the order Carnivora, for example. The final two group names are written in *italics* – this is a worldwide convention amongst scientists. The lion is called simba in Swahili, león in Spanish and leu in Romanian but is known as *Panthera leo* to scientists in each of these countries. This convention of giving organisms a two-part name made up of their genus and species was introduced by the Swedish biologist Carolus Linnaeus. He gave every organism known to science a two-part name based entirely on the body structure of the organism. This **binomial system of nomenclature** is still in use today (binomial = 'two name'). New species today may be given names based on characteristics such as chromosome number or gene sequence, which Linnaeus knew nothing about.

The pages that follow describe the characteristics that distinguish living organisms in some of the most important phyla and classes.

On moving down the hierarchy of groups, note that there are ...

More similarities and **fewer differences** between the members

Kingdom (Animalia)

Phylum (Chordata) — Other phyla

Class (Mammalia) — Other classes

Order (Carnivora) — Other orders

Family (Felidae) — Other families

Genus (*Panthera*) — Other genera

Species *Panthera leo* — Other species

Look! An ingestive heterotroph with a backbone, carnassial teeth, retractable claws which is about to...

Rrooaaarrrr!

All animals are ingestive heterotrophs.

All chordates have a notochord (becomes the backbone).

All mammals have fur and mammary glands.

All carnivores have well developed carnassial (flesh-cutting) teeth.

All Felidae have retractable claws.

All *Panthera* (big cats) can roar but cannot purr.

All lions can mate and produce fertile offspring with other lions. The English scientist John Ray used this feature to define the term 'species'.

The hierarchical classification of the lion

1 The scientific names for the weasel and mink are *Mustela nivalis* and *Mustela vison*, respectively. Both of these animals belong to the order Carnivora, as do the fox (*Vulpes vulpes*) and otter (*Lutra lutra*). The otter, mink and weasel all belong to the family Mustelidae.

   a Which feature must they have in common to belong to the order Carnivora?

   b Which two animals are most closely related?

   c Which animal is the most different from the other three?

   d Suggest one feature that places all of these organisms in the Animal Kingdom.

2 The scientific name for the human is *Homo sapiens*. Try to find out the meaning of this name.

1·3 Bacteria and viruses

Objectives

- To know the structure of a typical bacterial cell and a typical virus
- To know the requirements for bacterial growth
- To know how bacteria reproduce
- To understand some of the ways in which bacteria and viruses affect human activities
- To understand why viruses do not fit into the five kingdoms of living organisms

Bacterial structure

Bacteria (singular: bacterium) are single-celled organisms that **have no true nucleus**. Bacterial cells do not contain organelles like those found in typical animal and plant cells (see page 23), but are able to carry out all of their life processes without them. A few can photosynthesise, but most feed off other organisms. They may be **parasites**, feeding off living organisms, or **saprotrophs**, feeding off dead organisms.

Bacteria are very small, usually about 1–2 μm in length, and so are only visible using a high-powered microscope. The structure of a typical bacterium is shown in the diagram below.

Bacteria exist in a number of different shapes, some of which are shown below. Shape can be used to classify bacteria.

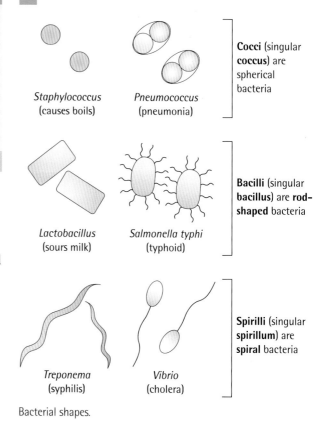

Cocci (singular **coccus**) are spherical bacteria

Staphylococcus (causes boils)
Pneumococcus (pneumonia)

Bacilli (singular **bacillus**) are rod-shaped bacteria

Lactobacillus (sours milk)
Salmonella typhi (typhoid)

Spirilli (singular **spirillum**) are **spiral** bacteria

Treponema (syphilis)
Vibrio (cholera)

Bacterial shapes.

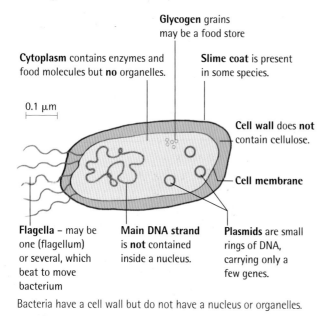

Glycogen grains may be a food store

Cytoplasm contains enzymes and food molecules but **no** organelles.

Slime coat is present in some species.

0.1 μm

Cell wall does **not** contain cellulose.

Cell membrane

Flagella – may be one (flagellum) or several, which beat to move bacterium

Main DNA strand is **not** contained inside a nucleus.

Plasmids are small rings of DNA, carrying only a few genes.

Bacteria have a cell wall but do not have a nucleus or organelles.

Requirements of bacteria

Bacteria have certain requirements that their environment must provide. An understanding of these requirements (see page 272) has been important in biotechnology and in the control of disease. If the environment supplies these needs, the bacteria can multiply rapidly by **binary fission** (see page 164). In this process each bacterium divides into two, then each of the two divides again and so on, until very large populations are built up. A bacterial colony can quickly dominate its environment, making great demands on food and oxygen and perhaps producing large quantities of waste materials.

The **generation time** (time taken for each cell to divide into two) can be as little as 20 minutes under ideal conditions. One *E. coli* cell in the human gut could **theoretically** become 2^{72} cells in 24 hours – this number of cells weighs about 8000 kg!

The importance of bacteria

Bacteria are important to humans in many ways.

- Some are **pathogenic** – they cause disease (see page 258). All pathogenic bacteria are parasites.
- Some are involved in **nutrient cycles** (see pages 240–3).
- Some are exploited by humans in **food production** and in **biotechnology** (see page 48).

Bacteria are probably the organisms that carry out the largest number of different activities, and are the most numerous organisms on Earth. There may be as many as 5000 undiscovered bacterial species in 1 m^3 of woodland soil, and more bacteria live on or in your body than all of the humans that ever existed!

Viruses

When the five-kingdom system of classification was devised, no one was able to find a place for the group of organisms called the **viruses**. This is because viruses do not show the typical features of living things – respiration, nutrition and reproduction, for example – unless they are inside the cells of another living organism. In other words, all viruses are parasites and therefore cause harm to their host. Some taxonomists have suggested that viruses belong in a sixth kingdom. There is great variation in the structure of viruses, but they all have certain common features. The structure of a typical virus is shown below.

Most viruses cause disease – they may infect humans, domestic animals or plants.

Virus and bacteria compared

	Virus	Bacteria
Covered by	Protein coat	Cell wall
Cell membrane	No	Yes
Cytoplasm	No	Yes
Genetic material	DNA or RNA – only a few genes	DNA – enough for several hundred genes
Living or non-living?	Non-living unless in host	Living

Viruses and bacteria also differ in the method of nutrition: *all* viruses are parasitic, but some bacteria feed as parasites, some as photosynthesisers and some feed like animals (as heterotrophs).

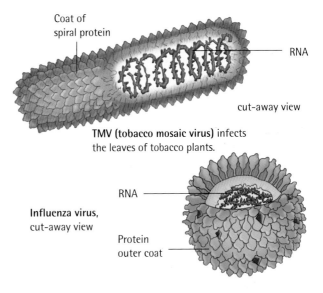

Coat of spiral protein

RNA

cut-away view

TMV (tobacco mosaic virus) infects the leaves of tobacco plants.

RNA

Influenza virus, cut-away view

Protein outer coat

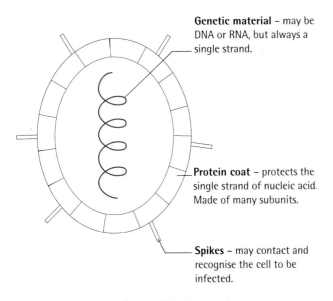

Genetic material – may be DNA or RNA, but always a single strand.

Protein coat – protects the single strand of nucleic acid. Made of many subunits.

Spikes – may contact and recognise the cell to be infected.

A typical virus has genetic material and a protein coat, but cannot carry out its life processes. It has no cytoplasm.

1 Look at the diagram of bacterial shapes. Make a dichotomous key that would enable a biologist to distinguish the different bacterial types on the basis of their structure.

2 Make a table to show which of the following structures are present in:
a an animal cell **b** a plant cell **c** a bacterial cell.
Write + if the structure is present and − if it is absent.
Cell wall, slime capsule, cell membrane, nucleus, chloroplast, mitochondrion, DNA, cytoplasm

3 Why is it difficult to classify viruses into one of the five kingdoms of living organisms?

4 If ten bacteria landed on a bowl of soup, and reproduced every 30 minutes, how many would be present after 5 hours?

1·4 Fungi

Fungal cells have a common structure

The fungi are a very large group of organisms. They range in size from single-celled yeasts to enormous fungi whose underground parts may occupy an area greater than a football or hockey field.

Fungal cells have a cell wall made of a mixture of substances including **chitin**. The cytoplasm contains many organelles, since the fungus manufactures digestive enzymes. It feeds by **saprotrophic** ('dead-feeding') **nutrition**, as illustrated below.

Reproduction in fungi

Single-celled yeasts reproduce asexually by binary fission (see page 164), but all other fungi reproduce by the production of **spores**, as shown above right.

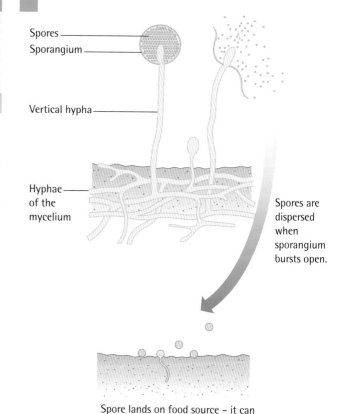

Spores

Sporangium

Vertical hypha

Hyphae of the mycelium

Spores are dispersed when sporangium bursts open.

Spore lands on food source – it can germinate and a new mycelium can develop.

Spore formation in a pin mould fungus

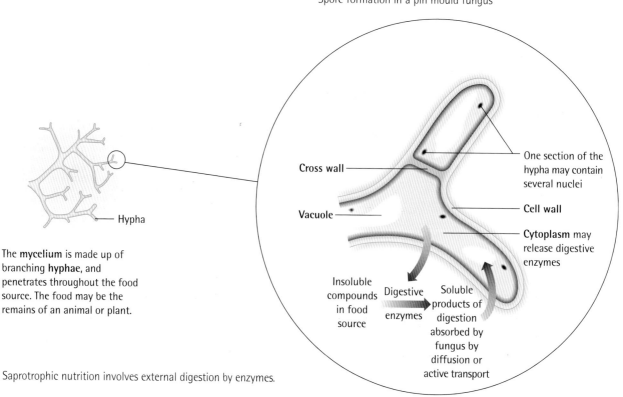

The **mycelium** is made up of branching **hyphae**, and penetrates throughout the food source. The food may be the remains of an animal or plant.

Hypha

Cross wall

Vacuole

One section of the hypha may contain several nuclei

Cell wall

Cytoplasm may release digestive enzymes

Insoluble compounds in food source

Digestive enzymes

Soluble products of digestion absorbed by fungus by diffusion or active transport

Saprotrophic nutrition involves external digestion by enzymes.

Characteristics and classification of living organisms

Requirements of fungi

Fungi have very similar requirements to those of bacteria, that is:

- a moist environment, so that they can absorb the soluble products of digestion of their food source in solution
- a warm environment, so that enzymes can work at their optimum temperature
- a nutrient source to provide the raw materials and energy required for growth
- Fungi do not require light since they do not rely on photosynthesis for the production of food compounds. This means that fungi are rarely found in light environments, since such environments are usually too warm and dry for fungal growth.

Parasitic fungi

Fungi may also feed by parasitic methods. These fungi produce digestive enzymes, but only once they have killed the host and can no longer obtain soluble foods directly from its tissues. An example of a parasitic fungus is shown right.

The importance of fungi

Fungi have a number of effects on the lives of humans, for example:

- They are **decomposers**, and play a vital role in **nutrient cycles** (see page 240).
- Their decomposing action may destroy materials. Wooden buildings, in particular, are at risk from wet and dry rot.
- Mould fungi consume food which might otherwise be eaten by humans.
- Fungi may be agents of disease, as in athlete's foot for example.
- They may themselves be a source of food, for example mushrooms.
- Fungi are used in biotechnology – the brewing and baking industries (see page 50) are entirely dependent on the activities of yeast, for example.

Single cell of a fungus such as yeast

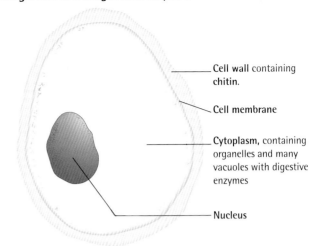

Cell wall containing chitin.

Cell membrane

Cytoplasm, containing organelles and many vacuoles with digestive enzymes

Nucleus

Yeast is a single-celled fungus.

Parasitic fungus

Feeding mycelium penetrates to vascular bundles of the host tree.

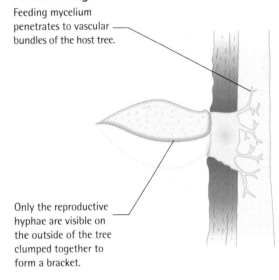

Only the reproductive hyphae are visible on the outside of the tree clumped together to form a bracket.

The best of both worlds! A bracket fungus eventually weakens and kills its host. It then feeds as a saprotroph on the **dead remains** of the tree.

---

1 Suggest why toadstools are likely to be found in dark areas of woodland where green plants are very limited.

2 Some fungi are saprotrophs, and secrete enzymes onto their food source. Suggest three such enzymes and name their substrates and products.

3 List, with examples, four ways in which fungi affect the lives of humans.

1.5 Plants

Objectives

▢ To recall that all plants are autotrophs, and are able to absorb light energy to drive photosynthesis

▢ To understand some of the steps in the adaptation of plants to life on dry land

▢ To recall the characteristics of the four main plant groups

Plants are autotrophs

As **autotrophs**, plants manufacture food molecules from simple, inorganic sources by the process of photosynthesis using light as a source of energy. Plants all **contain the light-absorbing pigment chlorophyll** (or similar molecules which perform the same function) inside cells which **have a definite cellulose cell wall.**

Adaptations to life on land

The first plants lived in water, but as living organisms evolved, plant forms developed that could live on land. The classification of plants into groups follows this sequence of evolution.

The Plant Kingdom may be divided into four main groups (phyla): **algae, mosses, ferns** and **seed plants.**

Seed plants

Algae, mosses and ferns all depend to some extent on a moist environment, especially for the transfer of gametes. The seed plants have proper roots, stems, leaves, vascular tissues and waterproof coverings, and **their gametes can be transferred without a film of moisture.** As a result the seed plants are able to live and reproduce in dry environments.

The two groups of plants that dominate our fields, woods and gardens are the **conifers** (cone bearers) and the **angiosperms** (flowering plants).

Conifers

The **conifers** dominate the landscape in colder climates where flowering plants cannot compete. Conifers have needle-like leaves with a very thick cuticle which prevents water loss (it is very difficult

Fungus or plant?

	Fungus	Plant
Nucleus in cell	Yes	Yes
Cell wall	Yes, but not made of cellulose	Yes, made of cellulose
Movement	No	No
Chlorophyll present	No	Yes
Method of nutrition	As saprotroph or parasite	By photosynthesis

to absorb water from cold soil). They do not rely on insects for pollination (flying insects are uncommon in cold areas) – conifers reproduce using structures called **cones.**

Angiosperms

The angiosperms or flowering plants are the most successful of plants – they have evolved into many species and have colonised almost every available habitat. More than 80% of all plants are angiosperms (plants with enclosed seeds). Many features of the lives of flowering plants are covered elsewhere in this book (see pages 60–73, 86–93, 160 and 186–199, for example). The diagram at the top of the opposite page summarises these features, and emphasises the adaptations of flowering plants to a successful life on land, including warmer habitats.

Two groups of angiosperms

There are two major subgroups within the angiosperms. In one group there is a single cotyledon in the seed (see page 195) – these are the **monocotyledons.** In the other group there are two cotyledons – these are the **dicotyledons.** There are other differences between monocotyledons and dicotyledons, as shown in the diagram on the next page.

Angiosperm adaptations

Growth, particularly of reproductive structures, can be very rapid. For example, pollination, pollen tube formation and fertilisation may take only one hour (compared with one year in some conifers), and some bamboos can grow 1m per day.

Flowers – the colour, pattern, shape, scent or nectar of the flower may attract insects, birds or mammals. These animals transfer pollen from male to female flower parts much more efficiently than wind or water.

Large **leaf surface** allows high rate of photosynthesis to supply energy for growth and fruit production. However, water losses by evaporation and diffusion through stomata are high.

Xylem vessels have no end walls and conduct water efficiently.

Roots form beneficial associations with other organisms. For example, legumes such as peas and beans form root nodules with nitrogen-fixing *Rhizobium* bacteria. See page 242.

The **ovary** protects the ovules and developing embryo, particularly from drying out. ('Angiosperm' means 'enclosed seed')

Endosperm is a store of nutrients for the developing plant embryo. It does not develop until after fertilisation so that food stores are not wasted, as they might be in conifers.

Fruits are formed from ripened ovaries. Their specialised shapes, colours, smells and textures aid seed dispersal by wind, water and animals.

Stomata with guard cells regulate loss of water vapour and exchange of oxygen and carbon dioxide between plant and atmosphere

Waterproof **cuticle** reduces water loss to atmosphere

Vascular system transports water, ions and organic solutes

Specialised **supporting tissues** (air has a low density and does not offer support as water does)

Extensive root systems anchor the shoot systems and absorb water and ions

Monocotyledons and dicotyledons – two groups of angiosperms (flowering plants)

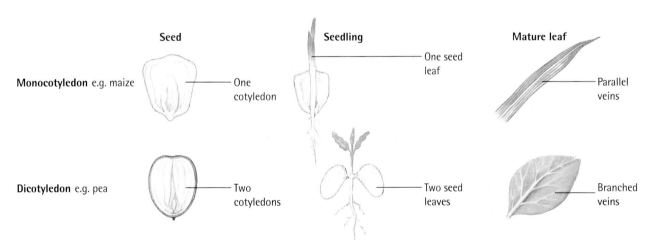

	Seed	Seedling	Mature leaf
Monocotyledon e.g. maize	One cotyledon	One seed leaf	Parallel veins
Dicotyledon e.g. pea	Two cotyledons	Two seed leaves	Branched veins

1 Name the four different plant groups. Why are algae confined to water, whilst ferns are well adapted to life on land?

2 Seed plants are well adapted to live and to reproduce in dry environments. What major adaptation allows reproduction on dry land?

Characteristics and classification of living organisms

15

1·6 Invertebrate animals

Objectives

- To know the difference between a vertebrate animal and an invertebrate animal
- To be able to describe the main characteristics of four invertebrate groups – annelids, nematodes, molluscs and arthropods
- To be able to distinguish between different classes of arthropods
- To understand the importance of metamorphosis in insects

Vertebrates and invertebrates

All animals share one characteristic – **they feed on organic molecules** (see page 76). Members of the Animal Kingdom can be divided into two large groups based on whether they have a backbone as part of a bony skeleton. Animals with a backbone are called **vertebrates** and those without a backbone are called **invertebrates**.

Four groups of invertebrates are described here:

Nematodes

Hookworms are nematodes with bodies that are specialised for feeding and reproducing; often they are parasites inside the gut of another animal.

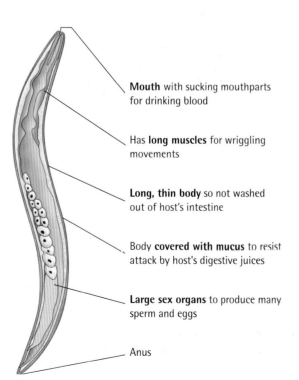

- **Mouth** with sucking mouthparts for drinking blood
- Has **long muscles** for wriggling movements
- **Long, thin body** so not washed out of host's intestine
- Body **covered with mucus** to resist attack by host's digestive juices
- **Large sex organs** to produce many sperm and eggs
- Anus

Annelids

Annelids such as the earthworm have a long segmented body and chaetae.

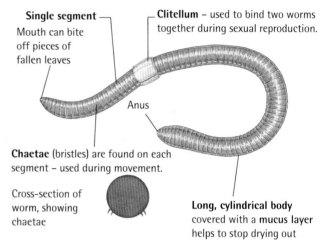

Single segment
Mouth can bite off pieces of fallen leaves

Clitellum – used to bind two worms together during sexual reproduction.

Anus

Chaetae (bristles) are found on each segment – used during movement.

Cross-section of worm, showing chaetae

Long, cylindrical body covered with a **mucus layer** helps to stop drying out

Molluscs

Molluscs have a hard shell protecting a soft body with no limbs.

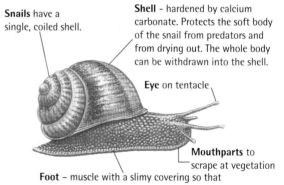

Snails have a single, coiled shell.

Shell - hardened by calcium carbonate. Protects the soft body of the snail from predators and from drying out. The whole body can be withdrawn into the shell.

Eye on tentacle

Mouthparts to scrape at vegetation

Foot – muscle with a slimy covering so that snail can move by creeping over the surface.

Arachnids are arthropods with four pairs of legs and no wings.

Annelid, nematode or mollusc?

	Annelid	Nematode	Mollusc
Body covering	Hard, slightly waterproof	Soft, not waterproof	Soft – shell helps to save water
Segments visible	Yes	No	No
Movement	Uses chaetae (bristles) to move from place to place	Wriggles but lives in one place	Creeps on foot from place to place
Feeding method	Herbivores	Mainly parasites	Mainly herbivores – some carnivores

Arthropods

The arthropods are the most numerous of all animals, both in terms of the number of different species and the number of individuals in any one species. The insects are arthropods that show an interesting adaptation in their life cycle called **metamorphosis** that allows them to use the resources of their habitat to the maximum.

Apart from insects, the arthropod phylum includes three other classes:

Crustacea

Crabs are slightly unusual because many of their segments are tucked under their body.

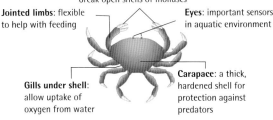

Hardened, serrated edge to claw: can hold onto slippery food, and break open shells of molluscs

Jointed limbs: flexible to help with feeding

Eyes: important sensors in aquatic environment

Gills under shell: allow uptake of oxygen from water

Carapace: a thick, hardened shell for protection against predators

Myriapods

Antennae: these are important sense organs in the millipedes' dark, damp environment. They can 'sense' chemicals and the level of moisture in the environment

Many body segments: body is flexible for movement and wriggling around and under leaves and stones

Mouthparts: these are modified legs! Have hard edges for biting vegetation (millipedes) or other animals (centipedes)

Hard exoskeleton: protection against predators

Walking legs: have many joints and internal muscles, and allow movement over rough surfaces

Body covering: waterproof, helping animal to live on land

Insects

e.g. housefly, mosquito (page 274)

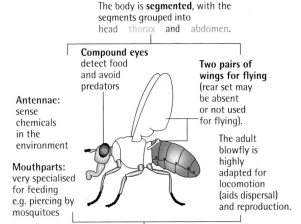

The body is **segmented**, with the segments grouped into head thorax and abdomen.

Compound eyes detect food and avoid predators

Antennae: sense chemicals in the environment

Mouthparts: very specialised for feeding e.g. piercing by mosquitoes

Two pairs of wings for flying (rear set may be absent or not used for flying).

The adult blowfly is highly adapted for locomotion (aids dispersal) and reproduction.

Three pairs of legs, attached to the thorax. Allow walking movements, over food or to avoid predators.

Metamorphosis (means 'change of body form') allows different stages which:
- do not compete for the same food sources
- can be highly specialised for different functions. The **larva** is adapted for **feeding** and **growth**, and the **adult** for **locomotion** and **reproduction**.

Arachnids

Head and thorax are combined into one body part, the **cephalothorax.**

Simple eyes (but more than one pair) help to detect prey

Four pairs of legs attached towards the rear of the cephalothorax. Allow chasing prey or holding onto web

Abdomen

Spinneret which produces long, thin strands of silk. (The word arachnid comes from the Greek goddess Arachne who was skilled at spinning.)

Powerful, piercing **jaws** – all spiders are predators

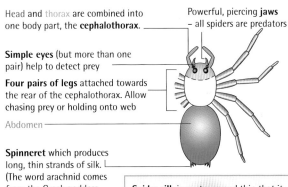

Spider silk is so strong and thin that it has been used to make the cross hairs in the telescopic sights of rifles.

---

1 Copy and complete the following paragraph.
   All animals have one common characteristic – _____. The invertebrates are animals that do not have _____. Examples of important invertebrate groups are _____, which are very clearly segmented with bristles called _____ to aid in movement; _____, which have a soft body inside one or two hard shells; and _____, which are the most numerous of all.

2 The arthropods include four classes – insects, arachnids, crustaceans and myriapods.
   a List three features that all of these classes possess.
   b List three features that only insects possess.
   c Compare insects and spiders under the headings 'Number of legs', 'Number of body sections', 'Number of wings' and 'Type of eyes'.

3 Insects are the most abundant of all animals on land. Many of them show an adaptation called complete metamorphosis. What does this term mean, and how does it help to explain why there are so many insect species?

1.7 Vertebrate animals: five classes

Objectives

- To know the characteristics of the vertebrates
- To understand how different classes of vertebrates show increasing adaptation to dry land
- To know the five classes of vertebrate, and to provide examples of each

If asked to name an animal, most people would probably name a mammal because these are the most familiar animals to us. Mammals are just one class of the phylum **Chordata**. The chordates are often called the **vertebrates**, although strictly speaking there are a few chordates that aren't vertebrates. Vertebrates have a hard, usually bony, internal skeleton with a backbone. The backbone is made up of separate bones called **vertebrae** which allow these animals to move with great ease.

There are five classes of vertebrates, which, like the members of the Plant Kingdom, show gradual adaptations to life on land. The classes are **fish**, **amphibians**, **reptiles**, **birds** and **mammals**.

Fish

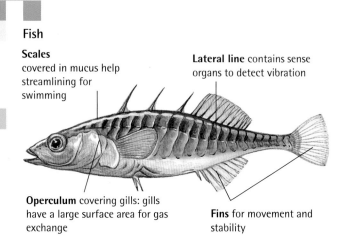

Scales covered in mucus help streamlining for swimming

Lateral line contains sense organs to detect vibration

Operculum covering gills: gills have a large surface area for gas exchange

Fins for movement and stability

Amphibians

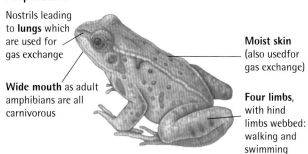

Nostrils leading to **lungs** which are used for gas exchange

Wide mouth as adult amphibians are all carnivorous

Moist skin (also used for gas exchange)

Four limbs, with hind limbs webbed: walking and swimming

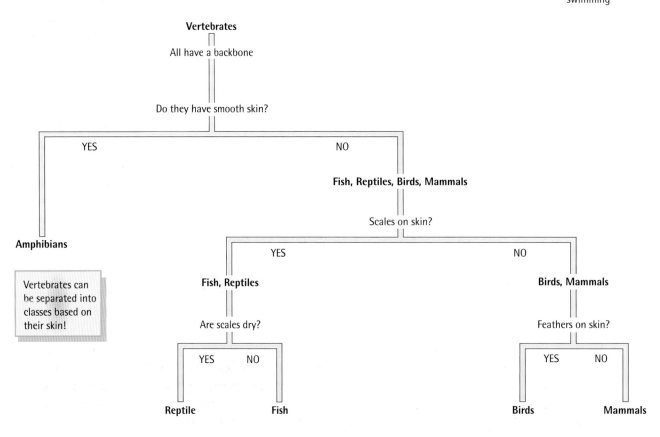

Vertebrates

All have a backbone

Do they have smooth skin?

YES — **Amphibians**

NO — **Fish, Reptiles, Birds, Mammals**

Scales on skin?

YES — **Fish, Reptiles**

Are scales dry?

YES — **Reptile**   NO — **Fish**

NO — **Birds, Mammals**

Feathers on skin?

YES — **Birds**   NO — **Mammals**

> Vertebrates can be separated into classes based on their skin!

Characteristics and classification of living organisms

Reptiles

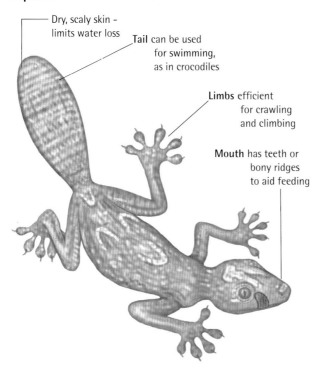

- Dry, scaly skin – limits water loss
- **Tail** can be used for swimming, as in crocodiles
- **Limbs** efficient for crawling and climbing
- **Mouth** has teeth or bony ridges to aid feeding

The crocodile has the typical dry scaly skin of reptiles, and the eyes on the top of its head and its sharp, pointed teeth adapt it for catching prey in water.

Birds

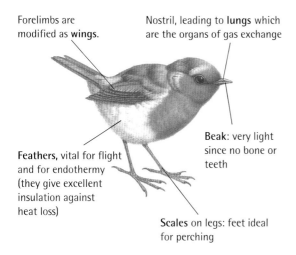

- Forelimbs are modified as **wings**.
- Nostril, leading to **lungs** which are the organs of gas exchange
- **Beak**: very light since no bone or teeth
- **Feathers**, vital for flight and for endothermy (they give excellent insulation against heat loss)
- **Scales** on legs: feet ideal for perching

The heron has typical bird features of feathers and a beak. It is well adapted to capture fish and frogs as it has large eyes to spot its prey, a long pointed beak to grab its prey and large feet for walking over soft, muddy ground.

Mammals

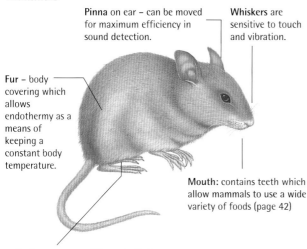

- **Pinna** on ear – can be moved for maximum efficiency in sound detection.
- **Whiskers** are sensitive to touch and vibration.
- **Fur** – body covering which allows endothermy as a means of keeping a constant body temperature.
- **Mouth**: contains teeth which allow mammals to use a wide variety of foods (page 42)
- **Penis** – an organ of the male that enables efficient internal fertilisation.

Mammals are endothermic vertebrates that have the characteristics shown in the diagram below.

A wide range of adaptations has allowed mammals to colonise many habitats as diverse as the polar wastes and the Arabian desert.

Humans are mammals

Humans show the typical mammalian characteristics of hair, mammary glands and a diaphragm, for example. Humans, though, are unique amongst all animals in that the adaptations they show allow them to modify their environment so that it is suitable for human occupation. As a result humans have been able to live and work in many habitats – no animal has a wider range. Human adaptation has allowed advanced development of the brain, and of all the complex activities that the brain can coordinate. The human brain is extremely sensitive to changes in temperature. Human adaptations include many that are concerned with the fine regulation of blood temperature (see page 130). Other features that make humans very special mammals include an upright posture, freeing the hands for complex movements including the use of tools.

Characteristics and classification of living organisms

Questions on characteristics and classification

1 South Uist is a small island which provides one of the few remaining summer habitats for a bird called the Corncrake *(Crex crex)*. It lives in grass fields, which are cut in the late summer for hay, where it feeds on insects, worms and seeds. South Uist provides a good habitat because there are plenty of grass fields where the Corncrake can nest and there are few predators.

However, a small mammal called the Hedgehog *(Erinaceus europaeus)* was released onto the island. The Hedgehog also has few natural predators and will feed on the eggs of Corncrakes, as well as on insects and worms. The number of Hedgehogs on South Uist has risen rapidly to 10 000 while Corncrakes are becoming endangered as their numbers worldwide are falling.

a State two features which birds and mammals have in common.
b State two features which distinguish birds from mammals.

(IGCSE 2004 [part])

2 Use the key to identify the five fish shown in the drawings. Write down the letter of each fish and its name.

(SEG June 1992)

Dorsal fins

Barbel

Key		
1. One dorsal fin		2
Two dorsal fins		4
2. Barbels (fleshy extensions) at corners of mouth		3
No barbels at corners of mouth	*Phoxinus phoxinus*	☐
3. Four barbels	*Barbus barbus*	☐
Six barbels	*Noemacheilus barbatulus*	☐
4. More than 10 bony rays in first dorsal fin	*Thymallus thymallus*	☐
10 or fewer bony rays in first dorsal fin	*Osmerus eperlanus*	☐

3 **a** What are you? Follow the branch points at 1, 3, 4, 8, 9 and 11 to identify yourself as a mammal.
b Name **two** additional characteristics of mammals.
c In what way are humans **special** mammals?

Keys and classification

*the FIVE KINGDOMS

A key enables identification of an organism by observation of its characteristics. Close observation allows a series of questions (the branch points in this key) to be answered, eventually leading to the organism being studied.

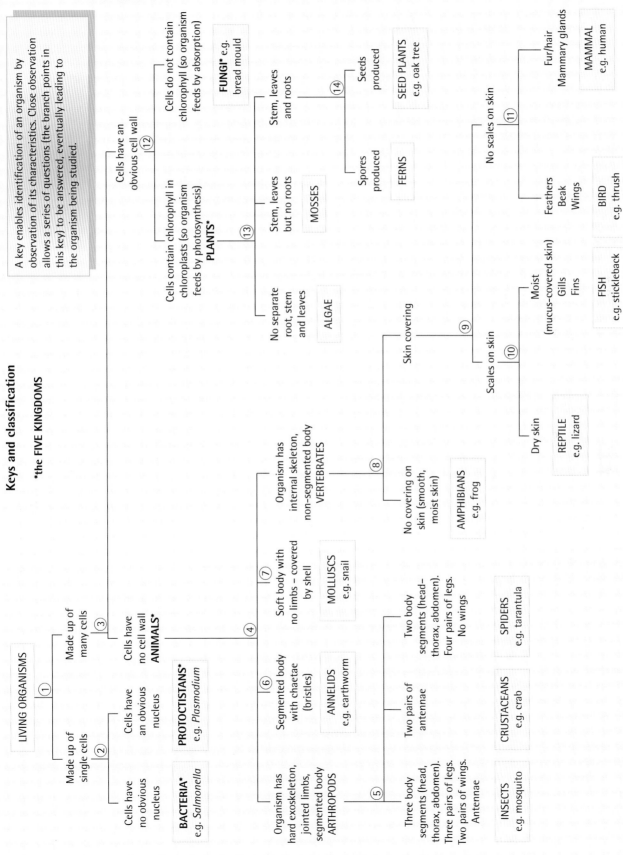

Characteristics and classification of living organisms

2·1 Organisms are made up of cells

Objectives

▶ To know that the basic unit of living organisms is the cell

▶ To know that all cells have certain features in common, but that there are differences between plant and animal cells

▶ To understand that the study of cells requires the use of a microscope

All living organisms are made up of units called **cells**. Although cells may take on very specialised functions, they have certain common features. These are shown on the opposite page. Both animal and plant cells have a **cell surface membrane**, **cytoplasm** and a **nucleus**. These three features can be seen on the photograph of a liver cell below. In addition, plant cells have a **cellulose cell wall**, a **vacuole** and may have **chloroplasts**. These features can be seen on the photograph of the palisade cell below.

A cell from the inside of the liver, viewed using a light microscope (magnified × 1500 times).

A palisade cell from a leaf, viewed using a light microscope (magnified × 500 times).

The light microscope

Cells are too small to see with the naked eye so a **microscope** is used to study them. Visible light passes through a suitable specimen, and a series of lenses magnify the image that is formed. A light microscope can give a useful magnification of about 400 times, which means the image seen is actually 400 times larger than the specimen. The contrast between different structures in the image can be improved by using dyes or stains. The nucleus of an animal cell, for example, shows up particularly well when stained with a dye called **methylene blue**, and plant cells often show up better when stained with **iodine** solution.

- Image viewed here
- Series of lenses which magnify and sharpen the image
- Specimen (living or prepared) on thin glass slide
- Source of visible light

A typical animal cell is about one-fortieth of a millimetre in diameter. This is rather a clumsy term, so scientists use smaller units: one metre (m) contains 1000 millimetres (mm), and one millimetre contains 1000 micrometres (µm). So a typical animal cell is about 25 µm in diameter.

The **size** of a structure or an organism is measured in **units of length** (such as mm or m). When a diagram is made, or a photograph taken, it may not be easy to directly show the correct size–for example, when a structure is extremely small or very large. The correct (or true) size of an organism can be calculated using a combination of actual measurement and a known magnification.

$$\text{Magnification} = \frac{\text{Measured length}}{\text{Actual length}}$$

or $$\text{Actual (true) length} = \frac{\text{Measured length}}{\text{Magnification}}$$

We can also use a **scale line** to work out magnification

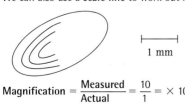

$$\text{Magnification} = \frac{\text{Measured}}{\text{Actual}} = \frac{10}{1} = \times 10$$

Calculating magnification and size

For example, look at this poppy seed.

● Mag × 50

$$\text{Actual length} = \frac{5}{50} = \frac{1}{10} = 0.1 \text{ mm}$$

Tips!

• 1 : make sure that measured and actual lengths are given in the same units

• 2 : to help remember the formula

$$\text{MAgnification} = \frac{\text{Measured}}{\text{Actual}}$$

Secretory vesicles containing cell products such as hormones or enzymes are much more common in animal cells.

Cytoplasm of animal cells is often denser, with many more organelles and dissolved substances.

Vacuoles are small and temporary. They can be involved with digestion (e.g. in phagocytes) or with excretion (contractile vacuoles may remove excess water).

Glycogen is the storage form of carbohydrates.

Animal cell features often relate to **heterotrophic nutrition** and high rates of **metabolic activity**. e.g. liver cell

The absence of the cellulose wall means that animal cells may be **very irregular in shape**. The amount of cytoplasm that can be controlled by the nucleus is limited, so that animal cells may be **quite small** – about 25 µm in diameter.

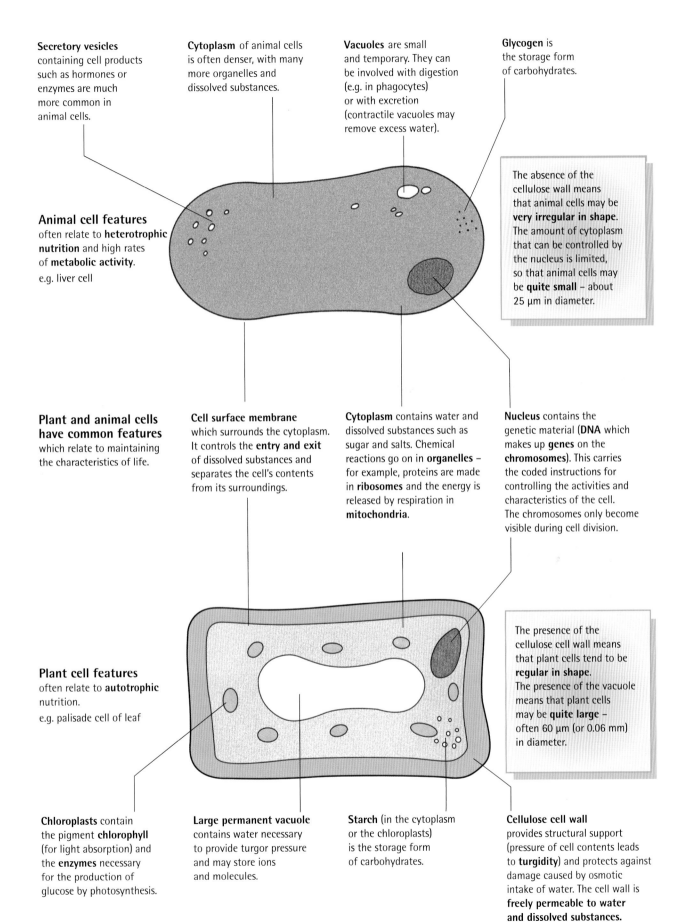

Plant and animal cells have common features which relate to maintaining the characteristics of life.

Cell surface membrane which surrounds the cytoplasm. It controls the **entry and exit** of dissolved substances and separates the cell's contents from its surroundings.

Cytoplasm contains water and dissolved substances such as sugar and salts. Chemical reactions go on in **organelles** – for example, proteins are made in **ribosomes** and the energy is released by respiration in **mitochondria**.

Nucleus contains the genetic material (**DNA** which makes up **genes** on the **chromosomes**). This carries the coded instructions for controlling the activities and characteristics of the cell. The chromosomes only become visible during cell division.

Plant cell features often relate to **autotrophic** nutrition. e.g. palisade cell of leaf

The presence of the cellulose cell wall means that plant cells tend to be **regular in shape**. The presence of the vacuole means that plant cells may be **quite large** – often 60 µm (or 0.06 mm) in diameter.

Chloroplasts contain the pigment **chlorophyll** (for light absorption) and the **enzymes** necessary for the production of glucose by photosynthesis.

Large permanent vacuole contains water necessary to provide turgor pressure and may store ions and molecules.

Starch (in the cytoplasm or the chloroplasts) is the storage form of carbohydrates.

Cellulose cell wall provides structural support (pressure of cell contents leads to **turgidity**) and protects against damage caused by osmotic intake of water. The cell wall is **freely permeable to water and dissolved substances**.

The features of plant and animal cells allow these cells to carry out the basic processes of life. The differences between plant and animal cells are due to the differences in lifestyle between animals and plants, especially to their different methods of nutrition.

2·2 The organisation of living organisms

Objectives

- To understand that the body of a living organism is a highly organised structure
- To understand that cells, tissues, organs and systems represent increasing degrees of organisation in living organisms

Specialised cells

Large organisms are **multicellular** – they are made up of many cells. Different types of cell have particular structures designed to help them carry out different tasks and functions – they have become **specialised**. Some examples of specialised cells, and their functions, are shown in the table.

Cell type	Appearance	Functions and adaptations
Animal cells		
Red blood cell (page 95)		**Transports** oxygen from the lungs to the tissues where aerobic respiration occurs. The cytoplasm is filled with the pigment haemoglobin, which carries oxygen. The cells have no nucleus, leaving more space for haemoglobin, and they are very flexible (they can be forced through even the narrowest of blood vessels).
Muscle cell (page 116)		**Contracts** so that structures can be brought closer together. Muscle cells are long, and have many protein fibres in the cytoplasm. These fibres can shorten the cell when energy is available.
Ciliated cell (page 121)		Has a layer of tiny hairs (cilia) which can **move and push mucus** from one place to another. The mucus can transport trapped dust and microbes when it is pushed by the cilia.
Motor nerve cell (page 138)		**Conducts nerve impulses.** The cell has a long fibre called an axon along which impulses travel, a fatty sheath which gives electrical insulation and a many-branched ending which can connect with many other cells.
Plant cells		
Root hair cell		**Absorbs minerals and water** from the soil water. The cell has a long extension (a root hair) which increases the surface area for the absorption of materials.
Xylem vessel		**Transports water and supports the plant.** The cell has no cytoplasm (so water can pass freely), no end wall (so that many cells can form a continuous tube) and walls strengthened with a waterproof substance called lignin.

Specialised cells combine to form tissues ...

Cells with similar structures and functions are massed together in **tissues**. Some plant and animal tissues are shown in the tables below.

Animal tissue	Main functions
Epithelium	Lines tubes such as the gut and covers surfaces such as the skin
Connective tissue	Binds and strengthens other tissues, such as tendons
Blood	Transports substances around the body, and defends against disease
Skeletal tissue	Supports and protects softer tissues, and allows movement
Nervous tissue	Sets up nerve impulses and transmits them around the body
Muscle tissue	Contracts to support and move the body

Plant tissue	Main functions
Epidermis	Protects against water loss, and may be involved in absorption of water and ions
Mesophyll	Photosynthesis
Parenchyma	Fills spaces between other plant tissues and may be involved in storage, as in the potato tuber
Vascular tissue	Transports materials through the plant body
Strengthening tissue	Supports the plant

... tissues combine to form organs ...

Several tissues may be combined to form an **organ**, a complex structure with a particular function, such as the small intestine shown right.

... organs combine to form organ systems

In complex organisms, several organs work together to perform a particular task. These organs form an **organ system**.

Each cell, tissue and organ in an organism has a specialised part to play (there is **division of labour**) but their activities must be coordinated.

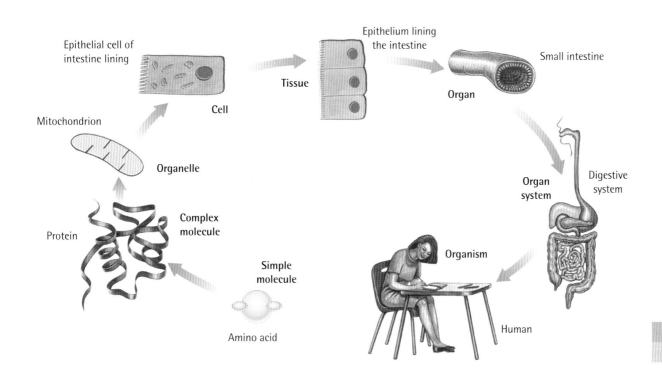

Questions on cells and organisation

1 Animals and plants are made up of cells, tissues and organs. This list contains some cells, tissues and organs:

phagocyte, sperm, epidermis, xylem, liver, blood, heart, leaf, ileum, ovary, neurone, brain, stem.

Make a table with these headings:

Cell	Tissue	Organ

Place each of the structures from the list into the correct column.

2 Arrange these biological terms in order of size (from the smallest to the largest):

organ, cell, organism, organelle, tissue, system.

3 Arrange these units of length in order, starting with the largest and ending with the smallest:

kilometre, micrometre, metre, millimetre.

An average plant cell is 50 micrometres long. How many plant cells could fit into one millimetre? Show your working.

4 The table below shows the percentage of different cells in a human body.

a Complete the table to show the percentage of 'other' cells in the body.

b Use the figures in the table to draw a pie chart to show the proportions of different cells in the body.

c The body contains about 100 000 000 000 000 cells. Work out how many red blood cells there would be – show your working.

5 Copy and complete this table by placing a tick if the structure is present and a cross if it is not.

Structure	Liver cell	Palisade cell
Cell surface membrane		
Chloroplasts		
Cytoplasm		
Cellulose cell wall		
Nucleus		
Starch granule		
Glycogen granule		
Large, permanent vacuole		

6 A biology book said that 'the structure of a cell is closely related to its function'. Using both plant and animal examples, comment on the validity of this statement.

7 The following list of the characteristics of living organisms can be matched with a series of definitions of these characteristics. Match up the two lists, so that you write out the definition of each of the characteristics.

Characteristics: respiration, sensitivity, growth, reproduction, nutrition, excretion, development

Definitions:
a change in size
the release of energy from organic molecules
the generation of offspring
the ability to detect changes in the environment
a change in shape or form
the supply of food
the removal of the waste products of metabolism

Cell type	Percentage in body
Bone	23
Red blood cell	13
White blood cell	0.5
Muscle	24
Nerve	8
Skin	11
Egg	0.1

8 Identify these cell structures from their descriptions:

a structures which contain chlorophyll

b cavity that is only found in plant cells

c contains cellulose, and surrounds a plant cell

d jelly-like material which fills most of the cell

e coloured threads found inside the nucleus

f the sites of aerobic respiration

g controls the entry and exit of substances

h carries the genetic information, and controls the activities of the cell

Cell structures: cell membrane; cell wall; chloroplasts; chromosomes; cytoplasm; mitochondria; nucleus; vacuole

9 Match these cells with their adaptations and/or functions.

Cells: red blood cell; white blood cell; cell lining bronchioles of lungs; motor nerve cell; palisade cell; root hair cell; phloem sieve tube; sperm cell; egg cell
Adaptations:

a has long extension to increase surface area for absorption of minerals and water

b contains haemoglobin for oxygen transport

c carries male parent's genetic information ready for fertilisation

d transports sugars through the body of a plant

e elongated, and transmits information from the central nervous system to a muscle

f has cilia to trap and remove mucus and dust particles

g contains powerful enzymes to digest bacteria

h carries female parent's genetic information, and has food stores in cytoplasm

i contains many chloroplasts

10 Say whether each of the following is an organelle, a cell, a tissue, an organ, a system or an organism:

a stomach

b mitochondrion

c cat

d onion bulb

e a carrot plant

f chloroplast

g neurone

h lung

i brain

j heart and circulation

k xylem

l the lining of the lung

11 On this diagram of a liver cell, identify

a which structure carries out aerobic respiration

b which structure controls the movement of salts into the cell

c which structure would carry the genes

d which feature increases the surface area of the cell

e which structure is a food store

2·3 Movement in and out of cells

On page 22 we saw that the cell cytoplasm is surrounded by a **cell surface membrane**. This acts as a boundary between the cell contents and its surroundings – it has very little strength, but it plays a vital role in regulating the materials that pass in and out of the cell. Materials may pass in and out of cells by:

- **diffusion**
- **osmosis**
- **active transport**
- in special cases, **phagocytosis**.

Diffusion – 'mixing molecules'

Molecules and ions in a liquid or a gas move continuously. The movement is quite random, and the particles change direction as they bump into one another. The particles collide more often when they are close together (when they are **concentrated**) and so they tend to **diffuse**, or spread out, until they are spaced evenly throughout the gas or liquid. The movement of the particles is due to their own **kinetic energy**. When diffusion happens in living cells, the cells themselves do not have to expend any energy for it to take place.

If there is a region of high concentration and a region of low concentration, we can say that there is a **concentration gradient** between the regions. We can therefore define **diffusion** as:

- the movement of particles within a gas or liquid
- from a region of high concentration to a region of lower concentration (down a concentration gradient)
- until an equilibrium is reached.

Partially permeable membranes

Not all particles can diffuse through cell surface membranes. Sometimes the particles are too big, or they have the wrong electrical charge on them, or the chemical composition of the membrane prevents them passing across. The diagram below shows a **partially permeable membrane** – it is **permeable** to glucose and water but **impermeable** to protein.

Diffusion and life processes

Diffusion is the main process by which substances move over short distances in living organisms. Some of the life processes that involve diffusion are shown in the diagram above right.

Living organisms have certain adaptations to speed up diffusion:

- **Diffusion distances are short** – the membranes in the lungs, for example, are very thin so that oxygen and carbon dioxide can diffuse between the blood and the lung air spaces.
- **Concentration gradients are maintained** – glucose molecules that cross from the gut into the blood, for example, are quickly removed by the circulating blood so that their concentration does not build up and equilibrium is not reached.
- **Diffusion surfaces are large** – the surface of the placenta, for example, is highly folded to increase the surface area for the diffusion of molecules between a pregnant female and the developing fetus in her uterus.

Key
- Protein
- Glucose
- Water

Partially permeable membrane – some, but not all, particles can diffuse across

The overall (net) movement of glucose and water molecules depends on their concentration gradient. Protein molecules cannot diffuse across this membrane, even though the concentration gradient suggests that they should move from right to left.

Life depends on the exchange of materials between different cells, and between cells and their surroundings. For example, a plant absorbs carbon dioxide from its surroundings by diffusion, and the carbon dioxide passes through the leaf to the photosynthesising cells by the same process.

From the lungs, oxygen enters the blood by diffusion. The continual movement of the blood keeps up a high concentration gradient between the air and the blood.

Glucose and amino acids pass from inside the gut into the blood, partly by the process of diffusion.

Many life processes depend on diffusion to move substances around. Diffusion has no 'energy cost' to a living organism.

Oxygen produced by photosynthesis diffuses out of the plant into the air. It enters the boy's lungs as he breathes in. The lungs are adapted to speed up the diffusion of oxygen into the blood, since they have thin surfaces with a very large surface area.

Mineral ions from the soil solution are absorbed by plant roots. This process depends upon diffusion as well as on active transport.

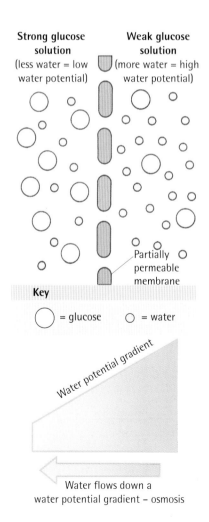

Strong glucose solution (less water = low water potential)

Weak glucose solution (more water = high water potential)

Partially permeable membrane

Key

◯ = glucose   ○ = water

Water potential gradient

Water flows down a water potential gradient – osmosis

Osmosis is a special case of diffusion

The biochemical processes in living cells always take place in a **solution**. A solution is made up of a **solvent** (the dissolving fluid) and a **solute** (the particles dissolved in the solvent). In living organisms, the solvent is water and the solution is called an aqueous solution.

Living cells are separated from their surroundings by the **partially permeable cell surface membrane**. The contents of the cell, the cytoplasm, is one aqueous solution and the surroundings of the cell, for example pond water, is another aqueous solution. If the two solutions do not have the same concentrations of various substances, molecules may move from one to the other by diffusion, if the membrane is permeable to these substances.

The diagram on the left shows two glucose solutions separated by a partially permeable membrane – this membrane will allow the diffusion of water molecules but not glucose (the solute) molecules. As a result water can move from the right, where there is a high concentration of water molecules, to the left, where there is a lower concentration of water molecules, by the process of diffusion. This diffusion of water is called **osmosis**, and will continue until a water equilibrium has been reached.

Because it is sometimes confusing to talk about water 'concentration', biologists use the term **water potential** instead. A solution with many water molecules has a **high water potential**, and a solution with few water molecules has a **low water potential**. In the diagram, a **water potential gradient** exists between the two solutions, and water molecules can flow down this gradient from right to left.

Osmosis can be defined as:

⬛ the diffusion of water molecules

⬛ from a region of higher concentration of water molecules to a region of lower concentration of water molecules down a water potential gradient

⬛ across a partially permeable membrane.

Cells and osmosis

A cell is surrounded by a partially permeable membrane, and water may cross this membrane easily. If a cell is placed in a solution of lower water potential, water leaves the cell by osmosis. If the cell is placed in a solution of higher water potential, water enters by osmosis.

Plant cells and osmosis

If water enters a plant cell by osmosis the cytoplasm will swell, but only until it pushes against the cellulose cell wall, as shown below. A plant cell will not be permanently damaged by the entry of water. If water leaves a plant cell by osmosis the cytoplasm will shrink, but the cellulose cell wall will continue to give some support. Plant cells rarely suffer permanent damage by the loss of water.

Water potential of surroundings

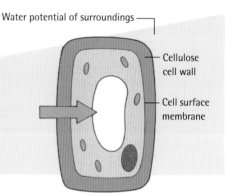

Cellulose cell wall

Cell surface membrane

Cell in solution of lower water potential than cell contents – water leaves by osmosis. The cytoplasm pulls away from the cell wall and the cell becomes **flaccid** ('floppy').

Cell in solution of equal water potential – no *net* movement of water; cytoplasm just presses against cell wall.

Cell in solution of higher water potential – water enters by osmosis. The cytoplasm pushes hard against the cell wall and the cell becomes **turgid** (firm).

Animal cells and osmosis

Animal cells have no cell wall, just a membrane. They are likely to suffer damage as a result of osmosis, as shown in the diagram below.

Osmosis is potentially damaging to animal cells, and animals have mechanisms to keep the blood plasma and the body fluids at the same water potential as the cytoplasm of cells. In mammals the kidney plays a vital part in this process of **osmoregulation** (see page 134).

Red blood cell

In a solution of lower water potential, the cell shrinks and becomes **crenated**

In a solution of the same water potential as the inside of the cell, the cell is in equilibrium

In a solution of higher water potential, the cell takes in water, swells and bursts (**haemolysis**)

The 'ghost' of a red blood cell; just the membrane is left behind

Crenated red blood cells

Red blood cells in equilibrium

Active transport requires energy to move materials

Molecules and ions can move from one place to another by diffusion, but only until an equilibrium has been reached. If no concentration gradient exists between the two places, no diffusion can occur – this means that if an equilibrium has been reached, useful particles cannot be absorbed by diffusion. **Active transport** is a method by which particles can cross membranes even against a concentration gradient. In active transport, protein molecules in the cell surface membrane pick up and carry particles across the membrane. These protein molecules are called **carriers**, and when they work they use energy supplied by the cell. Active transport is explained in the diagram below, and important examples of its use are the uptake of ions by plants (page 86) and the uptake of glucose by epithelial cells of the villi. To summarise – active transport:

- can move molecules against a concentration gradient but
- requires energy and
- involves protein carriers in membranes.

Some cells use phagocytosis

Some particles are too large to cross a membrane by diffusion or by active transport. A few very specialised cells have developed a method for taking up these particles – the particles are literally engulfed by the cell surface membrane flowing around them. This process of **phagocytosis** is used by white blood cells, and is described on page 98.

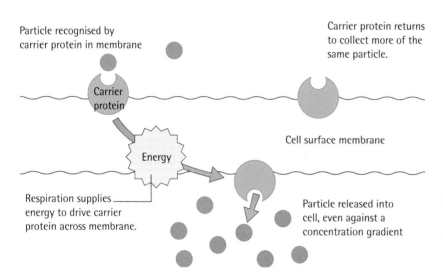

Particle recognised by carrier protein in membrane

Carrier protein returns to collect more of the same particle.

Carrier protein

Energy

Cell surface membrane

Respiration supplies energy to drive carrier protein across membrane.

Particle released into cell, even against a concentration gradient

Active transport uses energy to move substances against a concentration gradient. The protein carriers involved in active transport are rather like enzymes. They are able to recognise particular molecules and select them from a mixture. As a result active transport is specific, and the cell can 'choose' which molecules it will absorb from its surroundings.

---

1. Using an example, explain what is meant by a partially permeable membrane.

2. What is a concentration gradient?

3. Make a list of the processes in living organisms that are dependent on diffusion.

4. How are living organisms adapted to increase the possibility of diffusion?

5. Copy and complete the following paragraphs.
   Animal cells contain _____, a semi-fluid solution of salts and other molecules, and are surrounded by a _____. When in distilled water, the animal cells _____ because the cell has a _____ water potential than the surrounding water. Plant cells do not have this problem because they are surrounded by a _____.

In the gut, soluble food substances such as _____ cross the gut lining into the capillaries by the process of _____, which is the movement of molecules down a _____. When an equilibrium is reached between the gut contents and the blood, glucose may continue to be moved using the process called _____, which consumes _____ and can move molecules _____ a concentration gradient.

The leaves of green plants obtain the gas _____, which they require for the process of photosynthesis, by the process of _____. They also lose the gas oxygen, produced during _____, by the same process.

6. Make a table that compares diffusion with active transport. Include one example of each process in your table. Under what circumstances would an organism use phagocytosis rather than diffusion or active transport?

2·4 Enzymes control biochemical reactions in living organisms

Enzymes are biological catalysts

The sum of all the chemical reactions going on within a living organism is known as **metabolism**. **Anabolic** reactions build up large molecules from smaller ones, and usually require an input of energy. **Catabolic** reactions break down large molecules into smaller ones, and often release energy. The condensation of glucose molecules into the polysaccharide glycogen is an example of anabolism, and this happens in cells of the liver and skeletal muscle. The breakdown of glucose into carbon dioxide and water by respiration is an example of catabolism, and this also occurs in cells of the liver and skeletal muscle. What determines whether glucose molecules are built up into glycogen or broken down into carbon dioxide and water? The answer is **enzymes**. Enzymes are proteins, and they act as biological **catalysts** – (catalysts speed up reactions without themselves being affected by the reaction). The molecules that react in the enzyme-catalysed reaction are called **substrates**, and the molecules produced in the reaction are **products**. Different enzymes are involved in anabolic and catabolic reactions, and so the presence or absence of a particular enzyme controls what will happen to a particular molecule.

Enzymes and cells

Enzymes are synthesised in living cells. Most enzymes work inside the cell – examples of these **intracellular enzymes** are **catalase** (which breaks down harmful hydrogen peroxide in liver cells) and **phosphorylase** (which builds glucose into starch in plant storage cells). Other enzymes are made inside cells and then released from the cell to perform

their function – examples of these **extracellular enzymes** include the digestive enzyme **lipase** (which breaks down fats to fatty acids and glycerol) and **amylase**, which converts starch to maltose during germination (see page 194). Enzymes are **specific** – most enzymes work on one kind of substrate only. For example, proteases break down proteins but have no effect on carbohydrates or lipids, and lipases break down lipids but do not affect proteins or carbohydrates.

The mechanism of enzyme action (the lock and key hypothesis)

An **enzyme** is a protein, folded into a complex three-dimensional shape. The **active site** is the part of the enzyme that allows it to act as a catalyst, as shown below.

Molecules of substrate

Active site

Enzyme

The enzyme molecule is now free to bind with more molecules of substrate. Each enzyme molecule may be used many thousands of times.

Substrate molecules fit exactly into the active site of the enzyme. The active site brings the substrate molecules closer together.

Product

The substrates now react to form a molecule of product, which leaves the active site.

No enzyme

Enzyme present

Energy for reaction

Time

The enzyme lowers the energy needed for the reaction, and the reaction is then much more likely to take place.

Factors affecting enzyme activity

Temperature

Temperature affects the activity of enzymes since:

- a higher temperature speeds up the movement of substrate molecules, so that when they collide with the enzyme they have more energy and are more likely to bind to the active site. The enzyme activity increases with a rise in temperature, up to a point.

- the enzyme molecules themselves also gain in energy as the temperature rises so that they begin to vibrate. Eventually the enzyme molecules vibrate so much that they become **denatured** – they lose their three-dimensional shape and can no longer bind to their substrate. Because of this, high temperatures reduce enzyme activity. Each enzyme has an **optimum temperature**, which is a balance between these two effects, as shown in the graph below. Most human enzymes have an optimum temperature around 37 °C, whilst for most plants the optimum is rather lower at around 25 °C.

Denaturation is usually irreversible, and living cells make great efforts to keep the conditions suitable for their enzymes to work.

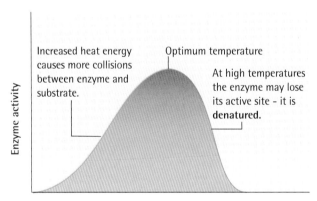

An enzyme-catalysed reaction gets faster, reaches a maximum rate and then slows down again as you increase the temperature.

pH

pH also affects enzyme activity since changing the acid or base conditions around an enzyme molecule affects its three-dimensional shape and can denature the enzyme. Each enzyme has its own **optimum pH**, as shown in the graph below, which depends on the environment in which the enzyme is working – **pepsin** is an enzyme that works in the stomach, and has an optimum pH around pH 2.0 (very acidic), whereas **amylase** works in the mouth and small intestine and has an optimum pH around 7.5 (slightly basic).

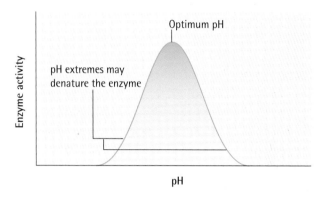

Activators and inhibitors

Some molecules change the likelihood of an enzyme being able to bind to its substrate. **Activators** make this binding more likely – for example, chloride ions are essential for the activity of salivary amylase. **Inhibitors** make it more difficult for the enzyme to bind to the substrate – for example, cyanide ions block the active sites of enzymes involved in respiration.

Humans exploit enzymes

Because enzymes are specific, and can be used over and over again, they are very useful in the fields of industry, food preparation and medicine – an enzyme from snake venom can break down blood clots, for example.

---

1 Copy and complete the following paragraph about enzymes.

Enzymes are _____ which speed up the biochemical _____ in living organisms. The enzymes themselves are not changed in these reactions, that is they are biological _____.

Enzymes are _____ – each one controls only one type of reaction. They are _____ by high temperatures and by extremes of pH.

2 Enzyme action is explained by the lock and key hypothesis (see box opposite). The example shows an enzyme that catalyses a condensation reaction – two small molecules are joined together to make a larger one. Redraw the diagram to show the action of an enzyme catalysing a hydrolysis reaction, and give an example of such an enzyme.

2.5 Humans use enzymes from microorganisms

Objectives

- To understand that enzymes have many roles which benefit humans
- To know examples of a range of uses of enzymes
- To understand the benefits of enzyme immobilisation

Enzymes in industry

Enzymes are biological catalysts that operate at the temperatures, pressures and moderate pH values found in living organisms (see page 32). Using enzymes for industrial processes therefore does not require extreme (and expensive) conditions. For example, the Haber process for producing ammonia requires a temperature of 750 °C and a pressure of 30 times atmospheric pressure whereas nitrogen-fixing bacteria can perform this process at 25 °C and at atmospheric pressure.

The majority of enzymes used commercially are obtained from microbial sources, usually fungi or bacteria. Sometimes the organism naturally secretes the enzymes onto its substrate; sometimes the microbial cells must be broken open to release the enzymes. Using genetic engineering (see page 224), genes for desirable enzymes such as chymosin (see page 48) can be inserted into organisms that do not use this enzyme, and so they secrete it into their environment.

Microorganisms that produce those valuable enzymes are grown under carefully controlled conditions in a fermenter (bioreactor), like the one shown on the opposite page.

Commercial applications of enzymes

Pharmaceuticals

The enzyme **catalase** is used in wound dressings. Catalase converts hydrogen peroxide in the dressing to oxygen and water. Oxygen speeds up healing and inhibits dangerous, anaerobic bacteria such as the species which causes gas gangrene.

Biological washing powders

The most difficult stains to remove from clothes often include **lipids** (e.g. from fatty foods or greasy fingerprints) or **proteins** (e.g. from blood). These can be washed out using biological washing powders that contain **lipase** and **protease**. These powders have the added advantage of working at lower temperatures (less water heating needed, and clothes don't shrink).

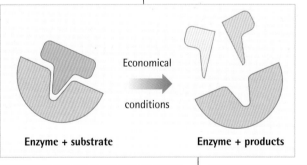

Enzyme + substrate → Economical conditions → Enzyme + products

Food production

- A **protease** from bacteria softens gluten, making the rolling of biscuits easier.
- **Isomerase** converts glucose to fructose – this is sweeter so less needs to be used in slimmers' biscuits.
- A **lipase** from fungi helps chocolate coverings to flow.

Textiles

Leather for clothing is softened using a **protease** from bacteria.

Stains are removed using **lipase, amylase** and **protease**.

A fermenter (or bioreactor)

Paddle stirrers continuously mix the contents of the bioreactor:
- ensures microorganisms are always in contact with nutrients
- ensures an even temperature throughout the fermentation mixture
- for aerobic (oxygen-requiring) fermentations the mixing may be carried out by an **airstream**.

Microbe input – the organisms that will carry out the fermentation process are cultured separately until they are growing well.

Nutrient input –
the microorganisms require:
- an energy source – usually carbohydrate
- growth materials – amino acids (or ammonium salts which can be converted to amino acids) for protein synthesis.

Heating/cooling water out

Sterile conditions are essential. The culture must be pure and all nutrients/equipment sterile to:
- avoid competition for expensive nutrients
- limit the danger of disease-causing organisms contaminating the product.

Heating/cooling water in

In **batch culture** there is a fixed input of nutrients and the products are collected by emptying the bioreactor. The process is then repeated. This method is **expensive**, since the culture must be replaced and the reactor must be sterilised between batches, but has the **advantages** that:
- the vessels can be switched to other uses
- any contamination results in the loss of only a single batch.

In **continuous culture** fresh nutrients are added as soon as they are consumed, and the reactor may run for long periods. Products are run off at intervals while the process continues. This is **more economical** but has the **disadvantages** that:
- contamination causes greater losses
- the culture may block inlet or outlet pipes.

Gas outlet – gas may be evolved during fermentation. This must be released to avoid pressure build-up, and may be a valuable by-product, e.g. carbon dioxide is collected and sold for use in fizzy drinks.

Constant temperature water jacket – the temperature is controlled so that it is high enough to promote enzyme activity but not so high that enzymes and other proteins in the microbes are denatured.

Probes monitor conditions such as pH, temperature and oxygen concentration. Information is sent to computer control systems which correct any changes to maintain the optimum conditions for fermentation.

Further processing of product
may be necessary:
- to separate the microorganism from the desired product. In some fermentation systems these microorganisms may then be returned to the vessel to continue the process.
- to prepare the product for sale or distribution – this often involves **drying** or **crystallisation**.

Objectives
- To understand how enzymes can work as biological catalysts
- To understand and apply the scientific method

What is the scientific method?

When scientists are faced with a problem, they tackle it using the **scientific method**. This starts off with an **observation**; for example, a farmer might notice that all his cows have stopped producing milk. The next step is to produce a **hypothesis**, a possible explanation for the observation (perhaps the cows' diet has been changed). Following this hypothesis, **predictions** are made, such as: *adding more protein pellets to the cows' feed will increase their yield of milk*. Then **experiments** are designed and carried out to test whether or not the predictions are true. The **data** (results of the experiment) are analysed and **conclusions** drawn. These conclusions will allow the experimenter to accept or reject the original hypothesis.

An illustration of the scientific method

In an experiment, apparatus is used to measure the effect of changing one factor (variable) on the value of a second factor (variable). For example, the experiment illustrated below is designed to test the hypothesis: *temperature affects the activity of catalase.*

Catalase is an enzyme that catalyses the breakdown of hydrogen peroxide:

Hydrogen peroxide → oxygen + water

Catalase is present in potato tissue. Discs of potato are put into a solution of hydrogen peroxide. The catalase breaks down the hydrogen peroxide into water and oxygen, and the oxygen passes into the manometer. The changing level of the manometer fluid shows how much oxygen is being produced, and gives a measure of the activity of the enzyme. The rate of oxygen production is measured at different temperatures.

An identical **control** experiment is also set up, in which the input variable (the temperature) is not changed. This confirms that the changes in temperature, and not an unknown variable, are causing the changes in enzyme activity. A control experiment ensures that the experiment is a **fair test**.

If the experimenter suspects that an error has been made, part of the experiment may be **repeated**. Taking a series of results and calculating the mean gives more accurate results than taking just one set, as any single inaccurate result then has less effect on the overall results.

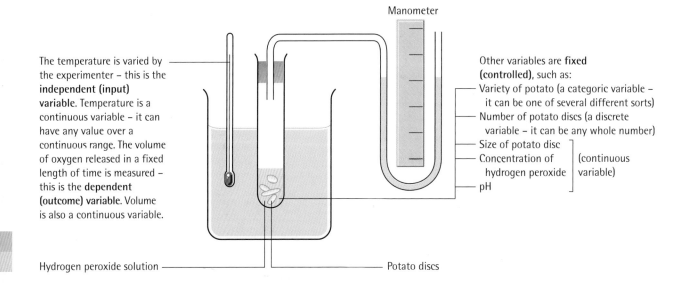

The temperature is varied by the experimenter – this is the **independent (input) variable.** Temperature is a continuous variable – it can have any value over a continuous range. The volume of oxygen released in a fixed length of time is measured – this is the **dependent (outcome) variable.** Volume is also a continuous variable.

Other variables are **fixed (controlled)**, such as:
- Variety of potato (a categoric variable – it can be one of several different sorts)
- Number of potato discs (a discrete variable – it can be any whole number)
- Size of potato disc
- Concentration of hydrogen peroxide
- pH

(continuous variable)

Manometer

Hydrogen peroxide solution

Potato discs

Dealing with data: recording results

Raw data are gathered in a table during the experiment. They may then be manipulated (converted into another form), and are often displayed as a graph to allow the experimenter to draw conclusions from the results.

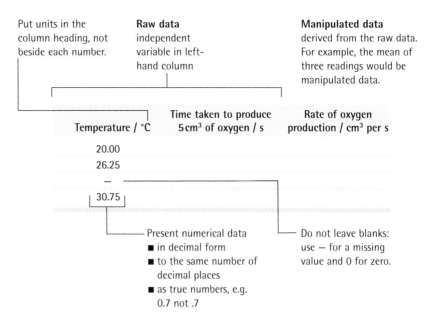

Put units in the column heading, not beside each number.

Raw data independent variable in left-hand column

Manipulated data derived from the raw data. For example, the mean of three readings would be manipulated data.

Temperature / °C	Time taken to produce 5 cm³ of oxygen / s	Rate of oxygen production / cm³ per s
20.00		
26.25		
–		
30.75		

Present numerical data
■ in decimal form
■ to the same number of decimal places
■ as true numbers, e.g. 0.7 not .7

Do not leave blanks: use – for a missing value and 0 for zero.

Results are recorded in a table during the experiment. Give an informative title, such as: *The effect of temperature on the activity of catalase.*

Drawing a graph

A graph is a visual representation of data which often helps to make a relationship more obvious.

Evaluating an experiment

Scientists often look back at the results of their experiments and the methods used to gather them. This **evaluation** process is an important part of the scientific method because the scientist needs to be sure that the techniques and apparatus used have given the most reliable results before he or she draws conclusions from them.

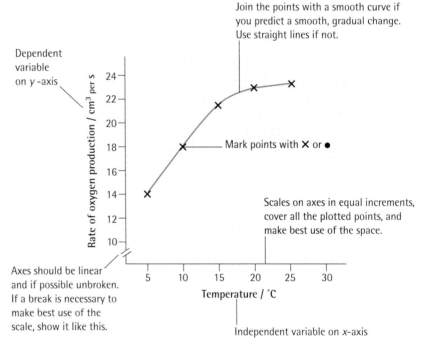

Join the points with a smooth curve if you predict a smooth, gradual change. Use straight lines if not.

Dependent variable on *y*-axis

Mark points with ✕ or ●

Scales on axes in equal increments, cover all the plotted points, and make best use of the space.

Axes should be linear and if possible unbroken. If a break is necessary to make best use of the scale, show it like this.

Independent variable on *x*-axis

Rule in the axes in black. Again, give an informative title.

1 Using the apparatus shown opposite, a student investigated the effect of temperature on the activity of the enzyme catalase. Here are his results:
a Copy and complete the table by calculating the rate of oxygen release.
b Present the data in the form of a graph.
c Explain the shape of the graph.

Temperature / °C	Time taken to evolve 10 cm³ of oxygen / s	Rate of oxygen release / cm³ per s
15	40	
25	20	
35	5	
45	20	
55	40	
65	120	
75	No gas evolved	

2·7   All living things are made up of organic molecules

Objectives
▪ To understand that the structures of living things depend on the molecules that make them up
▪ To list the types of molecule found in living organisms

Organic molecules

Biological molecules are often called **organic** molecules, since many of them were discovered in living organisms. Chemists have found that these compounds all contain carbon atoms, along with other elements. Carbon atoms bond strongly to other carbon atoms, so organic molecules can be large and show a wide variety of chain and ring structures, with many carbon atoms bonded together. Organisms need organic molecules to:

▪ provide **energy** to drive life processes
▪ provide **raw materials** for the growth and repair of tissues.

Nutrition supplies living organisms with the molecules that they need. There are four main groups of organic chemicals used by living things:

▪ **carbohydrates**
▪ **lipids**
▪ **proteins**
▪ **nucleic acids.**

The diagram on the next page shows the structures of these different groups of organic molecules.

Basic biochemistry

Living organisms also contain inorganic molecules (such as water) and a number of ions. The study of the organic and inorganic molecules that make up living organisms is called **biochemistry**. The sum of all the chemical reactions in living organisms is sometimes called **metabolism.**

Large organic molecules are usually made up of lots of similar smaller molecules called **subunits.** The subunits can be split apart by a reaction called **hydrolysis**, which uses water. They can be joined together again, perhaps in new combinations, by a reaction called **condensation**, which produces water (see opposite page).

In this way living organisms can take molecules from their environment and rearrange them into shapes that suit their own particular requirements, as illustrated below.

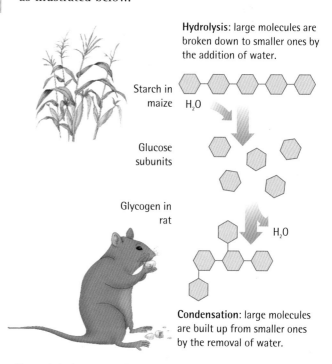

Hydrolysis: large molecules are broken down to smaller ones by the addition of water.

Starch in maize H_2O

Glucose subunits

Glycogen in rat H_2O

Condensation: large molecules are built up from smaller ones by the removal of water.

The carbohydrate starch in the maize is hydrolysed in the rat's cells into subunits called glucose. These are then built up into the carbohydrate glycogen by condensation reactions.

1 List the main groups of organic compounds found in living organisms. Suggest one important function for each group.

2 Using carbohydrates as an example, explain the meaning of the terms **hydrolysis** and **condensation.**

3 Some molecules such as glucose and amino acids are **soluble**, whereas others such as starch and fats are **insoluble**. Why is this physical property important in living organisms?

4 Some scientists would say that nucleic acids are the most important molecules in living cells; others might suggest that proteins are more important; and some might say that life could not continue without a supply of carbohydrates. Write a sentence in support of each of these points of view.

Carbohydrates (page 43)

Monosaccharides are the simplest carbohydrates, for example, glucose. Glucose is soluble so it is easily transported in blood and dissolves in the cytoplasm of cells. Monosaccharides are the main source of energy for many cells.

Hydrolysis　Condensation

Polysaccharides are formed from many monosaccharide molecules – for example, starch and glycogen are two polysaccharides both made of many thousands of glucose molecules. Polysaccharides are insoluble, so they are good stores of energy and can form important structures such as cellulose cell walls.

Lipids (page 43)

Lipids are formed by the condensation of three molecules of **fatty acid** with one molecule of **glycerol.**

Glycerol　Fatty acids

Hydrolysis　Condensation

Fats (which are solid at room temperature) and oils (which are liquid at room temperature) are insoluble in water. As a result they are excellent stores of energy, and form barriers between watery environments, such as between a cell and its surroundings.

Some contain only carbon (C), hydrogen (H) and oxygen (O)

All organic molecules contain the elements **carbon, hydrogen** and **oxygen**. The biological function of a molecule depends on its shape and structure.

Some also contain nitrogen (N) and sometimes sulphur (S)

Some also contain nitrogen (N) and phosphorus (P)

Proteins (page 43)

Proteins are made up of long chains of subunits called **amino acids**, joined together in particular sequences which are coded for by genes. The 20 different amino acids can be joined together in a vast number of different orders, and some proteins are thousands of amino acids long. The sequence of amino acids determines the shape of the protein molecule – some are long and thin (such as **keratin**, the protein in hair and nails), whilst others are more egg shaped or spherical (such as **haemoglobin**, the oxygen-carrying protein in red blood cells).
Amino acids are soluble so they are easily transported in living organisms, and can take part in reactions in the watery cytoplasm of the cell.

Hydrolysis　Condensation

Nucleic acids (page 202)

Base
Sugar
P
Phosphate

Nucleic acids are made up of long chains of subunits called **nucleotides**. Each nucleotide is made up of a base, a sugar and a phosphate group. In **deoxyribonucleic acid (DNA)**, there are four different nucleotides, each containing a different base.

Hydrolysis　Condensation

In DNA these chains are coiled around one another. The sequence of bases forms a code which carries the genetic information. This code is passed from one generation to the next and instructs a cell or an organism to carry out a particular task.

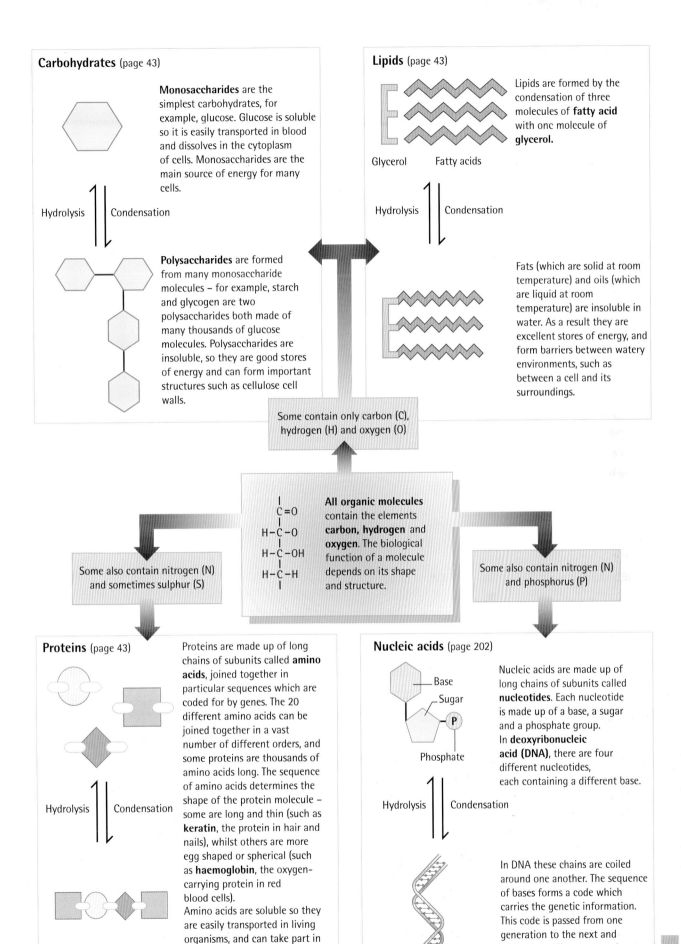

2·8 Testing for biochemicals

Objective
- To describe simple chemical tests for the molecules of living organisms

Scientists often need to know whether or not a particular type of molecule is present in a solution. For example, a doctor might try to detect glucose in a urine sample (glucose in the urine suggests the patient has diabetes), or an environmental scientist might test for starch in the outflow from a food factory. There are a number of simple chemical tests that can be carried out on biological solutions. Some of these tests are described on the opposite page.

A special test for lipids

An important feature of fats and oils is that they are insoluble in water. This means that you cannot make an aqueous solution of a fat or oil on which to carry out a biochemical test. However, the fact that lipids are insoluble forms the basis of a **physical test**.

This is known as the **emulsion test**:

- 2 cm³ of ethanol are added to the unknown solution, and the mixture is gently shaken.
- The mixture is poured into a test tube containing an equal volume of distilled water.
- If a lipid is present, a milky-white emulsion is formed.

A milky emulsion shows that a lipid is present.

---

1. **a** What is the difference between a fat and an oil?
   b Both lipids and carbohydrates contain carbon, hydrogen and oxygen. How do they differ from one another?
   c Draw a diagram to show a molecule of fat. Suggest why it is possible to have many kinds of fat.

2. Here are the results of a series of tests on biological solutions.
   Suggest, giving your reasons, which of these solutions might be:
   a the washings from a laundry   **d** urine from somebody who has sugar diabetes
   b milk   **e** sweetened tea.
   c crushed potato solution

Solution	Colour after testing with reagent:			
	Iodine solution	Benedict's reagent	Biuret reagent	Benedict's reagent after acidification and neutralisation
A	Blue-black	Clear blue	Clear blue	Clear blue
B	Straw yellow	Orange	Purple	Orange
C	Straw yellow	Clear blue	Clear blue	Orange
D	Blue-black	Clear blue	Faint purple	Clear blue
E	Straw yellow	Orange	Clear blue	Orange

3. Describe the two types of control which are used in food tests and explain why they are needed.

Testing for vitamin C: using DCPIP
Vitamin C takes the colour out of a blue dye called DCPIP.

VITAMIN C →

The number of drops of vitamin C solution needed to make this happen depends on how concentrated the vitamin C solution is.

So
few drops: strong vitamin C solution

many drops: weak vitamin C solution

A **control** is needed to make sure that results are valid.

- To show that the test is working properly, a solution that is known to contain the substance is tested (for example, the Biuret reagent is used with a solution known to contain protein). This should give a positive result.

- To show that the test solutions are not contaminated, each test should be carried out on a sample of water. This should give a negative result.

To test for **protein,** a few drops of **Biuret reagent** are added to 2 cm³ of the unknown solution, and the mixture is gently shaken. A **mauve/purple** colour is a positive result (protein is present).

To test for **starch**, a few drops of **iodine solution** are added to 2 cm³ of the unknown solution, and the mixture is gently shaken. A **deep blue–black** colour is a positive result (starch is present).

To test for **glucose** (a **reducing sugar**), 2 cm³ of **Benedict's reagent** are added to 2 cm³ of the unknown solution, and the mixture is heated in a boiling water bath for 2–3 minutes. An **orange/brick-red** colour is a positive result (glucose is present).

When **making comparisons** between different solutions – for example, to compare the glucose content of different urine samples – it is important to carry out all tests under the same conditions. For example, a series of Benedict's tests should be performed:

- on equal volumes of unknown solutions
- using equal volumes of Benedict's solution
- with all mixtures heated to the same temperature
- for the same length of time.

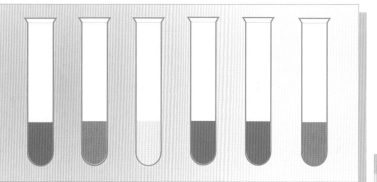

2·9 Food and the ideal diet: carbohydrates, lipids and proteins

Food

All living organisms are made up of molecules, organised so that they can carry out the characteristics of life. Food supplies them with:

- molecules that are the **raw materials** for repair, growth and development of the body tissues
- molecules that can be oxidised in respiration, and act as a **source of energy**
- elements and compounds that enable the raw materials and energy to be used efficiently.

All living organisms need food, but some, green plants in particular, can manufacture their own organic molecules. These organisms are said to be **autotrophic** (or 'self feeding'). Green plants use a form of autotrophic nutrition called **photosynthesis** to supply them with all the organic molecules they need (see page 60). Other organisms cannot make their own food, and must take in food molecules from their surroundings. These molecules have been made by another organism, so living things that feed in this way are said to be **heterotrophic** (or 'other feeding'). Humans, like all animals, are totally dependent on other organisms for their food.

A balanced diet

The total of the molecules or **nutrients** that we need is called the **diet**. A **balanced diet** provides all the nutrients, in the correct amounts, needed to carry out the life processes. If the diet does not provide all the nutrients in the correct proportions, a person may suffer from **malnutrition** (see page 54, for example).

Food can be analysed to find out what chemicals it contains, using quite simple chemical techniques (see page 40). A balanced diet should contain the correct proportions of **carbohydrates**, **lipids**, **proteins**, **vitamins** and **minerals**, **water** and **dietary fibre**. We shall look at each in turn.

Balanced and adequate diet

fat

protein

carbohydrate

- CARBOHYDRATE
- PROTEIN
- FAT
- WATER
- VITAMINS
- MINERALS
- FIBRE

An adequate diet provides sufficient **energy** for the performance of metabolic work, although the 'energy' could be in any form.

A balanced diet provides all dietary requirements **in the correct proportions**. Ideally this would be 1/7 **fat**, 1/7 **protein** and 5/7 carbohydrate.

In conditions of **under**nutrition the first concern is usually provision of an adequate diet, but to avoid symptoms of **mal**nutrition a **balanced diet** must be provided.

1. Give three reasons why living organisms need food.
2. Write one sentence to explain the difference between autotrophic and heterotrophic nutrition.
3. What is a balanced diet?
4. Which are the main energy foods for humans?
5. State four functions of proteins, using particular examples to illustrate your answer.

Organisation and maintenance of organisms

Carbohydrates, lipids and proteins: three food types

Good source	Functions in humans	Comments
Carbohydrates		
Rice, potatoes, wheat (e.g. pasta) and other cereals provide **starch**. Food sweetenings, such as those in desserts, sweets and soft drinks, and preservatives provide **refined sugars**, such as **sucrose (cane sugar)** and **glucose**.	A **source of energy**. Glucose is oxidised in **respiration** (see page 114) to release **energy** for active transport, cell division, muscle contraction and the manufacture of large biological molecules. Excess carbohydrate can be stored as **glycogen** (see page 158) and as **fat**.	Carbohydrates are digested in the mouth and small intestine and absorbed as **glucose**. Refined sugars are absorbed very rapidly, giving a sudden boost of 'energy source'. Starch is digested and absorbed more slowly, giving a steady supply of energy source: starches are called **slow release carbohydrates**.
Lipids		
Meat and animal foods (eggs, milk, cheese) are rich in **saturated fats** and **cholesterol**. Plant sources such as sunflower seeds and peanuts are rich in **unsaturated fats**.	Fats and oils are an important source of energy (see p. 52). They are especially valuable as an **energy store** because they are insoluble in water. They also provide **insulation** – electrical insulation around nerve cells (see p. 139) and thermal insulation beneath the skin (p. 131) – and form part of cell membranes. **Steroid hormones**, including sex hormones, are made from cholesterol.	Fats and oils are digested in the small intestine and absorbed as fatty acids and glycerol. Some lipids contain **saturated fatty acids** and others contain **unsaturated fatty acids** (with at least one carbon–carbon double bond). The body can store unlimited amounts of fat, contributing to obesity (see p. 54). The incorrect balance of saturated and unsaturated fatty acids, or an excess of cholesterol, can cause diseases of the circulation (see p. 110).
Proteins		
Meat, fish, eggs from animals, and legumes (peas and beans) and pulses from plants. One of the best sources of protein is the soya bean. This contains very little fat (unlike most animal sources) and so is suitable for people with health problems caused by fat (see p. 110). Soya beans can be flavoured and textured to make them taste and feel like meat – this **textured vegetable protein** is used as 'artificial' meat. Mycoprotein (see p. 48) is also a low-fat substitute for meat.	Many functions, including • catalysts (enzymes) p. 32 • transport molecules, e.g. haemoglobin p. 94 • structural materials, as in muscles (p. 116) • hormones, such as insulin (p. 159) • in defence against disease, as antibodies (p. 100)	Digested in the stomach and small intestine, and absorbed as amino acids. 20 different amino acids are needed to make up all of the different proteins in the human body. Some of these must be supplied in the diet as the body cannot make them – these are the **essential amino acids**. Proteins from animal sources usually contain all 20 amino acids, but plant proteins often lack one or two of the essential amino acids. Deficiency of protein causes poor growth – in extreme cases may cause **marasmus** or **kwashiorkor**.

Essential amino acids – cry baby

One factor that determines how comfortable babies feel is the supply of a 'pleasure chemical', called **serotonin**, in the brain (see neurotransmitters, page 139). An essential amino acid called **lysine** is needed to make serotonin. Lysine is in short supply in some artificial milks. Babies fed on these milk substitutes can't manufacture enough serotonin, they feel uncomfortable and they CCCRRRYYY! Natural mother's milk contains an adequate supply of lysine.

Vegetarians must ensure that their diet contains a wide range of protein sources since very few plants contain all the essential amino acids. An ideal vegetarian meal containing all the essential amino acids is baked beans on toast (which also contains a high proportion of dietary fibre).

Key

☐ % protein in the food   ■ % essential amino acids in the protein

The protein values of some common foods.

2·10 Food and the ideal diet: vitamins, minerals, water and fibre

Objectives
- To list the constituents of an ideal diet
- To know the functions of each component of an ideal diet

Vitamins and minerals

Vitamins and minerals are essential for the body to be able to use the other nutrients efficiently. They are needed in only very small amounts. There are many different vitamins and minerals, and they are usually provided in the foods of a balanced diet.

Too much can be harmful! Never eat a polar bear's liver! It contains so much stored vitamin A that it is poisonous to humans!

Vitamins

Fat-soluble	Food source	Symptoms of deficiency	Comments
A (retinol)	Liver, dairy products, eggs	Poor night vision	The yellow pigment, carotene, found in leafy vegetables and carrots can be turned into retinol by the body.
D (calciferol)	As vit. A, plus fish liver oil	Rickets – bones are soft and may bend, because vit. D is needed for the absorption of calcium.	Can be made by the body, just under the skin, but only if there is plenty of sunlight.
Water-soluble			
B (actually there are several different B vitamins)	Corn, whole cereals (ie with the 'husk' on), peas, beans, yeast extract	Respiration is affected so energy supplies are reduced e.g. Beri-beri (an African word meaning 'I cannot') causes muscle weakness and paralysis.	Polished rice or milled maize do not supply enough B vitamins.
C (ascorbic acid)	Cherries, citrus fruits e.g. limes, lemons, oranges, and fresh green leafy vegetables	Scurvy – production of fibres in the body is affected (see page 76).	Vitamin C also seems to protect cells from ageing.

Minerals

	Food source	Symptoms of deficiency	Comments
Iron	Red meat, liver, some leafy vegetables, e.g. spinach	Anaemia – iron is needed to produce **haemoglobin** for red blood cells. A shortage causes weakness as oxygen needed for respiration cannot be transported efficiently.	Iron is added to foods when metal utensils are used in cooking – the amount of iron in a piece of beef is doubled when the meat is minced in an iron mincer ready for making burgers!
Calcium	Milk, cheese and fish	Several problems • weak bones and teeth • poor clotting of blood • uncontrolled muscle contractions ('spasms').	Calcium shortage causes **rickets**, the same deficiency disease caused by insufficient vitamin D.

Organisation and maintenance of organisms

44

Water

Water forms about 70% of the human body. Two-thirds of this water is in the cytoplasm of cells, and the other third is in tissue fluid and blood plasma. Humans lose about 1.5 litres of water each day, in urine, faeces, exhaled air and sweat – this must be replaced by water in the diet. It is obtained in three main ways:

- as a drink
- in food, especially salad foods such as tomatoes and lettuce
- from metabolic processes (think back to the equation for aerobic respiration – water is one of the products).

A loss of only 5% of the body's water can lead to unconsciousness, and a loss of 10% would be fatal. We shall look further at how the body conserves water on page 134.

Fibre

Dietary fibre is the indigestible part of food, largely cellulose from plant cell walls, which provides bulk for the faeces. Plenty of fibre in the diet stretches the muscles of the gut wall and helps push the food along by peristalsis (see page 78). A shortage of fibre can cause constipation, and may be a factor in the development of bowel cancer.

Summary of a balanced diet

Key

○ Fat (naturally occurring and added to food)

◉ Sugars (added to food)

Food guide pyramid: choosing to eat these amounts of different kinds of foods each day provides a balanced diet.

---

1 Table 1 shows the daily energy needs of different people. Table 2 shows the energy content of four foods.
  a What is the daily energy need for an active 8-year-old boy?
  b How many grams of Food 3 would meet the energy needs of an office worker?
  c How much more energy does a labourer need than a male office worker each day? Show your working.
  d i From the foods given in Table 2, which ONE would be the best for the labourer to eat? Give a reason for your choice.
  ii If the labourer ate only the food you have suggested in your answer to i, what is the least amount he should eat to meet his daily energy need? Show your working.
  e The heat energy in foods can be measured experimentally by burning food under a known mass of water. The temperature rise of the water is recorded. The number of joules received by the water from 1 gram of food can be calculated using the following formula:

$$\text{Heat gained by water from Y grams of food} = \frac{\text{mass of water} \times \text{temperature rise} \times 4.2}{Y} \text{ J per g}$$

Use the following data and the formula to work out the number of joules released from 1 gram of food which caused the rise in temperature of the water.
Mass of water = 20 g
Temperature rise = 18 °C
Mass of food = 2 g   [MEG June 1994 (part)]

Person	Occupation	Daily energy need / kJ
Active girl aged 8 years	School girl	8 000
Active boy aged 8 years	School boy	8 400
Woman	Office worker	9 500
Man	Office worker	10 500
Active girl aged 15 years	School girl	11 800
Active boy aged 15 years	School boy	14 700
Man	Labourer	18 900

Table 1

Food	1	2	3	4
Energy content / kJ per 100 g	3 800	130	1 050	400

Table 2

Processed foods contain other substances

Natural foods contain mixtures of carbohydrates, lipids, proteins, vitamins, minerals and water. Many foods consumed in the developed world also contain other substances. These 'additional' substances fall into two main categories:

Fortification adds extra nutrients to processed foods.

- **fortifiers**: these are substances added to increase the nutrient value of the food ('fortification' means 'strengthening');
- **additives**: substances with no nutrient value but which are added to improve the appearance, flavour, texture and/or the storage properties of the food.

All food packages in European Union countries must carry a full list of additives so that consumers know exactly what they are getting when they buy a processed food.

Food additives may be natural or synthetic.

Ingredients

Whole wheat, malted barley extract, sugar, salt, niacin, iron, thiamin (B1), riboflavin (B2), folic acid

Allergens

Contains gluten and wheat

Nutrition

Typical values	per 37g serving with 150ml of semi-skimmed milk	per 100g
Energy	831kJ	1427kJ
	197kcal	336kcal
Protein	9.4g	11.8g
Carbohydrate	32.7g	68.0g
of which sugars	9.0g	4.7g
Fat	3.1g	1.9g
of which saturates	1.7g	0.6g
Fibre	3.8g	10.1g
Sodium	0.18g	0.27g
Niacin	5.9mg	15.3mg
% RDA	33	85
Thiamin (B1)	0.5mg	1.2mg
% RDA	36	85
Riboflavin (B2)	0.8mg	1.4mg
% RDA	49	85
Folic Acid	73mg	170mg
% RDA	36	85
Iron	4.5mg	11.9mg
% RDA	32	85

per 37g serving with 150ml of semi-skimmed milk		
197 calories	3.1g fat	0.5g salt

*RDA = recommended daily allowance

Guideline daily amounts for average adults

	Women	Men
Calories	2000	2500
Fat	70g	95g
Salt	5g	7g

Nutrition information from a packet of breakfast cereal.

Flavourings and flavour enhancers (usually E600 numbers)
- most common food additives
- some are natural (e.g. vanilla), some are artificial (e.g. propyl pentanoate – pineapple flavour)
- flavour enhancers make existing flavours stronger, by stimulating the taste buds (e.g. MSG – monosodium glutamate)

Colouring (E100 numbers)
- added to improve colour which may have been lost during cooking (e.g. peas become paler) or by dilution
- may be natural e.g. β carotene (E160) from tomatoes
- may be synthetic e.g. tartrazine (E102) from coal tar
- **cannot** be added to baby foods

NEW
NUTRI-LOW
Guaranteed to contain no food
but
High in additives

Prevention of spoilage – Preservatives (E200 numbers)
- inhibit growth of fungi or bacteria e.g. sulphur dioxide (E220) controls the browning of potatoes

Anti-oxidants (E300 numbers)
- slow down deterioration caused by atmospheric oxidation e.g. vitamin C (ascorbic acid – E300) added to fruit drinks

Additives may be dangerous For example
- tartrazine (E102) – linked to hyperactivity and poor concentration in children
- sulphur dioxide (E220) – may cause sensitivity in asthma sufferers
- monosodium glutamate (E621) – may cause vomiting, migraine and nausea

Improvement of texture
- thickeners alter the consistency of food e.g. cellulose E460
- stabilisers prevent components of emulsions separating out e.g. Xanthan E415 with yoghurt

All additives
- have an E (European) number
- must be pre-tested on animals

What about residues?

Additives are used to improve food *quality,* as described above. **Residues,** on the other hand, are added to increase food *production.* Because of their widespread use, or because of poor food production techniques, these substances may remain in food presented to humans. Some chemicals which may remain as residues, and which cause concern for human health, are:

- **Pesticides:** may become concentrated in food chains, causing harm to the top consumers (including humans) – see page 256.

- **Fertilisers:** nitrates and phosphates may leach into water supplies (see page 254). This has caused problems (**blue baby syndrome** in which babies' blood does not become properly oxygenated) in babies fed on reconstituted powdered milk.

- **Antibiotics:** used to prevent infection of cattle and poultry. May lead to the selection of antibiotic-resistant strains of microbes (see page 273).

- **Hormones:** oestrogen is used to boost the growth rate of chickens. This may cause human males to develop feminine characteristics.

---

1 Table 1 shows the composition and energy content of four common foods.

Food	Energy content / kJ per g	Composition per 100g					
		Protein / g	Fat / g	Carbohydrate / g	Vitamin C / mg	Vitamin D / mg	Iron / mg
A	3700	0.5	80	0	0	40	0
B	150	1.2	0.6	7	200	0	0
C	400	2.0	0.2	25	10	0	8
D	1200	9.0	1.5	60	0	0	0

Table 1

a Which food would be best to prevent rickets?
b Which food would be best for a young man training for cross-country running?
c Which food would be most needed by a menstruating woman?
d Which food would be the most useful to a body-builder?
e Which food would be most dangerous for a person with heart disease?

2 Breast milk contains all the nutrients a baby needs except for vitamin C and iron. However, the baby has sufficient iron stored in its liver for the first months of its life. The first milk a breast-fed baby receives is called colostrum. After a few days, normal breast milk is produced. Table 2 compares the composition of colostrum and normal breast milk.

	Nutrient / g per 100 cm³		
	Fat	Protein	Sugar
Colostrum	2.5	8.0	3.5
Normal breast milk	4.0	2.0	8.0

Table 2

a Use data from Table 2 to describe how the amounts of fat, protein and sugar are different in colostrum and normal breast milk.
b A baby feeding on normal breast milk drinks one litre of milk per day. Calculate how much protein the baby receives per day. Show your working.
c Suggest a suitable fruit juice a mother could give her baby to provide vitamin C.

(IGCSE May-June 2004 [part])

Food from microorganisms: fungi, bacteria and fermentation

Microbes carry out useful metabolic processes

Most microbes are **heterotrophic** – they take in ready-made food molecules from their environment. Fungi such as yeast and *Fusarium*, and many bacteria, secrete enzymes onto their food source, absorb the digested products and then use these products in their metabolism – they are **saprotrophic**. The enzymes they secrete, and any toxic or excess products which they excrete, may be of use to humans. This makes some microbes useful in food production, for example:

- *Acetobacter* in vinegar manufacture
- *Lactobacillus* in yoghurt and cheese production
- 'Ripening' bacteria in cheese production
- *Fusarium* and mycoprotein

Some of these processes are carried out on an enormous scale in special factories. The microbes (most commonly bacteria or fungi) are usually cultured separately and then added to their food source in a very large sterilised container. These containers are called **fermenters** or **bioreactors**, and the principles involved in their efficient use are described on page 35.

Commercial food production

The fermentation processes used to grow the microbes must be economical and efficient, and methods are always being improved.

Cheese production is a traditional process that has been updated by the use of modern scientific techniques. The curds are formed more quickly if the coagulation of the milk protein casein is catalysed by an enzyme. Traditionally **rennin** was used, extracted from the stomach contents of calves slaughtered for meat. Genetic engineers have now produced a strain of the bacterium *E. coli* which contains the gene for the enzyme **chymosin**. This enzyme can be used instead of rennin to produce a cheese that is acceptable to vegetarians.

The second phase of cheese production also involves the action of bacteria or fungi – hard cheeses such as Stilton are formed by bacterial action from the *inside*, whereas soft cheeses are usually the result of fungal action from the *outside*. The characteristic smells of strong cheeses are usually due to metabolism of fatty acids, sometimes the same as those found on human skin. The warm, moist conditions on the feet produce an odour which the producers of Camembert cheese call 'les pieds de dieu' (God's feet). Bread and beer are produced using yeast to ferment a sugar source (see page 50).

Excess yeast produced during alcoholic fermentation is sometimes used as cattle food – the cattle are actually eating the bodies of the fungus. Fungi may also be grown in a bioreactor to produce food for humans. The product is called **mycoprotein** or Quorn®, and is made from the compacted hyphae (see page 12) of the fungus *Fusarium graminearum*. This fungus offers a number of advantages as a food source:

- it can be produced very quickly – the fungus doubles its mass within hours
- it can be produced cheaply – the fungus can grow on waste materials from other processes, such as the waste carbohydrate from flour production or cheaply available 'foods' such as sugar beet
- fermenters take up very little land area, so valuable agricultural land is not used
- fermenters offer a controlled environment, independent of the local weather conditions
- the product is always of the same quality
- it has a high protein content (40%), at least as high as beef steak
- it has a much lower fat content (only 13%) but much higher fibre content than meat, offering numerous health advantages to humans
- the mycelium of hyphae can easily be shaped and flavoured.

Bacteria are involved in the production of food. **Vinegar** is produced by **aerobic fermentation of alcohol** in a suitable bioreactor (see page 35).

Oxygen ➡

Culture of *Acetobacter* ➡

Ethanol ➡

Wood shavings increase surface area for microbial fermentation.

Ethanoic acid (acetic acid) (vinegar) ➡

Ethanol + oxygen ➡ ethanoic acid

Cheese production involves several stages to provide both texture and flavour.

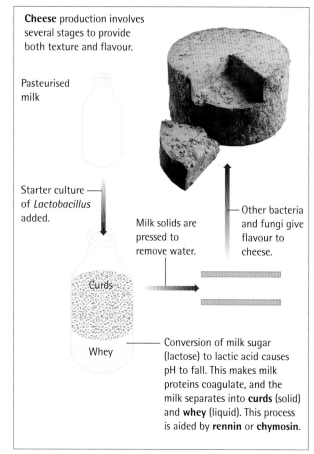

Pasteurised milk

Starter culture of *Lactobacillus* added.

Milk solids are pressed to remove water.

Other bacteria and fungi give flavour to cheese.

Curds

Whey

Conversion of milk sugar (lactose) to lactic acid causes pH to fall. This makes milk proteins coagulate, and the milk separates into **curds** (solid) and **whey** (liquid). This process is aided by **rennin** or **chymosin**.

Yoghurt is milk that has been soured by **fermentation of lactose** and thickened by **denaturation of protein**.

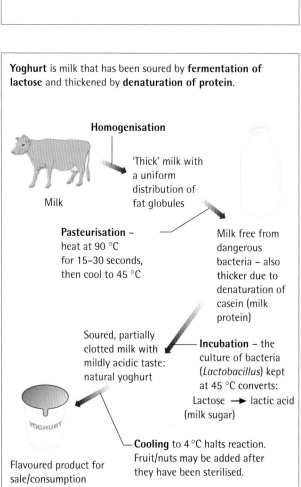

Homogenisation

Milk

'Thick' milk with a uniform distribution of fat globules

Pasteurisation – heat at 90 °C for 15–30 seconds, then cool to 45 °C

Milk free from dangerous bacteria – also thicker due to denaturation of casein (milk protein)

Soured, partially clotted milk with mildly acidic taste: natural yoghurt

Incubation – the culture of bacteria (*Lactobacillus*) kept at 45 °C converts:

Lactose ➡ lactic acid (milk sugar)

Cooling to 4 °C halts reaction. Fruit/nuts may be added after they have been sterilised.

Flavoured product for sale/consumption

A wide range of fermentations is used in food production, but they all share common features:

▪ The organisms require a source of food, including carbohydrate for energy and amino acids for protein synthesis.

▪ The organisms require optimum conditions of temperature, pH, oxygen concentration and water availability for most efficient activity.

1 What is meant by the term fermentation?

2 Several bacterial processes use milk as a starting point. Why is it important to pasteurise this milk?

3 Make a table to summarise the processes described on this page. Use these headings: Product, Starting material, Microbe involved, Special conditions.

4 Give one example of the importance of:
a genetic engineering
b technology
in the commercial production of foods.

5 Both cheese and yoghurt are available in many flavours. How do you think these different flavours might be obtained?

The economic importance of yeast: baking and brewing

Objectives

▸ To appreciate that some microorganisms are useful to humans

▸ To recall an equation for anaerobic respiration

▸ To understand the industrial production of alcohol and bread

Bread production

Flour, sugar, water and salt are mixed with **yeast**. This process is called **kneading** and produces **dough**.

The dough is rolled into shape, then kept in a warm (about 28 °C), moist environment. The yeast ferments the sugar, and the bubbles of carbon dioxide are trapped by the sticky proteins of the dough. The dough expands or **rises**.

Cooking at 180 °C – **baking**:

■ kills the yeast and stops fermentation
■ causes alcohol to evaporate
■ hardens the outer surface to form a crust.

The product is **bread**, which should be:

■ spongy in texture, because of trapped carbon dioxide
■ fresh smelling (partly alcohol vapour!).

If a loaf is not left to rise, it will be small and dense.

If a loaf is left to rise for too long too much carbon dioxide is produced and there are too many large holes.

The perfect loaf.

'Wholemeal' bread is made with flour which has **not** had the husk removed from the wheat – hence 'whole' meal. It is rich in B vitamins and dietary fibre.

Bread may be fortified – in Britain, bread often has added protein, calcium and vitamins A and D – not to mention preservatives and whitening agents.

Yeast performs alcoholic fermentation

Much of the commercial use of microorganisms is based on the process of **fermentation**. This term covers *any* metabolic process carried out by microorganisms using carbohydrate as a starting material. The best-known fermentation reaction is the anaerobic respiration of glucose by the single-celled fungus **yeast**:

$$\text{Glucose} \longrightarrow \text{carbon dioxide} + \text{ethanol} + \text{energy}$$

Since one of the products is ethanol (ethyl alcohol), this process is often known as **alcoholic fermentation**. As well as making alcohol, the carbon dioxide produced is valuable commercially. For the yeast, the useful product is energy – the alcohol and carbon dioxide are by-products.

Alcohol has a high energy content and is toxic

Alcohol contains a great deal of energy, a fact that is exploited when alcohol is used as a fuel source (see page 271). Alcohol is also toxic (poisonous) and the yeast excretes it into the surrounding liquid medium. If the alcohol concentration in the medium gets higher than 8–9%, the yeast is killed and fermentation stops.

Baking and brewing use fermentation

The processes of **baking** and **brewing** have both been around for thousands of years. These processes are outlined on the left and opposite.

Fine tuning the fermentation process

Because of the enormous commercial significance of these processes, much research has gone into making them as efficient as possible. For example:

▸ strains of yeast that are tolerant to higher concentrations of alcohol have been developed
▸ high-yielding strains of barley have been selectively bred
▸ genetic engineers have developed yeasts which can convert starch to maltose, and thus remove the need for the 'malting' stages.

Brewing

Barley is the source of **sugar**.

Barley is **ground** to separate husks from starchy interior.

Husks are collected, dried and sold to make cattle food

Enzymes in the barley convert
Starch → **maltose** (sugar)

Hops provide the **flavouring** and **bitterness**.

Hops are **roasted** – time depends on type of beer

Roasted hops and **colourings** (e.g. caramel)

Yeast and **extra sugar** – different yeast strains for different beers, e.g. *Saccharomyces carlsbergensis* for lager

Wine making uses similar processes. Grapes provide the sugar, and are 'pressed' to allow enzymes to begin the fermentation. Only 'sparkling' wines such as Champagne have a second 'in the bottle' fermentation.

Fermentation vat
- copper for beer (wood for wine)
- yeast + hops + sugar = **wort**
- here sugar is fermented to alcohol. The carbon dioxide escapes to form a froth which keeps the mixture anaerobic.

Typical fermentation temperature: 28–30 °C

'Live' beers – some yeast remains so that a second fermentation occurs in the barrel or bottle. CO_2 cannot escape and gives 'fizz' to beer.

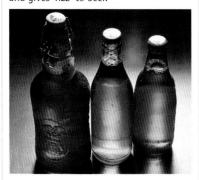

As the alcohol rises to 9 or 10% the beer yeast are killed. Much higher alcohol concentrations are achieved by:
- **distillation** – to remove water, as in the production of spirits such as whisky and gin
- **fortification** – addition of alcohol, as in production of port and sherry (fortified wines).

'Container' beers – fermented wort is sterilised to kill yeast. CO_2 is added from gas cylinders.

1. Yeast ferments glucose ($C_6H_{12}O_6$) to ethanol (C_2H_5OH) and carbon dioxide. Write out a balanced chemical equation for this process.

2. Bread may be fortified with vitamins A and D, and the mineral calcium. What benefit would these give to the consumer? Suggest why bakers often add: **a** preservative and **b** whitener to their product.

3. Brewing is a very competitive business. Name two possible by-products of the process which might generate some income for the brewer.

Organisation and maintenance of organisms

2·13 Food is the fuel that drives the processes of life

Objectives
- To know that food has an energy value
- To know how to calculate the energy value of different foods
- To understand that different people have different demands for energy

Measuring the energy in food

Energy is released from food by respiration, which is an oxidation process, similar in some ways to combustion – if food is combusted (burned), it releases energy, mainly as heat. We can work out the energy value of any particular type of food by assuming that respiration releases the same amount of energy in total as combustion does. The energy value is found using a **food calorimeter** or **bomb calorimeter**, shown in the diagram opposite.

A weighed sample of food is completely burned in an atmosphere of oxygen. The heat released by this combustion is transferred to a known volume of water, which rises in temperature as a result.
The energy value of the food can be calculated as follows:

To suction pump
Thermometer
Lid
Water
Stirrer
Coil – heat from the food is transferred to the water through this.
Crucible containing food
Heat-proof base
To heating element for igniting the food
Oxygen in here

$$\text{Energy value of food in calories per gram} = \frac{\text{temperature rise} / °C \times \text{volume of water} / cm^3}{\text{mass of food sample} / g}$$

$$\text{Energy value in kilojoules per gram} = \frac{\text{energy value in calories per gram}}{1000} \times 4.2$$

Energy values of different foods

The three main energy-providing organic molecules found in food are fats, carbohydrates and proteins. Each has a different energy value:

Fats	39 kJ per g
Proteins	20 kJ per g
Carbohydrates	17 kJ per g

Carbohydrates provide most of our energy, not because there is most energy available per gram in carbohydrates, but because we eat more grams of carbohydrates than of proteins or fats.

Units of energy

The SI unit of energy is the joule (J). The amount of energy contained in food is measured in either joules (J) or calories (cal).

1000 J = 1 kJ (kilojoule) 1000 cal = 1 kcal (kilocalorie)

A calorie is an older unit of energy that is still often used. A calorie is the amount of energy needed to raise the temperature of 1 cm^3 of water by 1 °C.

1 calorie = 4.2 joules

Joules and calories are small amounts of energy so kilojoules and kilocalories are more frequently used to describe the energy values of foods. In popular nutrition guides, the calories referred to are actually kilocalories and are often spelt Cal, with a capital C.

The energy content information given on the packaging of many foods has been calculated by burning a sample of the food in a food calorimeter.

Organisation and maintenance of organisms

Our energy requirements

The total of all the chemical reactions in the body is called **metabolism**. It is driven by the energy from respiration, so the amount of energy needed depends on how many metabolic reactions a person is carrying out. The amount of metabolism depends on three factors:

▪ the processes required simply to stay alive. These processes include breathing, excretion, thinking and keeping a constant body temperature. The energy consumed in one day by these processes is called the **basal metabolic rate** (BMR). The BMR is different for males and females, and gets less as a person gets older.

▪ the amount of **activity** or **exercise** – this requires muscular work and extra temperature regulation. This energy demand can be very little (in a sedentary office worker, for example) or very great (in a road worker, for example).

▪ the amount of food eaten – eating food means extra work for the digestive system and the liver. The energy demand simply caused by eating is called the **dynamic action of food**.

$$\text{Energy requirement per day} = \text{BMR} + \text{activity} + \text{dynamic action of food}$$

The bar chart below illustrates the energy demands for different people. Three factors affect the body's energy requirements – **age**, **sex** and **occupation**.

Energy requirements for different people.

Key: ▨ Male   ▨ Female

Energy in food

A class of students used the apparatus shown here to investigate the energy content of a peanut.
They first recorded the temperature of the water (T_1) and weighed the nut.
The nut was held in a Bunsen burner flame until it caught fire, and then placed under the boiling tube.
The students recorded the maximum temperature the water reached (T_2), and then repeated the experiment twice more. A typical set of results from one pair of students is shown in the table at the bottom of the page.

Boiling tube

20 cm³ of water

Burning peanut

---

1 a Copy and complete the table of results.
   b Add a further column and include the energy value of the peanut in kJ per g.
   c Calculate the mean energy value of the peanut as found by these students. Why is the mean value more valid than any single value that they obtained?

   d Can you suggest any improvements to the apparatus so that the students' value might be closer to the 'professional' one (24.5 kJ per g)? Redraw the apparatus showing your suggestions.
   e What features of the method helped to improve the validity of the results? How could the students have treated the results differently to improve their validity further?

T_1 / °C	T_2 / °C	$T_2 - T_1$ / °C	Volume of water / cm³	Energy transferred to water / kcal	Mass of nut / g	Energy value / kcal per g
22	78				0.45	
22	74				0.52	
21	75				0.47	

2·14 Balancing energy intake and energy demand: problems causing malnutrition

Malnutrition means literally 'bad feeding'. This 'bad feeding' could include:

☞ eating too much of all foods, so having a balanced diet but consuming more than is needed

☞ having too little food

☞ eating foods in the wrong proportions, for example, gaining too many kilojoules from fats and too few from carbohydrates.

Too much energy

The need for energy is related to **age, sex** and **activity** (see page 53).

If the diet contains more energy than the body needs, the excess will be stored as **glycogen** or **fat**; if it contains less energy than the body needs, then the body's own tissues will be broken down to be respired. The diagram below shows the importance of an **energy balance**.

A 'couch potato' has a poor diet and takes little exercise.

An athlete must take care that a balance is achieved between exercise and eating.

Storing excess food: overnutrition

The body can store a limited amount of glycogen, which allows the body to continue working even if the last meal was some time ago. However, the body can store an almost unlimited amount of fat to help the body survive periods without food. Our food intake should not be so great that we store an unhealthy amount of fat. A person whose fat storage is beyond a healthy limit is said to be **obese**.

The 'ideal' body mass differs from person to person, and depends on height and age. A person who is obese is at risk from a number of life-shortening diseases, including **diabetes, breathing difficulties, atherosclerosis** (narrowing of the arteries) and **arthritis**. Obesity is one of the most widespread results of malnutrition in the western world.

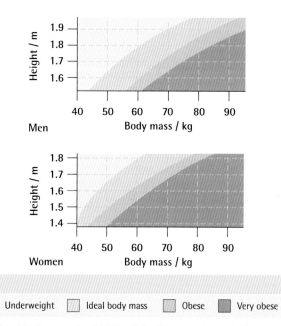

Key

☐ Underweight   ▨ Ideal body mass   ▦ Obese   ■ Very obese

The ideal body mass should fall within the range shown in these charts (designed for adults who have reached their full height).

Losing body mass

The energy balance diagram shows that to lose body mass, it is necessary to reduce energy intake below energy use. This can be done in two ways:

☞ by eating less 'high-energy' food, which will **reduce the energy intake**

☞ by taking more exercise, which will **increase the energy use.**

The best approach is to combine both methods, controlling the diet and also taking more exercise. Many people who rely on diet alone have great difficulty in controlling their body mass.

Malnutrition can also mean undernutrition: too little food

In the developing countries of the world, many people have diets which are neither adequate nor balanced. In other words, they do not receive enough energy to drive metabolism, nor do they take in the nutrients they need for growth and development. These people, often children, suffer from many deficiency diseases – shortage of iron means they are often anaemic, and a limited supply of vitamin C means that many of them have scurvy, for example. The most obvious signs of their malnourished state, however, are often caused by **protein deficiency**. There are two extremes of protein deficiency – **kwashiorkor** and **marasmus**.

Kwashiorkor

In kwashiokor, the child may not have received enough of its mother's milk (often because another child has been born) and may be forced onto a diet that is too high in carbohydrate (often maize). As a result the child may eat enough 'energy' food, but because the diet is poor in protein when its body should be developing quickly, the mental and physical development of the child may be impaired.

Marasmus

In marasmus, the child has symptoms of general starvation – there is not enough 'energy' food nor enough protein. All the body tissues waste away, and the child becomes very thin with a wrinkled skin.

Causes and treatments

Kwashiorkor and marasmus are both serious conditions. They are common in countries where drought conditions have led to poor harvests, or where people have left their homes because of civil war. Aid offered to these people must include both energy foods and the nutrients needed for growth. Powdered milk is often provided, because it is light and easy to transport. However it must be rehydrated with clean water otherwise water-borne diseases such as cholera (see page 258) may result.

Malnutrition in the developed world

As well as the problem of obesity, caused by taking in more energy than is needed for the body's metabolism and activity, there are other problems caused by an unbalanced diet for many people in developed countries. These problems, and the 'unbalanced diet' that causes them, are outlined in the figure.

This child has kwashiorkor. The absence of protein means that muscle development is very slow, and the limbs have a stick-like appearance. The swollen abdomen is caused largely by water from the blood plasma remaining behind in the body tissues. The liver is also swollen because it is working hard to make the proteins needed by the body from an inadequate dietary supply.

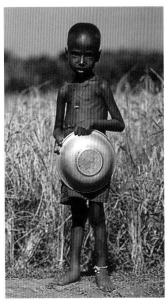

Marasmus is caused by insufficient levels of all nutrients in the diet.

Dangers of an unbalanced diet

High blood pressure
Too much **salt** in the diet can cause water to be drawn into the blood and blood pressure to rise, eventually damaging delicate blood vessels (page 102) including those in the brain.

Tooth decay
A diet with a high content of **acidic, sugary foods** can cause damage to tooth enamel and dentine (see page 77).

Coronary heart disease
Too much **saturated fat** and **cholesterol** can cause blockage to blood vessels supplying oxygen to heart muscle (page 110).

Constipation and bowel cancer
Too little **fibre** means that faeces are not passed as regularly as they should be – the person is **constipated**. Bacteria can work on some of the trapped faeces and release chemicals that cause **colon (large bowel) cancer**.

Don't forget obesity!
Too many kilojoules – the most common problem of nutrition in the developed world (see page 54)!

Questions on energy

1 The table below shows the energy value of a number of products from the Mars company.

a Copy and complete the table to show the energy value of each product in kJ per 100 g (take care – some energy values are shown for 25 g; others are for whole bars or packets).

b Draw a bar chart showing the products in descending order of energy value (the one with the highest energy value on the left).

c For a 50 g portion which product would be:
   i the least fattening
   ii the most fattening?

d A Mars bar weighs 65 g. What is its energy value in kilojoules?

e While sitting watching television, a boy of 15 uses about 6 kJ per minute.
   i How long would it take him to use all the energy obtained from the Mars bar?
   ii What is he using this energy for?

f While playing football the same boy uses, on average, 30 kJ per minute. How long would it take him to use up the energy obtained from the Mars bar?

g A football match lasts for 90 minutes. If the boy ran for half of the game, would he have used more energy or less than the Mars bar provided? How could his body cope with any difference between energy demanded and energy supplied?

Name of product	Energy value / kJ per 25 g, unless otherwise stated	Energy value / kJ per 100 g
Bounty, 60 g	490	
Maltesers	504	
Mars	454	
Milky Way	490	
Minstrels, 49 g	870	
Snickers	504	
Treets, 42 g	1040	
Twix	504	

2 Complete the following paragraph. Use terms from the list below – you may use each term once, more than once or not at all.

anaerobic, moist, living cells, animals, glucose, aerobic, oxygen, carbon dioxide, heat, water, energy.

Respiration is a process which occurs in all _____. The raw materials are _____ and, sometimes, _____. The purpose of the process is to release _____, and it is more efficient under _____ conditions.

3 Respiration is a feature of living organisms. Make a list of five other characteristics of living organisms.

4 Here are a number of statements about aerobic respiration. State whether each of them is TRUE or FALSE.

Aerobic respiration:

a uses water
b always requires oxygen
c occurs only in animal cells
d releases energy
e produces carbon dioxide
f is controlled by enzymes
g must have sugar as a starting material
h releases heat
i releases water
j is affected by temperature
k occurs in all living cells

5 Use words from this list to complete the following paragraphs. The words may be used once, more than once or not at all.

palisade cell, epidermis, tissues, excretory system, specialised, cells, blood, kidney, chloroplasts, leaf, red blood cell, division of labour, xylem, phloem, nervous, systems, endocrine, organ.

a Large numbers of _____ that have the same structure and function are grouped together to form _____, for example _____. Several separate tissues may be joined together to form an _____ which is a complex structure capable of performing a particular task with great efficiency. In the most highly developed organisms these complex structures may work together in _____, for example the _____ in humans is responsible for the removal of the waste products of metabolism.

b The structure of cells may be highly adapted to perform one function, i.e. the cells may become _____. One excellent example is the _____ which is highly adapted to carry oxygen in mammalian blood. If the different cells, tissues and organs of a multicellular organism perform different functions they are said to show _____ . One consequence of this is the need for close co-ordination between different organs – this function is performed by the _____ and _____ systems in mammals.

c In plants an example of a cell highly specialised for photosynthesis is the _____ which contains many _____ . These cells are located in the organ called the _____ which also contains other tissues such as _____ which limits water loss and _____ which transports water and mineral ions to the leaf.

2·15 Malnutrition and famine

Objectives
- To recall that malnutrition is a condition resulting from a defective diet where certain important food nutrients (such as proteins, vitamins, or carbohydrates) may be absent
- To remember that malnutrition can lead to deficiency diseases
- To understand some of the reasons why famines occur

A high global death rate linked to malnutrition has arisen from famine situations caused by a number of natural problems as well as by socio-political factors, such as alcohol and drug abuse, poverty, and war.

As well as suffering from a deficiency disease, a malnourished person is usually more at risk from other diseases (as the immune system may be very much reduced in efficiency) and a society with many malnourished individuals experiences mounting problems:

- Adults become ill and cannot work, so little money is available to buy food.
- Children become ill, and so adults must attempt to care for them (often going without food themselves).
- Older, weaker people will die and the society is deprived of their experience and knowledge.

Famine

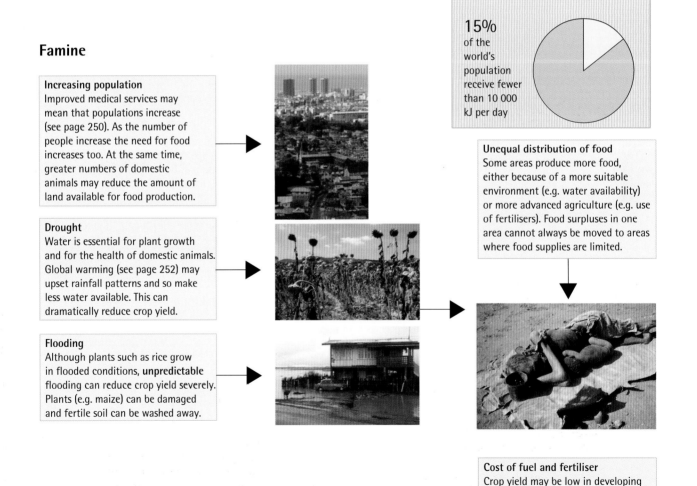

Increasing population
Improved medical services may mean that populations increase (see page 250). As the number of people increase the need for food increases too. At the same time, greater numbers of domestic animals may reduce the amount of land available for food production.

Drought
Water is essential for plant growth and for the health of domestic animals. Global warming (see page 252) may upset rainfall patterns and so make less water available. This can dramatically reduce crop yield.

Flooding
Although plants such as rice grow in flooded conditions, **unpredictable** flooding can reduce crop yield severely. Plants (e.g. maize) can be damaged and fertile soil can be washed away.

15% of the world's population receive fewer than 10 000 kJ per day

Unequal distribution of food
Some areas produce more food, either because of a more suitable environment (e.g. water availability) or more advanced agriculture (e.g. use of fertilisers). Food surpluses in one area cannot always be moved to areas where food supplies are limited.

Cost of fuel and fertiliser
Crop yield may be low in developing countries because poor farmers cannot afford fertiliser, or fuel to run machinery.

Can famine be stopped?

The world probably produces enough food to feed all of its inhabitants. Agriculture in developed parts of the world is extremely efficient (see page 260). Even so, as many as 15% of the world's inhabitants suffer from malnutrition because the available food is not evenly distributed among the world's population. Some people believe that all surplus food from developed countries should be made available to poorer countries, but many others (including EU agricultural ministers) argue that aid to poorer people should be mainly in the form of education and farming equipment. Direct food aid should only be reserved for disaster situations, such as the earthquake in Pakistan and flooding in Central America, where many individuals would quickly die if food were not made available. The problem of unequal food distribution is outlined in the figure.

Unequal distribution of food

Grain

Food mountains
in
rich countries

Milk

Transportation
Bulky foods are expensive to transport. Foods with a high water content (e.g. milk) do not give good 'food value per transport cost'. Perishable foods may not remain in good condition during long periods of transport.

Long distance transport can increase atmospheric pollution and global warming!

STOP

Self-sufficiency
It makes more sense to help poor people to grow food for themselves than to send food surpluses to them. For example
- **Education** about agricultural methods
- **Provision of water supplies** by digging wells

Price controls
Taking cheap food from a rich country to a poor one can artificially lower food prices in the poor region. This can upset the local economy, and reduce the incentive for indigenous people to grow their own food.

Organisation and maintenance of organisms

2·16 Photosynthesis and plant nutrition

Objectives

- To understand that plants, like all living organisms, must receive nourishment
- To know the basic definition for photosynthesis
- To know word and symbol equations for photosynthesis
- To remember that a plant body has organs that are well suited to carry out particular functions

Plants need food

All living organisms need food. Animals take in 'ready-made' food which they digest. They use the digested products for energy and to build new cells and tissues. Plants also require raw materials for building tissues and a source of energy. They manufacture everything they need out of simple ions and compounds available in the environment. The building up of complex molecules from simpler substances (**synthesis**) requires energy and enzymes. The enzymes are in the plant's cells, and the energy comes from sunlight. The process is therefore called **photosynthesis**. An outline of plant nutrition is shown in the diagram below.

Chloroplasts are energy transducers

Plants can absorb and use light energy because they have a green pigment, **chlorophyll**, contained in **chloroplasts** in some of their cells. Chlorophyll allows the energy in sunlight to drive chemical reactions. Chloroplasts act as **energy transducers**, converting light energy into chemical energy.

Defining photosynthesis

Photosynthesis is the process in which light energy, trapped by chlorophyll, is used to convert carbon dioxide and water into glucose and oxygen.

These equations summarise photosynthesis:

$$\text{Carbon dioxide} + \text{water} \xrightarrow[\text{chlorophyll}]{\text{light energy}} \text{glucose} + \text{oxygen}$$

$$6CO_2 + 6H_2O \xrightarrow[\text{chlorophyll}]{\text{light energy}} C_6H_{12}O_6 + 6O_2$$

These equations are simplified, and show only glucose as a food product of photosynthesis. In fact plants can make all of their food compounds by photosynthesis and other chemical processes.

Plants are **autotrophic** (self-feeding) – they take simple substances from their environment and use light energy to build them up into complex food compounds.

SUN

Light energy

Oxygen – a waste product released to the atmosphere

Carbon dioxide from the atmosphere

The plant makes **complex food compounds** which may be used for energy, growth, repair and reproduction. They include:
- glucose ⎤ contain carbon, hydrogen
- starch ⎦ and oxygen (**C, H,** and **O**).
- amino acids ⎤ contain nitrogen as
- and proteins ⎦ well as C, H and O
- nucleic acids – contain phosphorus as well as C, H, O and N
- lipids – contain C, H and O

Water from the soil

Minerals such as nitrate, phosphate and magnesium from the soil

Animals depend on plants
Autotrophic nutrition provides:
- a supply of **complex food compounds** which can be eaten by heterotrophic organisms, including animals
- a supply of **oxygen** which is essential for aerobic respiration in all organisms, including animals.

Some of the glucose produced is stored in the plant cells as **starch**. The experiment below shows how a starch test can be used to demonstrate the conditions needed for photosynthesis.

Testing leaves for starch

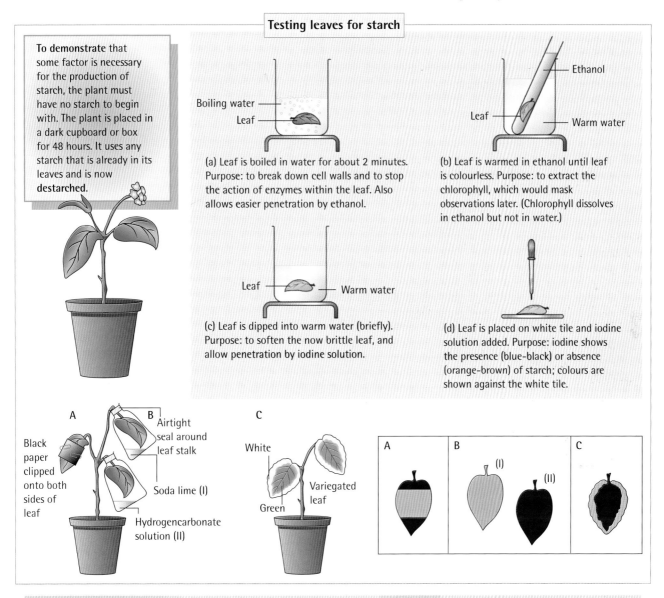

To demonstrate that some factor is necessary for the production of starch, the plant must have no starch to begin with. The plant is placed in a dark cupboard or box for 48 hours. It uses any starch that is already in its leaves and is now **destarched**.

(a) Leaf is boiled in water for about 2 minutes. Purpose: to break down cell walls and to stop the action of enzymes within the leaf. Also allows easier penetration by ethanol.

(b) Leaf is warmed in ethanol until leaf is colourless. Purpose: to extract the chlorophyll, which would mask observations later. (Chlorophyll dissolves in ethanol but not in water.)

(c) Leaf is dipped into warm water (briefly). Purpose: to soften the now brittle leaf, and allow penetration by iodine solution.

(d) Leaf is placed on white tile and iodine solution added. Purpose: iodine shows the presence (blue-black) or absence (orange-brown) of starch; colours are shown against the white tile.

These questions are about the diagram above.

1 Before testing for starch, the leaf is warmed in ethanol. The ethanol turns green. Why is this?

2 A group of students wanted to investigate the conditions needed for photosynthesis. They set up the three experiments shown as A, B and C. Each of the plants was given the same light conditions.
   a What does the result of experiment A suggest?
   b Soda lime removes carbon dioxide from the atmosphere, and hydrogencarbonate slowly releases it. What do the results of experiment B suggest about carbon dioxide and starch formation?
   c What is the purpose of experiment C?
   d From experiments A, B and C, list the factors necessary for starch formation by photosynthesis.

3 The students' teacher asked for some further tests to be completed before accepting their results as valid.
   a How could the students show that there was no starch in the leaves at the start of the experiment?
   b The teacher suggested that the black paper attached to the leaf in experiment A prevented the leaf from absorbing gases, and that was why no starch had been produced in the covered area. How could the students disprove this theory?

4 What additional experiment could be set up to show that the formation of starch by photosynthesis depends on the activity of enzymes? (There is a clue given in one part of the diagram above.)

2·17 The rate of photosynthesis

Objectives
- To understand a quantitative method of investigating photosynthesis
- To perform an exercise in experimental design

Measuring photosynthesis

The most straightforward way of showing whether or not photosynthesis has occurred is to test for the presence of starch. Starch is a product of photosynthesis and the blue-black colour of the iodine test is a simple method for detecting it. Unfortunately this is an 'all-or-nothing' test, that is, the colour is just as dark with a small amount of starch as it is with a large amount. The iodine test is said to be **qualitative** – it only shows whether or not starch is present. To find out *how quickly* photosynthesis is going on, we need to use a **quantitative** test.

The basic equation for photosynthesis is:

$$\text{Carbon dioxide} + \text{water} \xrightarrow[\text{chlorophyll}]{\text{light energy}} \text{glucose (starch)} + \text{oxygen}$$

This shows that as well as starch, there is another product of photosynthesis – oxygen. It is quite easy to measure amounts (volumes) of oxygen, and so the production of oxygen can be used as a quantitative test for photosynthesis.

Tracing photosynthesis

The rate of photosynthesis can be estimated by measuring how much carbon dioxide a plant absorbs. This is done using a radioactively labelled form of carbon dioxide, $^{14}CO_2$. Labelled carbon dioxide is absorbed by the leaf cells and converted into labelled carbohydrates in exactly the same way as 'normal' carbon dioxide. A Geiger counter is used to detect how much radioactive material has been incorporated by the plant in a fixed length of time – the rate of photosynthesis. This method is useful for studying the rate of photosynthesis in a 'real-life' situation – in the middle of a crop field, for example – where it is not possible to collect and measure volumes of oxygen.

Using radioactive tracers can also provide information about other compounds that plants make following photosynthesis, and about how plants transport food substances from one place to another in the plant.

Analysing the design of an experiment

The simplest apparatus for measuring oxygen release is shown in the next column. This method depends on counting the number of oxygen bubbles given off in a fixed length of time.

Apparatus that can be used to measure the *volume* of oxygen released in a fixed length of time is shown on the opposite page. When looking at this, remind yourself of the principles of experimental technique.

Simple estimation of photosynthesis

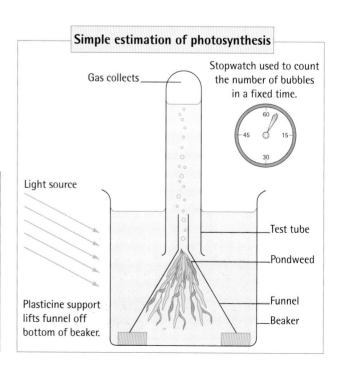

Gas collects

Stopwatch used to count the number of bubbles in a fixed time.

Light source

Plasticine support lifts funnel off bottom of beaker.

Test tube

Pondweed

Funnel

Beaker

Measuring the rate of photosynthesis

The volume of oxygen released in a fixed length of time can be used to calculate the rate of photosynthesis. This is the **dependent (outcome) variable**.

Scale

There are other variables that must be **fixed (controlled)** so that they do not influence the results, and the experiment remains a **fair test**.

e.g. Water temperature (continuous)

Concentration of hydrogencarbonate in vessel (continuous)

Wavelength of light (continuous)

Species of plant used (categoric)

Number of leaves on plant (discrete)

The light intensity can be varied by the experimenter: this is the **independent (input) variable**.

Light intensity is an example of a **continuous variable**.

A more accurate method for measuring the rate of photosynthesis. This apparatus can be used to investigate the effect of light intensity on the rate of photosynthesis.

---

1. What important assumption about the bubbles is being made, when using the method shown on the page opposite, to measure the rate of photosynthesis?

2. Using the apparatus above, Samantha and Jane obtained the results shown in the table.
   a Plot this information in the form of a graph.

Light intensity /arbitrary units	Volume of oxygen released / mm³ per minute
1	7
2	14
3	21
4	28
5	34
6	39
7	42
8	44
9	45
10	45

   b At what light intensity did the plant produce 25 mm³ of oxygen per minute?
   c What levels of light intensity had the greatest effect on the rate of photosynthesis? How could this information be useful to a grower of greenhouse tomatoes?

   Samantha and Jane wanted to investigate whether the wavelength of the light would affect photosynthesis, and decided that they could use the same apparatus.

   d What would be the input variable in this investigation? How could the two students change this variable?
   e What would be the fixed variables in this investigation?
   f The students decided to repeat their experiment, and then to pool their results with the results of other students in the same class. Why was this pooling of results important?
   g The teacher said that if the students were going to pool their results then they must remove the plants from the apparatus and weigh them. Why should they do this?
   h State the input, outcome and fixed variables in an investigation into the effect of temperature on the rate of photosynthesis.

3. This question is about the box 'Tracing photosynthesis' on the opposite page.
   a What important assumption is being made when using the rate of uptake of $^{14}CO_2$ as a measure of the rate of photosynthesis?
   b Why is it important that radioactively labelled carbon dioxide, $^{14}CO_2$, is treated by leaf cells in exactly the same way as 'normal' carbon dioxide?
   c Which process might release $^{14}CO_2$ from the plant?

Objectives

- To understand how the structure of the leaf is adapted for photosynthesis
- To recall the structure of a palisade cell
- To understand how whole plants can be adapted to make the most of light energy

- a way of **delivering water** to the leaf
- a system for the **removal of glucose** so that it can be transported to other parts of the plant
- an efficient means of **absorbing light energy**.

The diagram below shows how the structure of the leaf meets these requirements.

Features of the leaf

In order to photosynthesise efficiently a leaf needs:

- a method for **exchange of gases** between the leaf and its surroundings

Waxy cuticle reduces water loss. It is thicker on the upper surface since this surface is usually more exposed to the warming rays of sunlight.

Upper epidermis – a complete covering which is usually one cell thick. It is transparent to allow the free passage of light, and has the major function of preventing the entry of disease-causing organisms such as bacteria and fungi.

Palisade mesophyll – tall thin cells arranged in columns and separated by very narrow air spaces. Cells contain many chloroplasts, and the dense packing of these cells allows the **absorption of the maximum amount of light energy.**

Vein – the transport system in and out of the leaf. The **xylem** vessels **deliver water and mineral salts,** and the **phloem** sieve tubes **carry away the organic products of photosynthesis, such as glucose.**

Spongy mesophyll – these cells are rather loosely packed, and are covered with a thin layer of water. The air spaces between them aid the diffusion of gases through the leaf. The air spaces are saturated with water vapour so water diffuses out of the leaf.

Stomata – these minute pores **allow the entry of carbon dioxide and the exit of oxygen.** They are mainly present in the **lower epidermis.** This surface is less exposed to the Sun's radiation so that evaporation of water is kept to a minimum. The stomata can be closed when no carbon dioxide intake is needed (in the dark, for example).

When a plant is short of water, the guard cells become flaccid, closing the stoma.

When a plant has plenty of water, the guard cells become turgid. The cell wall on the inner surface is very thick, so it cannot stretch as much as the outer surface. So as the guard cells swell up, they curve away from each other, opening the stoma.

Closed

Flaccid guard cell

Stoma closed

Open

Turgid guard cell

Stoma open

Thick cell wall

Thin cell wall

Leaf structure is a compromise between maximising photosynthesis and minimising water loss.

This diagram shows how leaf, palisade cell and chloroplast are adapted for photosynthesis.

Leaf blade has a **large surface** to trap light and is **thin** so that light can penetrate

Interior of leaf magnified x300 with a light microscope

Cells of the upper epidermis do not have chloroplasts. Light passes easily through them.

Palisade cells are packed together and filled with chloroplasts. Best site for photosynthesis since **light** penetrates, **carbon dioxide** and **water** are delivered and **chlorophyll** is present.

Leaf stalk holds leaf in the best position to receive light

Chloroplasts can move within the cell to make best use of available light

Waxy cuticle is transparent

CO₂ from the air

Cell wall and cell membrane are freely permeable to CO₂ and water

Vein

Thin layer of water on cell surface can dissolve CO₂

Lower epidermis

Single palisade cell magnified x800 with a light microscope

Spongy cells have few chloroplasts. Large spaces between them allow easy diffusion of water and CO₂ through leaf to palisade cells.

Stomata are pores that allow CO₂ to diffuse into the leaf.

Water from the soil

2 Light energy reaches the chlorophyll molecules.

4 Oxygen is released as a waste product.

Key
- Water
- Carbon dioxide
- Oxygen
- Hydrogen

Membrane contains the **chlorophyll** molecules that can trap light energy.

5 Carbon dioxide can diffuse into the region between the green membranes.

7 Glucose is often stored as **starch grains**.

1 Water is a raw material for photosynthesis.

1 µm

3 Light energy splits the water molecules into oxygen and hydrogen: **the light reaction**.

6 Hydrogen and carbon dioxide react to form **glucose**, catalysed by enzymes: **the dark reaction**.

Photosynthesis goes on in two main stages – the **light reaction** and the **dark reaction**.

Chloroplasts are the site of photosynthesis.

---

1 Work out the magnification of the single chloroplast. Show how you reached your answer.

Objectives

- To understand that photosynthesis is affected by a number of different factors
- To appreciate that photosynthesis is affected most by the factor that is in shortest supply – the limiting factor
- To know that an understanding of limiting factors can be used in the efficient growth of greenhouse crops

Requirements for photosynthesis

The process of photosynthesis depends upon:

- the availability of light
- the presence of a pigment to absorb the light
- a supply of carbon dioxide and water
- a temperature suitable for enzyme activity.

The need for each of these requirements or **factors** is outlined in the diagram below.

If any of these factors is in short supply, the rate of photosynthesis will be less than its maximum possible rate. One factor can cause a 'bottleneck' in the overall process as shown at the top of the page opposite. The factor that is furthest from its optimum level is controlling the rate of the overall process. This factor is called the **limiting factor**. The limiting factor varies at different times and under different conditions.

- In Britain, during the summer, light and temperature may be ideal for photosynthesis but the carbon dioxide concentration may be the limiting factor.

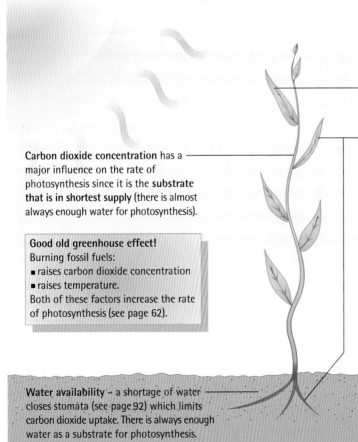

Availability of light – light provides the energy that drives photosynthesis (by splitting water molecules). The light energy absorbed by a plant depends on:
- the **intensity** of the light source
- the **wavelength** of the light
- the **length of time** (duration) that the light is available.

Chlorophyll is essential for the absorption of light energy. The synthesis of chlorophyll requires **magnesium ions**, which must be supplied from the soil (see page 86).

Temperature affects the rate of enzyme activity. A 10°C rise in temperature can cause a doubling in the rate of enzyme activity (although higher temperatures cause denaturation). This is important both in **leaves** (enzymes involved directly in photosynthesis) and in **roots** (enzyme systems involved in active transport of mineral ions – see page 87).

Carbon dioxide concentration has a major influence on the rate of photosynthesis since it is the **substrate that is in shortest supply** (there is almost always enough water for photosynthesis).

Good old greenhouse effect!
Burning fossil fuels:
- raises carbon dioxide concentration
- raises temperature.
Both of these factors increase the rate of photosynthesis (see page 62).

Poisons and photosynthesis
Photosynthesis may be inhibited by poisons, e.g.
- paraquat (a weed killer) prevents light energy being used to convert carbon dioxide to sugars
- sulphur dioxide (in acid rain) damages the palisade cells of the leaf.

Water availability – a shortage of water closes stomata (see page 92) which limits carbon dioxide uptake. There is always enough water as a substrate for photosynthesis.

Well balanced plants! Plants are autotrophic ('self-feeding') and can carefully regulate their food production. Plants need nitrate to be able to convert glucose from photosynthesis into amino acids. If there is a shortage of nitrate, the plant will reduce its rate of photosynthesis since it will need fewer sugars to make amino acids.

Factors affecting photosynthesis.

3 If the bottleneck is widened, in this case by raising the temperature, more substrate molecules can be converted to product.

1 The **rate of the reaction**, i.e. how many molecules of product (☐) are formed, is limited by the number of available substrate (carbon dioxide) molecules (○), since they can all pass through the enzyme 'channel'. The reaction will go faster if more substrate becomes available – in this situation **substrate concentration is the limiting factor**.

2 As the concentration of substrate is increased, a **second limiting factor** acts like a 'bottleneck'. No matter how many molecules of the substrate (○) are available, the number of molecules of product (☐) formed is limited by how quickly the enzymes (△) can work. In this example the temperature might be the limiting factor, since enzymes work less quickly at lower temperatures.

Limiting factors control the rate of reactions in living organisms.

- During any 24-hour period, light will be the limiting factor from dusk to dawn.
- During a British winter, plants may not photosynthesise on a bright, sunny day because temperature is the limiting factor.

The availability of water is rarely a limiting factor for photosynthesis, since there are so many other physiological processes in plants that depend on water that these processes will usually halt in a water shortage before photosynthesis does.

Controlling the limiting factors
In an open field, there is very little that farmers can do to speed up photosynthesis – they cannot change the degree of cloud cover or warm up the air, for example. However, in an enclosed environment such as a greenhouse, it is possible to control the factors affecting photosynthesis and so get the maximum yield from crops. This requires an understanding of the principle of limiting factors – it is no good simply increasing the light availability by having lights on in dull weather without making sure that carbon dioxide concentration and temperature are adequate, for example. A greenhouse grower will also try to use strains of plants selected for their high yield (see page 222), control any potential pests (see page 268) and will probably use automatic systems to control the factors that might limit the crop yield. The management of a greenhouse ecosystem is outlined on page 268.

---

1. List the three most important factors that control the rate of photosynthesis.
2. The burning of fossil fuels can both help and hinder photosynthesis. Explain this statement.
3. Which ion deficiency is most likely to affect photosynthesis? Why?

4. What is a limiting factor? Which limiting factor is most likely to affect photosynthesis:
   a on a cloudy, spring day
   b on a bright, sunny day in winter
   c in the middle of a crop field on a sunny, warm July day?

Objectives

- To understand that plants both photosynthesise and respire
- To understand that these processes affect the composition of the atmosphere
- To appreciate that photosynthesis plays an important part in the carbon cycle

Photosynthesis and respiration

From the equation for photosynthesis (see page 60) we know that this process removes carbon dioxide from the atmosphere and at the same time releases oxygen. This is the opposite of the exchange of gases in respiration:

> Glucose + oxygen → carbon dioxide + water

Green plants both photosynthesise and respire:

- if photosynthesis exceeds respiration (in the light) plants will, overall, remove carbon dioxide and add oxygen
- if photosynthesis is less than respiration (in the dark) plants will, overall, remove oxygen and add carbon dioxide.

Demonstrating gas exchange

The overall change in carbon dioxide levels in the atmosphere can be demonstrated using **hydrogencarbonate indicator**, as shown in the diagram below. Carbon dioxide produces a weak acid, **carbonic acid**, in water and this indicator is sensitive to the changes in pH caused by the acid.

In the dark, the rate of respiration greatly exceeds the rate of photosynthesis – the plant cells are living on the sugars they manufactured during previous periods of photosynthesis. As the light intensity increases after dawn, there comes a point where the rates of respiration and photosynthesis exactly balance one another and there is no net uptake or loss of carbon dioxide or oxygen. This is called the **compensation point**, and at this point the glucose consumed by respiration is exactly balanced by the glucose produced during photosynthesis. Beyond the compensation point the plant begins to gain glucose, as photosynthesis exceeds respiration.

Experiment on effect of light intensity

Colour of hydrogencarbonate indicator solution

Even source of light

Black paper cover

Tissue paper cover

Boiled leaf

As **carbon dioxide concentration decreases**, the indicator solution turns purple.

pH rises (less acidic)

Processes going on in living plant cells

O_2 CO_2
Respiration

O_2 Respiration CO_2
Photosynthesis

O_2 Respiration CO_2
Photosynthesis

No living cells

pH falls (more acidic)

As **carbon dioxide concentration increases**, the indicator solution turns orange–yellow.

Experiment to demonstrate the effect of light intensity on the balance between photosynthesis and respiration.

Hydrogencarbonate indicator reacts to changes in carbon dioxide in the air.

The products of photosynthesis

Plants manufacture all of their food requirements, starting from the glucose molecule. The diagram shows some of the products that the plant makes.

These products are available to the plant, and to any organism that eats the plant. An animal that eats plant material will use most of it to obtain energy by respiration. The carbon dioxide released as a waste product is then available for plants as a substrate for photosynthesis. An atom of carbon in carbon dioxide could be taken in by a plant, built up to a complex food molecule, and then eaten by an animal which breaks it down to carbon dioxide again. Thus atoms are **recycled** between simple and complex molecules, through the bodies of plants, animals and other living organisms. The **carbon cycle** is described simply in the diagram at the bottom of the page, and more fully on page 240.

Plants produce all their food molecules from the products of photosynthesis by metabolic reactions.

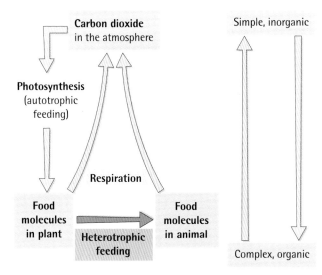

Photosynthesis and the carbon cycle – carbon is recycled between simple inorganic and complex organic compounds.

1. Name an indicator that can be used to measure carbon dioxide concentrations in solution. What colour change would you predict for this indicator in the presence of an actively photosynthesising plant? Explain your answer.

2. What is meant by the term compensation point? Why is it important that a grower of greenhouse crops should understand this term?

3. 'Photosynthesis provides plants with sugars' – is this true, and is it the whole story?

4. Plants take up carbon dioxide, which they convert to carbohydrate. Explain how it is possible for the plant to take in the same molecule of carbon dioxide more than once.

Questions on photosynthesis

1. The diagram shows apparatus which can be used to investigate the effect of different light intensities on the rate of photosynthesis.

   Bubbles of gas containing oxygen were produced by the pond plant during photosynthesis. These bubbles rose to the top of the test-tube. This forced water into the capillary tube, causing the air bubble to move along the tube.

   The lamp was placed at different distances from the plant. The intensity of light reaching the test-tube, and the distance moved by the air bubble in 4 minutes, were measured and recorded each time the lamp was moved.

   The syringe was used to bring the bubble back to 0 on the scale, at the start of each 4 minute period.

   The results are shown in the table.

Gas collects here
Test-tube
Pond plant
Syringe
Scale
Air bubble in capillary tube
Heat filter
Movable lamp

a Plot the results as a graph.

b Why was a heat filter needed?

c Each time the lamp was moved to a new position, an interval of 5 minutes was allowed before starting to time a 4 minute period for movement of the air bubble. Suggest a reason for this 5 minute interval.

d Suggest why the rate of movement of the air bubble was the same at 6.0 units as at 7.0 units of light intensity.

e Suggest why the air bubble did not move when the light intensity was 0.5 units.

f Suggest a suitable control for this investigation.

light intensity / arbitrary units	distance moved by bubble in the 4 min period / mm
0.5	0
1.0	6
2.0	18
3.0	30
4.0	42
5.0	54

(IGCSE June 1997)

2. Copy and complete the following paragraphs.

   a The cells of green plants absorb water by _____. Plant cells rely on water for _____, as a medium for biochemical reactions, as a _____ and as a raw material for _____.

   b Water is obtained by plants from the soil solution. The water enters the plant through its _____. These structures are well adapted to the absorption of water. There are _____ growing on their epidermis which greatly increase the _____ over which water absorption can take place. In addition to water, these structures also absorb _____ such as _____ which is required for the synthesis of chlorophyll and _____ which is required for the manufacture of amino acids and proteins. These substances are absorbed by a process called _____ since it requires a supply of energy.

   c Water is used as a transport medium for both ions and sugars. Mineral ions are transported within the main water flow through the plant in the _____ tissue. Sugars are transported in the living cells of the _____. These specialised tissues are grouped together into _____ bundles.

3 This question is about support in plant cells.

The plant cells are in the root of a carrot.

The following diagram shows three carrot root cells placed in a concentrated sugar solution.

a **i** Name the parts of the cell labelled **A**, **B** and **C**.

  ii What is filling the space labelled **D** on the diagram?

Concentrated
sugar solution
outside the cells

b Below are descriptions of plant cells which have turgor pressure and plant cells which do not.

List the **three** descriptions of cells with turgor pressure.

☞ the cell membrane is pressed against the cell wall
☞ the cell membrane is not in contact with the cell wall
☞ the cell wall is stretched
☞ the cell wall is not stretched
☞ the vacuole is pushing against the cytoplasm
☞ the vacuole is not pushing against the cytoplasm

c People do not like buying carrots which are split.

Scientists can use a wedge test to find out how easily a carrot splits.

The diagram shows a wedge test.

The graph shows the results of many wedge tests.

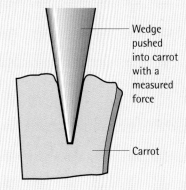

Wedge pushed into carrot with a measured force

Carrot

i What does the graph tell you about the relationship between turgor pressure and the amount of force needed to split carrot roots?

ii Suggest why carrots grown in low-rainfall areas are less likely to split.

(MEG June 1998)

Force needed to split carrot

Turgor pressure of carrot

2.21 Plants and minerals

Objectives
- To know that plants require minerals such as nitrate and magnesium
- To know the functions of minerals in plants
- To appreciate how information about plants' mineral requirements can be obtained

Plants need a number of minerals. The plant uses minerals to make food molecules such as amino acids, proteins and nucleic acids out of the carbohydrates made by photosynthesis (see page 69). Plants absorb minerals from the soil in the form of **ions**. The mechanism of ion uptake is described on page 86. Here we shall consider *why* the ions are required, and how scientists might work out the function of each different mineral nutrient.

Minerals in soil
The minerals present in soil depend on the type of rock beneath the soil and on the decomposition of animal and plant remains lying on the soil.

Minerals are taken out of the soil by plants, and are also washed out by rain. In natural, uncultivated soils there is a balance between the formation and the loss of mineral ions, as shown below.

In *cultivated* soils the ground is prepared and then the crop is harvested. There are few plant remains left to decompose and replace the minerals taken up into the plant body. Levels of minerals such as nitrate and phosphate fall, so farmers add these back in the form of **fertilisers**. These may be **natural fertilisers**, such as sewage sludge, animal manure or compost, or they may be **artificial fertilisers**. The most common artificial fertiliser is NPK fertiliser which contains three main nutrients – nitrogen (N), phosphorus (P) and potassium (K). The role of some of these minerals, and the effect on the plant of mineral deficiencies, is shown in the diagram on the opposite page. Providing these minerals is one of the most important aspects of preparing soil for agriculture.

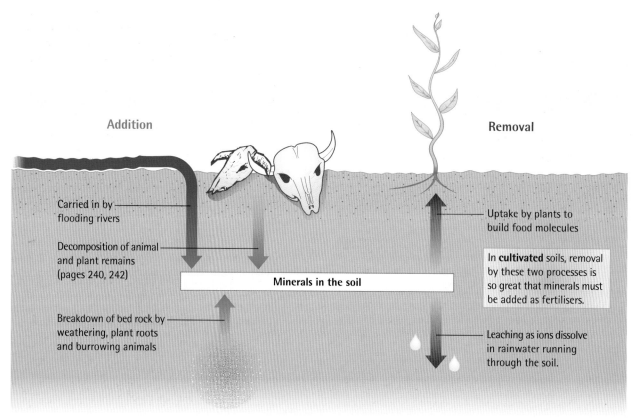

Addition

Removal

Carried in by flooding rivers

Decomposition of animal and plant remains (pages 240, 242)

Breakdown of bed rock by weathering, plant roots and burrowing animals

Minerals in the soil

Uptake by plants to build food molecules

In **cultivated** soils, removal by these two processes is so great that minerals must be added as fertilisers.

Leaching as ions dissolve in rainwater running through the soil.

Minerals are added to the soil and also removed by natural processes.

Magnesium is absorbed from the soil as **magnesium ions (Mg^{2+}).** Magnesium forms part of the chlorophyll molecule. Deficiency causes **chlorosis** – the leaves turn yellow, usually from the bottom of the plant first.

Leaves turn pale green or yellow.

Roots normal

Nitrogen probably has the greatest effect on plant growth. Farmers use expensive NPK fertilisers to replace nitrogen removed from the soil when crops are harvested.

Nitrogen is absorbed from the soil as **nitrate ions (NO$_3^-$)** or **ammonium ions (NH$_4^+$).** Because nitrogen is required for so many food molecules, especially proteins (including enzymes), deficiency causes severe symptoms. The whole plant is stunted, with a weak stem and yellowing, dying leaves.

Leaves pale

Lower leaves dead

Roots only slightly affected

Plant growth and mineral deficiencies.

Problems with fertilisers

Excessive use of fertilisers can cause problems of eutrophication (see page 254). The fertiliser runs off into nearby streams, rivers and lakes and boosts the growth of algae. As algae die they are decomposed by bacteria, which use all of the oxygen dissolved in the water for aerobic respiration. As a result the water becomes oxygen-deficient, and larger animals such as fish and insects die.

Plants and minerals – investigation

The apparatus shown on the right can be used to investigate the effects of mineral deficiencies on plant growth. Cereal plants of equal age and size are grown in a series of culture solutions. One of the solutions contains all known mineral nutrients in the correct proportions; each of the others is missing a single mineral. All the vessels are placed in identical conditions of temperature and light intensity, and the plants are allowed to grow for equal lengths of time.

1 Why is the vessel surrounded by black paper?

2 The bubbled air supply provides oxygen to the roots. Why might this be important in mineral uptake?

3 What is the independent variable in this investigation, and what is the dependent variable?

4 Suggest some fixed variables, and state how you would attempt to control them.

5 Cereal plants such as grasses are useful in this sort of investigation, since many identical plants can be obtained from a single clump. Why is this important in providing valid data?

6 The plant nutrients used in this investigation are supplied as salts. How could you make up a culture solution that is only lacking a single element?

Plant – a cereal such as grass is usually chosen since growth is rapid

Cotton wool support for plant

Glass vessel with black paper cover

Culture solution – minerals dissolved in distilled water

Air supply – provides oxygen to roots, and bubbles keep culture solution well mixed

2·22 Nutrition converts food molecules to a usable form

Objectives
- To know that the process of nutrition involves several stages
- To know the basic layout of the human alimentary canal

Definition: nutrition is the set of processes used by an organism to provide itself with food.

Nutrition involves a sequence of processes

Living things obtain food molecules from the environment. These molecules are not usually exactly the same as the biological molecules the organism needs to carry out its life processes. The processes of nutrition convert the food molecules into a form that can be used by the organism. In humans and many other animals, these processes take place in the **alimentary canal** (sometimes called the **gut**). The alimentary canal is a specialised tube running from the front of the animal (starting at its **mouth**) to the rear (ending at its **anus**). While the food is inside the tube it is not available to the body tissues. The food molecules must be changed into a form that can cross the gut wall and then be transported to the places where they will be used or stored. The processes of nutrition are described in the diagram below.

The alimentary canal is highly specialised in humans. The food molecules are converted to a usable form in a clear sequence, with each part of the gut being adapted to carry out particular functions. The layout of the alimentary canal is shown in the diagram opposite, and we shall see how its organs work in the next few pages.

1. List, in their correct sequence, the processes that make up nutrition.
2. What is the difference between the following?
   a chemical and mechanical digestion
   b absorption and assimilation
   c egestion and excretion
3. Why are the epiglottis and the soft palate important in efficient feeding?
4. Name three glands that add juices to the alimentary canal.

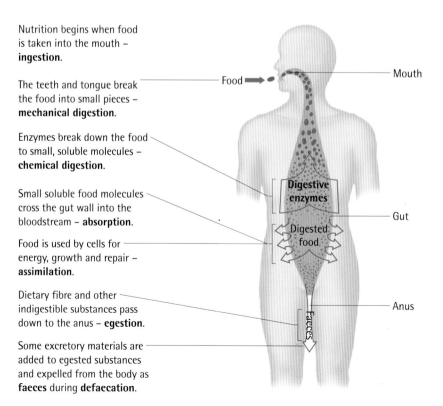

Nutrition begins when food is taken into the mouth – **ingestion**.

The teeth and tongue break the food into small pieces – **mechanical digestion**.

Enzymes break down the food to small, soluble molecules – **chemical digestion**.

Small soluble food molecules cross the gut wall into the bloodstream – **absorption**.

Food is used by cells for energy, growth and repair – **assimilation**.

Dietary fibre and other indigestible substances pass down to the anus – **egestion**.

Some excretory materials are added to egested substances and expelled from the body as **faeces** during **defaecation**.

Food — Mouth
Digestive enzymes — Gut
Digested food
faeces — Anus

Nutrition is a sequence of processes involving ingestion, digestion, absorption and egestion.

INGESTION

DIGESTION

ABSORPTION

EGESTION

Salivary glands – three pairs, produce saliva and pour it into the mouth through **salivary ducts**.

Oesophagus – muscular tube which helps food move to stomach by peristalsis.

Liver – produces **bile**, which helps to neutralise acidic chyme and also emulsifies fats. Important in assimilation.

Stomach – muscular bag which stores food for a short time, and mixes food with acidic digestive juices to form the creamy liquid called **chyme**.

Duodenum – first part of the small intestine, where semi-liquid food is mixed with pancreatic juice and bile.

Pancreas – produces pancreatic juice (contains enzymes, mucus and hydrogencarbonate which neutralises acidic chyme) which is poured into the small intestine through the **pancreatic duct**.

Mouth – here food enters the alimentary canal. It is converted to a **bolus of food** – produced by teeth, tongue and saliva during **mastication** (see page 76) – ready for swallowing.

Epiglottis – flap of muscle which closes the entry to the trachea during swallowing (see page 79).

Ileum – longest part of the small intestine, where digested food is absorbed into the blood and lymphatic system.

Large intestine – (wider than the small intestine) The **colon** is part of the large intestine. It reabsorbs water from gut contents; also absorbs some vitamins and minerals.

Rectum – stores faeces before expelling them at a convenient time.

Anus – exit for faeces; defaecation is controlled by two anal sphincters.

Ingestion provides food for the gut to work on

Objective
⬛ To understand the part played by teeth and the tongue in preparing food for the alimentary canal

Mastication produces a bolus

The first stage in processing food for use by the organism is taking the food into the gut. Once the food has been caught or collected, and perhaps cooked or processed in some other way, it is placed in the mouth. Here it is cut up by the teeth, and the pieces are mixed with saliva by the tongue. This cutting and mixing is called **mastication**, and produces a ball of food called a **bolus**. The bolus is swallowed and passed on to the next parts of the gut. The teeth play an important role in mastication, and it should be no surprise that:

⬛ the structure of a tooth is closely related to its function

⬛ there are different types of teeth adapted to deal with all types of food.

Human teeth and their function

The structure and function of a human tooth are shown in the diagram below. This type of tooth is called a molar, found towards the back of the jaw. The diagram above right shows the four different types of human teeth, and the part each of them plays in mastication.

The teeth in the skull

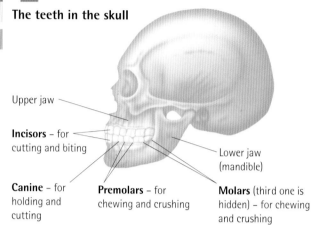

Upper jaw

Incisors – for cutting and biting

Lower jaw (mandible)

Canine – for holding and cutting

Premolars – for chewing and crushing

Molars (third one is hidden) – for chewing and crushing

Side view of the four types of tooth

Crown

Root

Incisor   Canine   Premolar   Molar

Surface view of the lower jaw

3 molars

2 premolars

1 canine

2 incisors

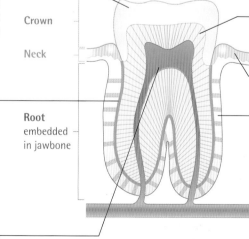

Enamel – the hardest tissue in the body. Produced by **tooth-forming cells** and made of calcium salts. Once formed, enamel cannot be renewed or extended.

Crown

Neck

Cement – similar in composition to dentine, but without any canals. It helps anchor the tooth to the jaw.

Root embedded in jawbone

Pulp cavity contains:
■ **tooth-producing cells**
■ **blood vessels**
■ **nerve endings** which can detect pain.

Dentine – forms the major part of the tooth. Harder than bone and made of calcium salts deposited on a framework of **collagen fibres**. The dentine contains a series of fine canals which extend to the pulp cavity.

Gum – usually covers the junction between enamel and cement. The gums recede with age.

Periodontal membrane – bundles of collagen fibres, anchoring the cement covering of the tooth to the jawbone. The tooth is held firmly but not rigidly. The periodontal membrane has many nerve endings which detect pressures during chewing and biting.

Vitamin C deficiency impairs production of collagen fibres, including those in the periodontal membrane, so that the teeth become loose and may fall out – a classic symptom of scurvy (see page 44).

Organisation and maintenance of organisms

Decay begins in enamel – **no pain**.

Decay penetrates dentine and reaches pulp – **severe toothache**.

Bacteria now infect pulp and may form abscess at base of tooth – **excruciating pain**.

Decayed part of tooth is drilled out by a dentist.

Hole is filled with amalgam or plastic, and may be coated with plastic.

Two sets of teeth

Humans, like other mammals, have two sets of teeth during their life. The first set is the milk dentition, which begins to grow through the gums one or two teeth at a time at around five months old. By about 18 months most children have a set of 20 teeth – there are fewer molars ('cheek teeth') than in an adult since the jaw is too small to hold any more. Between the ages of seven and twelve years these milk teeth fall out and are replaced by larger adult teeth. Eight new cheek teeth are added, with a further four (the wisdom teeth) appearing at the back of the jaw by about the age of 17 years. The individual now has the complete adult or permanent dentition of 32 teeth.

Western-style malnutrition may cause dental decay

A diet that provides too much energy can cause obesity (see page 54). Much of this energy-rich food will be in the form of refined sugars such as sucrose (cane sugar) which is used to sweeten many foods. These sugars may also be used by bacteria in the mouth to carry out their own life processes.

The bacteria produce a sticky matrix which traps food particles and forms a coating of **plaque** on the teeth. The bacteria in the plaque convert sugars in the food to acids. These acids remove calcium and phosphate from the enamel, allowing bacteria to reach the softer dentine beneath. This is the start of **dental decay** or **dental caries**. The dentine decays rapidly and the pulp cavity may become infected. The tooth will need dental treatment, as shown in the diagrams on the left.

Dental decay, and the gum disease that often goes along with it, can be prevented by:

- eating food with a low sugar content
- regular and effective brushing of teeth at least twice a day to prevent the build-up of plaque – plaque begins to reform after about 24 hours
- if brushing is not convenient, finishing a meal with a crisp vegetable or fruit, followed by rinsing with water.

The mineral fluoride can be added to drinking water. Tests have shown that this mineral reduces the risk of dental decay, although some people say that they should not be forced to consume it.

1. How do we know that a tooth is a living structure?
2. Imagine yourself on a British warship several hundred years ago. Explain, simply, why the sailors were losing their teeth.
3. a What is dental caries?
   b How does it begin?
   c Suggest **two** ways in which caries can be prevented or reduced.

Organisation and maintenance of organisms

2·24 Digestion prepares useful food molecules for absorption

Objectives
- To know that digestion converts large insoluble molecules into smaller, soluble molecules
- To understand that enzymes catalyse the breakdown of food
- To list examples of enzymes involved in digestion of carbohydrates, proteins and fats, and to know where they perform their tasks
- To understand that undigested food must be expelled from the gut

The diet contains three types of food molecule in large amounts – carbohydrates, proteins and fats. When ingested, these molecules may be too large to cross the gut wall and too insoluble to be transported in the watery blood plasma. **Digestion is the process that converts these ingested foods into a form that can be absorbed and transported.**

Digestive enzymes
In digestion, food molecules are broken down by **hydrolysis** reactions (breakdown with water), catalysed by a series of enzymes. There are different enzymes for the hydrolysis of each food type; each enzyme works in different regions of the gut. The basic process of hydrolysis is the same for all the food molecules (see page 39):

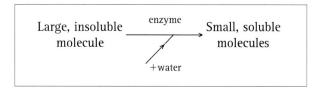

Carbohydrate digestion begins in the mouth
The saliva contains an enzyme called **salivary amylase** (a carbohydrase). This enzyme catalyses the conversion of the insoluble polysaccharide starch to the soluble simpler sugar called maltose:

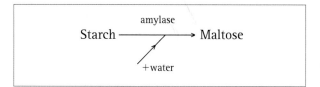

The saliva also contains mucus, which lubricates the food, and hydrogencarbonate, which provides the ideal conditions of pH (alkaline) for amylase to work. The starch is not usually all converted to maltose in the mouth since the food does not remain there for very long.

Passing to the stomach
Mastication produces a bolus of food, as we saw on page 76. The tongue pushes the bolus to the back of the mouth, and it is then swallowed (see opposite page) and enters the **oesophagus**. The oesophagus or gullet is a muscular tube leading from the mouth to the stomach. The bolus is forced down the oesophagus more quickly than can be explained by gravity alone. (It is even possible to swallow food when standing on your head!) Waves of muscular contraction push the bolus down towards the stomach, as shown in the diagram below. These waves of contraction are known as **peristalsis**, and they occur throughout the length of the gut. The reason why fibre is important in the human diet is that without it the gut contents are very liquid, and the muscles of the gut cannot squeeze the food along by peristalsis.

Cross-section of gut showing muscle layers

Longitudinal muscles (running down length of gut wall)

Circular muscles (running around the gut wall)

Longitudinal section of gut showing peristalsis

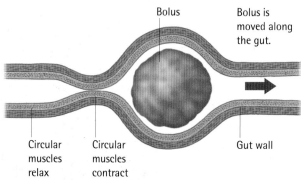

Bolus

Bolus is moved along the gut.

Circular muscles relax

Circular muscles contract

Gut wall

Peristalsis is a wave of muscular contraction that moves food along the gut. Mucus lubricates the bolus, helping it to move along.

Protein digestion begins in the stomach

The stomach is a muscular bag with a lining that contains digestive glands. These glands produce three important secretions:

- **mucus**, which protects the walls of the stomach from attack by gastric (stomach) juices
- pepsin, a **protease** or protein-digesting enzyme
- **hydrochloric acid**, which provides the acidic conditions needed for the action of pepsin.

Inside the stomach the food is churned up with the gastric juices. The long protein molecules are broken down by hydrolysis to smaller molecules called peptides, as shown in the diagram below.

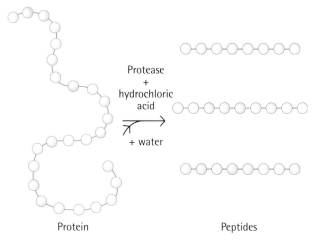

Protease
+
hydrochloric
acid

+ water

Protein   Peptides

The pH in the stomach is too low (too acidic) for the action of amylase, so the digestion of carbohydrate comes to a halt whilst the food is in the stomach. The churning action of the stomach muscles mixes the food into a creamy liquid called **chyme**. Once the food is sufficiently liquid, it squeezes past a ring of muscle at the foot of the stomach, the **pyloric sphincter**, and enters the **duodenum**, the first part of the small intestine.

pyloric sphincter

This X-ray was taken after the patient swallowed a barium meal. The barium makes the stomach show up on the X-ray. Food is passing through the pyloric sphincter.

The swallowing reflex

It is important that the bolus of food travels down the oesophagus and not down the trachea (windpipe), or it might block the trachea and prevent breathing. A flap of muscle, the **epiglottis**, is forced across the top of the trachea whenever food is swallowed, ensuring food does not enter the trachea. We don't have to think about this swallowing reflex, but it can be overruled if we try to eat and talk at the same time!

At the bottom of the oesophagus, just where it joins the stomach, is a ring of muscle called the cardiac sphincter. When the bolus reaches this sphincter, the ring of muscle relaxes to allow the bolus through into the stomach. If the stomach contents pass upwards through this sphincter and make contact with the wall of the oesophagus, they cause a burning sensation known as 'heartburn'. This can be treated using an alkaline ('antacid') solution.

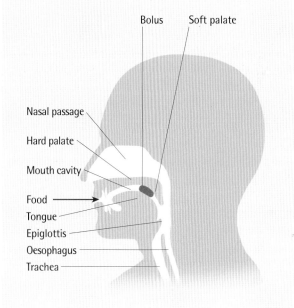

Bolus   Soft palate

Nasal passage

Hard palate

Mouth cavity

Food

Tongue

Epiglottis

Oesophagus

Trachea

Food bolus is moved down the oesophagus.

Digestion of food molecules is completed in the small intestine

The liquid chyme contains partly digested food molecules. The digestion of these food molecules is completed in the small intestine, using digestive juices which contain:

- enzymes from the pancreas
- enzymes from the intestine wall
- bile from the liver.

The enzymes from the pancreas carry out three tasks – **amylase** completes the conversion of starch to maltose, **protease** completes the breakdown of peptides to amino acids, and **lipase** converts fats to fatty acids and glycerol. These enzymes work best at around pH 8 (slightly alkaline conditions), and the juice from the pancreas also contains hydrogencarbonate which neutralises the acid coming through from the stomach.

Lipase is helped in its action by **bile**, which is made in the liver and stored in the gall bladder from where it is released when needed. Bile **emulsifies** the fats – it converts them from large globules into much smaller droplets, giving a greater surface area for the lipase to work on, as shown in the diagram.

Bile also contains hydrogencarbonate to help neutralise the acid from the stomach. Enzymes on the wall of the small intestine include **maltase**, which completes the breakdown of maltose to glucose. All the starch has now been converted to glucose. The table opposite lists the digestive juices and their actions.

Water and digestion

The digestive juices are largely made up of **water** – this is one of the major requirements for water within the body. This water is the solvent for the biochemical reactions of digestion and is also used in the hydrolysis reactions that split up the large, insoluble food molecules. The juices also contain **mucus** which protects the wall of the gut from being digested by its own enzymes.

Egestion removes undigested food

Food may contain some molecules that cannot be digested by the enzymes of the human gut. Examples include substances in plant cells, such as the cellulose in cell walls and the lignin in wood. These make up 'dietary fibre' (page 45). Water is first absorbed from the gut contents that remain after digestion, and this indigestible food is then expelled. This process is called **egestion**. Some excreted materials, such as salts in the bile, may be added to the indigestible foods to form the **faeces**. The faeces are stored temporarily in the rectum. When full, the rectum sets off a reflex action which causes its muscles to contract and squeeze the faeces out through the anus. Humans have a sphincter at the anus which can prevent this **defaecation** happening at an inconvenient time! The control of this sphincter has to be learned, and babies simply fill their nappies when the rectum is full.

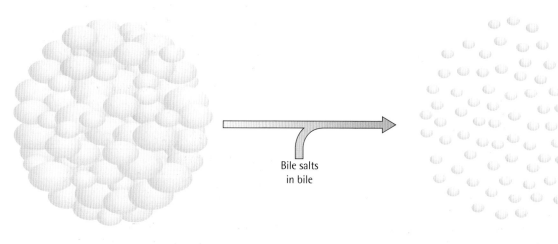

Large fat globule – relatively small surface area

Bile salts in bile

Many small fat droplets – relatively large total surface area

Emulsification of fats provides a larger surface for lipase to act on.

Region of gut	Digestive juice	Enzymes	Substrate	Product(s)	Other substances in juice	Function of other substances
Mouth	Saliva from salivary glands	Salivary amylase	Starch	Maltose	Hydrogencarbonate	Alkaline (pH 7.5) environment for amylase
Stomach	Gastric juice from glands in wall of stomach	Pepsin (protease)	Proteins	Peptides	Hydrochloric acid	Acidic (pH 2) environment for pepsin; kills bacteria
Small intestine (duodenum)	Pancreatic juice from pancreas	Pancreatic amylase Trypsin (a protease) Lipase	Starch Peptides Emulsified fats	Maltose Amino acids Fatty acids and glycerol	Hydrogencarbonate	Neutralises chyme: alkaline environment for enzymes
	Bile from liver (stored in gall bladder)	None			Bile salts	Emulsifies fats – converts globules to smaller droplets
					Hydrogencarbonate	Neutralises chyme
Small intestine (ileum)	Intestinal juice from cells on villi	Maltase Lactase Sucrase	Maltose Lactose Sucrose	Glucose Glucose and galactose Glucose and fructose		

The human digestive juices and their actions.

1 In 1822 Alexis St Martin, a Canadian fur trapper, was wounded in his left side by a shotgun blast. Luckily the accident occurred close to an army fort where one of the surgeons, William Beaumont, was able to treat St Martin. The wound healed very slowly, and left a small hole in the side of the young man. Beaumont realised that this gave him a unique opportunity to study what was happening in his patient's stomach.

a Which letter on the outline above represents the most likely position of the hole?

b Beaumont described one of his investigations as follows: 'Juice was extracted from the stomach and placed in a small vial. A solid piece of boiled, recently salted beef weighing three drachms was added. The vial was corked and kept under controlled conditions. A similar piece of beef was suspended on a string into the man's stomach.'

  i Suggest one condition around the vial that Beaumont would have kept constant.
  ii What control experiment should Beaumont have performed?
  iii Why did Beaumont use 'boiled, salted beef'?

c After two hours, Beaumont recorded the following results: 'Beef in vial – the cellular texture seemed to be entirely destroyed, leaving the muscular fibres loose and unconnected, floating about in fine, small shreds, very tender and soft. Beef in stomach – I drew out the string, but the meat was all completely digested and gone.'

Use your knowledge of digestion to explain the difference between the changes in the vial and those in the stomach.

2 The liver produces a liquid which is added directly to the partly digested food in the small intestine.
a Name the liquid.
b Describe how it helps digestion.

3 Describe, in the correct sequence, how the protein and starch in a ham sandwich are broken down ready for absorption.

4 Digestive juices contain enzymes, water and some other substances. Name two of these other substances. State which digestive juice contains them, and state what function they perform.

Objectives

- To understand that digested food in the gut is still 'outside' the body
- To know how the small intestine is adapted to the function of absorption of digested food
- To understand the part played by the liver in the assimilation and distribution of absorbed foods

Absorption of the products of digestion

Enzymes in the gut convert large, insoluble molecules to small, soluble molecules. These soluble molecules are transported across the lining of the gut into the bloodstream, a process called **absorption**. They can then be distributed to the parts of the body where they will be used.

Most absorption happens from the **ileum**, the lower part of the small intestine. The ileum is very well adapted to perform this task:

- It is **very long**, about 6 m in an adult human, so food takes a long time to pass through it, and there is enough time for absorption to occur.
- The surface of the ileum is **highly folded**, which gives a much larger surface area for absorption than a simple tube would.

The lining of the ileum is folded into hundreds of thousands of tiny finger-like structures, the **villi**, which project out into the liquid digested food. The structure of a villus, and its adaptations to increase absorption, are shown in the diagram below.

Following absorption in the small intestine, the contents of the gut are little more than water and indigestible matter. Most of the water is reabsorbed into the bloodstream from the colon, part of the large intestine. Some minerals and vitamins are also absorbed here.

The liver and assimilation

Digested food is absorbed into the bloodstream. Each type of absorbed food has a particular function in the body, so it is important that food molecules of the right type are available at the right time in the right place. The **liver** 'sorts out' digested food molecules, and all foods absorbed into the capillaries of the villi are sent first to the liver. The veins leaving the villi join together into one blood vessel called the **hepatic portal vein** ('hepatic' means 'to do with the liver' and 'portal' means 'carrying'). This arrangement, shown in the

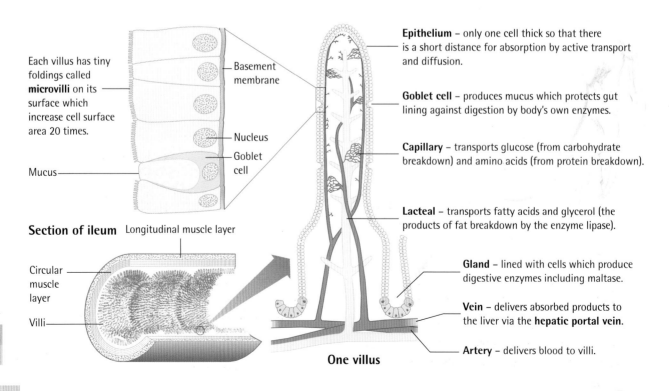

Each villus has tiny foldings called **microvilli** on its surface which increase cell surface area 20 times.

Basement membrane

Nucleus

Goblet cell

Mucus

Section of ileum Longitudinal muscle layer

Circular muscle layer

Villi

One villus

Epithelium – only one cell thick so that there is a short distance for absorption by active transport and diffusion.

Goblet cell – produces mucus which protects gut lining against digestion by body's own enzymes.

Capillary – transports glucose (from carbohydrate breakdown) and amino acids (from protein breakdown).

Lacteal – transports fatty acids and glycerol (the products of fat breakdown by the enzyme lipase).

Gland – lined with cells which produce digestive enzymes including maltase.

Vein – delivers absorbed products to the liver via the **hepatic portal vein**.

Artery – delivers blood to villi.

diagram below, means that the liver can sort out absorbed food molecules and make sure that the other tissues of the body receive exactly what they need.

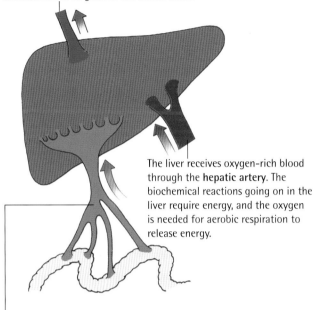

Blood returned to general circulation through **hepatic vein**. This blood contains a **constant** and **ideal** concentration of food molecules such as glucose and amino acids.

The liver receives oxygen-rich blood through the **hepatic artery**. The biochemical reactions going on in the liver require energy, and the oxygen is needed for aerobic respiration to release energy.

Blood from the intestine is delivered to the liver in the **hepatic portal vein**. This blood contains **variable** and **possibly dangerously high** concentrations of food molecules, depending on what has been absorbed from the gut.

The liver has many functions – at least 500 different biochemical reactions go on inside its cells. These functions include:

- manufacture of bile, which is important for the digestion of fats
- storage of glucose as glycogen
- interconversion of glucose and glycogen, which keeps the glucose concentration constant for the working tissues of the body (see page 158)
- interconversion of amino acids – the liver can convert some amino acids into others that the body might require in a process called **transamination**
- excretion of excess amino acids – the amino part of the amino acid is removed in a process called **deamination** (see page 132) and excreted in the urine as urea
- removal of old red blood cells from the circulation and storage of the iron they contained.

A combination of transamination and deamination makes sure that there is always a 'pool' of amino acids available for use by the cells of the body.

As a result of these and other activities, the liver provides ideal concentrations of food molecules for the working of the body tissues. Each type of tissue uses food molecules for different purposes – for example, muscle cells manufacture muscle protein, bone cells take up calcium and phosphate to make bone, and all cells use glucose to release energy by respiration. The processes of using up food molecules in these various ways are together called **assimilation**.

Alcohol and the liver

The liver receives all the molecules that the gut absorbs from food. As well as useful molecules such as glucose and amino acids, this may include harmful molecules such as drugs or poisons. **Alcohol** is a drug (a molecule that affects the normal working of the body – see page 152) which passes quickly to the liver after being absorbed from the stomach and ileum. The cells of the liver convert this alcohol to another substance which does not pass through to the rest of the body's circulation. Unfortunately, in working to protect the other tissues, the liver is likely to harm itself. The substance produced from alcohol can be dangerous to liver cells in high concentrations and can cause a serious disease called cirrhosis of the liver. If the liver is damaged by excessive alcohol consumption, then the whole body is affected. For example, the blood glucose concentration cannot be controlled efficiently if the liver has been damaged.

Alcohol has other effects on the body – these are described on page 154.

1 In what way is the blood supply to the liver unusual?

2 Name two substances stored in the liver, and two that are converted to different substances.

3 How is the structure of the villus adapted to its function?

4 What are goblet cells? Where else do you think they might be found apart from in the gut?

5 Some microorganisms infect the gut lining so that water cannot be absorbed. What effect(s) might this have on the infected person?

Questions on nutrition and health

Food	Energy / kJ	Animal protein / g	Plant protein / g	Calcium / mg	Iron / mg	Vitamin C / mg
Biscuits	2000	2	5	100	1.5	0
Bread	900	0	9	100	1.7	0
Butter	3000	0.5	0	15	0.2	0
Cheese	1600	26	0	800	0.4	0
Cucumber	40	0	0	25	0.3	8

Table 1

1 John and Paul were eating their school lunch.
Later, they decided to look up the nutritional value of some of the foods in a book. The book had a table showing what 100 g of each food contains.

a Use Table 1 above and your biological knowledge to answer the following questions.

  i Which food shown in the table would be the best for preventing scurvy?

  ii John ate a sandwich containing 100 g of bread, 50 g of cheese and 10 g of butter.

    How much energy did he take in?

    Show how you work out your answer.

b Paul had been complaining of pain after eating and so went to the doctor.
The doctor wanted to find out if Paul was allergic to any foods.
She asked Paul to eat two different foods at each meal and record whether he suffered any pain afterwards.
This is what he noted down.

Food eaten	Pain
Bread and butter	yes
Bread and cheese	yes
Cheese and biscuits	yes
Cheese and cucumber	no
Bread and cucumber	yes

  i The doctor asked Paul to complete a chart.
Using Paul's notes, copy and complete the chart according to the key given. The result for bread and butter has been done for you.

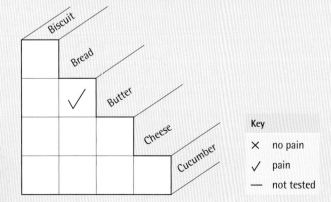

Key
× no pain
✓ pain
− not tested

  ii From the chart the doctor could identify the foods to which Paul was allergic. Which are they?

  iii Use Table 1 to identify which substance in the foods was the cause of the allergy.

  iv The doctor said that the substance which caused Paul's allergy was destroying the villi in his small intestine. She said that this might slow down Paul's growth.

    Explain why the destruction of the villi may slow down Paul's growth.

[MEG (June 1996)]

2 The diagrams below show plans of the teeth in the upper and lower jaw. Plan A is from a 27-year-old woman called Hannah; plan B is from a 27-year-old woman called Caitlin.

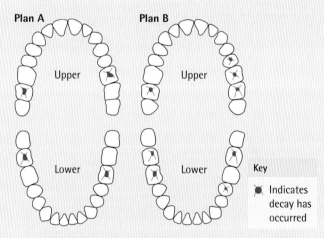

Plan A — Upper, Lower
Plan B — Upper, Lower

Key
🐛 Indicates decay has occurred

The two women live in different towns. In one town the natural drinking water contains fluoride salts, but there are no fluoride salts in the drinking water of the other.

a Which woman lives in the town with fluoride in the drinking water? Support your answer with numerical data.

b Suggest other reasons for the difference in the number of decayed teeth between the two women.

c Why is it important that both plans are from women, and each is aged 27?

d Explain why decay is more likely in the cheek teeth.

e How would these plans have been different if they had been taken when the women were 10 years old?

3 The table below shows the effect of pH on the time taken for the complete breakdown of a starch solution in the presence of an enzyme.

pH	5.0	5.5	6.0	6.5	7.0	7.5	8.0	9.0
Time taken / min	20.00	15.00	8.00	4.00	1.25	1.25	3.00	8.00
Rate of reaction								

a Copy and complete the table. Assume that the rate of reaction is the same as $1/\text{time taken}$.

b Plot the results in the form of an appropriate graph.

c What is the optimum pH for this enzyme?

d Name one region of the gut where this pH would be found. How is this pH kept constant?

e Suggest two chemical tests that could be carried out on samples of the solution to show that starch is being broken down.

f In this experiment pH is the input or independent variable, and rate of reaction is the outcome or dependent variable. Suggest three fixed variables which must be kept constant if these results are to be valid.

4 Study the following table. It shows the number of deaths in Paris from 1934 to 1966. Wine was rationed during the Second World War, and wine production was not back to normal until the early 1950s.

a Plot these results on a suitable graph.

b Do the results suggest any link between alcohol consumption and cirrhosis? Support your answer with figures from the table.

Year	Deaths / number per 100 000 population	
	All causes	Cirrhosis of liver
1934	1000	45
1938	1010	44
1942	1435	6
1946	1100	7
1950	1000	23
1952	998	35
1958	1012	43
1962	1000	42
1966	1188	45

5 During the 16th and 17th centuries, sailors were as likely to die from the disease **scurvy** as from enemy action. A chance observation that sailors who were transporting citrus fruits did not develop scurvy led Admiral Nelson to insist that all British ships should carry plenty of limes on long voyages. (This is why British sailors were called 'Limeys'.)

Clearly limes and other citrus fruits contained a substance that prevented scurvy, but it was not until the middle of the 20th century that this substance was shown to be **ascorbic acid** (also called **vitamin C**). At that time an American surgeon called John Crandon carried out an experiment on himself:

1 He cut himself with a sterile scalpel – the cut healed in 3 or 4 days.

2 He had no vitamin C in his diet for 3 months – a similar cut took 3 months to heal.

3 He had no vitamin C for 6 months – a cut would not heal at all.

Do you think that Crandon's results were valid? How could this experiment have been improved?

We now know that long-term deficiency in vitamin C makes it difficult for the body to manufacture the connective tissues that hold body structures together – thus skin damage is difficult to repair. The recommended daily amount (RDA) of vitamin C is the amount required to prevent scurvy, but many scientists believe that vitamin C has other functions in the body and that this RDA is probably too low. Higher doses of vitamin C help the immune system to fight off viruses, prevent cells ageing, and prevent anaemia by increasing the absorption of iron from food.

2.26 Uptake of water and minerals by roots

Objectives

- To understand that water may enter and leave cells by osmosis
- To understand that dissolved substances may enter and leave cells by diffusion and active transport

Plants need water and minerals

Plants need to obtain certain raw materials from their environment. The roots of the plant are adapted to absorb both minerals and water from the soil. **Water** is essential to support the plant, as a reagent in many biochemical reactions and also as a transport medium (see page 244). The diagram below shows how water enters the plant through **root hair cells**.

Minerals have a number of individual functions and together have a great effect on the water potential of the plant tissues. Minerals from the soil are absorbed in the form of **ions**, for example, magnesium enters the root as Mg^{2+} ions and nitrogen enters as nitrate NO_3^- ions. If the soil solution contains higher concentrations of these ions than the root hair cell cytoplasm, the ions can enter by diffusion (see page 28). However, plants can continue to take up ions even if the concentration gradient is in the wrong direction, that is, if the concentration of the ions is higher inside the cell than in the soil solution.

Leaves have a large surface area for photosynthesis. When the stomata are open, water is lost by evaporation from spongy mesophyll cells (see page 92).

Roots have an enormous surface area and penetrate between the particles of soil.

1 Water is drawn up the xylem to replace water lost at the leaves. This upward flow of water is the **transpiration stream** (see page 90).

Root hair cells have an enormous surface area. This helps them absorb water and minerals from the soil. The photograph shows root hair cells magnified ×300. The root hairs are very delicate and easily damaged.
When plants are transplanted they recover much more quickly if the roots are kept in a ball of soil or compost so that the root hairs are not disturbed.

Note: Water movement through the plant occurs in the sequence 1–2–3–4: it **begins** with loss from the leaves, and is **completed** with water absorption from the soil solution.

2 Water (with any substances dissolved in it) is forced to cross the membrane and cytoplasm of cells of the **endodermis**. The cell walls in the endodermis contain a waxy material which makes them impermeable to water. This allows the membranes of the endodermis cells to **select** which substances can enter the xylem and be distributed through the body of the plant.

3 Water crosses the living cells of the **cortex** by (a) osmosis through the cells and (b) 'suction' through the freely permeable cellulose cell walls. Almost all of the water moves across the cortex by route (b).

4 Water enters root hair cells by **osmosis**, from the thin film of water surrounding the particles of soil. The soil water has a **higher water potential** than the cytoplasm of the root hair cell, so that water moves down a water potential gradient (see page 29).

Uptake of water by root hair cells.

Organisation and maintenance of organisms

Osmosis: a reminder

A cell's membrane controls the entry and exit of materials to and from the cell (see page 29). A typical plant cell such as that found in the mesophyll layer of the leaf has a high concentration of solutes. As a result water will enter a plant cell by osmosis from an environment with a high water potential, until the water inside the cell forces the cell membrane up against the cellulose cell wall.

When a plant cell contains plenty of water, the internal pressure of the cell contents against the cell wall supports the cell. The cell is said to be **turgid**, and turgidity helps support the plant. If the plant does not have a good supply of water, the cells lose their turgidity and slowly collapse. The cells are said to be **flaccid** and the plant is wilted.

Experiments on the uptake of ions also show that:

☞ the cells can select which ions enter from the soil solution

☞ any factor that affects respiration, for example lack of oxygen or low temperature, can reduce the uptake of ions. The diagram opposite shows some results that support these observations.

The explanation of these observations is that the root hair cells use **active transport** to carry out the selective uptake of ions against a concentration gradient, using energy from respiration (see page 31).

'Plateau' suggests that active transport of ions is limited by some other factor that limits respiration, such as temperature.

Ion uptake by **active transport** – energy is supplied by respiration so ions are taken up more quickly when more oxygen is available.

Ion uptake by **diffusion** – no energy is required so process is not affected by the low concentration of oxygen that limits respiration.

Ion uptake depends on respiration.

Active transport: application

To increase crop yields, farmers may drain fields that are liable to flooding. If the soil is not waterlogged, more oxygen in soil air spaces is available to the plants, so the rate of aerobic respiration in root cells is faster. This provides more energy for active transport, so that the growing plants will more quickly absorb mineral ions present in the soil. Farmers may also cover their fields with black polythene. This absorbs heat and helps to raise the soil temperature, so that seed germination and ion uptake by young roots will be faster.

1 Does a solution containing many molecules of dissolved sugar and amino acids have a high or a low water potential? Explain your answer.

2 Define osmosis in terms of water potential.

3 How does the strength of the cellulose cell wall help plants to support themselves?

4 A scientist investigated the uptake of magnesium ions by the roots of young cereal plants. He made the following observations:

a The rate of uptake was increased by raising the temperature, so long as it did not exceed 40 °C.

b Uptake stopped if the roots were treated with cyanide, an ion that prevents respiration.

c Ions were taken up even if they were present at a lower concentration in the solution around the roots than in the root cells themselves.

d If ion uptake continued for some time, the concentration of sugars in the root cells decreased.

What conclusions can be drawn from each of these observations?

2.27 Transport systems in plants

Objectives
▶ To appreciate that water and dissolved substances are transported around the plant in specialised transport tissues

Xylem and phloem
Substances need to be transported for long distances throughout a plant's body – sugars, for example, are produced in the photosynthesising cells of the leaves and may need to be transported to storage cells in the roots. The water and ions absorbed by the roots may be required by cells at the growing tip (the **meristem**) of the shoot. These long-distance transport functions are carried out by two specialised plant tissues – the **xylem** and the **phloem**. These are tubes running through the plant,

collected together in groups in the **vascular** (transport) **bundles**, as shown in the diagram opposite.

Moving vital substances from sources to sinks
The transport tissues are arranged in the stem and root as shown opposite, to offer:

▶ the most efficient transport of materials from **sources** (where they are taken in or made) to **sinks** (where they are used or stored)

▶ the most effective support in air (the stem) and soil (the root).

The transport functions of xylem and phloem have been investigated in a number of ways, as shown in the diagram below.

Tracing xylem

Procedure
1 Cut a piece of celery and stand it in a coloured solution (suitable stains include eosin [red] and methylene blue [blue!]).

2 Leave for a few hours.

3 Carefully (CARE! SHARP SCALPELS) cut off about 5 cm of the celery, and use a hand lens to look for the stain. The coloured solution has been carried up the **xylem**.

Extension: You could also try:
a Carefully (using the scalpel) scrape away the outside tissues of the celery to trace the xylem. What happens as the stem branches to the leaves?
b Use a pale-coloured (e.g. white) flower, such as a carnation. You can change its colour, just as florists do!

Transport of the products of photosynthesis
Aphids (greenfly) are serious pests of many crops. They can take food meant for the growing regions of plants by inserting their mouthparts (the **stylet**) into the plant tissues.

If feeding aphids are anaesthetised with carbon dioxide their bodies can be 'flicked away' from the plant surface, leaving the stylet in place. The contents of the phloem, the **sap**, will slowly leak out of the stylet and can be analysed. The results show that the phloem transports sucrose (sugar), the main product of photosynthesis.

Application: aphids eat themselves to death!
Many insecticides kill useful insect species as well as pests. **Systemic** insecticides are sprayed onto the plant and absorbed into the phloem tissues, so they only kill aphids.

TOXOBUG (SYSTEMIC)

Xylem tissue contains long **xylem vessels** adapted for the rapid transport of **water** and **dissolved mineral ions.** Movement is always **up** the stem.

Longitudinal section of xylem vessels

Walls are thickened with **lignin**. This is waterproof and strong enough to prevent the cells collapsing inwards. In the shoot, the xylem is on the **inside** of the vascular bundle, helping support the stem.

No cytoplasm or organelles – cells are dead. There is no obstruction to the flow of water and mineral ions.

End walls removed – cells join to form long tubes called **xylem vessels.**

Cambium tissue (see page 204) contains cells which divide by mitosis to produce more phloem and xylem.

Vascular bundle (× 100).

Phloem tissue contains **sieve tubes** and **companion cells.** It is adapted for transport of the **organic products of photosynthesis** i.e. sugars (transported as **sucrose**) and amino acids. This transport is called **translocation.**

Longitudinal section of phloem sieve tubes

Sieve tube

Thin cytoplasm – cell must remain alive or sugar transport stops.

No nucleus or organelles, so sugar flow is not impeded.

Pores in **sieve plates** allow sugars to pass from one cell to the next.

Companion cell does not transport sugar but carries out some life processes of the sieve tubes.

Stem – vascular bundles are arranged in a ring with soft cortex in the centre, helping to support the stem.

Phloem
Xylem } Vascular bundle
Cambium

Cortex – cells become turgid and help to support non-woody parts.

Epidermis – protects against infection by viruses and bacteria, and dehydration.

Direction of transport varies with the seasons!
Sucrose is transported **from** stores in the root **to** leaves in spring, but **to** stores in the root **from** photosynthesising leaves in the summer and early autumn. Whatever the time of year the movement of sugars and amino acids (translocation) is from **source** to **sink**. In other words, sucrose and amino acids are translocated from the region where they are made or absorbed to the region where they are stored or used.

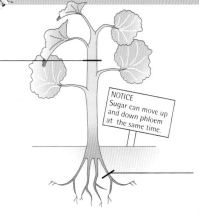

NOTICE
Sugar can move up and down phloem at the same time.

Root – root hairs are extended cells of the epidermis.

Endodermis

Epidermis – protects against infection by fungi.

Phloem
Xylem } Together form a strong central rod.

Cortex (pith) can act as a winter store for starch.

The transport tissues xylem and phloem are arranged in vascular bundles. They transport water and dissolved substances around the plant.

---

1. Name the two vascular tissues in flowering plants. Which tissue divides to form the vascular tissues?

2. What is a **source**? Suggest two examples in a flowering plant.

3. Why does the direction of sugar transport vary from season to season?

4. Why must sugar be transported to **sinks** such as growing points and roots?

5. Many dyes are water soluble. Xylem vessels reach up from roots to flower petals. How could these two observations be useful to a florist?

Objectives

- To recall that water movement through a plant begins with water loss from the leaves
- To understand that water is lost from leaves via the stomata, through which the exchange of gases between the leaf and the atmosphere also occurs
- To describe how the leaf surface most involved in water loss can be identified
- To understand how environmental conditions can affect water movement through plants

Evaporation from leaves

Water evaporates from the parts of a plant that are exposed to the atmosphere – for example, the whole shoot system of a terrestrial plant and the upper leaf surfaces of a floating aquatic plant. The greatest loss of water takes place through the **stomata** (singular **stoma**), minute pores on the leaf surface (see page 64). There are usually more stomata on the lower surface of leaves than on the upper surface. The lower surface is less exposed to

Water movement through a plant begins with the diffusion of water vapour out of the leaf and evaporation from the leaf surface (spongy mesophyll). 98% of the water taken up by a plant is lost to the atmosphere by transpiration.

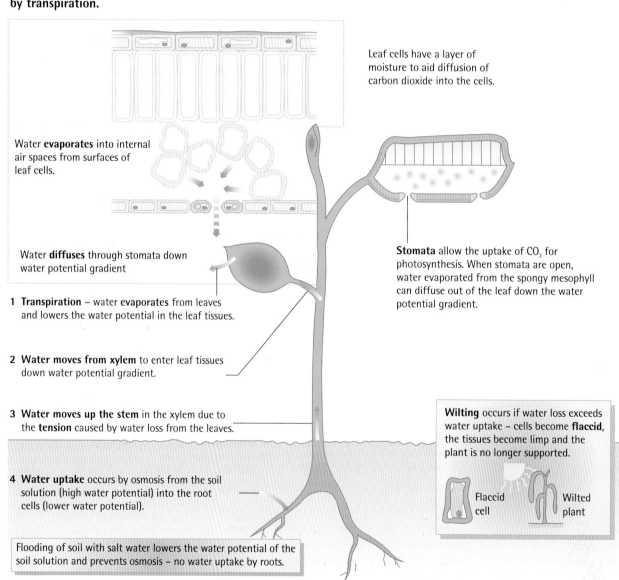

Leaf cells have a layer of moisture to aid diffusion of carbon dioxide into the cells.

Water **evaporates** into internal air spaces from surfaces of leaf cells.

Water **diffuses** through stomata down water potential gradient

Stomata allow the uptake of CO_2 for photosynthesis. When stomata are open, water evaporated from the spongy mesophyll can diffuse out of the leaf down the water potential gradient.

1 **Transpiration** – water **evaporates** from leaves and lowers the water potential in the leaf tissues.

2 **Water moves from xylem** to enter leaf tissues down water potential gradient.

3 **Water moves up the stem** in the xylem due to the **tension** caused by water loss from the leaves.

Wilting occurs if water loss exceeds water uptake – cells become **flaccid**, the tissues become limp and the plant is no longer supported.

Flaccid cell

Wilted plant

4 **Water uptake** occurs by osmosis from the soil solution (high water potential) into the root cells (lower water potential).

Flooding of soil with salt water lowers the water potential of the soil solution and prevents osmosis – no water uptake by roots.

the warming effects of the Sun's radiation, which would speed up the evaporation rate. Loss of water from the leaf is shown in the diagram on the opposite page.

Water cannot diffuse *into* the leaf through the stomata, because the air spaces inside the leaf are completely saturated. Instead, water must be absorbed from the soil solution and drawn up through the plant (see page 86). This flow of water through the plant to replace the losses by evaporation from the leaf is called the **transpiration stream**, shown in the diagram on the opposite page.

Since water is lost through the stomata to the atmosphere, transpiration is affected by **leaf structure** and by **conditions in the atmosphere** (see opposite). These factors can be investigated using the **potometer** shown below.

Leaf structure may reduce transpiration
- Thick, waxy cuticle reduces evaporation from epidermis
- Stomata may be sunk into pits which trap a pocket of humid air
- Leaves may be rolled with the stomata on the inner surface close to a trapped layer of humid air

Humid air

- Leaves may be needle shaped to reduce their surface area.

Atmospheric conditions may affect transpiration
- **Wind** moves humid air away from the leaf surface and increases transpiration
- **High temperatures** increase the water-holding capacity of the air and increase transpiration
- **Low humidity** increases the water potential gradient between leaf and atmosphere and increases transpiration
- **High light intensity** causes stomata to open (to allow photosynthesis) which allows transpiration to occur.

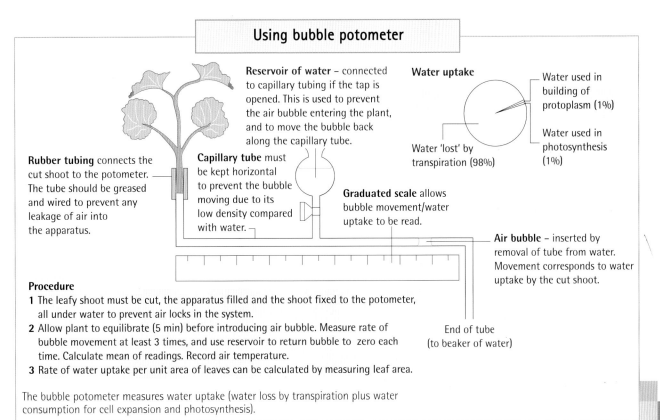

Using bubble potometer

Reservoir of water – connected to capillary tubing if the tap is opened. This is used to prevent the air bubble entering the plant, and to move the bubble back along the capillary tube.

Water uptake

Water used in building of protoplasm (1%)

Water 'lost' by transpiration (98%)

Water used in photosynthesis (1%)

Rubber tubing connects the cut shoot to the potometer. The tube should be greased and wired to prevent any leakage of air into the apparatus.

Capillary tube must be kept horizontal to prevent the bubble moving due to its low density compared with water.

Graduated scale allows bubble movement/water uptake to be read.

Air bubble – inserted by removal of tube from water. Movement corresponds to water uptake by the cut shoot.

End of tube (to beaker of water)

Procedure
1. The leafy shoot must be cut, the apparatus filled and the shoot fixed to the potometer, all under water to prevent air locks in the system.
2. Allow plant to equilibrate (5 min) before introducing air bubble. Measure rate of bubble movement at least 3 times, and use reservoir to return bubble to zero each time. Calculate mean of readings. Record air temperature.
3. Rate of water uptake per unit area of leaves can be calculated by measuring leaf area.

The bubble potometer measures water uptake (water loss by transpiration plus water consumption for cell expansion and photosynthesis).

Objectives

■ To understand that stomata are opened to allow carbon dioxide to enter the leaf, and that this allows water vapour to diffuse out of the leaf

■ To describe adaptations of leaves to reduce water losses

dioxide as a raw material for photosynthesis. Plants can open and close the stomata, which helps to minimise water loss whilst allowing photosynthesis to continue. The position and operation of the stomata is explained on page 64, which also shows the adaptations of the leaf to photosynthesis.

Stomata and water loss

Water is lost by evaporation and diffusion from the leaf surface. This water loss happens because the stomata need to open so the leaf can take in carbon

Adaptations of plants

The diagrams opposite show how plants may be adapted to the availability of water.

Investigation of water loss from leaf surfaces

Cobalt chloride paper is blue when dry, and pink when wet. It is handled with forceps to avoid dampness from the fingers affecting its colour. The paper is attached to the upper and lower leaf surfaces using microscope slides. The paper attached to the lower surface of the leaf turns pink, showing that water is lost mainly from the lower surface. This technique gives a *qualitative (non-quantitative)* comparison.

Measuring the mass changes of leaves can be used to give a quantitative comparison of water loss from different leaf surfaces. A number of leaves are smeared

with Vaseline as shown in the diagram below. They are weighed and then left in a drying atmosphere for 48 hours, and reweighed at intervals. Some typical results from this investigation are shown in the table.

Leaf number	Initial mass / g	Final mass / g	Percentage change in mass
1	4.2	4.1	
2	4.6	4.4	
3	3.9	2.5	
4	4.1	2.5	

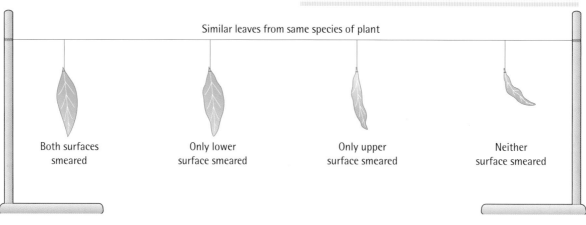

Similar leaves from same species of plant

Both surfaces smeared · Only lower surface smeared · Only upper surface smeared · Neither surface smeared

These measurements are made on leaves which have been detached from the plant. It is difficult to measure water loss from the leaves of an intact plant, but relatively simple to measure water uptake using a **potometer** (see page 91).

Questions 1 to 4 refer to the investigation above.

1 Copy the table above. Calculate the percentage change in mass for each leaf.

2 Why did leaf 3 lose a greater proportion of its mass than leaf 2?

3 Why was it important that leaves of the same species were used?

4 How could the results be made more reliable or valid?

Adaptations of plants to reduce water loss in different environments.

Cacti are well adapted to hot, dry environments.

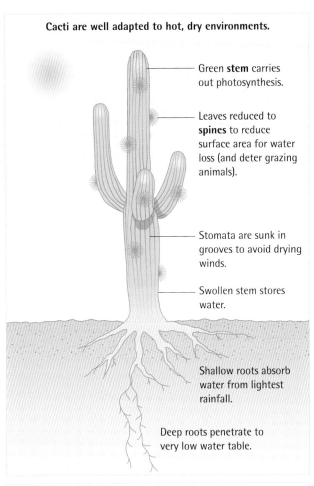

Green **stem** carries out photosynthesis.

Leaves reduced to **spines** to reduce surface area for water loss (and deter grazing animals).

Stomata are sunk in grooves to avoid drying winds.

Swollen stem stores water.

Shallow roots absorb water from lightest rainfall.

Deep roots penetrate to very low water table.

Aquatic plants have leaves with:
- little lignin in the xylem, since the leaf is supported by the water
- a very thin cuticle, since water conservation is not a problem
- stomata on the **upper** surface to allow CO_2 uptake from the atmosphere.

Wilting and leaf fall

When water is in short supply, plants may reduce water loss by:
- wilting – leaves collapse and stomata close to reduce heat absorption and evaporation/ diffusion of water

- leaf fall – in very severe conditions, e.g. when water is frozen during winter, plants allow the leaves to fall off so that no water loss can occur. No photosynthesis can take place, but the plants can remove chlorophyll from the leaves for storage before allowing leaves to fall.

Modern Christmas trees are bred so that the needles don't fall – a disadvantage in a natural habitat, but good news when clearing up after Christmas!

---

1 The diagram shows a leaf of marram grass, a plant that grows in dry, windy environments on sand dunes. The photograph shows a transverse section of marram grass leaf as seen under a microscope.

a Copy the diagram of the leaf, and draw a line to show the direction in which a transverse section is cut.

b The positions of several stomata are labelled on the photograph. If sufficient light is available, oxygen is released from the leaf through the stomata.
  i Name the process that produces oxygen.
  ii Which gas is consumed during this process?
  iii Name and define the process by which the oxygen moves from leaf to atmosphere.

c When the stomata are open, water vapour will also be lost from the leaf's internal surfaces. Use the diagram and the photograph to suggest three ways in which the structure of the marram grass leaf helps to reduce water loss.

d Give three reasons why plants require water.

e Why is it particularly important that a plant growing in sand dunes should reduce water loss?

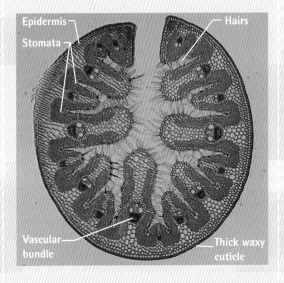

Epidermis

Hairs

Stomata

Vascular bundle

Thick waxy cuticle

2 Copy and complete the following paragraph.
The movement of water through the plant begins at the leaf surface, and a stream of water called the ——— is drawn up through the plant to replace these losses. The gas ——— is required for photosynthesis, and enters the leaves through pores called ———. These pores allow the loss of ——— to the atmosphere, and leaves show many adaptations to reduce this loss. These adaptations include ———, ——— and ———.

2.30 Transport systems in animals use blood as the transport medium

All living organisms require energy, which is released from food and oxygen in the process of respiration (page 115). All living cells in the body (for example in the brain, liver, kidney and muscle) need energy, and so glucose and oxygen must be transported throughout the body. In some small animals (especially those with a flat body such as the flatworm in the photograph), substances are transported in and out of the body, and from one tissue to another, by the process of **diffusion**.

The flatworm is very thin and has a high surface area to volume ratio. Its volume is made up of working cells that need various substances including oxygen, which can diffuse in across the large surface. The distance from the surface to all the cells is small.

Large complex organisms, such as humans, have a small surface area in relation to their relatively large volume. As a result, cells near the centre of the body are some distance away from contact with the atmosphere, and may also be some distance from the gut where food is digested. Cells inside such large organisms cannot gain enough oxygen and glucose by diffusion alone.

A mass flow system

To supply oxygen and glucose, as well as other substances, large organisms have a specialised **transport system**. This system, called the **blood system** in all vertebrate animals, is an example of a **mass flow system**. A mass flow system carries large volumes of fluid to all parts of the organism. A system like this has four parts:

☞ A **medium** – the fluid that flows in the system and carries materials around the body. This is the **blood**.

☞ A **system of tubes** that carries the fluid from place to place. These are the **arteries** and **veins**.

☞ A **pump** that supplies pressure to keep the fluid moving through the tubes. This is the **heart**.

☞ **Sites of exchange** that allow materials delivered by the blood to enter the tissues that need them. These are the **capillaries**.

A whale has a large surface area, but its volume is too large for materials to be moved to and from its body cells by diffusion. It has a circulatory system made up of 4000 dm³ of blood, pumped through 50 000 km of blood vessels by a heart the size of a small car, which beats 40 000 times a day. The main artery can be 20 m long and wide enough for a child to crawl through!

Blood is the circulatory medium

The average adult human has about 5 dm³ of blood, which contains a number of blood cells suspended in a watery liquid (**plasma**). If a sample of blood taken from the body is allowed to stand, and a chemical added to prevent it clotting, it will separate into layers as shown opposite.

If a drop of blood is placed on a microscope slide and stained with a special dye, these different types of cell can be seen, as the photograph below shows.

Blood cells are first formed in the bone marrow of long bones such as the femur (thigh bone), although they may go on to other parts of the body before they become fully developed. The structure and function of different types of blood cell are shown in the table below.

Red blood cells are pink, white blood cells have purple-stained nuclei, of several different shapes (platelets are not visible)

The red blood cells sink to the bottom, and the white blood cells and platelets settle on top of the red blood cells, rather like a layer of dust. The plasma forms a clear, straw-coloured layer at the top.

Cell type	Appearance	Function	How the structure is suited to the function
Red blood cells (erythrocytes)		■ Transport oxygen from lungs to all respiring tissues. Prepare carbon dioxide for transport from all respiring tissues to lungs.	■ Contain **haemoglobin**, an iron-containing pigment which picks up oxygen at the lungs and lets go of it at the tissues. ■ Have no nucleus, leaving more space for haemoglobin. ■ Cells are small and flexible, so can squeeze through narrow capillaries.
White blood cells (phagocytes)		■ Remove any microorganisms that invade the body and might cause infection. The phagocyte engulfs the microorganism (see page 98).	■ Irregular shaped nucleus allows cell to squeeze through gaps in walls of capillaries. ■ Enzymes in cytoplasm digest microorganisms once engulfed. ■ Sensitive cell surface membrane can detect microorganisms.
White blood cells (lymphocytes)		■ Produce antibodies – proteins that help in the defence against disease (see page 292).	■ Large nucleus contains many copies of genes for the control of antibody protein production.
Platelets		■ Cell fragments involved in blood clotting.	■ Can release blood-clotting enzymes (see page 98).

Functions of the blood

The table on page 95 shows that one function of red blood cells is the transport of the respiratory gases, oxygen and carbon dioxide, between the lungs and the respiring tissues. The **plasma** also has transport functions. This watery liquid carries dissolved food molecules such as glucose and amino acids, waste materials such as urea, and some control molecules such as hormones. Because the plasma is largely water, it has a very high specific heat capacity (see page 244). This means that the plasma is able to distribute heat around the various parts of the body.

Defence against disease is another important function of the blood. The different roles of the blood are summarised below.

Functions of the blood

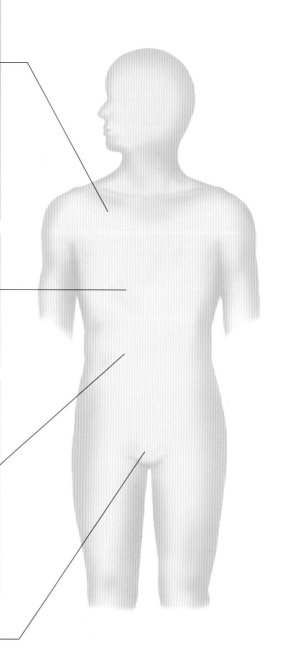

Regulatory functions – homeostasis

Blood solutes affect the water potential of the blood, and thus the water potential gradient between the blood and the tissue fluid. The size of this water potential gradient is largely due to sodium ions and plasma proteins. The blood solute level **regulates the movement of water** between blood and tissues.

Water plays a part in the **distribution of heat** between heat-producing areas such as the liver and areas of heat loss such as the skin.

Blood also helps to maintain an **optimum pH** in the tissues.

> Too much alcohol in the blood can cause water to leave brain cells, causing the pain and sensation of thirst called a **hangover!**

Protective functions

Platelets, plasma proteins (e.g. fibrinogen) and many other plasma factors (e.g. Ca^{2+} ions) protect against **blood loss** and the **entry of pathogens** by the clotting mechanism.

White blood cells protect against **disease-causing organisms**:
- **phagocytes** engulf them
- **lymphocytes** produce and secrete specific antibodies against them.

Transport functions

Soluble products of digestion/absorption (such as glucose, amino acids, fatty acids, vitamins and minerals) are transported from the gut to the liver and then to the general circulation.

Waste products of metabolism (such as urea, creatinine and lactate) are transported from sites of production to sites of removal, such as the liver and kidney.

Respiratory gases (oxygen and carbon dioxide) are transported from their sites of uptake or production to their site of use or removal.

Hormones (such as insulin) are transported from their sites of production in the glands to the target organs where they have their effects.

Support function

Erection of the penis is achieved by filling large spongy spaces with blood. The penis becomes flaccid when blood flows out more quickly than it flows in.

The blood detectives

A scientist who specialises in the study of blood is called a **haematologist**. A haematologist can tell a great deal from a tiny sample of blood. For example:

- **Anaemia**, an inability to transport enough oxygen, can be detected by noting a lower than normal number of red blood cells.

- **Sickle cell anaemia** shows some red blood cells shaped like sickles, as the photograph below illustrates.

- **Leukaemia**, a cancer of white blood cells, can be detected by high numbers of oddly shaped white blood cells.

- **AIDS** may be detected in its early stages by the presence of antibodies to the human immunodeficiency virus (HIV) in the plasma – the affected person is HIV positive. In the later stages of the disease, the number of white blood cells is very much reduced.

- **DNA fingerprinting**, which can be important in criminal investigations, can be carried out on nuclei extracted from white blood cells.

- **Diabetes** may be detected by a high glucose concentration in the plasma.

- **Eating disorders** may be detected by higher than normal concentrations of urea in the plasma.

Using modern techniques of biochemistry, a single drop of blood can yield information about all the conditions described above.

Sickle-shaped red blood cells show the person has sickle cell anaemia. A sickle is a long hooked tool used for cutting crops.

1. Why do large organisms require a transport system?

2. A sample of human blood is collected and placed in a tube and centrifuged. The blood separates into two distinct layers.
   a What are the two layers?
   b Suggest one dissolved food substance found in the upper layer. Choose a substance for which there is a simple chemical test. Describe the test for this substance, and state what a positive result would be.
   c There is a third, rather thin, layer between the two main components. What is this layer made of?

3. 'The structure of a cell is closely related to its function.' Is this statement correct for blood cells? Explain your answer.

4. The table shows the cell composition of three samples of blood.

Cell count / number per mm³	Sample from		
	Jill	Jenny	Jackie
Red blood cells	7 500 000	5 000 000	2 000 000
White blood cells	500	6000	5000
Platelets	250 000	255 000	50

   a Which person is most likely to have lived at high altitude recently? Explain your answer.
   b Which person would be the most likely to become ill if exposed to a virus? Explain your answer.
   c Which person's blood is least likely to clot efficiently? Explain your answer.
   d Which person is likely to have an iron deficiency in her diet? Explain your answer.
   e These three samples were all taken from 23-year-old women. Explain why this makes comparisons between them valid.

5. Use words from this list to complete the following paragraphs. The words may be used once, more than once or not at all.

   epidermis, tissues, specialised, cells, blood, red blood cell, division of labour, organ

   Large numbers of _____ that have the same structure and function are grouped together to form _____, for example _____. Several separate tissues may be joined together to form an _____ which is a complex structure capable of performing a particular task with great efficiency.

   The structure of cells may be highly adapted to perform one function, i.e. the cells may become _____. One excellent example is the _____ which is highly adapted to carry oxygen in mammalian blood. If the different cells, tissues and organs of a multicellular organism perform different functions they are said to show _____.

2·31 Combating infection: blood and defence against disease

Objectives
- To recall what is meant by disease
- To recall that disease can be caused by pathogens, which must first invade the body
- To understand that the body may be able to defend itself against pathogens

Disease is often caused by the invasion of the body by another organism. Organisms that cause disease in this way are called **pathogens** and their attacks on the body result in **infections**.

The skin and defence against disease

The outer layer of the skin, the epidermis, is waxy and impermeable to water and to pathogens (although microorganisms can live on its surface). Natural 'gaps' in the skin may be protected by **chemical** secretions, for example:

- the mouth leads to the gut which is protected by hydrochloric acid in the stomach
- the eyes are protected by lysozyme, an enzyme that destroys bacterial cell walls, in the tears
- the ears are protected by bactericidal ('bacteria-killing') wax.

Physical defences against the entry of microorganisms include the cilia and mucus-secreting cells of the respiratory pathways (see page 120). If the potential pathogens do penetrate these first lines of defence, they might reproduce quickly in the warm, moist, nutrient-filled tissues. Further defence depends upon the **blood**.

Bleeding and clot formation

Blood clotting seals wounds. The blood clot limits the loss of blood and also prevents entry of any pathogens. Clotting depends on **platelets** and **blood proteins,** as outlined in the diagram below.

White blood cells and defence

Organisms that gain entry to the tissues are removed or destroyed by **white blood cells**. These white blood cells must attack only invading organisms and not the body's own cells (although this does happen sometimes, see page 101). The white blood cells recognise foreign particles such as bacteria, or perhaps large molecules such as proteins in snake venom, and react against them. These foreign particles are called **antigens**. Potential pathogens have antigens on their surface, and they are

Blood clotting reduces loss of blood and seals the wound against pathogens.

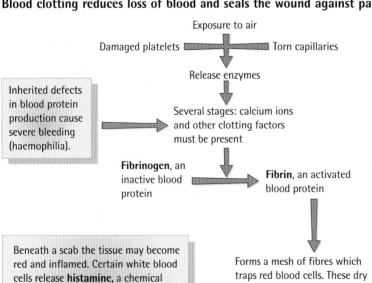

Exposure to air

Damaged platelets — Torn capillaries

Release enzymes

Inherited defects in blood protein production cause severe bleeding (haemophilia).

Several stages: calcium ions and other clotting factors must be present

Fibrinogen, an inactive blood protein

Fibrin, an activated blood protein

Forms a mesh of fibres which traps red blood cells. These dry out to form a **scab** which closes the wound and prevents the entry of pathogens.

Beneath a scab the tissue may become red and inflamed. Certain white blood cells release **histamine**, a chemical messenger which allows plasma to leak out of the capillaries. The extra plasma dilutes any toxins which may have entered the wound.

Fibrin fibres trap blood cells to form a scab.

Phagocyte action

Blood vessel

- Digestive enzymes are poured into the sac.
- The pathogen is destroyed.
- The phagocyte may absorb the digested products, and use them for its own metabolism.

Sometimes phagocytes die as they accumulate toxins from the pathogens. The pus underneath a scab, or in a spot, contains many of these dead phagocytes.

Infected tissue

- Phagocytes are large white blood cells.
- They are attracted to wounds or sites of infection by chemical messages.
- The long, lobed nucleus allows them to squeeze out between cells which line the capillaries.
- They contain sacs full of powerful digestive enzymes.

Phagocyte recognises pathogen and flows round it, enclosing it in a sac

Some pathogens escape the phagocytes by:
- hiding inside the host's cells, e.g. *Plasmodium* in liver cells
- staying in phagocyte-free areas, e.g. inside the gut

recognised and destroyed by **phagocytes** and by **antibodies**. Phagocytes engulf and then destroy the pathogens with digestive enzymes, as outlined above. Antibodies are described on page 100.

There are many phagocytes present in areas of the body likely to suffer infection. The exposed surfaces of the lungs, for example, are patrolled by phagocytes. If the lungs are regularly attacked by the free radicals in tobacco smoke, large numbers of phagocytes collect and may become disorganised.

They can destroy lung tissue rather than foreign particles, leading to the disease **emphysema** (see page 127).

First aid can save lives

Severe blood loss, or haemorrhage, can cause a number of problems. Following an accident there may be so much blood loss that the blood pressure falls to dangerously low levels. This may affect the function of vital organs such as the heart, brain and kidney.

If the victim has no pulse or is not breathing, steps are taken to restart these essential functions.

If there is considerable bleeding, the first-aider applies firm pressure to the site of the injury. The victim should not be moved unless he or she is in danger. No attempt should be made to clean wounds – this may force a foreign body such as a glass fragment deeper into the wound.

Organisations such as the St John's Ambulance Brigade in the UK provide training in first aid.

1. Suggest how the skin may limit the entry of pathogens to the body. Why is it necessary to prevent the entry of pathogens?

2. This question concerns the process of blood clotting.
   a Why might blood clotting be necessary?
   b When could blood clotting be a disadvantage?
   c Blood clotting occurs in a number of stages. This is quite common in biological processes, since it allows **amplification**. Each step produces a product which can trigger many repeats of the next step – for example, each enzyme molecule released from a platelet can catalyse the conversion of 100 inactive protein molecules to their active form.
      i Suggest how this amplification might be an advantage in a rapid response to wounding.
      ii If there were five steps, each allowing an amplification of 100, how many 'product' molecules would be present at the end of the complete process for each 'signal' molecule released at the start of the process?

3. Describe the process of phagocytosis. Suggest two ways in which the structure of a phagocyte is related to its function. Suggest two ways in which a pathogen might avoid phagocytosis.

2·32 Antibodies and the immune response

Objectives

- To know what an antibody is
- To understand how antibodies are involved in defence against disease
- To understand how memory cells protect against infections
- To know how the immune response can be enhanced

An antibody is a protein

An **antibody** is a protein produced by the body in response to an antigen. Each different antigen stimulates the production of the particular type of antibody that will destroy that antigen. Antibodies are made by white blood cells called **lymphocytes**. They defend the body as shown below.

Once the lymphocytes have learnt to make a particular type of antibody in response to the antigens on an infective organism, the body begins to recover as the organisms are destroyed. It takes a few days to produce antibodies, so the infected individual will show some symptoms of the disease (a high temperature, for example).

Immunity

After an infection, some lymphocytes are kept as 'memory cells', which help the body to defend itself against further attacks by the same antigen. This 'memory' may last for years, and the body is said to be **immune** to the disease. There are different types of immunity, as shown opposite.

The action of white blood cells – lymphocytes

There are several types of lymphocyte:
- only **B-lymphocytes** produce antibodies
- **T-lymphocytes** either attack pathogens directly, or produce chemicals which coordinate the activity of all cells in the immune system
- one kind of T-lymphocyte, T-helper cells, are invaded by HIV to cause AIDS (see page 181).

Scientists estimate that humans can make up to 1 000 000 different antibodies – enough to account for every pathogen or 'foreign' substance we might ever meet!

This end of the antibody acts as a signal to phagocytes, or to T-lymphocytes, to destroy the pathogen.

The forked end of the antibody recognises and binds to the surface antigen on the pathogen to 'label' it.

Lymphocytes are a type of white blood cell:
- found in circulating blood and in the lymph nodes (see page 105)
- have a large nucleus and no granules in the cytoplasm
- stimulated by contact with pathogens to produce **antibodies**.

Antibodies are:
- proteins produced by lymphocytes
- able to recognise, bind to and help to destroy pathogens
- always Y-shaped.

'Labelled' pathogens may be destroyed by:
- sticking together in clumps so they can be **ingested by phagocytes**
- T-lymphocytes, which **burst membranes around the pathogen**
- antibodies directly – a few antibodies may actually destroy the pathogen's cell walls or membranes.

An **antigen** is:
- a protein or carbohydrate on the surface of the pathogen
- able to provoke the immune system of the host.

Pathogens may evade the immune system by mutation – they change and produce different antigens which the host has not learned to recognise and has no antibodies for.

Organisation and maintenance of organisms

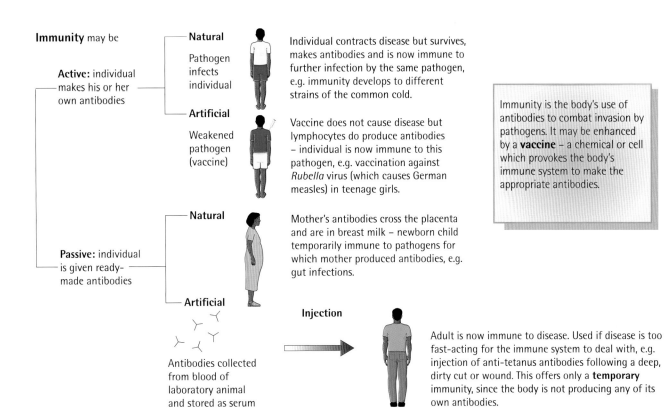

Immunity may be

Active: individual makes his or her own antibodies

— **Natural**

Pathogen infects individual

Individual contracts disease but survives, makes antibodies and is now immune to further infection by the same pathogen, e.g. immunity develops to different strains of the common cold.

— **Artificial**

Weakened pathogen (vaccine)

Vaccine does not cause disease but lymphocytes do produce antibodies – individual is now immune to this pathogen, e.g. vaccination against *Rubella* virus (which causes German measles) in teenage girls.

Passive: individual is given ready-made antibodies

— **Natural**

Mother's antibodies cross the placenta and are in breast milk – newborn child temporarily immune to pathogens for which mother produced antibodies, e.g. gut infections.

— **Artificial**

Antibodies collected from blood of laboratory animal and stored as serum

Injection

Adult is now immune to disease. Used if disease is too fast-acting for the immune system to deal with, e.g. injection of anti-tetanus antibodies following a deep, dirty cut or wound. This offers only a **temporary** immunity, since the body is not producing any of its own antibodies.

Immunity is the body's use of antibodies to combat invasion by pathogens. It may be enhanced by a **vaccine** – a chemical or cell which provokes the body's immune system to make the appropriate antibodies.

Some problems with the immune response

The activity of the immune system saves all our lives, many times over. There are occasions, however, when it may actually reduce the likelihood of survival. These are described below.

Autoimmune diseases are caused by the body producing antibodies which destroy its own cells. Why this should happen is not known. Examples include:

- diabetes – underactive pancreatic gland – the body destroys its own insulin-producing cells by an immune reaction
- rheumatoid arthritis – white blood cells destroy connective tissues in joints and make movement extremely painful.

Allergies are conditions in which the body becomes sensitive to a substance and over-reacts to it. This may cause swelling and tissue damage. Examples include

hay fever and sensitivity to bee and wasp stings. Allergies are treated with drugs such as antihistamines to reduce the immune response.

Transplant rejection – the most common organ transplant in Britain is the kidney transplant (see page 135), but heart, intestine, lung, liver and pancreas transplants are becoming more common. The recipient's lymphocytes may recognise antigens on the surface of the donor organ as foreign and slowly destroy it. This problem of rejection is being overcome by:

- drugs that suppress the immune system of the recipient long enough to allow the transplanted organ to become established
- matching tissues wherever possible, for example by seeking out relatives of people needing bone marrow transplants, since relatives are more likely to have similar antigens to the recipient.

1 How do antibodies recognise pathogens?

2 State one difference in structure between a lymphocyte and a phagocyte, and one difference in function between a B-lymphocyte and a T-lymphocyte.

3 Explain how a single infection by a pathogen can provide lifelong protection against a disease.

2.33 The circulatory system

Objectives

- To understand that the blood is directed around the body in a set of vessels
- To know the structure and function of arteries and veins
- To understand why humans have a double circulatory system
- To know the names of the main arteries and veins in the human body

Blood vessels – arteries and veins

Blood flows around the body in a system of tube-like **blood vessels**, arranged in such a way that they all eventually lead back to the heart. The blood flows *away* from the heart in vessels called **arteries**, and it flows back *towards* the heart in vessels called **veins**. Joining the arteries and veins are the **capillaries**, and we shall look at these on page 104.

In humans (and in many other animals), the main artery is called the **aorta** and the main vein is called the **vena cava**. The structure and functions of arteries and veins are shown in the table below.

The human double circulation

The human circulation is outlined at the top of the page opposite. The arrangement is called a **double circulation** because the blood passes through the heart twice for each complete circuit of the body. The blood flows to the lungs under high pressure (so a large volume of blood flows past the lung surfaces in a short time). Then, having picked up oxygen at the lungs, the blood receives another 'boost' of pressure from the heart to drive it out to the tissues, where the oxygen is needed.

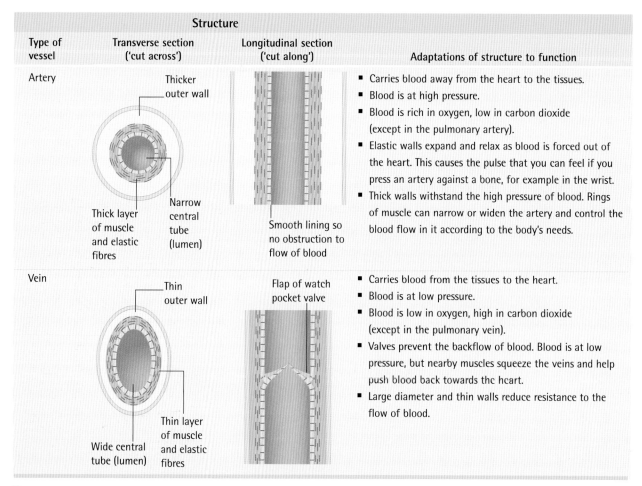

	Structure		
Type of vessel	Transverse section ('cut across')	Longitudinal section ('cut along')	Adaptations of structure to function
Artery	Thicker outer wall / Thick layer of muscle and elastic fibres / Narrow central tube (lumen)	Smooth lining so no obstruction to flow of blood	• Carries blood away from the heart to the tissues. • Blood is at high pressure. • Blood is rich in oxygen, low in carbon dioxide (except in the pulmonary artery). • Elastic walls expand and relax as blood is forced out of the heart. This causes the pulse that you can feel if you press an artery against a bone, for example in the wrist. • Thick walls withstand the high pressure of blood. Rings of muscle can narrow or widen the artery and control the blood flow in it according to the body's needs.
Vein	Thin outer wall / Wide central tube (lumen) / Thin layer of muscle and elastic fibres	Flap of watch pocket valve	• Carries blood from the tissues to the heart. • Blood is at low pressure. • Blood is low in oxygen, high in carbon dioxide (except in the pulmonary vein). • Valves prevent the backflow of blood. Blood is at low pressure, but nearby muscles squeeze the veins and help push blood back towards the heart. • Large diameter and thin walls reduce resistance to the flow of blood.

The structure and functions of arteries and veins.

Organisation and maintenance of organisms

Pulmonary artery – unlike other arteries, this vessel carries **deoxygenated blood** which also has a **high carbon dioxide concentration.**

The heart (see also page 106)

| Right atrium | Left atrium |
| Right ventricle | Left ventricle |

This wall separates oxygenated blood from deoxygenated blood.

Vena cava – the main vein of the body; returns deoxygenated blood at low pressure from organs and tissues to the heart.

Hepatic vein – returns blood with a regulated, optimum concentration of food substances to the circulation.

Renal vein – blood with reduced urea concentration is returned to the circulation.

High pressure - both ventricles pump out blood at high pressure, but the 'body' circuit has a pressure about 5x that in the 'lung' (pulmonary) circuit. This is because blood in the body circuit has so far to travel, and there are many branches in the circuit to take the high pressure blood.

Too high! If pressure in the pulmonary artery is too high, tissue fluid or plasma can leak into the lungs. This sometimes happens to climbers at high altitude.

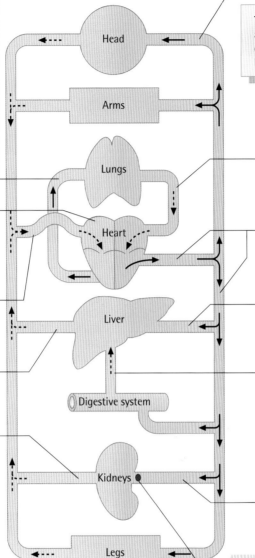

Head

Arms

Lungs

Heart

Liver

Digestive system

Kidneys

Legs

Pulmonary vein – unlike other veins, this vessel carries **oxygenated blood.** It has the **highest oxygen** and **lowest carbon dioxide** concentration in the circulation.

Aorta – the main artery of the body; supplies oxygenated blood, at high pressure, to the organs and tissues of the body.

Hepatic artery – carries oxygenated blood to the liver.

Hepatic portal vein – carries blood containing variable amounts of the absorbed products of digestion from the digestive system to the liver.

Renal artery – carries oxygenated blood with a **high concentration of urea** to the kidneys.

Key

Blood at low pressure ◄- - - - - - - -

Blood at high pressure ◄———

Capillaries link arteries and veins. They are present in all organs and tissues and are the site of exchange of materials between blood and tissue fluid (see next page).

1 State two differences between arteries and veins, and say how these differences are related to the functions of these blood vessels.

2 Look at the diagram above. Follow the path of the red blood cell in the renal artery around the circulation and back to the renal artery. How many times does it pass through the heart? List the blood vessels and chambers of the heart that the cell passes through.

Organisation and maintenance of organisms

2·34 Materials are exchanged between blood and tissues at the capillaries: tissue fluid is formed

Objectives

- To understand that substances carried in the blood must leave the circulation to reach the tissues
- To know that materials are exchanged between tissues and blood in the capillary beds
- To know how the structure of the capillaries is suited to the transfer of materials between blood and tissues

Tissue fluid leaves the capillaries

To reach the cells that need them, dissolved substances carried in the blood must leave the blood vessels and enter the tissues. At the same time, waste materials produced by the tissues need to enter the blood to be carried away. Dissolved substances move between the blood and tissues by **diffusion** across the walls of very fine blood vessels called **capillaries**. Networks or **beds** of capillaries extend through all the tissues, so every body cell is near to a capillary. The capillary beds are adapted to their function of exchange of substances in a number of ways:

- the walls of the capillaries are only one cell thick – substances do not have very far to diffuse through them
- the capillaries are highly branched so they cover an enormous surface area, giving more 'space' for diffusion to occur
- the capillary beds are constantly supplied with fresh blood, keeping up the concentration gradients of dissolved substances between blood and tissues. Without these concentration gradients diffusion could not occur.

The diagram shows how materials are exchanged between the blood and the tissues, and how **tissue fluid** is formed.

Artery – delivers oxygenated blood, rich in nutrients and at high pressure. Can be narrowed or widened to control blood flow (for example, during exercise). Continuous supply of blood keeps up the concentration gradients of substances between the blood plasma and the tissue fluid.

Cells of tissue
Need: oxygen and nutrients such as glucose and amino acids.
Produce: wastes such as carbon dioxide and some useful products such as hormones.

Vein – carries away deoxygenated blood, low in nutrients and at low pressure. Has high concentration of waste products.

Tissue fluid
- formed from plasma
- contains no blood cells or plasma proteins.

Formation of lymph

Useful substances move out from plasma – formation of tissue fluid

Substances collected from cells

Capillary has:
- wall only one cell thick
- very large surface area

Capillary walls are about 1 μm thick. The central tube (lumen) may only be the same diameter as the red blood cells, so they have to squeeze through the capillary in single file as they unload their oxygen.

Remember how substances cross membranes

Diffusion is:
- the movement of molecules
- down a concentration gradient
- until equilibrium is reached.

Osmosis is:
- the movement of water
- down a water potential gradient
- across a partially permeable membrane.

Problems with the return of tissue fluid

The diagram below shows in detail how tissue fluid is formed and returned to the blood. This tissue fluid is essential for the transport of dissolved substances between blood and cells. If anything goes wrong with this return of tissue fluid, the tissues swell up.

In **elephantiasis**, for example, a parasitic worm lodges in the lymph vessels in the groin and causes fluid to build up in the legs.

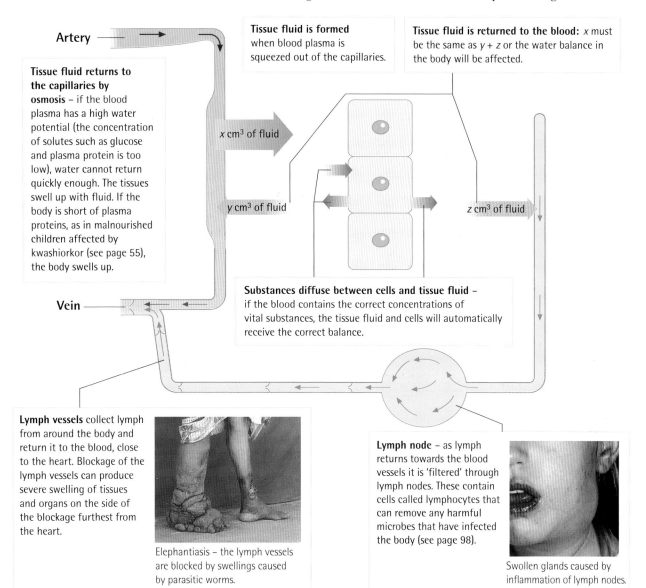

Artery

Tissue fluid is formed when blood plasma is squeezed out of the capillaries.

Tissue fluid is returned to the blood: x must be the same as $y + z$ or the water balance in the body will be affected.

Tissue fluid returns to the capillaries by osmosis – if the blood plasma has a high water potential (the concentration of solutes such as glucose and plasma protein is too low), water cannot return quickly enough. The tissues swell up with fluid. If the body is short of plasma proteins, as in malnourished children affected by kwashiorkor (see page 55), the body swells up.

x cm³ of fluid

y cm³ of fluid

z cm³ of fluid

Vein

Substances diffuse between cells and tissue fluid – if the blood contains the correct concentrations of vital substances, the tissue fluid and cells will automatically receive the correct balance.

Lymph vessels collect lymph from around the body and return it to the blood, close to the heart. Blockage of the lymph vessels can produce severe swelling of tissues and organs on the side of the blockage furthest from the heart.

Elephantiasis – the lymph vessels are blocked by swellings caused by parasitic worms.

Lymph node – as lymph returns towards the blood vessels it is 'filtered' through lymph nodes. These contain cells called lymphocytes that can remove any harmful microbes that have infected the body (see page 98).

Swollen glands caused by inflammation of lymph nodes.

---

1. This diagram represents a group of body cells and some parts of the circulatory system. The arrows show movement of fluids.
   a Name the fluids contained in spaces **A**, **B** and **C**.
   b Name two substances that the cells remove from the fluid in **B**. Suggest two substances that the cells might add to the fluid in **B**.
   c Describe how the fluid in **C** is returned to the circulation.
   d Give a reason why the process shown at **D** might be inefficient. What would be the result of this for the body? How could it be corrected?

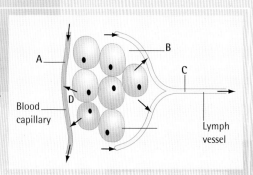

A

B

C

Blood capillary

D

Lymph vessel

2·35 The heart is the pump for the circulatory system

Objectives
▪ To know that the blood is pumped around the circulatory system by the action of the heart
▪ To know that the heart is a muscular organ with four chambers
▪ To understand how the flow of blood through the circulation is maintained

The heart of a mammal pumps blood through the circulatory system. It provides the pressure that forces the blood through arteries, capillaries and veins. The pressure is generated by the squeezing of the walls of the heart against the incompressible fluid blood. The heart walls can squeeze the blood because they are made of **muscle**, and the muscle contracts rhythmically.

A double pump
The heart is divided into two sides, each of which acts as a pump. The right side of the heart pumps deoxygenated blood coming from the tissues out to the lungs. The left side pumps oxygenated blood coming from the lungs out to the tissues. A much greater pressure (about five times as much) is needed to force blood out to the extremities of the body than is needed to drive blood to the lungs. Because of this, the left side of the heart is much more muscular than the right side (page 103).

Even though the two sides of the heart generate different pressures, they work in the same way and have the same parts, as shown in the diagram below.

Pulmonary arteries – carry deoxygenated blood to the lungs.

Semilunar valves – prevent blood running back into the ventricles when pressure falls during relaxation.

Vena cava – the main vein of the body; returns deoxygenated blood from the head and lower body to the right atrium.

Right atrium – receives deoxygenated blood from the vena cava. The **pacemaker** is found in the wall of the right atrium.

Three flaps of tricuspid valve – prevent blood flowing back from ventricle to atrium during contraction.

Tendons which are tightened to make sure that the valve does not turn inside out when the ventricle walls contract.

Chamber of **right ventricle**

Aorta – the main artery of the body; carries oxygenated blood out to the tissues. Blood pressure is at its highest in the aorta, and the strongest pulse is felt here.

Pulmonary vein – returns oxygenated blood from the lungs. A vein from each lung join together before entering the left atrium.

Left atrium – receives oxygenated blood returning from the lungs. Atria have thin walls since they need only pump blood to the ventricles.

Two flaps of **bicuspid valve** – when this valve is closed and the ventricle contracts, the blood **must** leave through the aorta.

Chamber of **left ventricle**

Wall of left ventricle – thick and muscular since it must force blood through the arteries to all the tissues of the body.

Wall of right ventricle – less muscular than left ventricle since it need only force blood along the pulmonary arteries to the lungs.

Think about it! The left ventricle can push out about 70 cm^3 of blood with each beat, and in a normal healthy person at rest the heart beats 70 times per minute. How much blood is pumped out of the heart per hour? How much per day?

Key
▨ Deoxygenated blood	◀--- Blood at low pressure
■ Oxygenated blood	◀— Blood at high pressure

Note that:

- The **atrium** receives blood at low pressure from the veins (coming from the lungs or tissues).
- The **ventricle** pumps blood at high pressure out to the arteries (to the lungs or tissues).
- **Valves** make sure that the blood flows in the right direction.

The beating of the heart is controlled by a pacemaker

In a healthy person the heart beats about 70 times a minute during normal levels of activity. This rate is enough to supply blood containing oxygen and nutrients to tissues.

The muscular walls of the heart differ from other muscles in that they never become tired or **fatigued**, because each contraction of the heart is immediately followed by a relaxation. Even when the heart is beating at its fastest during severe exercise (see page 109), the period of relaxation allows the muscle to recover so it does not fatigue.

The pattern of contraction and relaxation is kept going by electrical signals sent from a region of the heart called the **pacemaker**. This is a specialised piece of tissue in the wall of the right atrium. It is sensitive to the swelling of the heart wall as blood enters the heart from the main veins. The signals from the pacemaker make sure that:

- the atria contract just before the ventricles, so that blood flows from atria to ventricles
- the heartbeat is fast enough to meet the demands of the tissues for oxygen and nutrients, and for the removal of wastes.

If the pacemaker does not work as well as it should, an artificial electronic pacemaker can be fitted inside the chest (see box opposite).

Artificial pacemakers – help for the heart

The beating of the heart is controlled by the natural pacemaker in the wall of the right atrium. If this pacemaker is damaged, pumping goes on automatically at about 30 beats per minute. This is less than half the normal rate, and is only enough to keep a very inactive person alive.

An artificial pacemaker can help people whose natural pacemaker does not work well. This artificial pacemaker is made up of a box containing batteries and an electronic timing device. It is placed in a cavity under the muscle of the upper chest as shown below, and a wire is fed down a vein into the right ventricle. The timing device sends a small electrical charge which triggers the beating of the heart. This is set to give a basic rate of 72 beats per minute. The latest pacemakers can sense changes in breathing, movement and body temperature, and make exactly the right adjustments to heart rate. The battery in the pacemaker is usually replaced every year or so, under local anaesthetic.

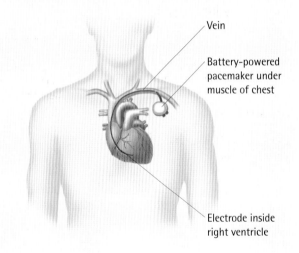

An artificial pacemaker.

---

1 a Name the chamber of the heart that receives blood from the lungs.
   b Explain what happens to the blood in the ventricles when the muscle in the ventricle walls contracts.
   c The muscle around the atria is thinner than the muscle around the ventricles. Suggest a reason for this.

2 A doctor listening to the heartbeat through a stethoscope hears two sounds as the blood flows through the heart: 'lup-dup lup-dup lup-dup'.
   a From your knowledge of the working of the heart, suggest how these two sounds are produced.
   b The doctor records 72 beats per minute. How long a period would there be between two consecutive 'lup' sounds? Explain your answer.

Objectives
- To understand how the flow of blood through the circulation is maintained
- To understand how the regular beating of the heart can be adjusted according to the body's needs

Blood pressure

As the ventricles of the heart contract they force blood at high pressure into the arteries. This pressure needs to carry blood to the working tissues, but it must not be so high that it damages the blood vessels. Blood pressure can be varied, such as to force more blood to muscles during exercise. The blood pressure is raised by:

- making the ventricles contract more powerfully
- narrowing the diameter of the arteries.

Stress or excitement also raise the blood pressure. A diet with too much saturated fat can cause high blood pressure by clogging up the arteries.

Measuring blood pressure

The blood pressure naturally goes up and down during the heart's cycles of contraction and relaxation. The blood pressure is highest when the ventricles contract (**systolic pressure**) and lowest when the heart walls are relaxed as blood returns into the atria (**diastolic pressure**). A person's blood pressure is expressed as a fraction, systolic pressure divided by diastolic pressure. A typical healthy young person would have a blood pressure around 120/80 – this means that systolic pressure is 120 mm of mercury and diastolic pressure is 80 mm of mercury.

The high pressure generated when the ventricles contract forces blood out into the arteries. The elastic walls of the arteries expand and then relax. This causes a **pulse** in the arteries – this can be felt wherever an artery can be pressed against a solid surface, such as a bone. The pulse should always be felt with the index or ring fingers, since the thumb has a pulse of its own. There is no pulse in the veins since the blood no longer has spurts of pressure (it is now a long way from the heart) and the walls of veins are not elastic.

Blood flow through the veins

The pressure generated by the beating of the heart, together with the elastic recoil of the walls of the arteries, drives the blood out to the tissues. At the capillaries, some of the plasma leaks across the capillary walls to form the tissue fluid (see page 104). As a result of this the volume of blood in the vessels falls, and so too does its pressure. The pressure is no longer great enough to return the blood to the heart through the veins. How does blood return to the heart? There are a number of factors that help it to flow in the veins, as shown in the diagram below.

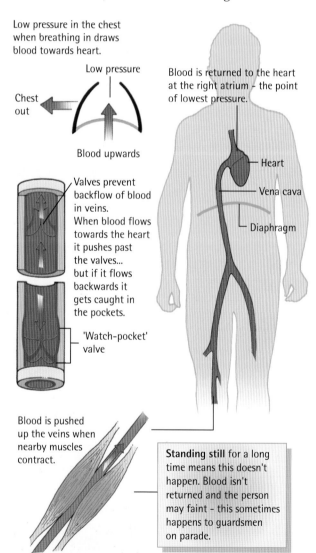

Low pressure in the chest when breathing in draws blood towards heart.

Low pressure

Chest out

Blood upwards

Blood is returned to the heart at the right atrium - the point of lowest pressure.

Heart

Vena cava

Diaphragm

Valves prevent backflow of blood in veins. When blood flows towards the heart it pushes past the valves... but if it flows backwards it gets caught in the pockets.

'Watch-pocket' valve

Blood is pushed up the veins when nearby muscles contract.

Standing still for a long time means this doesn't happen. Blood isn't returned and the person may faint - this sometimes happens to guardsmen on parade.

Blood from the veins is returned to right atrium of the heart via the vena cava. At this point blood pressure is at its lowest.

DANGER!
Exercise, especially if sudden and unplanned, can overstress the heart. This can lead to chest pain (**angina**) or even death. Those who are especially at risk include:
- the elderly
- people with coronary heart disease (CHD)
- people who do not exercise regularly.

Anticipation of exercise such as a warm-up can prepare the body for action. The hormone **adrenaline**:
- increases blood flow to muscles, and reduces blood flow to 'non-vital' organs such as the gut
- allows the heart to expand more to give 'deeper' beats – greater volume of blood is forced out with each beat.

During exercise the concentration of carbon dioxide in the blood rises. This is detected automatically (no 'thought' is necessary) by the brain, and nerve messages are sent out to...

Long-term benefits
Regular, carefully planned training can:
- increase the size of the heart
- increase the power of heart muscle
- keep artery walls flexible
- increase the size of capillary beds, including the ones that supply the heart muscle itself.

The heart, which beats more quickly and more deeply, pumping more blood out into the circulation each minute.

The capillary beds, which can be opened up in vital working organs such as muscle, and closed down in non-vital organs such as the gut.

Sphincter muscles control blood flow to capillaries.

Result?
More oxygen and **more glucose** can be delivered for **respiration** in working muscles.

Well-trained athletes often have a lower pulse rate than people who are less fit because their heart and circulation are more efficient.

The heart and exercise

During strenuous exercise such as running, the muscles work hard. They need more oxygen and glucose to release energy by respiration, so they need an increased circulation of blood to supply the oxygen and glucose. This is achieved in two ways:

- **the heart pumps more blood each minute** – it beats more quickly and more deeply
- **sphincters control the distribution of blood** – rings of muscle open to increase the blood flow to the muscles, and close to decrease the blood flow to less important areas such as the gut.

1 During exercise the heart pumps out a greater volume of blood per minute than at rest. Suggest two ways in which the heart can increase the volume of blood pumped out.

2 'Exercise has both short- and long-term effects on the heart.' Explain what is meant by this statement.

3 When a doctor takes a patient's blood pressure the result is expressed as two figures, for example, 120/80 mm of mercury. Explain why there are two figures.

Organisation and maintenance of organisms

Objectives

- To know that the heart muscle requires a supply of oxygen, glucose and other nutrients
- To know that the heart muscle has its own blood supply through the coronary arteries
- To understand that factors such as lifestyle, diet and family history may affect the efficiency of the coronary arteries
- To know that coronary heart disease is one of the major causes of death in the developed world

Cast of the heart showing the coronary circulation

The supply of blood to the heart muscle

Heart muscle contracts to push blood through the vessels of the circulation. This contraction is work, and it requires energy. The energy is made available by aerobic respiration, so the working cells of the heart need glucose and oxygen for respiration.

The blood passing through the chambers on the left side of the heart carries oxygen and glucose, but the heart cells cannot use these because the muscular walls are very thick and the blood is too far away. The heart muscle has its own blood supply, delivered to capillary beds in the walls of the heart through the **coronary arteries**. The coronary arteries branch off from the aorta, just where the aorta leaves the left ventricle. The heart therefore has a high-pressure supply of blood loaded with oxygen and glucose. Once these useful substances have been

removed by the heart muscle cells and replaced with wastes such as carbon dioxide, the blood returns to the circulation through **coronary veins** which pour blood into the vena cava. The coronary circulation is shown below left. The photograph above shows a cast of the heart with all the coronary circulation picked out after the heart muscle has been removed.

Coronary heart disease

If any of the coronary arteries become blocked, the supply of blood to the heart muscle may be interrupted. The heart muscle cells are deprived of glucose and oxygen, and poisonous wastes such as lactic acid build up (see page 116). Part of the heart muscle stops contracting, causing a **heart attack**. This can be damaging or even fatal, since other tissues in the body no longer receive their supplies of oxygen and nutrients if the heart stops beating.

What causes the coronary arteries to become blocked? A healthy coronary artery may be narrowed by atheroma so that blood flow through it is restricted. This person has **coronary heart disease (CHD)**.

The risk of developing CHD is increased by:

- **poor diet** – high levels of cholesterol or saturated fatty acids in the blood
- **poor lifestyle** – smoking, lack of exercise, stress
- **genetic factors** – being male; having a family history of heart disease.

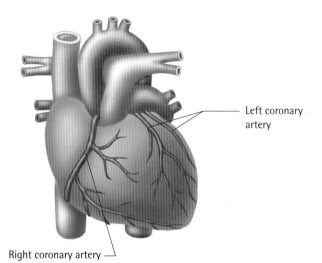

Left coronary artery

Right coronary artery

The coronary arteries branch off the aorta, supplying the surface of the heart with oxygenated blood at high pressure.

Anyone with a genetic risk of developing heart disease should obviously take care that he or she does not have a poor diet or lifestyle. Many middle-aged men, the highest risk group, help to prevent heart disease by taking half an aspirin a day (this seems to help stop small clots forming which could block the arteries) and/or by drinking a small quantity of alcohol (red wine may be the most beneficial).

If a doctor suspects that a patient has CHD, an **angiogram** is carried out. This gives a picture of the state of these arteries (see below). If the coronary arteries are blocked, a **coronary artery bypass** operation may be carried out, as shown below.

Aortic arch

Grafted 'bypass'

Blocked part of coronary artery

Coronary artery

Avoid the problem!
- Don't smoke
- Avoid fatty foods
- Take regular aerobic exercise

Men are more at risk of CHD than women – but men can't avoid CHD by changing their gender!

In a **coronary artery bypass operation** a blood vessel is removed from another part of the body and stitched into place between the aorta and the unblocked part of the coronary artery. Sometimes an artificial vessel is used. The bypass increases blood flow and reduces the likelihood of angina (chest pain).

1 a The heart muscle has its own supply of blood from vessels that run all over its surface. What is the name of these vessels?

   b In some people these vessels can become blocked with a fatty substance containing cholesterol. Explain the effects that blocking these blood vessels would have.

2 Look at the graphs. Graph A shows the relationship between the death rate for CHD and the blood cholesterol level. Graph B shows the relationship between cholesterol levels and age, for men and women.

   a At which ages do men and women show the same blood cholesterol level?

   b Use the information in the graphs to explain why the death rate from CHD is higher for men than for women between the ages of 25 and 45 years.

   c Use the graphs to determine the level of blood cholesterol that would keep the death rate from CHD at a minimum.

   d What does your answer to c suggest about cholesterol as the only cause of CHD?

   e What sort of person is most at risk from CHD?

Questions on circulation

1 Read the following article carefully, then answer the questions based on it.

Blood plasma carries red blood cells, white blood cells and platelets to all parts of the body. It also carries many solutes (dissolved substances) – these include oxygen, carbon dioxide, urea, hormones, glucose and amino acids.

In a normal healthy person the number of white blood cells may vary, but is usually no more than 8000 per mm^3 of blood. If a person has an infection, the number of white blood cells may rise to 40 000 per mm^3 of blood.

In a healthy person living at sea level there are about 5 000 000 red blood cells per mm^3 of blood. The cells are regularly replaced from the bone marrow. Old, worn out red blood cells are removed from the blood by the liver, after about 120 days of carrying out their function. Each cell carries oxygen from the lungs to the tissues, combined with a protein called haemoglobin. Haemoglobin will also combine with carbon monoxide, a gas in car exhaust fumes and cigarette smoke. Carbon monoxide combines with haemoglobin about 250 times more readily than oxygen does, and the combination does not break down.

a Name two soluble substances transported in the blood plasma. For each substance you name, suggest where it might be coming from and where it might be going to.

b What is the maximum number of white blood cells normally found in 1 mm^3 of blood? What can cause this number to increase?

c In a healthy person, what is the ratio of red blood cells to white blood cells?

d Name two sources of carbon monoxide.

e What happens to the amount of oxygen transported if a person breathes in carbon monoxide? Explain your answer.

f How long would it take the blood of the person in part **e** to regain its full ability to carry oxygen? Explain your answer.

g Liver is a good dietary source of iron. Why?

2 Name the blood vessel in a human that has:

a the highest pressure

b the highest oxygen concentration

c the highest carbon dioxide concentration

d the highest temperature when the body is at rest

e the function of removing deoxygenated blood from the leg

f the highest concentration of glucose following a meal

g blood at high pressure but with a low oxygen concentration.

3 These diagrams are concerned with the exchange of materials between the blood and tissues.

Part of the circulatory system

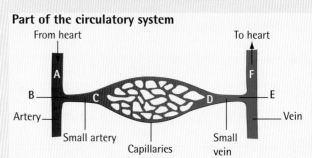

Sections through blood vessels *(not to scale)*

Average blood pressure at different positions in the circulatory system

a What happens to the blood pressure as the blood travels from A to F?

b The highest pressure is found in the artery. Why is this important for the delivery of materials to the cells?

c Veins have structures along them, not shown in the diagram, to help return blood to the heart. What are these structures called?

d How can the small arteries help control the distribution of blood to tissues which have a high demand for oxygen and nutrients?

e Use information shown in the diagrams to explain how the structure of capillaries allows substances to pass from them to surrounding cells.

4 List the blood vessels and chambers of the heart through which:

a a molecule of glucose absorbed through the gut passes on its way to an active muscle in the leg

b a red blood cell passes as it delivers oxygen from the lungs to the brain and returns to be oxygenated again.

5 On a visit to a sports physiology laboratory, a student underwent a series of tests. He was made to exercise on a rolling road, and the following information was collected.

Heart rate / beats per minute	Total heart output / dm³ per minute	Output per beat / cm³
55	4.0	
70	4.8	
80	5.2	
90	5.6	
120	6.0	
140	6.0	
150	5.8	
170	4.6	

a Copy the table and complete it by calculating the output per beat for each heart rate value.

b Plot a graph of total output (vertical axis) against heart rate (horizontal axis). On the same graph plot output per beat (vertical axis) against heart rate.

c Describe the relationship between:
  i heart rate and total output
  ii heart rate and output per beat.

d **i** Even during severe exercise, the heart rate seldom rises above 140 beats per minute. Use the data in the table to explain why this is so.
  ii Well trained athletes can keep up a heart rate of 170 beats per minute. Suggest how their output per beat may be different from that of an untrained person such as the student.

e Distance runners often have low resting heart rates. How might this be of advantage to them?

f Increased total output means that more blood can be delivered to active tissues. As heart rate increases, so does breathing rate. Suggest why.

6 The bar chart below shows how the risk of CHD varies in different parts of the world.

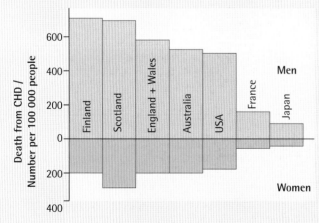

A USA citizen is almost three times as likely to develop CHD as a French citizen. Medical scientists suggested that this difference could be due to either diet or inheritance. They set up a study of 1000 French nationals who had emigrated to the USA, and who had taken up the American lifestyle, including diet.

a How many of these people would you expect to develop CHD if:
  i diet is responsible
  ii inheritance is responsible?
b All the people in this study were male, and non-smokers. Why was this important to the validity of the results?

7 The following tables show the effects of smoking and blood cholesterol levels on the risk of developing CHD.

Cigarettes smoked per day	Relative risk of CHD
0	1
5	1.2
10	1.5
15	2.0
20	2.5
25	2.9
30	3.2

Effect of smoking.

Cholesterol level	Relative risk of CHD
Male, normal	1
Female, normal	0.3
Male, 30% above normal	1.4
Male, 45% above normal	2.0
Male, 75% above normal	3.1

Effect of blood cholesterol level.

a Plot the two sets of results in an appropriate way.
b **i** Which appears to carry greater risk, smoking 10 cigarettes per day or having a blood cholesterol level 45% above normal?
  ii How much more likely is a man who smokes 30 cigarettes per day and has a 75% higher than normal blood cholesterol level to develop CHD than a non-smoking woman with normal blood cholesterol level?

8 Suggest how:
a lifestyle
b diet
c inheritance
may cause problems with the circulatory system.

Objectives

- To understand that energy is needed to carry out work
- To appreciate that different forms of energy can be interconverted
- To be able to list some of the energy-demanding processes in living organisms
- To describe how the process of respiration releases energy from chemical foods

in greater detail on page 60, but in energy terms it can be described simply as:

> Light energy from the Sun
> ⇓
> Converted in green plants
> ⇓
> Chemical energy in organic molecules

Energy conversions in living things

Energy can be defined as 'the capacity for doing work'. The processes that keep organisms alive (for example, pumping ions from one side of a membrane to another) usually require work to be done. It is clear, therefore, that life requires energy.

Life also depends on energy **conversions**. The first and most important energy conversion in living things is **photosynthesis**. This process is described

A second energy-conversion process releases the chemical energy stored in organic food molecules and converts it to energy forms that organisms use to stay alive. This process is called **respiration**. The diagram at the bottom of the page shows some of the energy conversions carried out by living organisms.

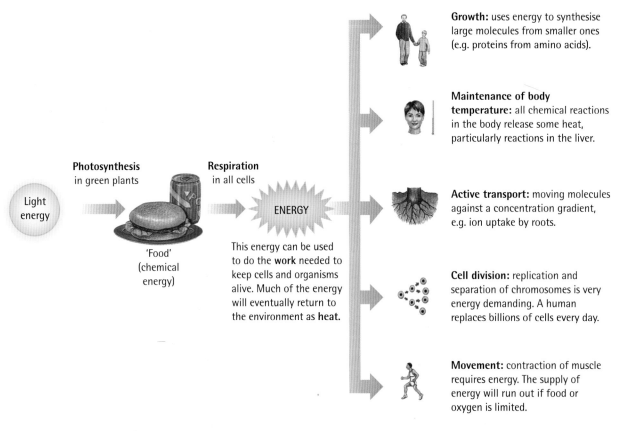

Growth: uses energy to synthesise large molecules from smaller ones (e.g. proteins from amino acids).

Maintenance of body temperature: all chemical reactions in the body release some heat, particularly reactions in the liver.

Active transport: moving molecules against a concentration gradient, e.g. ion uptake by roots.

Cell division: replication and separation of chromosomes is very energy demanding. A human replaces billions of cells every day.

Movement: contraction of muscle requires energy. The supply of energy will run out if food or oxygen is limited.

Photosynthesis in green plants

Respiration in all cells

Light energy

'Food' (chemical energy)

ENERGY

This energy can be used to do the **work** needed to keep cells and organisms alive. Much of the energy will eventually return to the environment as **heat**.

Living organisms obtain their food by nutrition (see page 42). They release energy from food in the process of respiration, and use it to carry out the work needed for life.

What is respiration?

Respiration involves the **oxidation** of food molecules, and energy is released during the process. These food molecules all contain carbon, hydrogen and oxygen and the complete oxidation process converts these to carbon dioxide and water. Complete oxidation occurs only if oxygen is present. For example:

Words: glucose + oxygen → energy + carbon dioxide + water

Symbols: $C_6H_{12}O_6 + 6O_2 →$ energy $+ 6CO_2 + 6H_2O$

Definition: respiration is the release of energy from food substances, and goes on in all living cells.

So much energy is released in this process that, if it was all released at once, the cell might be damaged.

The energy is released in small 'packets' which can then drive the reactions that keep the cell alive. These energy packets act as a short-term store of energy. The one used most commonly by cells is a molecule called **adenosine triphosphate (ATP)**.

The reactions are summarised in the following equation.

glucose + oxygen

├──→ ATP → 'work' in cells

carbon dioxide + water

This process, which releases energy in the presence of oxygen, is called **aerobic respiration** ('aerobic' means 'in air'), and takes place in the **mitochondria** (see page 23). Some energy is 'lost' as heat.

Vacuum flask experiment

A   B

Vacuum flasks: prevent heat loss from contents or gain from surroundings

Equal masses of peas

Cotton wool plugs: support thermometers and allow gas exchange between flask contents and surroundings

Thermometers: positioned so that they can be read without removal from flask

Living peas, previously soaked in water and washed with dilute disinfectant

Dead peas, killed by boiling or by strong disinfectant

- Apparatus is assembled as shown.
- Temperature readings are taken immediately, and then every day for 4–5 days.

In an experiment like this one, the following results were obtained:

Time/days	Temperature/°C	
	A	B
0	20	20
1	23	20
2	25	20
3	27	21
4	28	21
5	28	21

a Explain these results.
b Why is it important to include flask B?
c Disinfectant kills bacteria – why is this important?

Organisation and maintenance of organisms

2.39 Contraction of muscles requires energy supplied by respiration

Objectives
- To know that respiration is the source of energy for muscular work
- To understand that anaerobic respiration is less efficient than aerobic respiration and produces a toxic product
- To understand that exercise is limited by the build-up of lactic acid

How muscles contract

Muscles contract and pull on bones to move the skeleton. Muscles are collections of very long **muscle fibres**.

When lots of fibres shorten at the same time, the muscle contracts.

Muscular work requires energy

Aerobic respiration

Work must be done to contract muscle. **The energy for this comes from aerobic respiration.** The equation is a reminder of how this energy is released:

> Glucose + oxygen → energy + carbon dioxide + water

The oxygen comes from the air. It is taken in at the lungs and carried around the body in the blood, pumped by the heart. Glucose comes from food digested in the gut, and is also carried in the blood. Muscles have extensive capillary beds to supply glucose and oxygen for respiration, and to carry away carbon dioxide. The blood also carries away heat that is produced during respiration.

Anaerobic respiration

When we work very hard our muscles use up a lot of energy. The heart and lungs, even working flat out, cannot supply enough oxygen to provide this energy by aerobic respiration. Muscles can release energy from food without using oxygen, by a process called **anaerobic respiration**:

> Words: glucose → energy + lactic acid
> Symbols: $C_6H_{12}O_6 \rightarrow$ energy $+ 2C_3H_6O_3$

Anaerobic respiration has two drawbacks:
- It gives only about one-twentieth of the energy per glucose molecule that aerobic respiration yields.
- Lactic acid is poisonous – if it builds up in the cells it inhibits muscular contraction, which leads to fatigue and, eventually, death.

This harmful lactic acid is carried out of the muscles in the blood. It is transported around the body to the heart, liver and kidneys where it is oxidised to **pyruvate**, which can be used to release energy by aerobic respiration. The heart, the liver and the kidneys will need extra oxygen to get rid of this lactic acid, provided by the deep fast breathing that follows hard exercise. This extra oxygen is the **oxygen debt**.

1. One of the comparisons between aerobic and anaerobic respiration shown below is incorrect. Which one?

Respiration

	Aerobic	Anaerobic
A	Uses oxygen gas	Does not use oxygen gas
B	Produces ethanol or lactic acid	Produces no ethanol or lactic acid
C	Large amount of energy released	Small amount of energy released
D	Mitochondria involved	Mitochondria not involved
E	Carbon dioxide always produced	Carbon dioxide sometimes produced

2. What is meant by energy transformation? Briefly describe one energy transformation that is important to living organisms. What eventually happens to all of the energy taken in by living organisms?

The diagram below shows the part played by aerobic and anaerobic respiration during rest, exercise and recovery.

Rest – all respiration is aerobic. Normal breathing and heart rates can supply the tissues with all the oxygen they need, Glucose + oxygen → energy + carbon dioxide + water

Heart rate
70 beats per minute

Breathing
15 breaths per minute

Hard exercise – respiration is mainly anaerobic. Very high breathin and heart rates still cannot provide the muscles with enough oxygen for aerobic respiratin.
Glucose → energy + lactic acid

Heart Rate
140 beats per minute

Breathing
50 breaths per minute

The muscles are getting energy without 'paying for it with oxygen. They are running up an oxygen debt.

Recovery – paying off the oxygen debt. The breathing and heart rates remain high, even though the muscles are at rest. The extra oxygen is used to convert the lactic acid into carbon dioxide and water, paying off the oxygen debt.

Heart rate
140 beats per minute falling to normal after some minutes

Breathing
50 breaths per minute falling to normal after some minutes

Panting and rapid heartbeat continue until the lactic acid has been romoved. Physically fit people recover faster.

Blood levels of oxygen and lactic acid

| Rest | Exercise | Recovery |

No lactic acid builds up since there is enough oxygen for aerobic respiration.

This is the 'extra' oxygen required to pay off the oxygen debt.

This is the shortfall in oxygen – making lactic acid builds up an **oxygen debt.**

Oxygen

Lactic acid

Time / min

Anaerobic respiration is
important in other organisms

- yeast, for brewing and baking (page 50)

- bacteria, for making yoghurt for example (page 49)

Trained athletes can exercise for longer than confirmed couch potatoes before they build up an oxygen debt.

---

3 The concentration of lactic acid (lactate) in the blood of a runner was measured at intervals before, during and after she ran for 10 minutes. The results are shown in the table below.

Time / minutes	Concentration of lactic acid / arbitrary units
0	18
10	18
15	56
25	88
35	42
50	21
65	18

a Plot this information in the form of a graph.
b What was the lactic acid concentration at the end of the run?
c For how long did the concentration of lactic acid increase after the end of the run?
d Why did the blood still contain lactic acid after the run?
e In which tissues was the lactic acid produced?
f How long after the run was it before the oxygen debt was paid off?

The measurement of respiration

Since respiration is essential for life, an obvious 'sign of life' is that respiration is taking place. We can demonstrate that respiration is happening, and we can even measure how quickly it is going on.

The equation for aerobic respiration suggests methods that we might use to demonstrate this process.

To demonstrate that respiration is going on, we need to use some living organisms. Germinating seeds are useful for this experiment since they are chemically very active (the fast growth during germination requires a great deal of energy). Animals such as blowfly larvae (maggots) or woodlice can also be used, although they are rather more difficult to handle.

| 1 | **Measurement of oxygen consumption using a respirometer** |

The apparatus shown in the diagram on the next page is used.

a A measured mass of living organisms is put in the chamber.

b First the spring clip is open, so that an equilibrium of temperature and pressure is set up between the chamber and the surroundings.

c After five minutes or so, the spring clip is closed and the movement of the coloured liquid along the capillary tube is observed. The time taken for it to move a measured length along the tube is noted.

d The living organisms are removed and the experiment is repeated.

Using this apparatus, a group of students obtained the following data.

Experiment	Distance moved / mm	Time taken / s	Relative oxygen consumption / mm per s
1 Seeds	39	100	
2 Seeds	42	100	
3 Seeds	24	60	
4 Maggots	46	90	
5 Maggots	55	100	
6 Maggots	30	60	

Principle: Carbon dioxide produced during respiration is absorbed by potassium hydroxide solution. If the system is closed to the atmosphere, a change in volume of the gas within the chamber must be due to the consumption of oxygen. The change in volume, i.e. the oxygen consumption, is measured as the movement of a drop of coloured liquid along a capillary tube.

Spring clip – when open, contents of chamber are in equilibrium with atmosphere.

Rubber stopper – can be made more airtight by smearing Vaseline along seal between chamber and stopper.

Filter paper wick ensures that maximum surface area of potassium hydroxide solution is available to contents of chamber.

Potassium hydroxide solution absorbs carbon dioxide evolved during respiration.

Graduated scale against which movement of coloured liquid can be measured

Coloured liquid – narrow-bore capillary tube means that any small change in volume of gas in chamber produces a large movement of liquid.

Gauze basket to hold respiring material must be porous to allow free exchange of gases.

Respiratory chamber has relatively low volume, so that changes in volume due to respiration are significant enough to be measured.

Weighed amount of respiring material – the mass, m, of the respiring material should be known so that results can be compared with other experiments.

Glass rod to keep respiring material out of direct contact with potassium hydroxide solution

---

2 Measurement of carbon dioxide release

To detect carbon dioxide released by respiring organisms, we can use an **indicator solution**. For example **hydrogencarbonate indicator** is purple at high pH (alkaline), red around neutral pH and orange-yellow at low pH (acidic).
The diagram shows the apparatus.

A	B	C	D
Potassium hydroxide solution	Hydrogencarbonate indicator		Hydrogencarbonate indicator

---

1. **a** In experiment **1** why did the students take more than one set of readings for each group of organisms?

   b Calculate the mean relative oxygen consumption for the seeds and for the maggots. Suggest a reason for the difference.

2. The students repeated the experiment with no living organisms in the chamber. The coloured liquid did not move at all. Why was this important?

3. In an extension of this investigation, the students measured the effect of temperature on the rate of oxygen consumption by the maggots. They obtained the following results:

Temperature / °C	Relative oxygen consumption / mm per s
15	0.3
25	0.6
35	1.1
45	0.8
55	0.2
65	0.0

   a Plot these results on a graph, and explain the shape of the curve.

   b In this investigation, identify the **independent variable** and the **dependent variable**.

   c Suggest any **fixed variables**. (Refer to page 36 if you are unsure about these terms.)

In experiment 2:

4. What is the purpose of the potassium hydroxide solution?

5. What does the indicator solution in flask B show?

6. How can you explain the change in flask D?

7. Suggest a control for this investigation, and explain why it is a suitable control.

8. Suggest any visible change that might happen in flask **C**. Explain your answer.

2.41 Gas exchange supplies oxygen for respiration

Objectives

- To understand why living organisms must obtain oxygen from their environment, and why they must release carbon dioxide to their environment
- To know the properties of an ideal gas exchange surface
- To be able to identify the parts of the human gas exchange system

Exchanging oxygen and carbon dioxide

Respiration uses oxygen to 'burn' (oxidise) food and so release the energy that cells need to stay alive. Respiration produces carbon dioxide and water vapour as waste products:

$$\text{Glucose} + \text{oxygen} \rightarrow \text{energy} + \text{carbon dioxide} + \text{water}$$

Living organisms must be able to take oxygen from the air and get rid of carbon dioxide to the air. Swapping oxygen for carbon dioxide in this way is called **gas exchange** (or **gaseous exchange**).

Gas exchange takes place through a **gas exchange surface**, also known as a **respiratory surface**. The diagram below shows how the process happens. The properties of an ideal respiratory surface are given in the table on the right.

Gas exchange surface is thin – dissolved gases can pass through it easily.

Layer of water on gas exchange surface

Oxygen

Carbon dioxide

Oxygen dissolves in moist layer

Carbon dioxide is changed to a gas

Carbon dioxide produced by respiration dissolves in body fluids to form hydrogen-carbonate ions (HCO_3^-).

A gas exchange surface allows cells to obtain the oxygen they need for respiration, and get rid of the carbon dioxide they produce.

Property of surface	Reason
Thin (ideally one cell thick)	Gases have a short distance over which to diffuse.
Large surface area	Many molecules of gas can diffuse across at the same time.
Moist	Cells die if not kept moist.
Well ventilated	Concentration gradients for oxygen and carbon dioxide are kept up by regular fresh supplies of air.
Close to a blood supply	Gases can be carried to and from the cells that need or produce them.

Gas exchange in humans

Like other mammals, humans are active and maintain a constant body temperature. This means they use up a great deal of energy. Mammals must have a very efficient gas exchange system.

The gas exchange system in humans is shown opposite and is made up of:

- a **respiratory surface** – membranes lining the alveoli (air sacs) in the lungs
- a **set of tubes** to allow air from the outside to reach the respiratory surface. This set of tubes has many branches, and is sometimes called the 'bronchial tree'
- a **blood supply** (carried by the pulmonary artery and pulmonary vein) to carry dissolved gases to and from the respiratory surface
- a **ventilation system** (the intercostal muscles and the diaphragm) to keep a good flow of air over the respiratory surface.

1. What are the properties of an ideal gas exchange surface?
2. List the structures through which a molecule of oxygen passes to get from the atmosphere to the cytoplasm of a named working cell.
3. Most larger animals transport oxygen in red blood cells. What are the advantages of transporting oxygen in this way? How is a red blood cell adapted to its function of oxygen transport?
4. What is the difference between respiration and gas exchange?

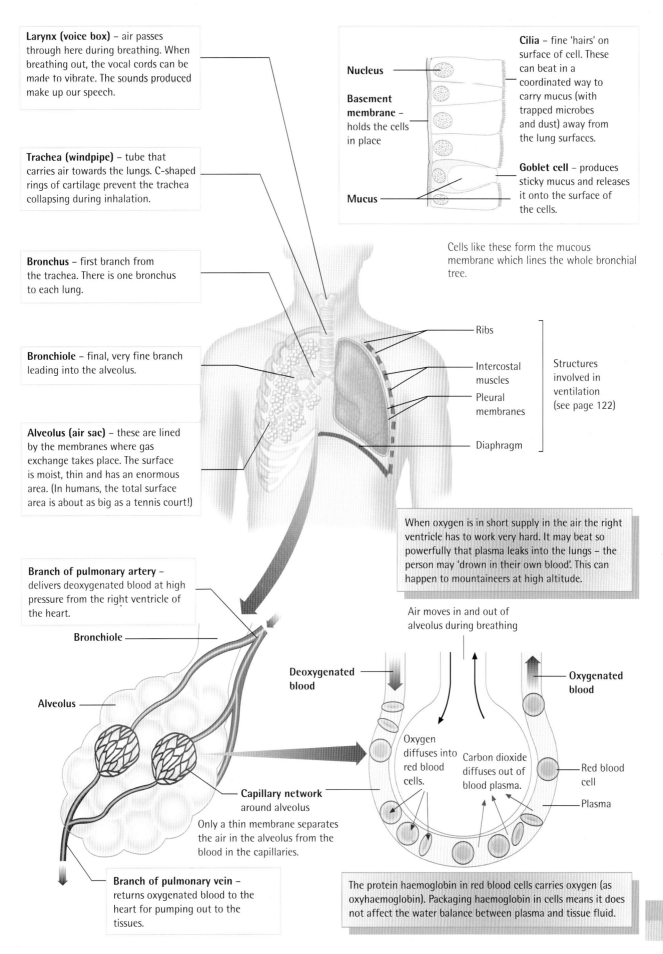

Larynx (voice box) – air passes through here during breathing. When breathing out, the vocal cords can be made to vibrate. The sounds produced make up our speech.

Trachea (windpipe) – tube that carries air towards the lungs. C-shaped rings of cartilage prevent the trachea collapsing during inhalation.

Bronchus – first branch from the trachea. There is one bronchus to each lung.

Bronchiole – final, very fine branch leading into the alveolus.

Alveolus (air sac) – these are lined by the membranes where gas exchange takes place. The surface is moist, thin and has an enormous area. (In humans, the total surface area is about as big as a tennis court!)

Nucleus

Basement membrane – holds the cells in place

Mucus

Cilia – fine 'hairs' on surface of cell. These can beat in a coordinated way to carry mucus (with trapped microbes and dust) away from the lung surfaces.

Goblet cell – produces sticky mucus and releases it onto the surface of the cells.

Cells like these form the mucous membrane which lines the whole bronchial tree.

Ribs

Intercostal muscles

Pleural membranes

Diaphragm

Structures involved in ventilation (see page 122)

When oxygen is in short supply in the air the right ventricle has to work very hard. It may beat so powerfully that plasma leaks into the lungs – the person may 'drown in their own blood'. This can happen to mountaineers at high altitude.

Branch of pulmonary artery – delivers deoxygenated blood at high pressure from the right ventricle of the heart.

Bronchiole

Alveolus

Capillary network around alveolus

Only a thin membrane separates the air in the alveolus from the blood in the capillaries.

Air moves in and out of alveolus during breathing

Deoxygenated blood

Oxygenated blood

Oxygen diffuses into red blood cells.

Carbon dioxide diffuses out of blood plasma.

Red blood cell

Plasma

Branch of pulmonary vein – returns oxygenated blood to the heart for pumping out to the tissues.

The protein haemoglobin in red blood cells carries oxygen (as oxyhaemoglobin). Packaging haemoglobin in cells means it does not affect the water balance between plasma and tissue fluid.

Organisation and maintenance of organisms

2.42 Breathing ventilates the lungs

Objectives

- To understand the muscular movements involved in the ventilation of the lungs
- To know how the efficiency of breathing can be measured
- To understand how breathing is affected by exercise
- To appreciate that the function of the lungs may sometimes need to be supported

Breathing is the set of muscular movements that gives the respiratory surface a constant supply of fresh air. This means there is always a concentration gradient between the blood and the air in the alveoli for both oxygen and carbon dioxide.

As shown below, breathing is brought about by:

- the action of two groups of muscles – the **intercostal muscles** and the **diaphragm**
- the properties of the **pleural membranes** that surround the lungs.

The pleural membranes 'stick' the outside of the lungs to the inside of the chest cavity. The lungs themselves do not have any muscles, but the 'stickiness' of the pleural membranes means that the lungs will automatically follow the movements of the chest wall. If the volume of the chest cavity increases, the volume of the lungs will increase at the same time. The pressure inside the lungs will decrease as the volume gets bigger.

Air always moves down a pressure gradient, from a region of higher air pressure to a region of lower air pressure. If the air pressure in the lungs is less than the pressure of the atmosphere, air will move into the lungs along a pressure gradient. In the same way, if the air pressure in the lungs is greater than the pressure of the atmosphere, air will move out of the lungs along a pressure gradient.

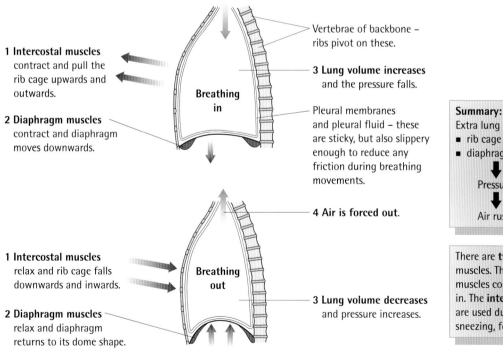

4 Air rushes in to fill the extra space and equalise the pressures.

Breathing in

1 Intercostal muscles contract and pull the rib cage upwards and outwards.

2 Diaphragm muscles contract and diaphragm moves downwards.

Vertebrae of backbone – ribs pivot on these.

3 Lung volume increases and the pressure falls.

Pleural membranes and pleural fluid – these are sticky, but also slippery enough to reduce any friction during breathing movements.

4 Air is forced out.

Breathing out

1 Intercostal muscles relax and rib cage falls downwards and inwards.

2 Diaphragm muscles relax and diaphragm returns to its dome shape.

3 Lung volume decreases and pressure increases.

Summary:
Extra lung volume created by
- rib cage moving up and out
- diaphragm moving down

↓

Pressure falls

↓

Air rushes into lungs

There are **two** sets of intercostal muscles. The **external** intercostal muscles contract during breathing in. The **internal** intercostal muscles are used during coughing and sneezing, for example.

The intercostal muscles ('intercostal' means 'between the ribs') and the diaphragm work together to alter the volume of the chest cavity. Changing the volume of the chest cavity will automatically change the pressure of air inside it. (It is a law of physics that pressure × volume is a constant – in other words, if pressure increases then volume must decrease, and vice versa.)

Air is breathed in, gas exchange happens in the alveoli, and the air is breathed out again. The composition of the inspired (breathed-in) air is therefore different from the composition of the expired (breathed-out) air, as shown in the table.

Component of air	Inspired (inhaled) air / %	Expired (exhaled) air / %	Reason
Oxygen	21	18	Oxygen has diffused from the air in the alveoli into the blood.
Carbon dioxide	0.04	3	Carbon dioxide has diffused from the blood into the air in the alveoli.
Nitrogen	78	78	Nitrogen gas is not used by the body.
Water vapour	Very variable	Saturated	Water evaporates from surfaces in the alveoli.
Temperature	Very variable	37 °C	Heat is lost to the air from the lung surfaces.

Composition of inhaled and exhaled air.

Asthma

Breathing is difficult, and an asthma sufferer may become very distressed. Air cannot easily move along the pressure gradient because:

- the muscles in the wall of the bronchi contract
- the lining of the bronchi 'leaks' a sticky mucus.

An asthma attack can be brought on by various factors including allergy to pollen or dust (or fur), emotion, breathing in cold air, smoke (page 126) and air pollution (page 251) and exercise. Treatment involves:

- removal of the factor causing the asthma
- use of a **bronchodilator** – usually a spray containing a drug which relaxes the bronchial muscles.

Measuring the efficiency of the lungs

The amount of air that enters and leaves the lungs is measured using a **spirometer**. A person breathes in and out of a mouthpiece connected to a chamber. Inside the chamber a piston moves up and down, and its movements are measured electronically. The changes in volume during breathing are plotted on a graph called a **spirogram**, shown below.

A spirogram gives a great deal of information about someone's breathing and the efficiency of their lungs. The lung volumes are expressed in the SI unit dm^3. 1 dm^3 is the same as 1 litre.

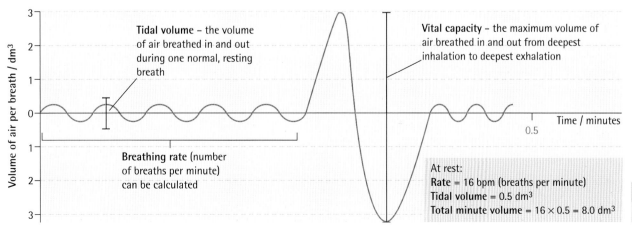

Tidal volume – the volume of air breathed in and out during one normal, resting breath

Vital capacity – the maximum volume of air breathed in and out from deepest inhalation to deepest exhalation

Breathing rate (number of breaths per minute) can be calculated

At rest:
Rate = 16 bpm (breaths per minute)
Tidal volume = 0.5 dm^3
Total minute volume = 16 × 0.5 = 8.0 dm^3

Organisation and maintenance of organisms

Exercise and breathing

During exercise the muscles work hard, and need to release more energy by respiration. Greater volumes of air must therefore be breathed in and out, by:

- increasing the **breathing rate** – more breaths per minute
- increasing the **tidal volume** – more air per breath.

These two changes can increase the volume of air passing in and out of the lungs from the typical 8 dm^3 per minute at rest to 50–60 dm^3 per minute during strenuous exercise.

The effect of exercise on breathing can be measured after a race.

1 Explain the part played by the intercostal muscles and diaphragm in breathing.
2 What can be learned from a spirogram?
3 Why are there differences in the oxygen and carbon dioxide compositions of inhaled air and exhaled air?

At rest: CO_2 concentration in blood, and blood pH, are kept at safe levels (see page 128 – homeostasis)

Exercise: • deeper, more rapid **breathing** (so more CO_2 lost from lungs)
• deeper, more rapid **heartbeat** (so more blood pumped to tissues to carry CO_2 away)

Changes in breathing and bloodflow keep CO_2 concentration and blood pH at safe levels.

Other factors affecting breathing rate

As well as **exercise** (see also page 109) some other factors affect breathing rate:

Factor	Effect
Smoking	Increase, due to the effect of **carbon monoxide** (see page 127)
Anxiety	Increase, due to the effect of **adrenaline** (see page 157)
Drugs	Some cause an increase e.g. **amphetamines** because they are stimulants (see page 152)
	Some cause a decrease e.g. **alcohol** and **barbiturates** because they are depressants (sedatives) (see page 152)
Environmental factors	Increased by **high CO_2 concentration** (see page 252)
	Sometimes increased by **high temperature or humidity**, as an attempt to lose body heat by panting (see page 117)
Altitude	Increased by **low O_2 concentration** in the atmosphere. Climbers at high altitude breathe quickly and with a low tidal volume – this can cause problems of dehydration
Weight	Can increase because fat makes lung ventilation harder (i.e. tidal volume falls)
	Can decrease if excess body weight is a symptom of low activity of the thyroid gland (see page 157)

Questions on gas exchange

1 Two boys were asked to take part in an investigation into the effect of exercise on breathing. The number of breaths they took in each half minute was measured and recorded, first of all while sitting still, then when recovering from two minutes of hard exercise. The results are shown in the table below.

Time / minutes	Activity	Number of breaths in each half minute	
		Tom	Alan
0.0		7	8
0.5		7	8
1.0	Sitting still	7	8
1.5		7	8
2.0			
2.5			
3.0	Exercise (step-ups)		
3.5			
4.0		24	24
4.5		23	17
5.0		18	13
5.5		15	10
6.0	Recovery (sitting)	12	10
6.5		12	9
7.0		10	8
7.5		8	8
8.0		8	8
8.5		7	8

a Draw a graph to show the changes in breathing rate over the time period of this investigation. Plot both lines on the same axes.

b Which boy appears to be fitter? Explain your answer.

The teacher of the class was interested in the changes in breathing during the exercise period. She used a sensor, computer interface, monitor and printer to obtain the following information on another member of the class.

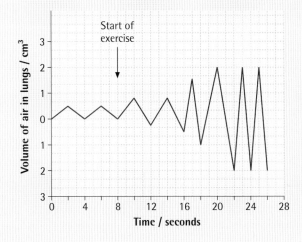

c What is the ratio of the volume of a breath during exercise to the volume of a breath at rest?

d Calculate the rate of breathing, in breaths per minute, during strenuous exercise.

e Using the data gathered, describe two effects of exercise on breathing.

f The computer could also measure the effects of exercise on heart rate. Suggest what these effects might be.

g What is the benefit to the body of the effects described in e and f?

2 These diagrams show apparatus that can be used to explain the mechanism of breathing.

Diagram A

Diagram B

Look at diagram A.

a What does the rubber sheet represent?

b What will happen to the balloons when the rubber sheet is pulled downwards?

c What phase of the breathing cycle is represented when the rubber sheet is allowed to return to its resting position?

d In what way is this model an incomplete demonstration of the mechanism of breathing?

Look at diagram B.

e What parts of the human ventilation system do the labels 1–4 represent?

f Use the information in your answers to a–e to comment on the statement: 'Breathing in is an active process, but breathing out is completely passive.'

2.43 Smoking and disease

Objectives
- To understand that smoking tobacco is harmful to health
- To list some of the harmful components of tobacco smoke and the damage they cause
- To understand why it is so difficult to give up smoking

The risks of smoking

Many national advertising campaigns stress that smoking is harmful. At the same time, the manufacturers of cigarettes emphasise the 'glamorous' side of smoking. However, manufacturers have to include, by law, a statement on their advertisements and cigarette packets that 'smoking can seriously damage your health'.

Life insurance companies routinely ask 'Do you smoke?' because they are aware that smokers are more likely to die younger. Whether or not to take up smoking is the most important health decision that many of us will ever make. For this reason everyone should know about the possible effects of smoking. Nobody who starts smoking now can say 'But I didn't know the risks' when they suffer the effects of their smoking habit later in life.

How is smoking harmful?

Smoking is inhaling the smoke from burning tobacco (and paper). This smoke can harm the lungs and respiratory passages for a number of reasons:

- it is hot
- it has a drying effect
- it contains many harmful chemicals.

The heat and dryness irritate the lungs, but the main dangers of smoking come from the chemicals in the burning tobacco. There are over 1000 known chemicals in tobacco smoke. These include tars, carbon monoxide, sulphur dioxide, nicotine and even small quantities of arsenic and plutonium! When doctors treat lung diseases with medicine, the molecules of the medicine are delivered in a spray; the droplets of water in the spray carry the medicine down through the respiratory tubes and deep into the lungs. Burning tobacco produces tiny droplets of water too, and these carry the harmful chemicals deep into the lungs in just the same way as a medicine spray. It would be hard to find a more efficient way of delivering harmful chemicals to the lungs than smoking! Some of these dangerous chemicals, and the effects they have on the body, are shown on the opposite page.

Why is it so difficult to give up smoking?

In many ways nicotine is the most dangerous of the chemicals in tobacco smoke. As well as affecting the heart and blood pressure directly, nicotine makes a person become **addicted** to smoking. Addiction comes in two forms:

- in **physical addiction**, the body cannot function properly in the absence of the chemical because it has partly replaced a natural body chemical
- in **psychological addiction**, the addicted person links smoking with comfort or lack of stress – when they feel stressed they may automatically reach for a cigarette.

---

1. How is smoke harmful to the lungs?

2. What is the difference between physical and psychological addiction? How can smokers be helped to overcome their addiction?

3. Suggest three harmful effects of smoking other than damage to the lungs and breathing passages.

4. Why are smokers more likely to develop infections of the lungs than non-smokers?

5. Draw a single cube with a side of 10 cm, and then the same cube divided into smaller cubes each with a side of 1 cm.
   a How many small cubes fit into the large cube?
   b What is the surface area of each small cube?
   c What is the total surface area of all of the small cubes?
   d What is the surface area of the large cube?
   e Use your answers to explain why emphysema sufferers are often very breathless.

Organisation and maintenance of organisms

Free radicals are extremely dangerous chemicals that damage proteins and DNA. They cause ageing of cells (smokers are often 'wrinkled', inside and out!) but smokers can reduce their effects with high doses of vitamin C.

Cancer of the mouth and larynx is 5 times more likely in smokers than non-smokers. Cancer of the tongue and oesophagus is particularly common in smokers who drink alcohol. **Laryngitis** (infection of the larynx) is more common in smokers than non-smokers. Laryngitis causes a husky voice, and makes speaking difficult and painful.

Nicotine is the chemical that causes **addiction**. It is also a **stimulant** which makes the heart beat faster and at the same time makes blood vessels narrow. Together these two effects **raise blood pressure** (causing long-term damage to the circulation). The increased heart rate increases the demand for oxygen, but carbon monoxide (see below) reduces oxygen availability – so heart muscle is more likely to be damaged.

Cilia are destroyed which means that mucus accumulates in the respiratory tubes. Dust and microbes, trapped in the mucus, slide down towards the lungs making the person cough. This coughing inflames the lining of the bronchi, causing **bronchitis**. A smoker is 20 times more likely to develop bronchitis than a non-smoker is.

Mucus, microbes and cell fragments build up

Carbon monoxide reduces the oxygen supply
Oxygen combines with haemoglobin to form **oxyhaemoglobin** in red blood cells. Carbon monoxide (CO) reduces oxyhaemoglobin formation because it binds very tightly to haemoglobin, and the effect is permanent since **carboxyhaemoglobin is very stable**. This:
■ reduces aerobic respiration (bad for sport)
■ reduces oxygen transport across the placenta (babies born to smokers have low birth-weight).
Carbon monoxide poisoning is especially likely when car engines are allowed to run in enclosed spaces (such as garages) and when the atmosphere is of poor quality (e.g. in smog).

Lung cancer is 10 times more likely in a smoker than a non-smoker. The tumour invades other tissues. This causes pain and loss of function of other tissues, often resulting in death.

The lung of a smoker destroyed by cancer (left), and a normal lung (right)

Tar causes cancer, which is uncontrolled division of cells. These cells, usually those lining the lower part of the bronchus, grow through the basement membrane and invade other tissues.
Tar is also an **irritant** which makes coughing more likely. This causes physical damage to the lungs, and makes the effects of emphysema even worse. Other irritants in tobacco smoke include **smoke particles**, **ammonia** and **sulphur dioxide**.

Smoking causes other diseases including:
■ cancer of stomach, pancreas and bladder
■ loss of limbs – amputated because of poor circulation
■ coronary heart disease
■ lower sperm counts in men.

Emphysema results when the walls of the air sacs are destroyed. This happens because smoke affects white blood cells which then destroy lung tissue. When the walls break down there is less surface for gas exchange, and breathing becomes very difficult. Somebody with emphysema may only be able to walk 2 or 3 metres before becoming breathless. Emphysema is almost unknown in non-smokers.

Healthy alveoli

Alveoli in person with emphysema

Organisation and maintenance of organisms

127

Objectives

- To be able to define the term homeostasis
- To understand why the body must keep constant conditions around its cells
- To remember that tissue fluid surrounds all cells
- To understand the principle of negative feedback
- To know the organs involved in homeostasis

The cells in any living organism will only function properly in the correct conditions. The conditions *outside* the body (the **external environment**) are continuously changing – for example, temperature on a cool day might vary from 0 °C out of doors to 20 °C indoors. The body has mechanisms for adjusting conditions *within* the body (the **internal environment**) so that conditions around the cells remain constant.

Keeping the internal environment constant

The blood cells lie in the blood plasma, and other cells are surrounded by tissue fluid (see page 104). Conditions in the blood (and therefore in the tissue fluid) are maintained at an **optimum** – the best values for the cells to function. Keeping constant conditions in the tissue fluid around the cells is called **homeostasis**.

Homeostasis involves several organs, but the basic principle is always the same, as shown below. The diagram on the right shows some of the organs involved in homeostasis, and the particular conditions in the tissue fluid which they regulate.

Cells change the composition of the tissue fluid as they remove food and oxygen and add carbon dioxide and other wastes.

Heart supplies the constant pressure needed to deliver blood to the tissues, and to form the tissue fluid.

Skin – the main organ for control of heat exchange (see page 130).

Kidneys regulate levels of water and salt (**osmoregulation**) and remove urea and other wastes (**excretion**) (see page 132).

Lungs regulate exchange of carbon dioxide and oxygen.

Intestines supply soluble foods and water.

Liver regulates the levels of many solutes in the blood, and removes poisons (see page 154).

Many organs play a part in homeostasis. (A more accurate diagram of the human circulation is given on page 103.)

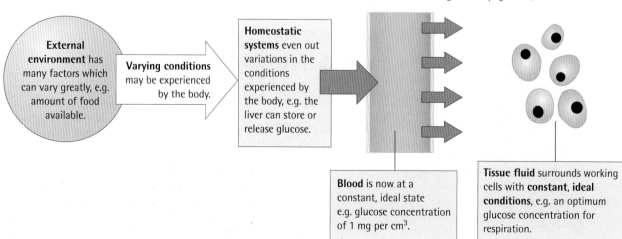

External environment has many factors which can vary greatly, e.g. amount of food available.

Varying conditions may be experienced by the body.

Homeostatic systems even out variations in the conditions experienced by the body, e.g. the liver can store or release glucose.

Blood is now at a constant, ideal state e.g. glucose concentration of 1 mg per cm^3.

Tissue fluid surrounds working cells with **constant, ideal conditions**, e.g. an optimum glucose concentration for respiration.

How is homeostasis brought about?

The work of these organs must be coordinated to achieve homeostasis. Information about the conditions in the body is continuously fed to the brain from **sensory receptors** around the body.

For example, if the body temperature rises, temperature receptors in the skin send information to the brain. In response, the brain starts off mechanisms that will lower the body temperature again. The same temperature receptors 'inform' the brain when the temperature is back to normal. Homeostasis depends on this continual **feedback** of information, as explained in the diagram below.

To summarise:

- Homeostasis is the maintenance of a constant internal environment.
- Homeostasis involves control by negative feedback.
- In negative feedback, a change sets off a response that cancels out the change.

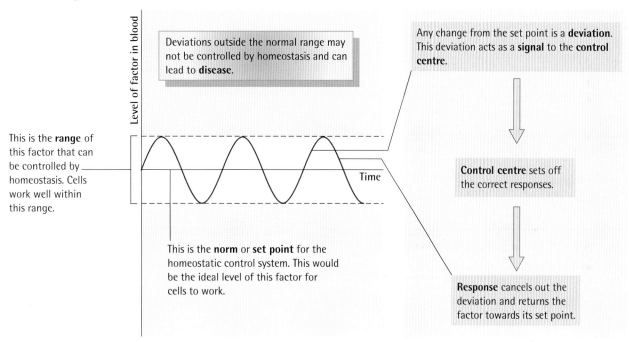

In homeostasis, deviation from a set point acts as the signal that sets off the correction mechanism. This negative feedback keeps variable factors within the narrow range suitable for life.

---

1. Copy and complete the following paragraph.

   Cells work best when conditions around them remain constant. Cells are bathed in _____ fluid, and many systems work to keep the composition of this fluid constant. Each system has _____, which detect any changes from the _____ (the ideal conditions for the cells). The changes are then communicated to the _____, usually along _____ neurones. The central control area then sets off the correct responses. These responses cancel out the original change and so this sort of control is often called _____.

2. Copy and complete the following table.

Homeostatic organ	Factor controlled
Liver	
Lungs	
	Water content of blood
	Heat loss or gain
Intestines	

3. Use the principle of feedback control to compare the regulation of blood glucose level in humans (see page 157) with the maintenance of a stable temperature in an aircraft cabin.

2.45 Control of body temperature

Objectives

⏵ To understand why body temperature must be controlled

⏵ To know the difference between heat and temperature

⏵ To understand the part played by the skin in control of temperature

⏵ To appreciate that control of body temperature is an example of negative feedback

Heat and temperature

Heat is a type of energy, so it can be 'held' by an object or passed from one object to another. Temperature is a measure of how concentrated the heat energy is in an object, such as the human body. A body will rise in temperature if it gains heat energy.

The importance of a constant temperature

Many biological and physical processes are affected by temperature. For example:

⏵ enzymes work best at their optimum temperature, and are denatured by wide deviations from this

⏵ cell membranes become more fragile as temperature rises

⏵ diffusion rates are increased by higher temperatures, and decreased by lower ones

⏵ liquids such as blood become more viscous (thicker) as the temperature falls.

Birds and mammals are **endotherms** ('inside heat') – they can maintain a constant body temperature by generating heat internally. Humans have several mechanisms which work non-stop to balance heat production against heat loss, as shown in the diagram below. This balance is achieved by a **temperature control centre** in the **hypothalamus**, a region of the brain. The diagram opposite shows the negative feedback systems that control body temperature in an endotherm.

The role of the skin

As the barrier between the body and its environment, the skin is also the main organ concerned with heat loss and heat conservation.

An endothermic animal maintains an ideal body temperature by balancing heat losses and heat gains.

Metabolism – many biochemical reactions, especially **respiration**, in the liver **generate heat**.

Movement **generates heat** by **respiration** and **friction** within the muscles.

Excretion: urine and faeces are at body temperature. Heat is **lost** when they are expelled from the body.

Heat is lost when water **evaporates** from the lungs and sweat evaporates from the skin.

Convection – transfer of heat to and from the body on air currents. Can be increased by 'fanning' air past the body.

Radiation – transfer of heat in the form of rays, usually infra-red rays.

Conduction – transfer of heat by direct contact with another object such as a cold rock or a hot oven door.

Heat can be **gained or lost** by these processes.

Fat! Fat is an important compound in temperature control:

■ each fat molecule provides about twice as much energy in respiration as a molecule of either protein or carbohydrate

■ fat stores under the skin insulate against heat loss.

Heat gains	Heat losses
Respiration	Evaporation
Conduction	Excretion
Convection	Conduction
Radiation	Convection
	Radiation

If heat gains exceed heat losses the body temperature will rise – may cause **hyperthermia**.

37°C

If heat losses exceed heat gains the body temperature will fall – may cause **hypothermia**.

During **fever**, the body's temperature may be reset 2–3 °C higher.

Higher temperatures denature proteins of infecting bacteria more rapidly than they affect human proteins. Blood flows to the hypothalamus through vessels at the back of the neck. A nosebleed can be stopped by placing a cold object on the back of the neck – the hypothalamus reacts to the 'cooled' blood by closing down skin blood vessels. As a result the nosebleed stops.

Skin increases heat loss by:

Evaporation (sweat)

Radiation (vasodilation of blood vessels leading to surface capillaries)

Convection (relaxation of hair erector muscles so hair lies flat)

Radiating heat

Increase → Detector → Integrator in brain → Corrective mechanisms: attempt to increase heat loss → Norm

The **optimum temperature** for the body's activities is about 37 °C.

Norm → Decrease → Detector → Integrator in brain → Corrective mechanisms: attempt to conserve heat ...

The structure of the skin is adapted for temperature control

Epidermis protects against water loss and entry of disease-causing organisms

Hair erector muscle

Hair

Nerve ending – receptor that detects temperature changes on the skin surface.

Subcutaneous ('under the skin') fat insulates against heat loss – only involved in long-term (e.g. seasonal) temperature control.

Capillary beds

Sensory neurone carries impulses to the hypothalamus.

Dermis

Sweat gland – produces sweat

Malpighian layer

... and to generate more heat
- **shivering** – muscular activity generates heat
- **adding extra clothing** – insulation reduces heat loss
- **eating more** – eating stimulates heat production by respiration ...
- ... or **turn on the central heating!** (Humans can control their **external environment** too.)

Skin reduces heat loss by reducing:

Convection (contraction of hair erector muscles raises hairs and traps a layer of still air)

Radiation (vasoconstriction of blood vessels leading to surface capillaries shunts blood away from skin)

Evaporation (sweat glands do not secrete sweat)

The structure of the skin is adapted for temperature control.

2.46 Excretion: removal of the waste products of metabolism

Objectives
- To understand that living cells produce wastes
- To name some human waste products
- To name the organs involved in excretion
- To understand the functions of the kidney

Homeostasis means keeping a constant environment around the cells of the body. This involves providing cells with essential raw materials, but also means removing waste products. These waste products can be very toxic (poisonous), for example:

- **Carbon dioxide**, produced during respiration, dissolves in plasma and tissue fluid to form a weak acid (carbonic acid, H_2CO_3) which can denature enzymes and other proteins at high concentrations.
- **Urea**, produced in the liver during deamination of excess amino acids, can denature enzymes.

The body expends a great deal of energy getting rid of these wastes, and has several specialised organs for this function of **excretion**.

The role of the kidney
The kidneys are specialised organs that:

- remove the toxic waste product **urea** from the circulating blood – they carry out **excretion**
- regulate the **water content** of the blood – they carry out **osmoregulation**.

The structure of the kidneys is well adapted to enable them to carry out these processes.

- Each kidney receives a good supply of blood at high pressure through the **renal artery**.
- Each kidney contains hundreds of thousands of tubes, the **nephrons**, that can filter substances from the blood.
- Each kidney has an exit tube, **the ureter**, to carry away the **urine** (a solution of wastes dissolved in water).
- The kidney is under close control by a **feedback system** so that water saving is always exactly balanced to the body's needs.

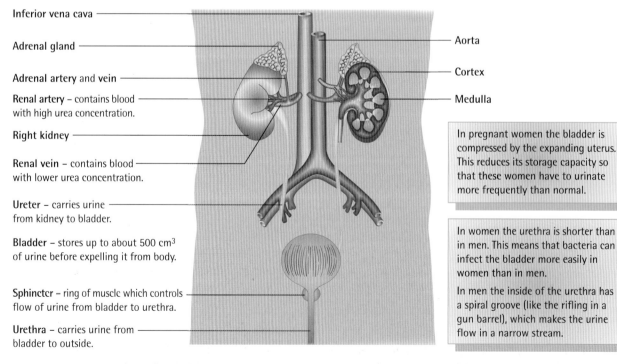

Inferior vena cava

Adrenal gland

Adrenal artery and vein

Renal artery – contains blood with high urea concentration.

Right kidney

Renal vein – contains blood with lower urea concentration.

Ureter – carries urine from kidney to bladder.

Bladder – stores up to about 500 cm³ of urine before expelling it from body.

Sphincter – ring of muscle which controls flow of urine from bladder to urethra.

Urethra – carries urine from bladder to outside.

Aorta

Cortex

Medulla

In pregnant women the bladder is compressed by the expanding uterus. This reduces its storage capacity so that these women have to urinate more frequently than normal.

In women the urethra is shorter than in men. This means that bacteria can infect the bladder more easily in women than in men.

In men the inside of the urethra has a spiral groove (like the rifling in a gun barrel), which makes the urine flow in a narrow stream.

The kidneys receive blood from the renal artery, remove urea and a variable amount of water from it and return the 'modified' blood to the circulation through the renal vein. The wastes removed from the blood are eventually expelled from the body through the urethra after being stored in the bladder.

The structure of the kidney

The kidneys and their blood vessels are located in the abdomen, as shown in the diagram opposite. The kidneys constantly produce urine which then passes to the **bladder**.

The functional unit – the nephron

Each kidney contains hundreds of thousands of long tubes called **nephrons**, each with its own branch of the renal artery and vein. Each nephron works in exactly the same way, so the function of the kidney can be explained by considering the working of just one nephron, as shown below.

The kidney is made up of many nephrons (kidney tubules). Substances are filtered out of the blood into the nephron. Useful molecules and most of the water are reabsorbed into the blood.

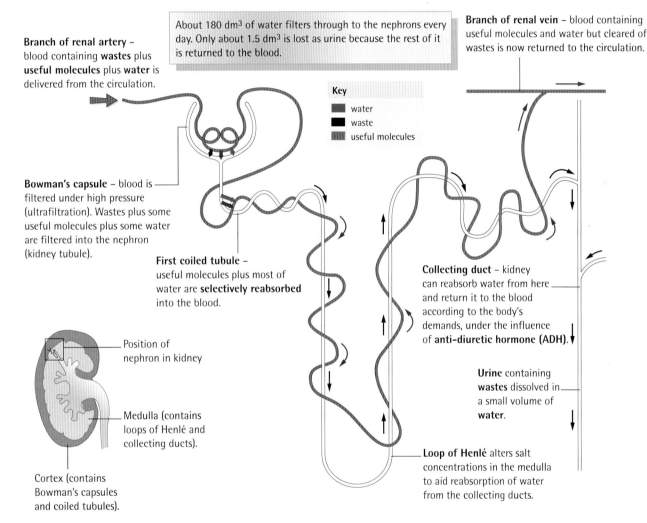

About 180 dm³ of water filters through to the nephrons every day. Only about 1.5 dm³ is lost as urine because the rest of it is returned to the blood.

Branch of renal artery – blood containing **wastes** plus **useful molecules** plus **water** is delivered from the circulation.

Branch of renal vein – blood containing useful molecules and water but cleared of wastes is now returned to the circulation.

Key
- water
- waste
- useful molecules

Bowman's capsule – blood is filtered under high pressure (ultrafiltration). Wastes plus some useful molecules plus some water are filtered into the nephron (kidney tubule).

First coiled tubule – useful molecules plus most of water are **selectively reabsorbed** into the blood.

Collecting duct – kidney can reabsorb water from here and return it to the blood according to the body's demands, under the influence of **anti-diuretic hormone (ADH)**.

Urine containing **wastes** dissolved in a small volume of **water**.

Loop of Henlé alters salt concentrations in the medulla to aid reabsorption of water from the collecting ducts.

Position of nephron in kidney

Medulla (contains loops of Henlé and collecting ducts).

Cortex (contains Bowman's capsules and coiled tubules).

1. Define the terms excretion and osmoregulation.
2. Name two waste products of metabolism. State their source and how they are removed from the blood.
3. Copy and complete the following paragraph.
   The main excretory organ in the mammal is the _____. There are two of these, each supplied with blood through the _____ and each composed of many thousands of tubules called _____ Each of these tubules receives materials from the blood after filtration in the _____ capsule. The tubules then remove useful substances such as _____ from this filtrate by the process of _____ The remaining waste or excess materials pass down the tubule and leave the excretory organ via the _____ They are collected for temporary storage in the _____ Eventually a dilute solution of these wastes, the urine, leaves the body through the _____

- To explain how body water is regulated
- To explain how kidney disease can be treated

Osmoregulation

The final part of each nephron, the **collecting duct**, removes water from the filtered solution passing down inside the tubule and returns it to the blood. The body can control the amount of water that is returned to the blood in this way, and balance it with the amount of water taken in in the diet and the amount of water lost from the body by other means. This vital control of water balance is called **osmoregulation**. Water is the most common substance in the body, and has many functions (see pages 244). The average daily intake and loss of water by different methods is outlined in the diagram below. The amount of water reabsorbed into the blood from the collecting ducts, and therefore the amount of water lost in the urine, is controlled by **antidiuretic hormone**. This is another example of control by negative feedback, as described in the diagram at the top of the page opposite.

Kidney failure

Damage to the kidneys, perhaps through infection or following an accident, can stop the nephrons working efficiently. The body can no longer control the composition or amount of urine formed, so the content of the blood plasma and tissue fluid is not kept at its optimum. Death may follow quite quickly if the kidney failure is not corrected. Two types of treatment are available:

- **dialysis** using a kidney machine (an artificial kidney)
- **kidney transplant**.

Dialysis and the artificial kidney

A kidney machine takes a patient's blood, 'cleans' it and returns the blood to the circulation. This process is called **dialysis**. Wastes diffuse out of the blood, across a partially permeable membrane, into a fluid that is constantly renewed. In this way urea is removed from the blood without altering any of its other features. The diagram on the opposite page shows the workings of a kidney dialysis machine.

The water excreted in the urine is adjusted so that total water intake and total water loss are balanced.

Intake varies greatly depending on the type of food available. Some desert animals gain 90% of their water from respiration. Camels don't store water in their hump, but fat. Water is released when the fat is respired.

Water intake

Drinks	1500 cm³
Water in foods	800 cm³
From respiration	200 cm³

Body contains about 40 dm³ of water.

15 dm³ in tissue fluid and blood plasma

25 dm³ inside the cells

Water loss

Urine	1500 cm³
Sweat	500 cm³
Exhaled air	400 cm³
Faeces	100 cm³

Isotonic sports drinks provide rapid rehydration. They contain:
- **glucose and salts,** which are quickly absorbed so that
- **water** follows by osmosis.

Volume of urine is greatly reduced if more water is lost through sweating.

Diarrhoea can greatly increase water loss. Severe cases can cause death by dehydration.

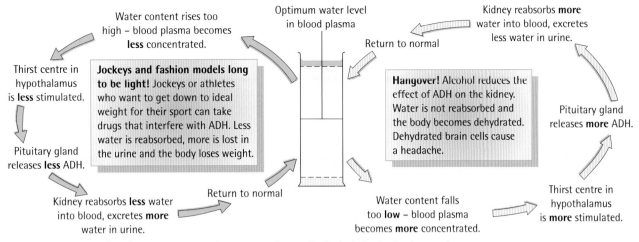

Water content rises too high – blood plasma becomes **less** concentrated.

Optimum water level in blood plasma

Kidney reabsorbs **more** water into blood, excretes less water in urine.

Return to normal

Thirst centre in hypothalamus is **less** stimulated.

Jockeys and fashion models long to be light! Jockeys or athletes who want to get down to ideal weight for their sport can take drugs that interfere with ADH. Less water is reabsorbed, more is lost in the urine and the body loses weight.

Hangover! Alcohol reduces the effect of ADH on the kidney. Water is not reabsorbed and the body becomes dehydrated. Dehydrated brain cells cause a headache.

Pituitary gland releases **more** ADH.

Pituitary gland releases **less** ADH.

Kidney reabsorbs **less** water into blood, excretes **more** water in urine.

Return to normal

Water content falls too **low** – blood plasma becomes **more** concentrated.

Thirst centre in hypothalamus is **more** stimulated.

Antidiuretic hormone (ADH) helps to regulate the amount of water in the body by feedback control.

Kidney transplants

A **kidney transplant** involves surgically transferring a healthy kidney from one person (the **donor**) to a person with kidney failure (the **recipient**). It is relatively simple to connect up the donor kidney in the recipient's body, but a problem arises with **tissue rejection**. The recipient's immune system will attack the donor kidney and slowly destroy it (see page 101) unless the recipient takes drugs to stop this happening. Blood groups and tissue types of donors and recipients are carefully matched to reduce the likelihood of rejection. Successful kidney transplants have advantages over dialysis treatment:

⚑ In the long term, a transplant is much cheaper.

⚑ The patient's life is less disrupted once they have recovered from the operation.

1 The body must maintain a water balance.
  a Why does the body need water?
  b How is water gained by the body?
  c How is water lost by the body?

2 The water balance of the body is maintained by negative feedback. Explain what this term means.

3 What is meant by the term water potential? Use a flow diagram to explain how measurement of the blood water potential allows control of the body's water balance.

4 Why is a kidney transplant considered better than dialysis? What problems are associated with kidney transplantation?

Blood returns to body through **vein** – this is easier since blood in vein is at low pressure.

Chamber – removes any blood clots and re-warms blood to body temperature so body is not 'shocked' when blood returns.

A patient usually has three dialysis sessions per week, each lasting 6–8 hours, which disrupts the person's life. There are never enough machines and trained staff to treat all the people who need dialysis, so difficult decisions have to be made about who receives treatment.

Dialysis fluid in

Blood taken from **artery** – leaves body under high pressure.

Dialysis fluid has a composition which means that urea and salts diffuse into it from blood but useful solutes and water do not.

Membrane is partially permeable so that urea can cross it but blood cells and large molecules such as proteins cannot.

Pump controls pressure and flow rate so that blood is 'cleaned' in 6–8 hours.

Dialysis fluid out – the fluid can be cleaned and then re-used.

Diffusion of urea out of blood is aided by **countercurrent flow** of plasma and dialysis fluid – they flow in opposite directions, maintaining the concentration gradient.

Questions on homeostasis

1 a What is hypothermia?

b Why are old people particularly at risk from hypothermia?

c Why do you think children lose heat very quickly?

2 This diagram shows how body temperature is controlled.

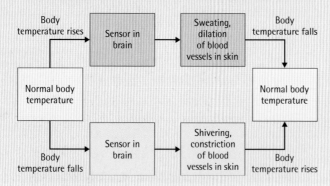

a Use this information to explain how humans control body temperature.

b Explain how shivering affects body temperature.

c How does the liver contribute to body heat?

d Use the diagram to explain the meaning of 'negative feedback'.

3 If a person's kidneys are diseased he or she may have a kidney transplant. The transplanted kidney is connected to blood vessels which go into and out of the leg.

a Copy and complete the diagram below to show clearly how the artery, vein and tube carrying urine should be connected in a transplant operation.

b Sometimes a transplanted kidney is rejected. Explain why rejection may occur.

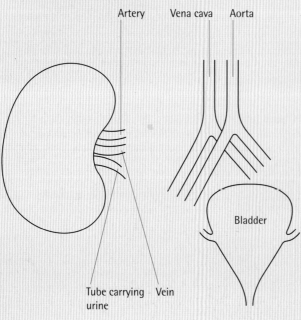

c Below is a record of how much urine a healthy man produced each day during one week. The man's diet included the same amount of water each day.

Day	Volume of urine produced / cm³
Monday	1540
Tuesday	1470
Wednesday	1510
Thursday	1240
Friday	1450
Saturday	1770
Sunday	1520

i Calculate the average (mean) volume of urine produced each day.

ii Suggest, with reasons, why the amount of urine produced was quite different on two of the days.

d Explain how the kidneys prevent sugar and useful ions being lost from the blood.

(NEAB June 1992)

4 A person who suffers kidney failure may be treated every few days by dialysis. This uses an artificial kidney machine. The diagram shows the working of a kidney machine. In this machine a special solution flows around the outside of an inner tube which carries the patient's blood.

a How is the waste substance urea removed from the blood by dialysis?

b i It is better for the body if a kidney transplant operation is performed instead of having to undergo dialysis every few days. Apart from the improved convenience, why is a kidney transplant better than dialysis treatment?

ii It is important to match carefully the tissue type of the kidney donor and of the patient before doing a kidney transplant. What would happen after the transplant if this matching were not done?

(SEG June 1992)

5 The table below summarises information about the excretion of urea by three mammals which live in different habitats.

Mammal	Habitat	Urine concentration / units urea per litre of urine	Length of kidney tubules
Beaver	Aquatic	500	Short
Human	Land	1150	Medium
Desert rat	Land (desert)	6000	Long

a What was the concentration of human urine?

b Which mammal had the most dilute urine?

c How many times more concentrated is the urine of the desert rat than that of the beaver? Show your working.

d What is the relationship between the length of kidney tubules and the amount of water available to each of the mammals in its habitat?

e What is the relationship between urine concentration and the amount of water available to each of the mammals in its habitat?

f One of the functions of a mammalian kidney tubule is to reabsorb water. The reabsorbed water may be important for survival. Suggest how the length of the kidney tubule may play a part in making beavers and desert rats successful in their particular habitats.

(MEG)

6 a During an investigation into heat loss, four tubes were set up as shown in the diagram below.

The same volume of very hot water was placed in each tube.

The temperature of each tube was recorded every two minutes for 10 minutes.

The results are shown in the table below.

	Temperature / °C			
Time / mins	Tube A	Tube B	Tube C	Tube D
0	83	84	82	83
2	81	83	81	80
4	80	82	80	75
6	78	82	79	71
8	75	81	78	66
10	72	80	76	61

i During the investigation, the thermometers were kept in the middle of the tubes and did not touch the glass.
Suggest a reason for this.

ii Explain the difference in the rate of temperature fall in tubes A and B.

b i A newborn baby is sometimes wrapped in aluminium foil. Use the results of the investigation in part a and your own knowledge to explain why this is done.

ii Explain why it could be harmful to go out in wet clothing on a windy day.

c Sweating is an important method of controlling the temperature of the body. Use the results of the investigation in part a and your own knowledge to explain how sweating helps to keep the body cool.

d i On a hot day, we sweat more but produce less urine than on a cold day, even if we drink the same amount of liquid. The change in the volume of urine produced is controlled by antidiuretic hormone (ADH).
Explain how ADH helps to maintain the correct amount of water in our bodies.

ii The control of the water level in the body by ADH is an example of negative feedback.
What is meant by **negative feedback**?

(Edexcel June 1997)

7 a What is homeostasis?

b Copy and complete this table to explain how the kidneys, lungs, liver and skin are involved in this process.

c For any one of the organs that you have described in your table, suggest how negative feedback is involved in its operation.

Name of organ	One body 'factor' controlled by this organ

A — Thermometer, Cotton wool
B — Aluminium foil
C — Dry absorbent paper
Fan blowing cool air
D — Wet absorbent paper

2.48 Coordination: the nervous system

Working together

There are millions of cells and scores of different tissues and organs in the body of an animal such as a mammal. The cells and organs do not all work independently – their activities are **coordinated**, which means that they work together, carrying out their various functions at certain times and at certain rates, according to the needs of the body.

Coordination in mammals is achieved through two systems, each with its own particular role. The **nervous system** deals with rapid but short-lasting responses, whereas the **endocrine system** brings about slower, longer lasting responses. The two systems are compared in the table below.

The nervous system

In mammals and other vertebrates, the nervous system is arranged as shown in the diagram on the left. It consists of a **brain** and **spinal cord**, which together form the **central nervous system (CNS)**, connected to the various parts of the body by the **peripheral nervous system**. This is made up of **nerves**, collections of many long thin nerve cells called **neurones**.

Information flows along the nervous system as follows. A **receptor** detects a change in conditions (a **stimulus**). A message is carried from the receptor to the CNS by a **sensory neurone**. After processing, a message is sent from the CNS to an organ (an **effector**) that carries out a **response**. A **motor neurone** carries this message.

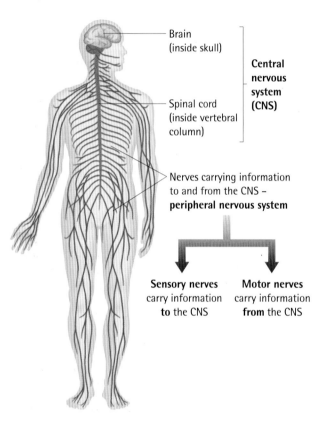

Brain (inside skull)

Spinal cord (inside vertebral column)

Central nervous system (CNS)

Nerves carrying information to and from the CNS – **peripheral nervous system**

Sensory nerves carry information **to** the CNS

Motor nerves carry information **from** the CNS

The arrangement of the human nervous system.

The endocrine and nervous systems compared

Comparison	Nervous system	Endocrine system
Speed of action	Very rapid	Can be slow
Nature of message	Electrical impulses, travelling along nerves	Chemical messengers, travelling in the bloodstream
Duration of response	Usually completed within seconds	May take years before completed
Area of response	Often confined to one area of the body – the response is **localised**	Usually noticed in many organs – the response is **widespread**
Examples of processes controlled	Reflexes such as blinking; movement of limbs	Growth; development of reproductive system

Organisation and maintenance of organisms

Nerves and neurones

All the information carried by the nervous system travels along specialised cells called neurones (sometimes just called nerve cells). The structure of a single neurone, and the ways in which it is adapted to its function of carrying information, are shown on the right.

Nerve impulses

Messages pass along neurones in the form of **electrical impulses,** called **action potentials,** which travel very quickly from one end of a nerve cell to the other. In a living mammal the impulses always travel along a neurone in a certain direction. They are then passed on to another neurone, to a muscle cell or to a gland cell. The end of the neurone is separated from the next cell by a tiny gap, visible under a microscope, and the impulses can only cross this gap in one direction. This gap, called a **synapse,** acts like a valve as explained in the diagram below.

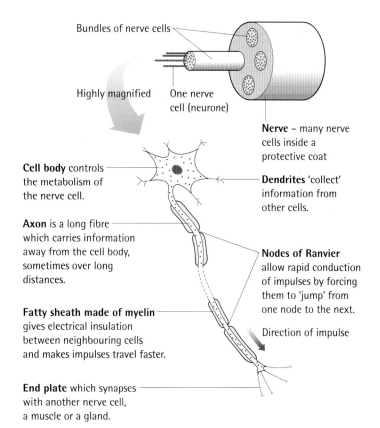

Bundles of nerve cells

Highly magnified

One nerve cell (neurone)

Nerve – many nerve cells inside a protective coat

Cell body controls the metabolism of the nerve cell.

Dendrites 'collect' information from other cells.

Axon is a long fibre which carries information away from the cell body, sometimes over long distances.

Nodes of Ranvier allow rapid conduction of impulses by forcing them to 'jump' from one node to the next.

Fatty sheath made of myelin gives electrical insulation between neighbouring cells and makes impulses travel faster.

Direction of impulse

End plate which synapses with another nerve cell, a muscle or a gland.

A nerve is made of many neurones. This **motor neurone** carries information from the CNS to an effector.

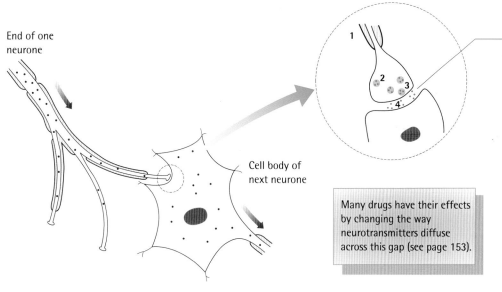

End of one neurone

Cell body of next neurone

The **synapse** is the junction between the end plate of one neurone and the dendrite of the next.
1   An impulse arrives at the synapse.
2   At the end plate are tiny sacs containing a chemical (**neurotransmitter**).
3   The chemical is released into the gap.
4   The chemical diffuses across the gap and the impulse restarts on the other side.

Many drugs have their effects by changing the way neurotransmitters diffuse across this gap (see page 153).

Impulses travel along a neurone in the direction that allows the mammal to respond to changes in its environment. They can only pass across the synapse in this direction.

1 Suggest two similarities and two differences between the endocrine system and the nervous system. What is the importance of these differences?

2 Explain how the structure of a neurone is related to its function.

3 Explain the difference between:
a motor and sensory neurones
b central and peripheral nervous systems.

4 How does a nerve impulse:
a pass along a neurone   b cross a synapse?

2·49 Neurones can work together in reflex arcs

Objectives

- To understand that neurones work together in a reflex arc
- To understand that all reflex arcs are important for survival

Neurones act together in many complex ways to bring about the correct response to a stimulus. The simplest type of response is called a **reflex action**. A reflex action is a rapid automatic response to a stimulus, for example jerking your hand away from a sharp or hot object. The nerve pathway involved in the reflex action is called a **reflex arc**, shown in the diagram on the opposite page.

Reflexes and survival

All reflex actions have evolved to help us survive. The table below lists four reflexes, and shows how each helps us survive.

The size of the pupil can change quickly and automatically in response to changes in the intensity of light. This reflex action, described in more detail on page 147, prevents damage to the retina.

Name of reflex	Stimulus	Response	Survival value
Coughing	Particles making contact with the lining of the respiratory tree	Violent contraction of the diaphragm and internal intercostal muscles	Prevents lungs being damaged or infected, so that gas exchange remains efficient
Pupil reflex	Bright light falling on the retina	Contraction of the circular muscles of the iris	Prevents bleaching of the retina so that vision remains clear
Knee jerk	Stretching of the tendon just under the knee, holding the kneecap in place (a doctor may tap this tendon to test the reflex)	Contraction of the muscles of the upper thigh so that the leg straightens	The leg can support the body's weight during walking
Swallowing	Food particles making contact with the back of the throat	Contraction of the muscle of the epiglottis, which closes off the entrance to the trachea	Prevents food entering the respiratory pathway, so that the lungs are not damaged

1 The diagram opposite shows the route taken by nerve impulses to bring about the knee-jerk reflex.
  a Name the structure tapped by the hammer. How does this set off the reflex action?
  b Name the structure that carries impulses towards the spinal cord.
  c Which structure A–E is responsible for the response in this reflex action?
  d The distance between structure B and the spinal cord is about 30 cm. Assuming that the impulses travel at 100 m/s, how long should it take for an impulse to travel through this reflex arc?
  e Careful measurement suggests that the actual time taken for the impulse to travel through this arc is 2 or 3 times this value. Can you explain why?

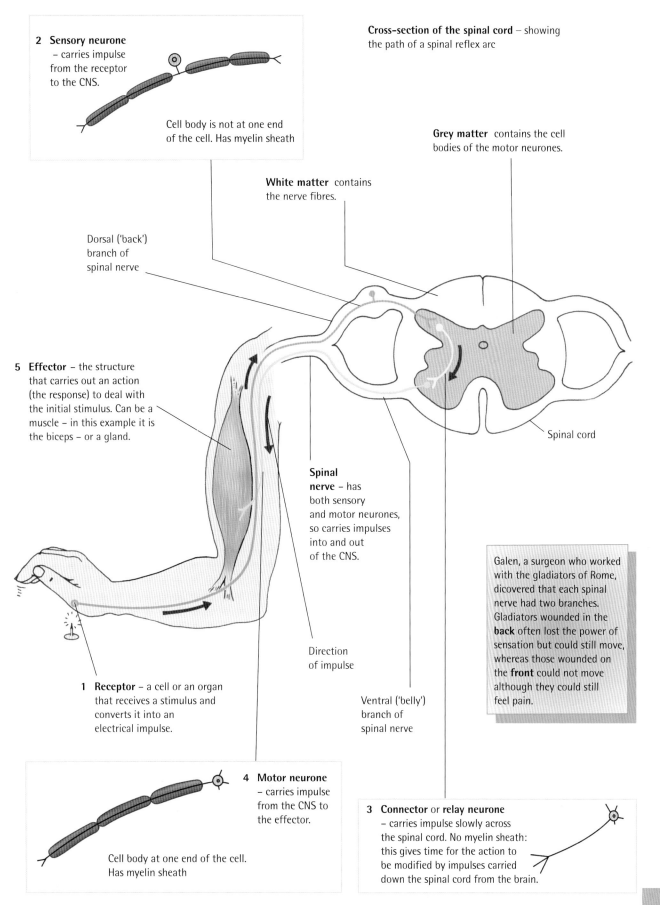

2 Sensory neurone – carries impulse from the receptor to the CNS.

Cell body is not at one end of the cell. Has myelin sheath

Cross-section of the spinal cord – showing the path of a spinal reflex arc

Grey matter contains the cell bodies of the motor neurones.

White matter contains the nerve fibres.

Dorsal ('back') branch of spinal nerve

5 Effector – the structure that carries out an action (the response) to deal with the initial stimulus. Can be a muscle – in this example it is the biceps – or a gland.

Spinal cord

Spinal nerve – has both sensory and motor neurones, so carries impulses into and out of the CNS.

Direction of impulse

Galen, a surgeon who worked with the gladiators of Rome, dicovered that each spinal nerve had two branches. Gladiators wounded in the **back** often lost the power of sensation but could still move, whereas those wounded on the **front** could not move although they could still feel pain.

1 Receptor – a cell or an organ that receives a stimulus and converts it into an electrical impulse.

Ventral ('belly') branch of spinal nerve

4 Motor neurone – carries impulse from the CNS to the effector.

Cell body at one end of the cell. Has myelin sheath

3 Connector or relay neurone – carries impulse slowly across the spinal cord. No myelin sheath: this gives time for the action to be modified by impulses carried down the spinal cord from the brain.

Organisation and maintenance of organisms

141

2.50 The brain is the processor for the central nervous system

Objectives

- To understand that the brain is made up of large numbers of neurones along with other cells which nourish and support them
- To be able to describe the functions of particular regions of the brain
- To know that our understanding of brain function depends upon the development of non-damaging investigation techniques

The central nervous system (brain and spinal cord) integrates the working of receptors and effectors to bring about appropriate responses. The brain controls all our voluntary actions and many of our involuntary actions. It is also the seat of awareness, knowledge, emotion and learning.

The structure of the brain

The **brain** develops as a swelling at the anterior (front) end of the spinal cord. In humans it weighs about 1.4 kg and is the most complex organ known. The brain is largely composed of neurones, typically containing about 25 000 000 000 cells, each connected to as many as 1000 others, forming a total of up to 10^{14} synapses. As well as these neurones, the brain contains many other cells with supporting roles – some form a barrier to prevent infection, others secrete cushioning fluids – and a well developed blood supply delivers the vital supplies of oxygen and glucose.

Grey matter

The brain gives instructions for responses by the body, some simple involuntary actions, others resulting from intelligent decisions. The brain delays the flow of information around the nervous system slightly. This is because the neurones of which it is made are not fast-conducting neurones covered by a myelin sheath. The absence of the fatty myelin sheath around the nerve fibres in the brain gives brain tissue a grey appearance, hence the name 'grey matter'.

Organisation of the brain

The brain is a highly organised structure, and contains three types of 'centre':

- **sensory centres** receive incoming messages from the sense organs
- **motor centres** carry instructions from the brain to the effectors, such as muscles and glands
- **association centres** interpret the information delivered to the sensory centres and make sure that appropriate instructions are given via the motor centres.

Magnetic resonance imaging

Magnetic resonance imaging (MRI) is a technique used by doctors for scanning the body, including the brain. This technique can be used to locate areas of brain damage, disease or unusual brain activity. The results can be used in research, for example to relate a loss of body function to an area of brain damage, and in medicine, for example to examine the effects on the brain of a particular treatment.

MRI is much less damaging to patients than the techniques that were available previously. Brain surgery is extremely complex, and may cause more damage than benefit as there are areas of the brain with unknown function. X-rays cannot be used to study the brain as the soft tissues in the brain do not show up without injection of dense materials. MRI works by measuring changes in positions of molecules in the body after being exposed to a strong magnetic field.

This MRI scan shows **atrophy** (shrinkage and wastage away) of the brain in the dark red area at the top.

Some association centres are little more than a collection of relay neurones involved in **cranial reflexes** such as blinking (see page 150) – the brain is acting like an extension of the spinal cord. Other association centres are more complex, involving the **learning centres** which can compare incoming information with previous experience.

What is behaviour?

Many of us use the term 'behaviour' without ever thinking what the term really means! A biologist could define behaviour as:

'the course of action produced by an organism in response to a stimulus'.

All living organisms, even plants, show a variety of behavioural activity – the extent of their behaviour depends on how much they are able to respond to stimuli. Behavioural scientists sometimes distinguish two types of behaviour. **Innate behaviour** is inherited, is not changed by the environment and is inflexible (always the same response to a given stimulus). **Learned behaviour**, on the other hand, is not inherited, is changed by the environment and may be quickly adapted to new circumstances.

1 Give an example of:
   a innate behaviour and
   b learned behaviour in humans.
2 How is the brain protected?
3 How does information reach the brain, and how is it carried away to other parts of the body?
4 a Magnetic resonance imaging (MRI) is a non-invasive technique. What does this mean?
   b What information can now be obtained using techniques such as MRI which could not be obtained before this technology was available?

Using choice chambers

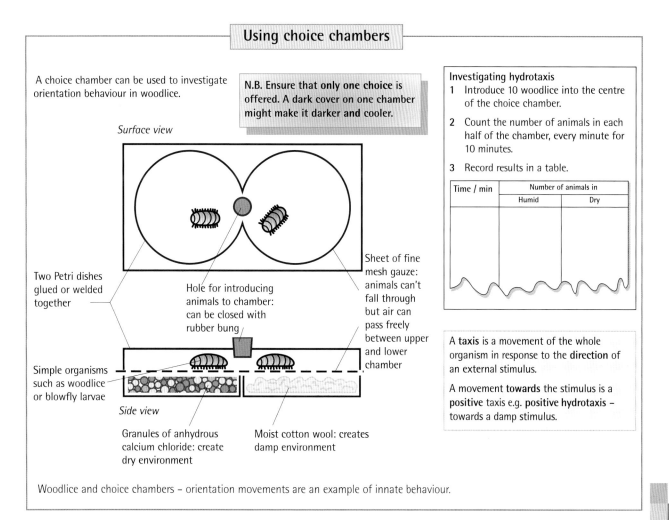

A choice chamber can be used to investigate orientation behaviour in woodlice.

N.B. Ensure that only one choice is offered. A dark cover on one chamber might make it darker and cooler.

Surface view

Two Petri dishes glued or welded together

Hole for introducing animals to chamber: can be closed with rubber bung

Sheet of fine mesh gauze: animals can't fall through but air can pass freely between upper and lower chamber

Simple organisms such as woodlice or blowfly larvae

Side view

Granules of anhydrous calcium chloride: create dry environment

Moist cotton wool: creates damp environment

Investigating hydrotaxis
1 Introduce 10 woodlice into the centre of the choice chamber.
2 Count the number of animals in each half of the chamber, every minute for 10 minutes.
3 Record results in a table.

Time / min	Number of animals in	
	Humid	Dry

A **taxis** is a movement of the whole organism in response to the **direction** of an external stimulus.

A movement **towards** the stimulus is a **positive** taxis e.g. **positive hydrotaxis** – towards a damp stimulus.

Woodlice and choice chambers – orientation movements are an example of innate behaviour.

Objectives

- To understand that receptors are the first stage in reflex arcs
- To know the different types of stimulus to which a mammal is sensitive
- To know that a sense organ combines receptors with other cells
- To know the structure and function of the eye

Receptors detect changes in the environment

A **stimulus** is a change in the environment that affects an organism. All living organisms are **sensitive** – they can respond to stimuli. Animals, including mammals, have a nervous system which receives information from the environment, decides how to respond and then tells the body. A **receptor** is a part of the nervous system that is adapted to receive stimuli. Receptors can be classified according to the type of stimulus they respond to, as shown in the table.

Receptor type	Responds to stimulus	Example in humans
Photoreceptor	Light	Rod cells in retina of eye
Chemoreceptor	Chemicals	Taste buds
Thermoreceptor	Changes in temperature	Thermoreceptors in skin
Mechanoreceptor	Mechanical changes such as changes in length	Hair cells in ear (hearing and balance)

Classification of receptors.

Receptors are transducers

All receptors are **transducers**, which means they convert one form of energy into another. They convert the energy of the stimulus (such as light energy) into the kind of energy that the nervous system can deal with (electrical impulses). The general principle of receptor action is outlined in the diagram opposite.

The senses

Our **senses** are our ability to be aware of different aspects of the environment. For example, the sense of sight allows us to be aware of light stimuli, detected by photoreceptors. The photograph opposite shows the different human senses, and the stimuli to which they are sensitive.

The receptor cells that provide our senses do not work on their own. They need a supply of blood to deliver nutrients and oxygen and remove wastes. Receptors may need help in receiving the stimulus, and receptor cells are often grouped together with other tissues to form a **sense organ**. The other tissues allow the receptor cells to work efficiently.

The working of the eye illustrates the involvement of other tissues in the operation of a sense organ, as described opposite.

Note that the senses are detected by receptors in structures on the outside of the body, and mainly around the head. This is because the stimuli come from outside the body, and the head is often the first part of the body that goes into a new environment. There are also many **internal** receptors inside the body. These detect blood temperature and pH, for example, and are vital in the process of homeostasis (see page 128).

> **Think about it!** We are not aware of any stimulus until the impulse reaches the correct area of the brain. The receptor can be working perfectly but unless the sensory nerve and brain are working, the 'sense' will be incomplete – we 'see' with our brain as much as our eyes.

All receptors work in the same way – they convert one form of energy (the stimulus) into another form that the nervous system can understand.

Temperature sensitivity depends on heat stimulation of the **skin**.

Balance and **hearing** depend on mechanical stimulation of the **ear**.

Sight depends on light stimulation of the **eye**.

Touch depends on mechanical stimulation of the **skin**.

Taste depends on chemical stimulation of the **tongue**.

Smell depends on chemical stimulation of the **nose**.

The body also has a **sense of position**. Each muscle and tendon sends information about how stretched it is to the central nervous system (CNS). The CNS interprets this so that we 'know' where each part of the body is in relation to the other parts (see how easy it is to clasp your hands behind your back, or to touch your nose with your eyes shut).

The eye as a sense organ

The eye is an example of a sense organ. It contains:

- ⚑ receptors – the rod and cone cells on the retina
- ⚑ systems for making the most of the light stimulus, including the lens and the iris
- ⚑ its own blood supply and physical protection via the choroid and the sclera.

The diagram below shows the arrangement of the structures in the eye.

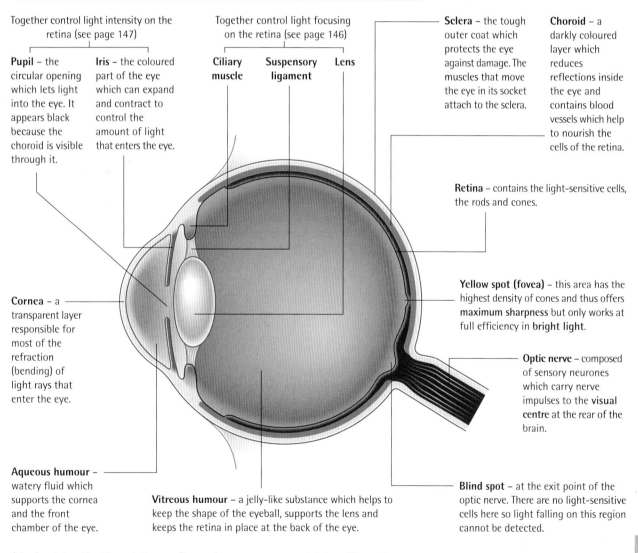

Together control light intensity on the retina (see page 147)

Pupil – the circular opening which lets light into the eye. It appears black because the choroid is visible through it.

Iris – the coloured part of the eye which can expand and contract to control the amount of light that enters the eye.

Together control light focusing on the retina (see page 146)

Ciliary muscle   **Suspensory ligament**   **Lens**

Sclera – the tough outer coat which protects the eye against damage. The muscles that move the eye in its socket attach to the sclera.

Choroid – a darkly coloured layer which reduces reflections inside the eye and contains blood vessels which help to nourish the cells of the retina.

Retina – contains the light-sensitive cells, the rods and cones.

Yellow spot (fovea) – this area has the highest density of cones and thus offers **maximum sharpness** but only works at full efficiency in **bright light**.

Cornea – a transparent layer responsible for most of the refraction (bending) of light rays that enter the eye.

Optic nerve – composed of sensory neurones which carry nerve impulses to the **visual centre** at the rear of the brain.

Aqueous humour – watery fluid which supports the cornea and the front chamber of the eye.

Vitreous humour – a jelly-like substance which helps to keep the shape of the eyeball, supports the lens and keeps the retina in place at the back of the eye.

Blind spot – at the exit point of the optic nerve. There are no light-sensitive cells here so light falling on this region cannot be detected.

A horizontal section through the eye. The eye is a sense organ, containing different tissues working together to perform one function.

Organisation and maintenance of organisms

Rods and cones are photoreceptors on the retina

Sclera
('white' of eye)

Opening of tear duct
(tears wash the surface
of the eye, and contain
a mild antiseptic)

Pupil
(transparent - 'black'
is the choroid at
the back of the eye)

Iris
('colour' of eye)

Eye: front/surface view

The retina contains two types of light-sensitive cell, **rods** and **cones,** as shown in the diagram below.

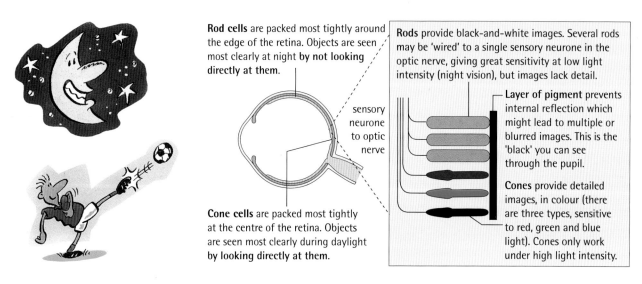

Rod cells are packed most tightly around the edge of the retina. Objects are seen most clearly at night **by not looking directly at them.**

Rods provide black-and-white images. Several rods may be 'wired' to a single sensory neurone in the optic nerve, giving great sensitivity at low light intensity (night vision), but images lack detail.

sensory neurone to optic nerve

Layer of pigment prevents internal reflection which might lead to multiple or blurred images. This is the 'black' you can see through the pupil.

Cone cells are packed most tightly at the centre of the retina. Objects are seen most clearly during daylight by looking directly at them.

Cones provide detailed images, in colour (there are three types, sensitive to red, green and blue light). Cones only work under high light intensity.

How a sharp image is formed on the retina

An **image** is formed when rays of light from an object are brought together (**focused**) onto the retina, as shown here.

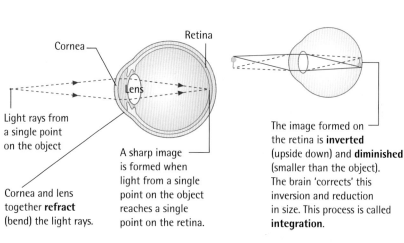

Retina

Cornea

Lens

Light rays from
a single point
on the object

Cornea and lens
together **refract**
(bend) the light rays.

A sharp image
is formed when
light from a single
point on the object
reaches a single
point on the retina.

The image formed on the retina is **inverted** (upside down) and **diminished** (smaller than the object). The brain 'corrects' this inversion and reduction in size. This process is called **integration**.

Accommodation – adjusting for near and distant objects

The amount of **refraction** (bending) of the light is adjusted depending on the distance between the object and the eye. The light rays coming from very distant objects are parallel. They only need to be refracted a little to form a single, sharp, focused image on the retina. However, the lens does not need to be very powerful for this. The light rays coming from close objects are diverging. They need to be refracted more to form a sharp image on the retina, and the lens needs to be more powerful. The ability of the lens system to produce a sharp image of objects at different distances is called **accommodation**. As people get older the lens becomes less elastic and loses its ability to change shape. This makes it harder to refocus quickly on objects at different distances. Smokers may experience this problem earlier than non-smokers because smoke 'ages' molecules in the lens.

The iris controls the light intensity at the retina

Light falls on the retina and stimulates the rods and cones to produce nerve impulses. These travel to the brain along the optic nerve. It is important that the rod and cone receptor cells are not over-stimulated. If too much light fell on them they would not recover in time to allow continued clear vision. The iris contains muscles that alter the size of the pupil, thereby controlling the amount of light that falls on the retina. This control is automatic, and is a good example of a reflex action. This **pupil reflex** is explained in the diagram opposite.

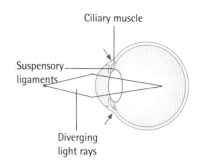

Distant object
- Light needs to be **refracted** (bent) **less**.
- Ciliary muscles **relax**, eyeball becomes spherical.
- Ligaments are **tight**.
- Lens is pulled **long and thin**.

Close object
- Light must be **greatly refracted** (bent).
- Ciliary muscles **contract**, pull eyeball inwards (eyeball 'bulges' forward).
- Ligaments **relax**.
- Lens becomes **short and fat**.

Relaxed or waking eyes are set for viewing distant objects so that images of close objects (such as alarm clocks!) are blurred.

Eyestrain is caused by long periods of close work. The ciliary muscles are contracting against the pressure of fluid in the eyeball.

Stimulus – light falls on retina

↓

Impulse in sensory neurones of optic nerve

↓

Integration in the visual centre of the brain

↓

Impulses in motor neurones

Low light intensity – radial muscles of iris contract and the pupil is opened wider, so more light can enter and reach the retina.

Circular muscles

Radial muscles

The muscles of the iris

High light intensity – circular muscles of iris contract and the pupil is reduced in size, so less light can enter and the retina is protected from bleaching.

Adrenaline (see page 158) imitates this part of the reflex – pupils dilate.

Heroin (see page 152) imitates this part of the reflex – pupils constrict.

The pupil reflex prevents bleaching of the retina by regulating the amount of light that enters the eye.

Questions on receptors and senses

1. What is a transducer? Explain how:
   a taste buds   **b** rod cells
   can be called transducers.

2. Copy and complete this paragraph.
   Light rays from an object are refracted by the _____ and the _____ which focus the light rays onto the _____. The amount of light that reaches this light-sensitive layer is controlled by the _____ which is able to adjust the size of the _____ (the black 'hole' in the front of the eye). There are two types of light-sensitive cells, the _____, which are responsible for _____ vision in low light intensity, and the _____, which are responsible for _____ vision in _____ light intensity. The image formed on the _____ is _____ and _____ than the object, but the nerve impulses that pass along the _____ nerve to the brain are interpreted so that they make sense. The ability of the brain to compare incoming information with previous experience, and to set off the correct response, is called _____.

3. Bimla was sitting in a well-lit room. She covered one eye with an eye patch. A pencil was held in front of her eye for 10 seconds. Bimla focused on it and at the same time the thickness of her eye lens was measured using an optical instrument. The pencil was then moved a different distance from the eye. This was repeated over a short period. The results are shown in the table.

Distance from eye / cm	Thickness of lens / mm
10	4.0
20	3.6
30	3.2
50	2.9
100	2.7
150	2.6
200	2.6

   a Name the structures in the eye that bring about the change in the thickness of the lens.
   b In this investigation, which is the independent variable and which is the dependent variable?
   c Suggest two important fixed variables. Explain why they must be fixed.
   d How could the experiment be improved to make the data more valid?

4. **a** Copy the diagram of the eye. Use arrows and the letters listed below to label the diagram.

   A Layer containing rods and cones
   B Muscles controlling the amount of light entering the eye
   C The source of tears
   D A black layer containing blood vessels
   E A very thin layer which protects the surface of the eye from bacteria
   F A tough white protective layer

   b In bright light the iris changes shape to reduce the size of the pupil.
   i What is the advantage of this?
   ii For this purpose, name the stimulus, receptor, coordinator and effector. Copy and complete the diagram below.

   Stimulus   Receptor   Coordinator   Effector

   c Rosie went from bright light into a dark room. The graph below shows the dimmest light in which she could see during the first half hour after entering the room.
   i How long was it before Rosie's eyes were completely 'used to the dark'?
   ii Rosie's friend, Matilda, suggests that Rosie's eyes become 'used to the dark' because her iris changes shape. From the evidence in the graph, do you think that this is likely? Explain your answer.

   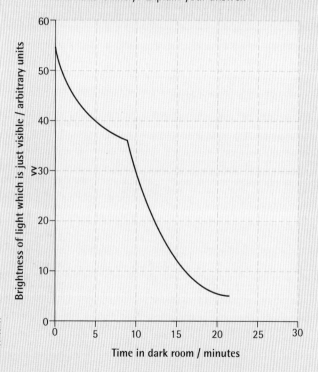

5. An experiment similar to that in question 3 was carried out. Data from a number of subjects were used to draw the graph below.

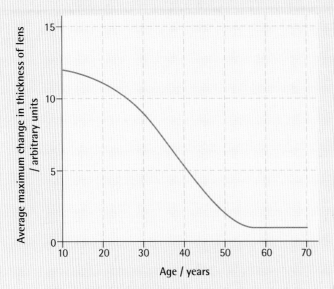

a At what age does the lens more or less lose the ability to change shape?

b What effect will this have on the person's eyesight?

c From the information in the graph, suggest why senior citizens (people over the age of 60) do not have to keep getting new glasses for reading.

d In the condition called **cataract** the lens becomes very cloudy and must be removed. Which structure will now be the only way to converge light onto the retina? How will this operation affect a person's eyesight?

e Scientists know that cigarette smoking hardens the arteries. Some scientists believe that smoking also hardens the lens, making a change of shape more difficult. How could you investigate this hypothesis? What controls would you need?

6. The figure shows a diagram of the human brain and the table shows the functions of some parts of the brain.

Part of brain	Function
P	controls body temperature
Q	is the master hormone-producer
R	controls unconscious activities such as heart beat
S	helps to control balance and give coordination
T	memory storage and conscious behaviour

a Label the figure using the letters P to T from the table.

b One of the hormones produced by Q regulates growth and the development of the reproductive organs.

 i Explain how a hormone made in the brain can have its effect in the reproductive organs.

 ii Suggest possible effects on a child of the region Q producing unusually high amounts of this hormone.

(CIE 'O' level May-June 2004)

Objective
▶ To understand that the central nervous system integrates and coordinates the responses of the body

The central nervous system (CNS) processes information from receptors and passes instructions to effectors to tell the organism how to respond. This complex series of operations, referred to as **integration**, is outlined below.

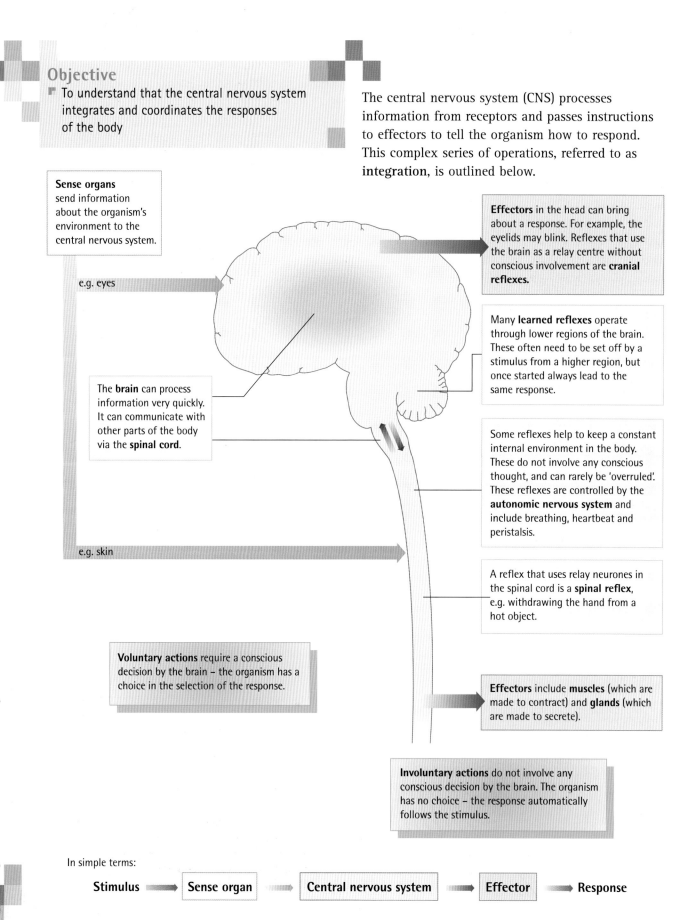

Sense organs send information about the organism's environment to the central nervous system.

e.g. eyes

The **brain** can process information very quickly. It can communicate with other parts of the body via the **spinal cord**.

e.g. skin

Effectors in the head can bring about a response. For example, the eyelids may blink. Reflexes that use the brain as a relay centre without conscious involvement are **cranial reflexes.**

Many **learned reflexes** operate through lower regions of the brain. These often need to be set off by a stimulus from a higher region, but once started always lead to the same response.

Some reflexes help to keep a constant internal environment in the body. These do not involve any conscious thought, and can rarely be 'overruled'. These reflexes are controlled by the **autonomic nervous system** and include breathing, heartbeat and peristalsis.

A reflex that uses relay neurones in the spinal cord is a **spinal reflex**, e.g. withdrawing the hand from a hot object.

Voluntary actions require a conscious decision by the brain – the organism has a choice in the selection of the response.

Effectors include **muscles** (which are made to contract) and **glands** (which are made to secrete).

Involuntary actions do not involve any conscious decision by the brain. The organism has no choice – the response automatically follows the stimulus.

In simple terms:

Stimulus ⟹ **Sense organ** ⟹ **Central nervous system** ⟹ **Effector** ⟹ **Response**

Involuntary actions

Reflexes concerned with the 'housekeeping' tasks of the body, such as breathing, do not reach the conscious level of the brain. They are dealt with by the **autonomic** branch of the nervous system.

Responses may be more complex than a simple reflex arc. For example, the CNS may store information as **memory** and then compare an incoming stimulus with a previous one. It chooses the correct response for this particular situation, and sends information out to the effectors to bring about the appropriate action. Each time a particular stimulus leads to a certain response, the impulse passes along the same route, so that reflex actions become **learned reflexes**. Talking and cycling are examples of learned reflexes. Whether or not a reflex has been learned, it is an **involuntary action** – a particular stimulus always leads to the same response.

Voluntary actions

During evolution, the front of the spinal cord became highly developed to form the brain. The advanced development of the brain, particularly those parts that deal with learning, sets mammals (and especially humans) apart from 'lower' animals. The brain is involved in **voluntary actions**, in which a conscious choice is made about the response to a particular stimulus.

Conditioned reflexes

Conditioned reflexes are learned reflexes in which the final response has no natural relationship to the stimulus. In an experiment, a Russian scientist, Ivan Pavlov, rang a bell when he fed dogs. The dogs then salivated in response to the bell, even when no food was given. The natural stimulus (the food) had been replaced by an unnatural one (the sound of the bell). Conditioned reflexes can be 'unlearned' if the unnatural stimulus is not repeated with the natural one – if the food was produced without the bell over a period of time, the dogs would no longer salivate at the sound of the bell.

---

1. Reaction times for a class were measured using a computer to calculate the time taken for each student to press the space bar after seeing a light. The table opposite shows the results for student 1.

   a Calculate the mean reaction time of this student. Why is the mean value useful?

   The mean class results are shown in the table below. (You have just calculated the result for student 1.)

Student number	Reaction time / ms	Student number	Reaction time / ms
1		16	150
2	220	17	300
3	130	18	140
4	220	19	230
5	210	20	150
6	250	21	190
7	190	22	180
8	200	23	240
9	220	24	120
10	240	25	170
11	140	26	160
12	280	27	190
13	210	28	210
14	330	29	270
15	270	30	200

Attempt	1	2	3	4	5	6	7	8	9	10
Reaction time / ms	330	340	290	320	320	280	270	290	400	260

   b Place the students' reaction times into groups by copying and completing the table below. Draw a bar chart of the results.

Reaction time / ms	Number of students in group
110–150	
160–200	
210–250	
260–300	
310–350	

   c The teacher suggested that this reaction time could affect driving ability – a motorcycle travelling at 55 km per h would cover about 15 m in a second. How far would the motorcycle travel before:

   i the student with the shortest reaction time pulled the brake lever

   ii the student with the longest reaction time pulled the brake lever?

   d In a further experiment a loud noise was made at the same time as the light was shown. Eventually the student began to respond when just the noise was made. How does this result explain the meaning of the term 'conditioned reflex'?

2.53 Drugs and disorders of the nervous system

Objectives

- To know what is meant by a drug
- To be able to list the main types of drug
- To understand the effects of some drugs on the nervous system
- To appreciate that the nervous system may not always work perfectly

Types of drug

A **drug** is a chemical substance that can alter the way in which a part of the body works. A **medicine** is a chemical treatment for an illness or disorder. **Antibiotics** are drugs which are medicines (see page 272). All medicines contain drugs, for example, aspirin tablets contain the drug acetylsalicylic acid, but not all drugs are medicines. Nicotine and alcohol are drugs, for instance, but are not usually thought of as medicines.

There are many drugs, affecting different parts of the body. Some drugs act directly on the nervous system. These are often grouped according to the effect they have, for example:

- **Stimulants** promote (speed up) the action of the nervous system. Stimulants usually make the drug user feel more confident and alert, and include **amphetamines**, **caffeine** and **nicotine**.
- **Depressants** inhibit (slow down) the action of some part of the nervous system. The user feels sleepy and less anxious, but may become dependent on the drug. Examples of depressants are **barbiturates**, **alcohol** and **cannabis**.
- **Narcotics** act like depressants but particularly target the brain. They work as pain-killers and may bring about a feeling of drowsy well-being or **euphoria**. Narcotics such as **heroin** are very likely to bring about drug dependence in the user.
- **Analgesics** are mild pain-killers. **Aspirin** and **paracetamol** are widely used analgesics.
- **Hallucinogens** alter the passage of impulses through the brain, causing unusual sensations.

Some of these drugs and the effects that they have are described on the opposite page.

Social drugs may be abused

A drug that is taken for non-medical reasons can be described as a **social** or **recreational drug**. Examples include legal drugs, such as nicotine in cigarette smoke, and alcohol, and illegal drugs, such as amphetamines and LSD. These drugs are taken for the pleasurable sensations that they give the user. Users may become **dependent** on the drugs because they are unwilling to give up these pleasurable sensations. This **psychological** or **emotional addiction** may then be followed by a **physical addiction**. A person becomes physically addicted to a drug when the drug is necessary for the normal working of the body. If the person cannot get the drug, then he or she will get **withdrawal symptoms**. Someone suffering withdrawal from heroin, for example, may vomit, tremble, sweat profusely and have severe abdominal pain after as little as four hours without the drug.

The dangers of abusing social drugs

Many casual users of social drugs soon become dependent upon them (physically and/or psychologically), so that the drug becomes a dominant feature of everyday life. The user will do almost anything to satisfy the desire for the effects of the drug, and this may lead to problems such as:

- malnourishment as the drug depresses the appetite
- financial problems – drugs can be expensive and users often resort to stealing
- infections from shared needles used to inject drugs, including HIV and hepatitis
- dangers from other substances mixed with the drugs.

The drug may also lead to dangerous behaviour such as poorly coordinated driving after drinking alcohol or erratic behaviour when using a hallucinogen.

Organisation and maintenance of organisms

152

Drugs may affect the central and peripheral nervous system

Alcohol affects emotional centres in the forebrain. It acts as a **depressant** and overrules normal social restraints. At low concentrations alcohol therefore 'lifts' social inhibitions.

The brain is affected by several groups of drugs:
- **Narcotics** such as **heroin** mimic the action of the body's natural pain-killers. This gives a pleasurable sense of well-being (a 'high').
- **Alcohol** can upset normal sleep patterns by reducing the levels of a 'calming agent' in the brain.

At high concentrations, **alcohol** depresses the life-support centres in the medulla. Breathing may stop, causing brain damage or even death.

Alcohol slows down impulses in peripheral nerves, causing slower reactions. It also affects nerves that control blood flow to the skin, causing flushing of the skin.

Many drugs have their effects at synapses
Synapses transfer nerve impulses as chemicals called **neurotransmitters** (see page 139). Many drugs have their effects by changing the concentration of neurotransmitters, or by mimicking what they do.

Nicotine in tobacco smoke is a **stimulant** which mimics the natural neurotransmitters in the part of the nervous system concerned with control of heartbeat and blood pressure (see page 106).

Aspirin does not affect the nervous system directly but inhibits an enzyme involved in the response that leads to inflammation.

Ecstasy

- Ecstasy is known by many other names, including 'Disco burgers', 'Doves', 'Dennis the Menace' and 'Fantasy'.
- It provides a 'feeling of energy' which can enable people to dance for long periods. This causes **dehydration** – users need to drink a pint of non-alcoholic liquid each hour.
- Death or disability can result from high body temperatures, **but** rapid rehydration has also caused some deaths.
- Ecstasy is one of the most commonly 'cut' drugs. This means it is mixed with other substances, and its quality is extremely variable.
- Long-term use has been shown to reduce the number of nerve cell connections in the brain. This causes memory loss and inability to perform simple tasks.
- Is a powerful stimulant and so is especially dangerous for anyone with high blood pressure, heart problems or epilepsy.
- Affects coordination so users should never drive or use machinery.

Alcohol is the most widely used drug

Alcohol is an unusual drug in that it is widely available legally in many countries. Even young people that cannot buy alcohol legally may still be able to obtain it quite easily. Apart from some cultures which ban alcohol, very few people have never tried the drug, and most young people would not consider it a 'drug of abuse'. However, alcohol can be an addictive drug, and causes great harm when used in excess. Most people greatly underestimate how much alcohol they drink. The effects of alcohol on the body extend beyond the nervous system – these are described in the diagram below.

Alcohol has widespread effects throughout the body.

Cardiovascular effects include **anaemia** (alcohol poisons bone marrow) and increased **deposits of fat** in the coronary arteries.

Skin blood vessels dilate so warm blood flows to the skin. The body feels warm and comfortable, but **hypothermia** may result at low environmental temperatures.

One unit of alcohol is the amount that can be processed by the liver in one hour in the average person (see page 83). This is equivalent to one glass of wine, half a pint of beer, or one measure of spirits.

Sex organs are stimulated but do not work well. Sperm count may be reduced.

Intestines are irritated, causing indigestion, nausea, diarrhoea and ulcers.

In pregnant women, alcohol may cross the placenta to the unborn child. The child may develop slowly, especially its nervous system (this is called **fetal alcohol syndrome**).

Liver cells work harder to detoxify the alcohol. Cells lining blood vessels are damaged causing **cirrhosis** – liver function begins to fail.

Many effects on the nervous system – see page 153.

Kidneys cannot reabsorb water very well. Too much water is excreted and the body becomes dehydrated (this is responsible for the headache following a drinking bout).

Cancer of the tongue and oesophagus are much more likely in heavy drinkers (especially if they also smoke).

Because alcohol is a depressant, **withdrawal** leads to tremors, high pulse rate, sweating and visual hallucination. This is called **delirium tremens** (the DTs) and is treated with sedatives and multivitamins.

Disorders of the nervous system

We have seen that many drugs have their effects by altering the activity of the nervous system. The nervous system may also be damaged by medical conditions. Some of these are more likely in old age (such as Alzheimer's disease), some may strike at any time (such as multiple sclerosis), some are caused by infection (such as meningitis) while others may result from an injury (such as a broken back). Such problems may cause great hardship to the affected person, and to those who care for them.

1 a Several drug types affect the brain. These include stimulants, depressants, and narcotics. Give one example of each, and describe how it affects the brain.

b What is the difference between psychological and physical addiction to a drug?

c What is meant by drug tolerance?

Some drug users suggest that ordinary people are drug dependent. They claim that people who drink six or more cups of coffee per day may experience withdrawal symptoms if they stop. These symptoms are said to include headaches and poor concentration.

d Design an experiment that would allow you to investigate the validity of this claim. State clearly the independent (input) and dependent (outcome) variables, and say how you would manipulate or record them. Suggest some fixed variables that might improve the validity of your data.

2 Alcohol is a powerful and widely used drug. It affects the central nervous system, slows down reflex actions and causes small blood vessels in the skin to dilate. Most alcohol is absorbed in the small intestine, although its rapid effects are partly explained by the observation that up to 30% of it may be absorbed from the stomach. Alcohol is broken down in the liver, and most of it appears as carbon dioxide and water.

A medical student was given six units of alcohol to drink, then blood samples were taken over the next five hours. The table shows the blood alcohol level (BAL) over the time of the experiment.

Time since drinking / hours	BAL / mg of alcohol per 100 cm³ of blood
0.0	0.0
0.5	70
1.0	135
1.5	140
2.0	115
3.0	75
4.0	50
5.0	40

a Use these data to plot a graph.

b i What would be the likely BAL after 2.5 hours?

  ii The legal limit for driving is a BAL of 80 mg per 100 cm³ of blood. For how long would this student be above this limit?

iii How would driving be affected by a BAL of 100 mg per 100 cm³ of blood?

c Suggest one visible effect of the dilation of blood vessels in the skin.

d The liver detoxifies (breaks down) alcohol, and much of it is lost as carbon dioxide and water. How would these substances be lost from the body? Suggest one long-term effect of alcohol consumption on the liver.

e People who drink large amounts of alcohol over long periods often become malnourished. In particular they may be deficient in calcium and vitamin C. What symptoms might be seen in such people?

f What is delirium tremens? Does this condition suggest that alcohol is a stimulant or a depressant? Explain your answer.

3 Illegal or controlled drugs are classified in the UK into three groups – A, B and C. Group A contains the most harmful drugs, including the opiates such as heroin. Drugs seized by police and customs are put into these categories for the purposes of keeping records. The table shows the number of drug seizures by the police in the UK in 1980, 1985 and 1990.

a i Suggest one reason for classifying a drug as a group A drug.

  ii Calculate the percentage increase in the total quantity of cocaine seized by the police between 1980 and 1990. Show your working.

  iii Identify three main trends in the information shown in this table.

b Drug dependence is characterised by personal neglect – poor nutrition, lack of care in personal hygiene and being willing to share needles during injections. Infections such as hepatitis are common, as are vitamin deficiencies. Heroin users are 50 times more likely to commit suicide than non-users. A female user who becomes pregnant may pass on the dependence to her child. Users who are denied access to the drug show violent withdrawal symptoms that include convulsions, diarrhoea and vomiting.

  i What factors contribute to the early death of heroin users?

  ii Following withdrawal, users are treated with methadone (a drug similar to heroin but less likely to case dependence) and multivitamin supplements. Why?

Seizures of group A drugs in the UK

Drug	Number of seizures			Quantity seized / kg		
	1980	1985	1990	1980	1985	1990
Cocaine (Group A)	365	510	1410	4.2	6.7	49.6
LSD (Group A)	244	448	1772	0.003	0.006	0.020
Heroin (Group A)	612	3003	2321	1.8	32.2	26.9
Cannabis resin	6218	13734	43474	312.2	469.8	57164
Amphetamines	706	3401	4490	5.0	50.2	222.7

2·54 The endocrine system

Objectives

- To understand the need for a chemical system of coordination
- To define the terms hormone and endocrine organ
- To give examples of hormones in the human body

A second control system

The responses controlled by the nervous system happen quickly, but there are some responses that go on over a long period of time. Growth and development, for example, continue for years. Animals have a second coordination system, the **endocrine system**, which carries out this sort of control.

Ductless glands

The endocrine system is a series of organs called **glands**, which secrete chemicals called **hormones**. The endocrine glands are ductless glands – they secrete their hormones directly into the bloodstream. (Other glands, called exocrine glands (such as those in the digestive system), secrete substances through a duct or tube.) The hormones, once released, travel in the blood to any part of the body that is supplied with blood. The hormones affect only their **target organs,** as outlined in the diagram below.

1 Stimulus affects endocrine gland so that it releases a hormone (chemical messenger).

4 Target organ brings about an appropriate response to deal with the original stimulus.

Endocrine gland

Hormone

2 Hormones are distributed through the body in the bloodstream.

Hormone responses can last for a long time. The hormones are eventually removed from the blood. Some (such as adrenaline) pass into the urine; others (such as sex hormones) are first altered chemically by the liver.

3 Receptors on the cell membranes of the target organ recognise the circulating hormone molecules. Cells with different receptors are not affected by the hormone, so only the specific target organ can respond to the hormone.

The mechanism of hormone action.

Hormones in humans

The main hormone-producing glands, and the hormones they produce, are shown in the diagram on the opposite page.

A comparison between hormonal and nervous co-ordination is shown on page 138.

Hormones control puberty in humans

Hormones control long-term processes, and often have widespread effects on the body. At **puberty** a person becomes physically able to reproduce. The development of sexual maturity is a good example of a hormone-controlled process (see page 166).

As a young person develops physically, certain signals are processed by the brain, which then instructs the pituitary gland to stimulate the **primary sex organs** – the testes in males and the ovaries in females. Sex hormones - **oestrogen** (in females) and **testosterone** (in males) - are released into the bloodstream and circulate throughout the body. They only affect the target organs which have receptors that recognise them. These target organs then carry out responses, such as the growth of body hair, which may continue for many years.

Hormone production is under feedback control

The production and secretion of hormones is accurately controlled by **feedback** – the hormones regulate their own production. As the level of hormone in the blood rises, it switches off (**inhibits**) its own production so that the level never gets too high. As the level of hormone in the blood falls, it switches on (**stimulates**) its own production so that the level never gets too low. **Feedback control** is very important in biology, particularly in homeostasis (see page 128). It is outlined in the diagram opposite.

Hormones and food: growth hormones are widely used to increase meat production in domestic animals.

Organisation and maintenance of organisms

Endocrine organs and their secretions

Thyroid gland
- Thyroxine – controls the rate of metabolism, including heat production by the liver (see page 130). This hormone may also help to control body mass.

Adrenal glands
- Adrenaline – control of preparing the body for action (see page 158).

Ovaries in female
- Oestrogen and progesterone – control puberty in females, including development of breasts and hips. Also control the menstrual cycle and ovulation (see page 168).

Sex organs
secrete
sex hormones.

Human growth hormone
Sometimes the endocrine system does not function properly. An example is **pituitary dwarfism** – a person fails to grow and develop properly because of a lack of a hormone called **human growth hormone.** Treatment has been considerably improved in recent years by the production of human growth hormone by bacteria.

Pituitary gland
- Human growth hormone – controls growth and development
- Trophic hormones – control other endocrine organs, e.g. thyrotrophin controls the thyroid gland
- Antidiuretic hormone – controls kidney function (see page 133).

Pancreas
- Insulin and glucagon – control of blood sugar concentration (see page 158).

  The pancreas is also an exocrine organ! It secretes digestive enymes down a tube into the small intestine.

Testes in male
- Testosterone – controls puberty in males, including deepening voice, stronger muscles and growth of body hair. Also controls development and release of sperm (see page 167).

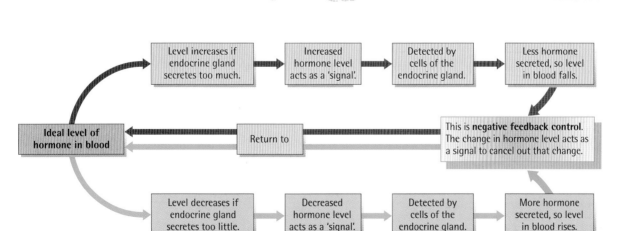

Feedback control regulates hormone levels in the blood.

Organisation and maintenance of organisms

Adrenaline

One hormone that has been widely studied is **adrenaline**. This substance seems to bridge the gap between nervous and endocrine control. It is definitely a chemical messenger, and is released directly into the bloodstream, yet its actions are often very rapid indeed and may only last for a very short time. The widespread and instant effects of adrenaline are described below.

Skin becomes pale as blood is diverted away.

Deeper, more rapid breathing and airways become wider.

Heart beats more rapidly.

Blood is diverted away from digestive system to muscles by using sphincters (see page 109).

Adrenal glands (on top of the kidneys) release the hormone adrenaline.

Glycogen in muscles is converted to **glucose**, and released into the blood.

Adrenaline is known as the 'flight or fight' hormone, released when the body is given a shock.

The overall effect is to provide more glucose and more oxygen for working muscles – preparation for action!

Control of blood glucose level

One of the functions of adrenaline is to increase the concentration of glucose in the blood for respiration. However, constant high concentrations of glucose in the blood are harmful.

The ideal concentration of glucose in the blood is normally maintained by two further hormones, **insulin** and **glucagon**. These are secreted by cells in the pancreas in response to changes in blood glucose concentration. They affect liver, fat tissue and muscle.

- **Insulin** is released when blood sugar is too high. It stimulates the removal of glucose from the blood.
- **Glucagon** is released when blood sugar is too low. It stimulates the release of glucose into the blood.

Insulin controls the conversion of **glucose** to **glycogen**; glucagon controls the conversion of **glycogen** to **glucose**. Glucose is a simple sugar and is soluble in blood plasma and cell cytoplasm. Glycogen is a polysaccharide (see page 38) and is insoluble. Glucose is therefore the usable form of carbohydrate and glycogen is the storage form of carbohydrate. The way in which the blood glucose level is kept within safe limits is shown in the diagram on the opposite page.

Hormones and sport

Athletes can improve their performance with the use of hormones. Although this is strictly illegal and may be harmful, some athletes are willing to take the risk in the pursuit of sporting success. Some 'abused' hormones are listed below.

Hormone	Sporting benefit	Possible harm to user
Adrenaline	Improved immediate performance, especially in 'power' events such as sprinting.	Rise in blood pressure may be harmful to the circulation.
Anabolic steroids	Increased growth of muscle. Allows rapid recovery between training sessions – more training can be completed.	Act as feedback inhibitors of 'natural' steroid production. May cause loss of sexuality, hair loss and possibly increase risk of cancer.
EPO (erythropoeitin)	Increase rate of production of red blood cells, so allowing more oxygen to be carried by the blood.	Blood 'thickens' and the rise in blood pressure can lead to strokes.

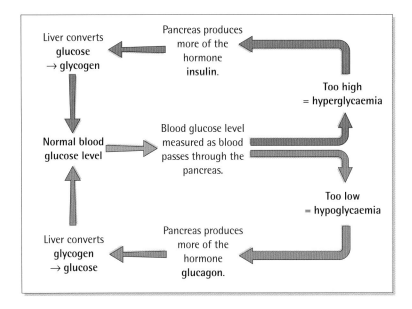

What is diabetes?

Diabetes is a condition in which the blood glucose concentration is higher than normal.

- It is usually the result of the pancreas failing to secrete enough insulin.
- Symptoms include
  - excessive thirst, hunger or urine production
  - sweet smelling breath
  - high 'overflow' of glucose into urine (test with **Clinistix**).
- Long-term effects if untreated include
  - premature ageing
  - cataract formation
  - hardening of arteries
  - heart disease.
- Treatment is by regular injection of pure insulin – much of this is now manufactured by genetic engineering (see page 224).
- A diet that contains too much fat and too much sugar can also cause a form of diabetes. This type of diabetes can be controlled by adjusting the diet to limit fat and sugar, and does not need injection of insulin. This 'non-insulin-dependent' diabetes is a common problem for obese people.

Blood glucose level

Glucose is the cells' main source of energy, and it must always be available to them for respiration ...

... so the body keeps a constant amount of glucose in the blood. This **blood glucose level** is usually maintained at about 1 mg of glucose per cm³ of blood.

Glucose + oxygen
↓
Carbon dioxide + water
+
⟨Energy⟩
↓
Cells may carry out work

Clinistix are thin strips of plastic with a small pad at the bottom. The pad contains an enzyme and a dye. If glucose is present the enzyme uses it to change the colour of the dye. A Clinistix dipped into a urine sample from a diabetic person will give a positive result within seconds. Clinistix are an excellent example of the medical uses of enzymes (see page 33).

Blood glucose level is under feedback control by the hormones insulin and glucagon.

1. Copy and complete the following paragraph.
   A human exposed to a severe shock responds by producing the hormone _____. This hormone causes the storage polysaccharide _____ to be converted to _____, a soluble sugar used to release energy via respiration. Aerobic respiration requires _____ as well as this sugar, and more of this gas is made available because the hormone causes _____ and _____ breathing. The body makes the most of its resources by adjusting blood flow to different organs – less blood flows to the _____, for example, and more flows to the _____. The face of a shocked person shows three effects of this hormone – the skin _____, the pupils _____ and the hair _____. Because of these effects this hormone is often called the _____ or _____ hormone.

2. A dangerously aggressive animal is unlikely to fit into society. Aggression may be an important part of puberty in male animals, and may help to win females. Explain how negative feedback (feedback control) would keep aggression within acceptable limits in a young male animal.

2.55 Sensitivity and movement in plants

Objectives

- To recall that plants, like all living things, are sensitive to their environment
- To know that plants respond to stimuli by changes in their growth patterns
- To know that plant growth responses are controlled by hormones
- To appreciate the importance of plant growth responses
- To understand how plant hormones may be used commercially

Plants respond to their environment

Plants respond to their environment – they show **sensitivity (irritability)**. Plant responses are rather slow compared with those of animals – plants respond to **stimuli** (to changes in their environment) by changing their growth patterns. These growth responses enable a plant to make the most of the resources available in its environment.

Plants respond to many stimuli, but two are of particular importance: **light** (the photo-stimulus) and **gravity** (the geo-stimulus). A growth response carried out by a plant in response to the direction of a stimulus is called a **tropism**.

A **positive** response is a growth movement towards the stimulus, and a **negative** response is a growth movement away from the stimulus. For example:

- a stem growing towards light is a **positive phototropism**
- a stem growing upwards (away from gravity) is a **negative geotropism**
- a root growing downwards (away from light but towards gravity) is a positive geotropism but a negative phototropism.

Roots are **positively geotropic**:

- They grow into the soil, which provides a source of water and mineral ions.
- They provide an extensive system of support and anchorage for the plant.

Shoots are **positively phototropic**:

- Leaves are in the optimum position to absorb light energy for photosynthesis.
- Flowers are lifted into the position where they are most likely to receive pollen. They will be held out into the wind, or may be more visible to pollinating insects.

Experiments provide clues about phototropism

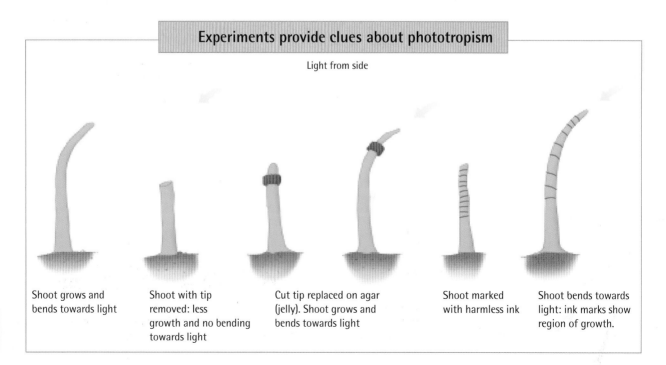

Light from side

Shoot grows and bends towards light

Shoot with tip removed: less growth and no bending towards light

Cut tip replaced on agar (jelly). Shoot grows and bends towards light

Shoot marked with harmless ink

Shoot bends towards light: ink marks show region of growth.

Organisation and maintenance of organisms

160

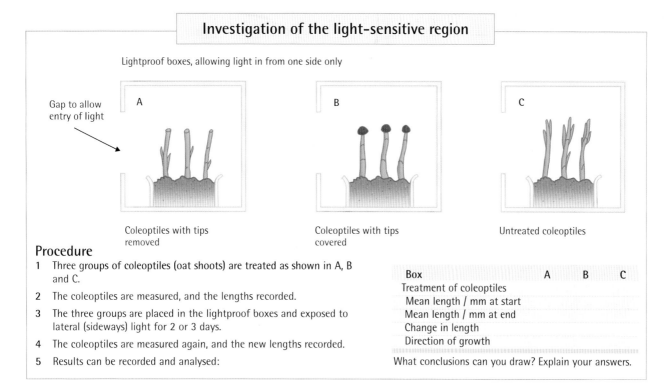

Lightproof boxes, allowing light in from one side only

Gap to allow entry of light

A — Coleoptiles with tips removed

B — Coleoptiles with tips covered

C — Untreated coleoptiles

Procedure

1. Three groups of coleoptiles (oat shoots) are treated as shown in A, B and C.
2. The coleoptiles are measured, and the lengths recorded.
3. The three groups are placed in the lightproof boxes and exposed to lateral (sideways) light for 2 or 3 days.
4. The coleoptiles are measured again, and the new lengths recorded.
5. Results can be recorded and analysed:

Box	A	B	C
Treatment of coleoptiles			
Mean length / mm at start			
Mean length / mm at end			
Change in length			
Direction of growth			

What conclusions can you draw? Explain your answers.

Phototropism is controlled by auxin

Growth is a relatively slow response to a stimulus in animals (see page 156) and plants. Growth in plants is controlled by **plant hormones** or **plant growth substances**. These are sometimes grouped together as **'auxin'**, which means 'growth substance'. The following observations have been made about auxin:

- If the tip of a young shoot is cut off, the shoot can no longer respond to stimuli. This suggests that the tip produces the auxin.
- A shoot responding to a stimulus always bends *just behind* the tip. The auxin appears to travel from the tip (where it is made) to a region behind the tip (where it has its action).
- Auxin can diffuse back from the tip and can be collected in blocks of agar jelly. These blocks can then allow a decapitated tip to respond to light.
- When shoot tips are exposed to light from one side, auxin accumulates on the 'dark' side of the shoot. The auxin is somehow affecting the growth of the 'dark' side of the shoot.

The role of auxin in phototropism is shown below.

The mechanism of phototropism

Light from one side

Light from all sides

More light means less growth!
Plants grown in the dark grow much taller and thinner than those grown in the light. This is called **etiolation**. Light reduces the amount of auxin and so reduces growth.

Auxin is produced at the tip and diffuses slowly down the plant. Cells on both sides are affected equally and the shoot grows straight upwards.

Light reduces the concentration of auxin on the 'light' side. The cells absorb **less** water, and so swell **less** than normal. The 'light' side therefore grows **less** quickly and the shoot bends towards the light.

Cells on the 'dark' side receive **more** auxin. They absorb **more** water, and so increase in size **more** than normal. The 'dark' side therefore grows **more** quickly and the shoot bends away from the dark, i.e. towards the light.

Organisation and maintenance of organisms

Plants respond to gravity: the mechanism of geotropism

Many experiments can be carried out to investigate a plant's response to gravity. A useful organism for this type of experiment is the broad bean. Soaked beans germinate (see page 194) to provide obvious roots and shoots. These can be fixed inside a clear glass jar and their growth observed over a series of days. A simple experiment of this type is shown in the figure below.

It is obvious *why* the shoot grows away from gravity (i.e. is negatively geotropic) because this means the leaves will be exposed to light energy for photosynthesis. It is more difficult to explain *how* the shoot grows in this way whilst the root is positively geotropic. One suggestion is that the root and the shoot are responding to different growth substances, but scientists believe that the same growth substance (auxin) affects both roots and shoots. It seems likely that the root and shoot cells have **different levels of sensitivity** to auxin, so that the same concentration of this substance reduces cell expansion in roots but stimulates cell expansion in shoots.

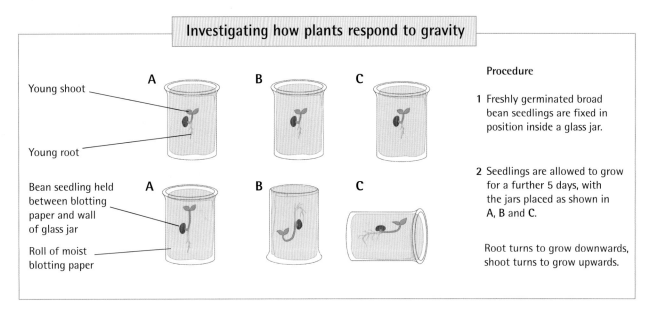

Investigating how plants respond to gravity

Young shoot

Young root

A   B   C

Bean seedling held between blotting paper and wall of glass jar

Roll of moist blotting paper

A   B   C

Procedure

1 Freshly germinated broad bean seedlings are fixed in position inside a glass jar.

2 Seedlings are allowed to grow for a further 5 days, with the jars placed as shown in A, B and C.

Root turns to grow downwards, shoot turns to grow upwards.

The mechanism of geotropism

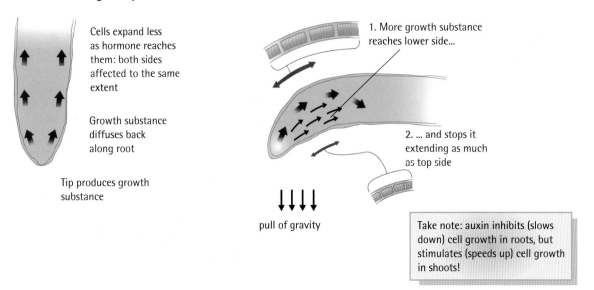

Cells expand less as hormone reaches them: both sides affected to the same extent

Growth substance diffuses back along root

Tip produces growth substance

1. More growth substance reaches lower side...

2. ... and stops it extending as much as top side

pull of gravity

Take note: auxin inhibits (slows down) cell growth in roots, but stimulates (speeds up) cell growth in shoots!

Plant hormones have commercial uses

Humans put their knowledge of how hormones work in plants to good use. Being able to control the growth of plants is valuable, since plants are at the base of all human food chains. Some examples of the commercial use of plant hormones are illustrated above and in the diagram below.

Synchronised fruiting – spraying hormone onto fruits can make them develop at the same rate. This allows efficient picking of the crop by machine.

This happens naturally!
One ripe fruit in a bowl releases a hormone gas which makes the other fruit ripen.

Weeds can be killed – spraying with high concentrations of hormone upsets normal growth patterns. Different plant species are sensitive to different extents, so this weed killing can be selective, e.g. grasses may be killed when shrubs survive.

Agent Orange worked like this!
During the Vietnam war, hormone sprays were used to clear areas of vegetation and make bombing of bridges and roads easier. These sprays can also be used to clear vegetation from overhead power lines, where removal by hand could be expensive and dangerous.

Seedless fruits can be produced – a hormone spray can make fruits such as apples and grapes develop **without fertilisation**. Since no fertilisation has taken place, no seeds are formed. This also reduces the grower's dependence on pollinating insects.

Cuttings can be stimulated to grow roots. In this way a valuable plant can be cloned (see page 198) to provide many identical copies.

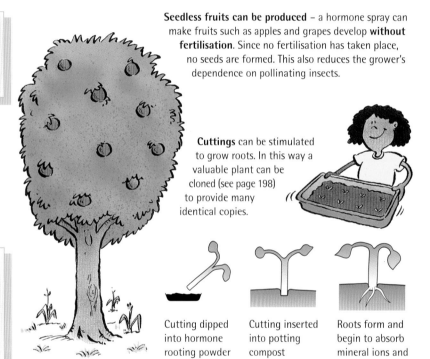

Cutting dipped into hormone rooting powder

Cutting inserted into potting compost

Roots form and begin to absorb mineral ions and water

Copy and complete the following paragraphs.

1 The _____ of a growing shoot produces a plant hormone or _____. This substance causes cells behind the tip to _____ by the absorption of _____. When the shoot is lit from one side, more _____ accumulates on the dark side. As a result the cells _____ more and the shoot bends towards the light. This response is called _____ and offers several advantages to the plant, including greater access to light energy to drive the process of _____.

2 Plant hormones have many commercial uses. These include:
- the stimulation of _____ on cuttings, which allows growers to produce many _____ of valuable plants
- the control of _____, which allows growers to harvest economically with machinery
- the destruction of _____, which could otherwise compete with crops for _____, _____ and _____. Careful selection of hormone concentrations allows this destruction to be _____: only pest plants are killed.
- the production of _____ fruits, since the hormone can make the plant develop a fruit without _____ taking place.

3·1 Reproduction is an important characteristic of living organisms

Objectives
▸ To understand the importance of reproduction
▸ To know that there are different methods of reproduction

It is possible to tell whether an organism is living or not by testing for certain characteristics (see page 6). Among these characteristics is included **reproduction**, although reproduction is *not* necessary for an *individual* organism to survive. However, no individual lives forever and if the *species* is to survive the individuals must replace themselves before they die. This generation of new individuals is called **reproduction**.

The simplest form of reproduction simply involves an organism splitting into two. This is called **binary fission** and is the method of reproduction most commonly used by bacteria and, in a slightly different form, by simple fungi such as brewer's yeast.

More complicated fungi reproduce by making **spores** in a specialised part of their bodies (see page 12) – a large fungus may make millions of spores each time it reproduces.

Both binary fission and spore formation are **asexual** – they do not involve the joining of gametes from two parents. Some animals and plants can use asexual reproduction (see page 196, for example), but many also have a form of sexual reproduction available to them. Asexual and sexual reproduction are compared on page 210. Mammals can *only* reproduce sexually – the sexual reproduction method in humans is described in the following pages.

The **generation time** (time taken for each cell to divide into two) can be as little as 20 minutes under ideal conditions. One *E. coli* cell in the human gut could **theoretically** become 2^{72} cells in 24 hours – this number of cells weighs about 8000 kg!

The number of cells in a population, starting from just one cell, is 2^n (where $n = $ number of generations).

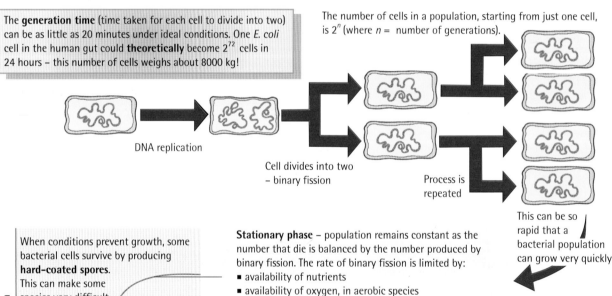

DNA replication

Cell divides into two
– binary fission

Process is repeated

This can be so rapid that a bacterial population can grow very quickly

When conditions prevent growth, some bacterial cells survive by producing **hard-coated spores**. This can make some species very difficult to kill.
▪ Sterilisation kills all bacteria and their spores

Number of bacteria (y-axis)

Time (x-axis)

Stationary phase – population remains constant as the number that die is balanced by the number produced by binary fission. The rate of binary fission is limited by:
▪ availability of nutrients
▪ availability of oxygen, in aerobic species
▪ temperature
▪ availability of water
▪ pH.
The number of deaths may be increased by:
▪ production of waste which increases in concentration as population becomes more dense.

Exponential phase – population grows rapidly, doubling perhaps as often as every 20 minutes.
The bacteria require:
▪ amino acids, for the synthesis of proteins
▪ carbohydrate, e.g. glucose, for the release of energy by respiration
▪ water, as a solvent and a reagent in biochemical reactions
▪ a suitable temperature, for optimum enzyme activity.

Understanding what bacteria need to reproduce can be useful in:
▪ preventing food spoilage – see page 46
▪ controlling infections
▪ providing the best conditions for growth of useful bacteria.

Development of organisms and the continuity of life

3·2 Reproduction in humans

Objectives
- To define the term 'sexual reproduction'
- To know the steps involved in sexual reproduction
- To describe the human reproductive systems

Reproduction may be sexual or asexual. In **sexual reproduction**, genetic information from two parents combines to produce a new individual. Humans, like all other mammals, only use sexual reproduction. Sexual reproduction produces individuals that are different from each other. The process involves a number of stages, as shown in the diagram below.

The male reproductive system
The male reproductive system has two functions:

- to manufacture the male gametes
- to deliver them to the site of fertilisation.

The male gametes, called **spermatozoa**, or **sperm** for short, are manufactured in the **testes**. These are enclosed in a sac of skin, the **scrotum**, which hangs outside the body between the legs. This position helps protect the testes from physical damage, and more importantly keeps them at a temperature

2–3 °C lower than body temperature, ideal for development of the sperm. The sperm are delivered inside the female body through a series of tubes that eventually release the sperm from the tip of the **penis**. The male reproductive system lies very close to the part of the excretory system that removes urine from the body; indeed the urethra is a tube used to expel urine and seminal fluid from the body. A valve prevents this happening at the same time! The two systems together are called the **urinogenital system**. The male reproductive system is shown in the diagram on page 167.

The female reproductive system
In addition to producing female gametes, the female reproductive system receives male gametes. It provides a site for fertilisation and for the development of the zygote. The female gametes, called **ova**, are produced one at a time by the two **ovaries**. The ovum travels along the **oviduct** or **Fallopian tube** towards the **uterus**. It may be fertilised while in the oviduct. The zygote grows and develops into a baby in the uterus. The female reproductive system is shown in the diagram on page 167.

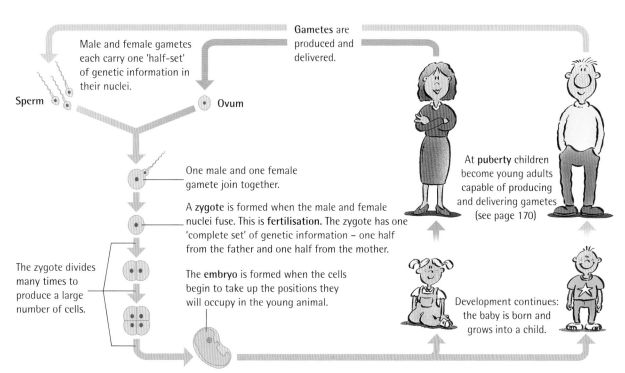

Male and female gametes each carry one 'half-set' of genetic information in their nuclei.

Gametes are produced and delivered.

Sperm

Ovum

One male and one female gamete join together.

A **zygote** is formed when the male and female nuclei fuse. This is **fertilisation**. The zygote has one 'complete set' of genetic information – one half from the father and one half from the mother.

The zygote divides many times to produce a large number of cells.

The **embryo** is formed when the cells begin to take up the positions they will occupy in the young animal.

At **puberty** children become young adults capable of producing and delivering gametes (see page 170)

Development continues: the baby is born and grows into a child.

Development of organisms and the continuity of life

Hormones control puberty in humans

Hormones control long-term processes, and often have widespread effects on the body. At **puberty** a person becomes physically able to reproduce. The development of sexual maturity is a good example of a hormone-controlled process.

As a young person develops physically, certain signals are processed by the brain, which then instructs the pituitary gland to stimulate the **primary sex organs** – the testes in males and the ovaries in females. Sex hormones - **oestrogen** (in females) and **testosterone** (in males) - are released into the bloodstream and circulate throughout the body. They only affect the target organs which have receptors that recognise them. These target organs then carry out responses, such as the growth of body hair, which may continue for many years. The effects of these hormones at puberty are explained further in the diagram below.

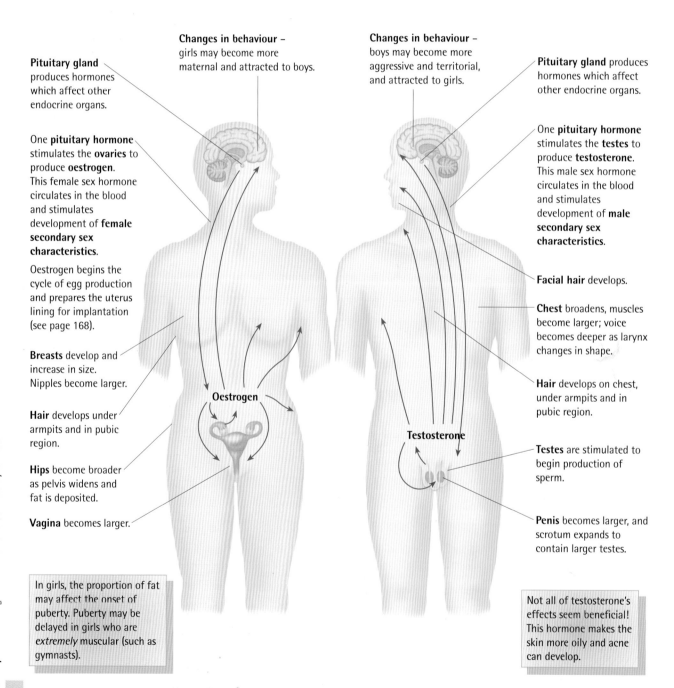

Pituitary gland produces hormones which affect other endocrine organs.

One **pituitary hormone** stimulates the **ovaries** to produce **oestrogen**. This female sex hormone circulates in the blood and stimulates development of **female secondary sex characteristics**.

Oestrogen begins the cycle of egg production and prepares the uterus lining for implantation (see page 168).

Breasts develop and increase in size. Nipples become larger.

Hair develops under armpits and in pubic region.

Hips become broader as pelvis widens and fat is deposited.

Vagina becomes larger.

Changes in behaviour – girls may become more maternal and attracted to boys.

Changes in behaviour – boys may become more aggressive and territorial, and attracted to girls.

Pituitary gland produces hormones which affect other endocrine organs.

One **pituitary hormone** stimulates the **testes** to produce **testosterone**. This male sex hormone circulates in the blood and stimulates development of **male secondary sex characteristics**.

Facial hair develops.

Chest broadens, muscles become larger; voice becomes deeper as larynx changes in shape.

Hair develops on chest, under armpits and in pubic region.

Testes are stimulated to begin production of sperm.

Penis becomes larger, and scrotum expands to contain larger testes.

Oestrogen

Testosterone

In girls, the proportion of fat may affect the onset of puberty. Puberty may be delayed in girls who are *extremely* muscular (such as gymnasts).

Not all of testosterone's effects seem beneficial! This hormone makes the skin more oily and acne can develop.

Oestrogen and testosterone are hormones – they are chemical messengers secreted directly into the bloodstream and bring about widespread and long-lasting effects.

The male urinogenital system.

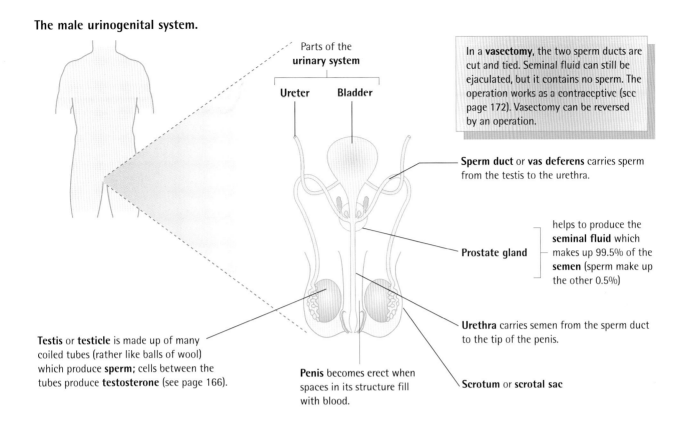

Parts of the **urinary system**

Ureter **Bladder**

In a **vasectomy**, the two sperm ducts are cut and tied. Seminal fluid can still be ejaculated, but it contains no sperm. The operation works as a contraceptive (see page 172). Vasectomy can be reversed by an operation.

Sperm duct or **vas deferens** carries sperm from the testis to the urethra.

Prostate gland helps to produce the **seminal fluid** which makes up 99.5% of the **semen** (sperm make up the other 0.5%)

Urethra carries semen from the sperm duct to the tip of the penis.

Testis or **testicle** is made up of many coiled tubes (rather like balls of wool) which produce **sperm**; cells between the tubes produce **testosterone** (see page 166).

Penis becomes erect when spaces in its structure fill with blood.

Scrotum or **scrotal sac**

The female urinogenital system.

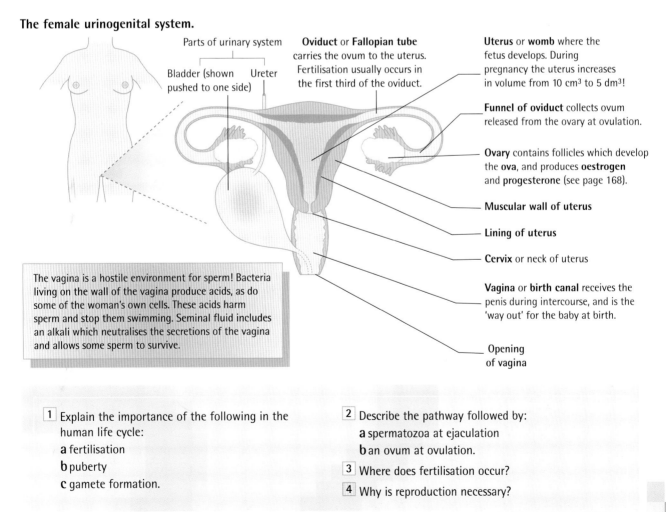

Parts of urinary system

Bladder (shown pushed to one side) Ureter

Oviduct or **Fallopian tube** carries the ovum to the uterus. Fertilisation usually occurs in the first third of the oviduct.

Uterus or **womb** where the fetus develops. During pregnancy the uterus increases in volume from 10 cm^3 to 5 dm^3!

Funnel of oviduct collects ovum released from the ovary at ovulation.

Ovary contains follicles which develop the **ova**, and produces **oestrogen** and **progesterone** (see page 168).

Muscular wall of uterus

Lining of uterus

Cervix or neck of uterus

Vagina or **birth canal** receives the penis during intercourse, and is the 'way out' for the baby at birth.

The vagina is a hostile environment for sperm! Bacteria living on the wall of the vagina produce acids, as do some of the woman's own cells. These acids harm sperm and stop them swimming. Seminal fluid includes an alkali which neutralises the secretions of the vagina and allows some sperm to survive.

Opening of vagina

1. Explain the importance of the following in the human life cycle:
   a fertilisation
   b puberty
   c gamete formation.

2. Describe the pathway followed by:
   a spermatozoa at ejaculation
   b an ovum at ovulation.

3. Where does fertilisation occur?

4. Why is reproduction necessary?

3·3 The menstrual cycle

Objectives
- To understand the female monthly cycle of ovulation
- To know the role of hormones in the menstrual cycle
- To describe the sequence of events in follicle development and ovulation

The testes produce sperm continually at a rate of about 100 000 000 per day from puberty to old age. Women produce only one ovum per month during their reproductive life, from puberty to middle age. The two ovaries take it in turns to produce an ovum, and one ovary releases a mature female gamete every 28 days. The cycle of producing and releasing mature ova is called the **menstrual cycle** (from the Latin word *menstrua* meaning month).

The menstrual cycle is a long-term process controlled by a number of hormones, which:

- prepare the uterus to receive any fertilised ova
- control the development of mature ova.

Hormones affect the wall of the uterus

During the menstrual cycle the wall of the uterus goes through four phases, under the influence of two hormones, **oestrogen** and **progesterone**. During the first phase, which lasts about five days, the lining of the uterus is shed, accompanied by a loss of blood. This time is a woman's **period**, or more correctly the **menstrual phase** or **menstruation**. The other phases of the cycle prepare the uterus to receive and protect a zygote, and are shown in the diagram below.

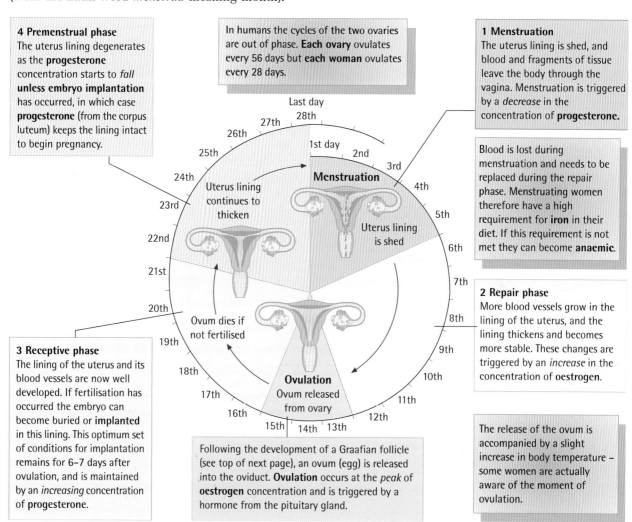

4 Premenstrual phase
The uterus lining degenerates as the **progesterone** concentration starts to *fall* **unless embryo implantation** has occurred, in which case **progesterone** (from the corpus luteum) keeps the lining intact to begin pregnancy.

In humans the cycles of the two ovaries are out of phase. **Each ovary** ovulates every 56 days but **each woman** ovulates every 28 days.

1 Menstruation
The uterus lining is shed, and blood and fragments of tissue leave the body through the vagina. Menstruation is triggered by a *decrease* in the concentration of **progesterone**.

Blood is lost during menstruation and needs to be replaced during the repair phase. Menstruating women therefore have a high requirement for **iron** in their diet. If this requirement is not met they can become **anaemic**.

2 Repair phase
More blood vessels grow in the lining of the uterus, and the lining thickens and becomes more stable. These changes are triggered by an *increase* in the concentration of **oestrogen**.

The release of the ovum is accompanied by a slight increase in body temperature – some women are actually aware of the moment of ovulation.

3 Receptive phase
The lining of the uterus and its blood vessels are now well developed. If fertilisation has occurred the embryo can become buried or **implanted** in this lining. This optimum set of conditions for implantation remains for 6–7 days after ovulation, and is maintained by an *increasing* concentration of **progesterone**.

Following the development of a Graafian follicle (see top of next page), an ovum (egg) is released into the oviduct. **Ovulation** occurs at the *peak* of **oestrogen** concentration and is triggered by a hormone from the pituitary gland.

Last day
28th
27th
26th
25th
24th
23rd
22nd
21st
20th
19th
18th
17th
16th
15th
14th
13th
12th
11th
10th
9th
8th
7th
6th
5th
4th
3rd
2nd
1st day

Uterus lining continues to thicken

Menstruation

Uterus lining is shed

Ovum dies if not fertilised

Ovulation
Ovum released from ovary

Development of organisms and the continuity of life

168

Hormones control the development of ova

The ova develop from cells lining the ovary. This is triggered by follicle stimulating hormone (FSH) released from the pituitary gland. FSH causes a special cell in the ovary to produce a sac around itself. The fluid-filled sac and the developing ovum inside it are together called a **Graafian follicle**. Once the follicle is mature, and there is a high concentration of oestrogen, it moves to the surface of the ovary and bursts, releasing the ovum into the funnel of the oviduct. This process is called **ovulation**. The remaining cells of the Graafian follicle become a structure known as the **corpus luteum**, which produces the hormone progesterone. This hormone keeps the wall of the uterus in good condition for the development of a zygote if implantation has occurred. It also prevents FSH secretion which prevents the release of any more mature ova by feedback inhibition. This ensures that only one fertilised ovum develops in the uterus at any one time. The processes taking place in the uterus and the ovary and their control by hormones are summarised in the diagram below.

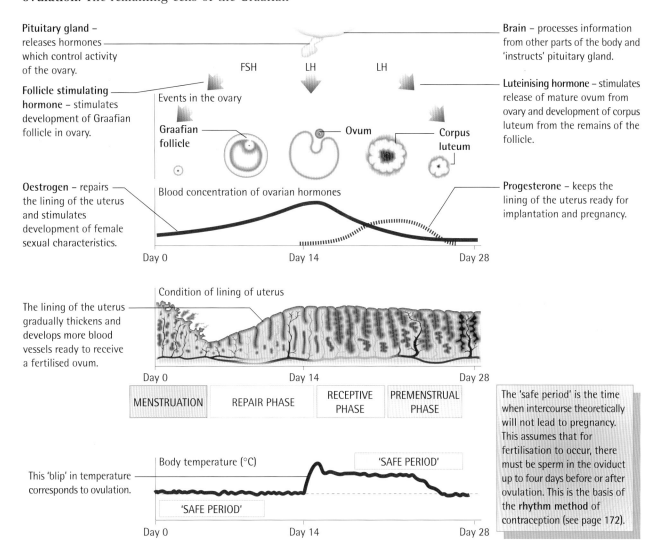

Pituitary gland – releases hormones which control activity of the ovary.

Brain – processes information from other parts of the body and 'instructs' pituitary gland.

Follicle stimulating hormone – stimulates development of Graafian follicle in ovary.

FSH   LH   LH

Events in the ovary

Graafian follicle   Ovum   Corpus luteum

Luteinising hormone – stimulates release of mature ovum from ovary and development of corpus luteum from the remains of the follicle.

Oestrogen – repairs the lining of the uterus and stimulates development of female sexual characteristics.

Blood concentration of ovarian hormones

Progesterone – keeps the lining of the uterus ready for implantation and pregnancy.

Day 0   Day 14   Day 28

Condition of lining of uterus

The lining of the uterus gradually thickens and develops more blood vessels ready to receive a fertilised ovum.

Day 0   Day 14   Day 28

| MENSTRUATION | REPAIR PHASE | RECEPTIVE PHASE | PREMENSTRUAL PHASE |

The 'safe period' is the time when intercourse theoretically will not lead to pregnancy. This assumes that for fertilisation to occur, there must be sperm in the oviduct up to four days before or after ovulation. This is the basis of the **rhythm method** of contraception (see page 172).

This 'blip' in temperature corresponds to ovulation.

Body temperature (°C)

'SAFE PERIOD'

'SAFE PERIOD'

Day 0   Day 14   Day 28

1 Define the terms **menstruation** and **ovulation**. What is the link between these processes?

2 Describe the role of the hormones FSH, LH, oestrogen and progesterone in the control of the menstrual cycle.

3 Use the term **feedback inhibition** to explain why contraceptive pills contain the hormone progesterone.

4 a List the phases of the menstrual cycle.
   b How long does the cycle last?
   c At what time in the cycle does ovulation occur?

Objectives

- To understand the difference between copulation and conception
- To describe the events of fertilisation
- To describe the processes of *in vitro* fertilisation and artificial insemination by donor
- To understand some of the moral and ethical questions posed by human intervention in reproductive processes

Ovulation provides a female gamete

During ovulation each month, an ovum is released from one of the ovaries. The ovum moves slowly along the oviduct towards the uterus. This movement is brought about by:

- **peristalsis** – rhythmic contractions of muscles in the wall of the oviduct
- **cilia** – fine hair-like structures on the lining of the oviduct which sweep the ovum along.

Sexual intercourse or copulation delivers male gametes to the female reproductive system.

It takes 4–7 days for the ovum to reach the uterus, and during this time fertilisation may take place in the oviduct (see below).

Copulation delivers male gametes

Before intercourse, sexual stimulation causes blood to flow into the man's penis. The penis becomes erect and hard enough to enter the woman's vagina (helped by lubricating fluids released by the walls of the vagina). This is called **copulation** or **sexual intercourse**. The rubbing of the tip of the penis (the **glans**) against the wall of the vagina sets off a reflex action that releases stored sperm from the testes, and squeezes them by peristalsis along the sperm ducts and the urethra. As the sperm pass along these tubes, seminal fluid is added to them and the complete **semen** is ejaculated in spurts from the tip of the penis. About 3 or 4 cm³ of semen is ejaculated, and this contains about 300 000 000 sperm. The diagram below illustrates how the male and female gametes arrive at the same place.

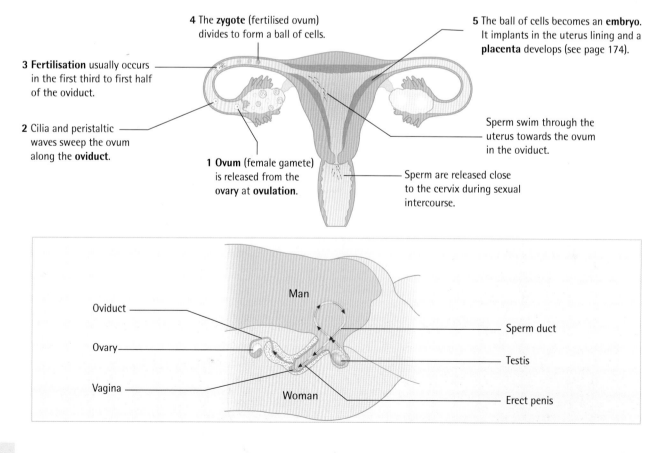

4 The **zygote** (fertilised ovum) divides to form a ball of cells.

5 The ball of cells becomes an **embryo**. It implants in the uterus lining and a **placenta** develops (see page 174).

3 Fertilisation usually occurs in the first third to first half of the oviduct.

2 Cilia and peristaltic waves sweep the ovum along the **oviduct**.

1 Ovum (female gamete) is released from the ovary at **ovulation**.

Sperm swim through the uterus towards the ovum in the oviduct.

Sperm are released close to the cervix during sexual intercourse.

Oviduct

Ovary

Vagina

Man

Woman

Sperm duct

Testis

Erect penis

1 Sperm swim towards ovum.

Ovum — Cells from the follicle surrounding ovum

Nucleus —

Outer membrane —

— Cytoplasm

2 Remaining follicle cells are scattered by sperm.

— Tail

— Sperm nucleus

— Ovum membrane

3 One sperm passes through the outer membrane. A barrier forms to prevent entry of more than one sperm.

4 Head of sperm crosses ovum cell membrane.

5 Sperm nucleus and ovum nucleus fuse at fertilisation. A zygote has been formed.

Fertilisation is the fusion of ovum and sperm.

Fertilisation is the fusion of ovum and sperm

Fertilisation is the joining together (fusion) of an ovum and a sperm. The new cell contains a set of genetic material from the mother and a set from the father. Fertilisation takes place in the oviduct, and although several hundred sperm may reach the ovum, only one of them will penetrate the membrane that surrounds it. Once this has happened a series of changes takes place:

▪ The ovum membrane alters to form a barrier to the entry of other sperm.

▪ The head of the sperm (the male nucleus) moves towards the nucleus of the ovum and the two fuse (join together).

▪ The fertilised ovum or **zygote** now starts to divide, first into two cells, then into four, and so on. It continues to move towards the uterus.

The events of fertilisation are summarised in the diagram opposite.

Conception is the implantation of the ball of cells

About six days after fertilisation the ball of cells, now called an **embryo**, becomes embedded in the thickened lining of the uterus. **Conception**, the beginning of the development of a new individual, takes place when this embedding or **implantation** is complete. Once the embryo is attached to the lining of the uterus, some of its outer cells combine with some of the mother's cells and a **placenta** begins to develop.

Infertility treatment

In vitro fertilisation (IVF)

The term *in vitro* means 'in glass', and is used to describe a procedure that takes place outside the body in some form of laboratory glassware. In *in vitro* fertilisation, an ovum is fertilised outside a woman's body in a special kind of dish (not a test tube, although the technique is sometimes called 'test-tube fertilisation'). The fertilised ovum is placed in the woman's uterus to develop. This procedure is used to treat couples who are unable to conceive. For example, a woman's oviducts may be blocked, preventing sperm reaching the ovum, or making it difficult for a fertilised ovum to get to the uterus.

Artificial insemination by donor (AID)

If a couple is unable to conceive naturally due to a problem with the man's sperm, they may try AID. Sperm from a donor is obtained from a sperm bank (where it is stored) and is inserted into the woman's uterus close to her time of ovulation.

1 Define the terms conception, copulation and fertilisation. In what order do these events occur?

2 It is possible for humans to intervene in the process of reproduction. Suggest how IVF and AID raise ethical problems for the medical profession.

3.5 Contraception

Objectives
- To define contraception
- To know about different methods of contraception
- To evaluate the effectiveness of different methods of contraception

Preventing pregnancy

Contraception (which literally means 'against conceiving') is defined as 'deliberately preventing pregnancy'. It is quite natural for two people who love each other to want to have intercourse (to 'make love' or 'have sex'). However, they may not want to have a baby. Using contraception allows a couple to choose when to have children and is an essential part of **family planning**.

Contraception may depend on:

- an understanding of the body's natural cycles (e.g. the **rhythm method**)
- a physical barrier between ovum and sperm (e.g. the **condom**)
- a chemical (e.g. a **pill**, or a **spermicide**)
- a surgical procedure (e.g. **vasectomy**).

The rhythm method: natural contraception

Couples who use the rhythm method avoid having intercourse during the **fertile period**. Instead they wait for the **safe period**, when fertilisation is unlikely to result. The diagram on page 169 shows the safe period. There are several methods of working out the time of ovulation:

- **Calendar method** – the time of ovulation is calculated after keeping a record of when the last six or more periods started.
- **Temperature method** – the woman measures her body temperature and looks for changes at ovulation.
- **Mucus method** – the woman notes changes that take place in the mucus lining of the vagina and cervix at ovulation.

The table opposite shows that the rhythm method is not very reliable. However, it is acceptable to religious groups opposed to artificial methods of contraception.

Male contraceptive methods

There are three methods of contraception for men:

- **Withdrawal (coitus interruptus)** – the penis is withdrawn from the vagina before ejaculation. This method is unreliable as small amounts of semen can leak out before the ejaculation.
- **Vasectomy** – the sperm ducts are cut or tied in a surgical operation (see page 167).
- **Condom or sheath** – this is a thin rubber covering that is fitted over the erect penis before intercourse. It prevents sperm being released into the vagina, and also protects against sexually transmitted diseases (see page 181).

The condom or sheath is unrolled over the erect penis, and semen is collected in the end.

Female contraceptive methods

The main methods of contraception used by women are shown in the diagram opposite.

Which method is best?

Choosing a method of contraception depends on a number of factors, including age, religious belief and whether a long- or short-term method is required. The table compares the failure rates of the different methods in the form of **HWY**, the number of pregnancies likely if a hundred women used the same method for one year.

Method of contraception	Failure rate / HWY
No method used	54
Rhythm method	15
Condom	8–10
Diaphragm with spermicide	2–3
IUD	1
Contraceptive pill	1
Female sterilisation	0
Vasectomy	0

Female sterilisation is difficult to reverse and should only be considered by couples who are sure that they do not want any more children.

Female sterilisation
The oviducts are tied and cut during an operation. Released ova cannot reach the part of the oviduct where sperm are present.
- A permanent method which is 100% reliable.

IUD (intrauterine device) or coil
This is a plastic-coated copper coil which may be left in the uterus for months or even for years. Strings attached to the lower end allow the coil to be removed via the vagina.
- Quite reliable, particularly for women who have already had children.
- Irritates the lining of the uterus so that implantation of the zygote does not occur.

A capsule inserted just beneath the skin can release progestogen over a 3 or 4 month period. This is useful for women who might forget to take the contraceptive pill.

The contraceptive pill
There are two kinds of contraceptive pill. The **mini-pill** contains **progestogen** (synthetic progesterone) which causes changes in the uterus lining so that implantation of a zygote is difficult. The **combined pill** contains **oestrogen** and **progestogen**, and prevents ovulation.
- Almost 100% reliable if used according to instructions.
- Diarrhoea or vomiting can remove the pill from the gut before it has been absorbed fully, reducing its effectiveness.

Spermicide
A chemical, applied as a cream, gel or foam, which kills sperm.
- Very unreliable on its own but makes barrier methods of contraception more effective.

Diaphragm or cap
A thin rubber barrier with a springy outer ring to ensure a close fit. Prevents sperm from entering the uterus.

- Very reliable if properly fitted and used with a spermicide.
- Correct size must be used – requires a trial fitting at a family planning clinic.
- Must be fitted before intercourse and remain in place for 6 hours afterwards.

Female condom or 'Femidom'
A thin sheath which lines the vagina, and prevents entry of sperm. The 'closed' end has a ring to make fitting easier, and the ring at the open end lies flat against the labia.

Morning-after contraception
These are pills used after intercourse has taken place. They are not for regular use, but a doctor might prescribe them if there is a risk of unwanted pregnancy which might lead to an abortion at a later date. The morning-after pill contains hormones which cause the uterus lining to be shed. It is taken 48–72 hours after intercourse. A **coil** fitted within 72–96 hours of intercourse usually prevents pregnancy as well.

Methods of contraception for women include physical, chemical and surgical methods.

1 List the methods of contraception mentioned on these two pages. Mark each one P, C or S for physical, chemical or surgical.

2 Which contraceptive method(s) might be suitable for a short-term relationship?

3 Why is sterilisation unsuitable for a short-term relationship?

4 Why do you think the rhythm method has such a high rate of failure?

Development of organisms and the continuity of life

Objectives

�F To know the sequence of events in the development of a baby

�F to understand the role of the placenta

Growth and development

From the time of conception it takes about nine months, or 40 weeks, for a fertilised ovum to become a fully formed baby. This progress involves two closely linked processes:

�F **growth** – the repeated division of the zygote to provide the many cells that make up the baby

�F **development** – the organisation of the cells into tissues and organs.

During growth, the zygote divides into many identical cells – one zygote at conception becomes 30 million million cells at birth! This type of cell division is called **mitosis** (see page 204). Each cell also takes up its correct position in the embryo. The cells become organised into tissues (see page 25) and start to take on special functions such as nerve cells and skin cells.

A controlled environment

The time taken for the development of a baby from an implanted zygote is called the **gestation period**. The developing fetus needs a stable environment which is provided by the **placenta**, a structure that is only found in mammals. The placenta forms early in pregnancy, partly from the lining of the uterus, and partly from the outside cells of the developing embryo. The fetus is attached to the placenta by the **umbilical cord** as shown below. It is surrounded by the **amniotic sac** which is filled with **amniotic fluid**; this protects the fetus from knocks and bumps.

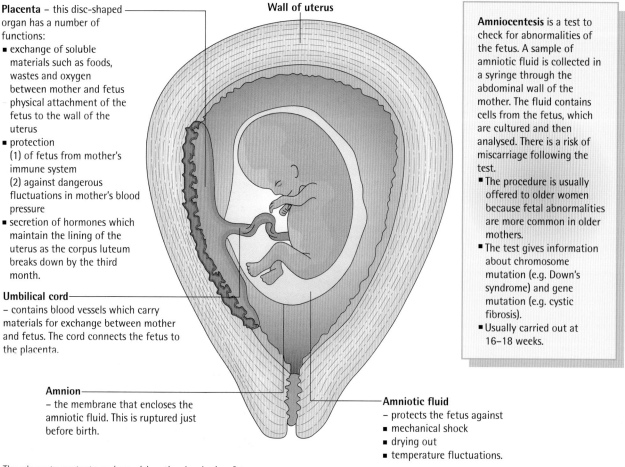

Placenta – this disc-shaped organ has a number of functions:
- exchange of soluble materials such as foods, wastes and oxygen between mother and fetus physical attachment of the fetus to the wall of the uterus
- protection
  (1) of fetus from mother's immune system
  (2) against dangerous fluctuations in mother's blood pressure
- secretion of hormones which maintain the lining of the uterus as the corpus luteum breaks down by the third month.

Wall of uterus

Umbilical cord – contains blood vessels which carry materials for exchange between mother and fetus. The cord connects the fetus to the placenta.

Amnion – the membrane that encloses the amniotic fluid. This is ruptured just before birth.

Amniotic fluid – protects the fetus against
- mechanical shock
- drying out
- temperature fluctuations.

Amniocentesis is a test to check for abnormalities of the fetus. A sample of amniotic fluid is collected in a syringe through the abdominal wall of the mother. The fluid contains cells from the fetus, which are cultured and then analysed. There is a risk of miscarriage following the test.
- The procedure is usually offered to older women because fetal abnormalities are more common in older mothers.
- The test gives information about chromosome mutation (e.g. Down's syndrome) and gene mutation (e.g. cystic fibrosis).
- Usually carried out at 16–18 weeks.

The placenta protects and nourishes the developing fetus.

The placenta begins to develop at implantation and after about 12 weeks it is a thick, disc-like structure with finger-like projections called **villi** that extend deep into the wall of the uterus. The placenta continues to grow to keep pace with the developing fetus and is about 15 cm across, weighing about 500 g, at the time of birth. After the baby has been born the placenta, amniotic sac and umbilical cord are expelled from the uterus as the **afterbirth**. The structure of the placenta, and some of its functions, are illustrated in the diagram below.

Exchange of materials across the placenta

At the placenta, materials are exchanged quickly and selectively between the mother's blood and that of the fetus to keep a constant internal environment inside the fetus. The placenta has adaptations that make this process efficient, as outlined in the diagram below. Towards the end of pregnancy, protective antibodies also cross the placenta so that the baby has some immunity to certain diseases.

A countercurrent system – blood flowing in the umbilical capillaries arrives at the placenta with a low oxygen concentration (0) but can pick up oxygen which diffuses across from the mother's side (2). Even at the end of the umbilical capillary bed the oxygen concentration is lower than in the mother's capillaries. The countercurrent flow system means there is always a concentration gradient which allows diffusion in the direction that favours the fetus.

Vein to mother takes away blood which is:
- low in nutrients and oxygen
- high in carbon dioxide and urea.

Wall of uterus is well supplied with blood vessels.

Blood-filled space in lining of uterus

Placental villi are finger-like projections which provide a large, thin surface for exchange of materials between mother and fetus.

There is **no direct contact between maternal and fetal blood** – they are separated by a membrane which can, to some extent, select the materials that cross it.

Umbilical cord

Umbilical artery – carries deoxygenated blood containing wastes such as urea away from fetus to placenta.

Umbilical vein – carries oxygenated blood cleared of wastes from placenta to fetus. Blood contains a high concentration of soluble foods such as glucose, amino acids and iron.

Artery from mother delivers blood which is:
- high in nutrients and oxygen
- low in carbon dioxide and urea.

The placenta is the site of exchange – useful substances such as glucose and oxygen pass from mother to fetus and wastes such as urea and carbon dioxide move in the opposite direction.

1. What name is given to the complete period from fertilisation to birth?

2. The growth of the fetus is due to an increase in the number of cells of which it is made. A newborn baby has about 30 million million cells. Remember that each cell divides into two, and each of those two into two more (a total of four), and so on. Calculate approximately how many divisions were necessary to produce the baby from the zygote.

3. Cell division is only part of the overall process of production of the baby. Which other process runs alongside cell division? Define this process.

3·7 Pregnancy: development and prenatal care

Objectives
- To understand why abortion may be necessary
- To know how abortion is carried out
- To know about prenatal care

Abortion

This is the common name for the medical process of ending pregnancy. It is sometimes called 'termination'.

Many people have religious, cultural or philosophical beliefs about abortion. Different countries have different laws about:

- whether abortion is legal
- up to which stage in pregnancy abortion is allowed.

The **reasons why abortion may be necessary** are:

- Continuing with the pregnancy would be a greater risk to the woman's life than ending the pregnancy.
- Continuing with the pregnancy would be a greater risk of injury to the woman's mental or physical health than ending the pregnancy.
- Continuing with the pregnancy would be a greater risk to the mental or physical health of any of the woman's existing children than ending the pregnancy.

- There is a real risk that the child, if born, would have a serious mental or physical disability.

This actually gives doctors a great degree of flexibility in deciding whether a woman should have an abortion or not.

When it should be done

If it is necessary then generally an abortion should be carried out as early in the pregnancy as possible (ideally, before twelve weeks) when it is easier and safer. If a woman's life is in danger or if the child, when born, would have a severe mental or physical disability, then there is no legal time limit.

How an abortion is carried out

There are different methods for abortion, as shown below. The time from conception is usually worked out by counting the number of weeks from the first day of the woman's last period.

Whichever method of abortion is used, there are two important rules:

- A woman should seek counselling from an appropriate guidance or advice centre.
- The abortion *must* be carried out under medical supervision in a licensed clinic or hospital.

Up to 9 weeks In the first nine weeks of pregnancy the abortion pill may be used. This is also called an early medical abortion. It involves taking two drugs 48 hours apart. The drugs used in this process can make some women feel sick and in some cases they may vomit or have diarrhoea.	**14–19 weeks** Between 14 and 19 weeks of pregnancy a process known as surgical dilatation and evacuation (referred to as D and E) may be used, under general anaesthetic. The neck of the uterus (the cervix) is stretched just wide enough for forceps to be used to remove the fetus. There may be some bleeding afterwards for up to 14 days. It is not normally necessary to stay in the hospital or clinic overnight.
9–14 weeks From 9 to 14 weeks of pregnancy, a process called vacuum aspiration (which means gentle suction) can be used to remove the fetus from the uterus, under local or general anaesthetic. There can be a little bleeding afterwards for up to 14 days. It is not normally necessary to stay in the hospital or clinic overnight.	**20–24 weeks** Between 20 and 24 weeks of pregnancy there are two alternative methods of abortion. The first method is a surgical two-stage abortion. The second method is a medically induced abortion and is similar to a late miscarriage. A drug is given to start an early labour and the woman remains awake. Both methods usually involve an overnight stay in hospital.

Prenatal care

Prenatal care includes
- advice on diet
- guidance on motherhood
- checks on fetus and mother

Signs of pregnancy
- first sign – a missed period
- second sign – another missed period, perhaps with feelings of nausea, tender breasts and more frequent urination.

Testing for pregnancy
Measures the amount of HCG hormone in the urine, using monoclonal antibodies

Checks on the fetus

Size and **position** can be felt by gentle pressure on the uterus. Towards the end of pregnancy the best position for the baby is head downwards and facing the mother's back.

Heartbeat can be measured, using a stethoscope, during the second half of pregnancy. The fetal heart rate is usually 120–160 bpm, about twice as high as its mother!

Ultrasound scanning is used to produce a picture of the fetus in the uterus. It provides information on
- baby's age, size, sex and position
- position of the placenta
- whether there are twins!

Amniocentesis (see page 174) provides valuable early information about the developing fetus

Checks on the mother

Weight check: from about the 3rd month of pregnancy a woman gains about 1 lb (450 g) per week. During the whole pregnancy she will gain about 30 lb (12 kg). This includes the weight of the baby, the placenta and the amniotic fluid, as well as some fat under the skin. If she gains too much weight she will be advised to diet.

Blood tests include
- Haemoglobin – to check that the mother is not anaemic (see page 95)
- Blood group – in case an emergency blood transfusion is needed, and to check for Rhesus compatibility (see page 101)
- German measles antibodies – to check that she is immune and there is no risk of the Rubella virus crossing the placenta (see page 101)

Urine tests
- Blood sugar (glucose) – to check for diabetes (see page 158)
- Protein (albumin) – to check for any damage to the kidneys (page 134)

Vaginal examination – on the first visit to the antenatal clinic the vagina is checked for
- presence of infection e.g. thrush
- to obtain a cervical smear to identify cancer cells
Late in pregnancy the vagina is checked to make sure that it will be big enough for the baby's head to pass through.

Blood pressure: checked at every visit as high b.p. may indicate **toxaemia of pregnancy** which can be very serious for both mother and baby.

Hormones: the level of **oestrogen** in the blood indicates how well the placenta is functioning to supply the fetus with food and oxygen.

From conception to birth: development of the human fetus

2 months   actual length 13 mm

Drugs administered during this period may severely affect development e.g. Thalidomide leads to loss of or abnormal limbs.

Birth is a compromise – the fetus has outgrown the placenta's supply systems but must adjust to a much more variable environment.

All adult organs are present, though tiny and immature. Muscles begin to differentiate and embryo is capable of movement. Sex organ distinguishable as ovary or testis. Bones begin to harden. From now on the developing organism is know as the **fetus**.

At this stage, **preterm** babies have a good chance of survival with apppropriate respiratory and thermoregulatory assistance.

1 month   actual length 7 mm

- nose
- eye
- umbilical cord
- heart
- forelimb
- hindlimb

By this time the basic pattern of the body has been laid down – the nerve tube is forming, the heart begins to beat, the limb buds appear and the three regions of the brain are formed. The developing organism is an **embryo**.

3 months
actual length 70 mm

Fetus may kick, curl toes, squint and frown. Sex can be determined by external inspection. Lymph nodes develop.

0 1 2 3 4 5 6 7 8 9

Time since fertilisation / months

4 months
actual length 95 mm

Face begins to look 'human'. Lobes of the forebrain develop. Eye, ear and nose begin to look 'normal'. Movements may begin to be vigorous, and may be detected by mother (the fetus 'kicks').

3.8 Birth and the newborn baby

Objectives
- To describe the events leading to birth
- To describe the early care of a young baby
- To appreciate the benefits of breast feeding

Hormones are responsible for birth

The sequence of events that leads to the birth of a baby is called **labour**. Labour begins with the **contractions** of the uterus muscle. These contractions are:

- prevented by **progesterone** – the level of this hormone *falls* as birth approaches
- stimulated by **oxytocin**, a hormone released from the pituitary gland of the mother
- helped by **oestrogen** (which makes the uterus more sensitive to oxytocin) – the level of this hormone *rises* as birth approaches.

Labour

By the end of pregnancy the baby normally lies with its head against the cervix. At first the contractions come every 20 minutes or so, but as birth approaches they become more frequent and more powerful. The contractions cause the amniotic membrane to break and release the amniotic fluid – this is known as breaking the waters – and the cervix to dilate (get wider). The first stage of labour is complete when the cervix is wide enough for the baby's head to pass through. Labour continues as the baby's head is pushed past the cervix into the vagina, which is now acting as a birth canal. From now on the process is quite rapid and needs only gentle contractions by the mother, helped by the midwife or the obstetrician (doctor who specialises in birth). The birth process is quite traumatic for the baby, and it may become short of oxygen as the umbilical cord is compressed by the walls of the birth canal. The baby's heartbeat is monitored during birth, and the blood soon reoxygenates once the baby begins to breathe. When the baby is breathing properly the umbilical cord is clamped (to prevent bleeding) and cut. The placenta comes away from the wall of the uterus and leaves the vagina as the **afterbirth**.

Feeding the newborn baby

When a newborn baby is placed close to its mother's breast it sucks at the nipple. This is known as the **suckling reflex**. Suckling stimulates the mother's brain to release more oxytocin. The hormone causes tiny muscles in the **mammary glands** to squeeze out milk. This process is **lactation**.

The mother's milk is an ideal food for the baby – it contains all the nutrients the baby needs in the correct proportions. It also contains some antibodies from the mother which help to protect the baby during its early months. Milk made in the first few days is called **colostrum**. It contains mainly antibodies and very little food. The mother continues to produce milk as long as the baby suckles. A newborn baby cannot eat solid food because it has no teeth and its digestive system is not developed enough to deal with solids. At around four to six months when the first teeth are starting to appear, the baby can begin to eat some solid food. The gradual changeover from milk to a solid food diet is called **weaning**.

Bottle feeding

The artificial or formula milks intended for use in bottle feeding are based on cows' milk. Various sugars and other substances are added to the dried powder to make it more like human milk. The differences between cow and human milk are shown opposite.

The main advantages of bottle feeding are that the exact quantity of the baby's food intake can be measured, and that people other than the baby's mother can help with feeding. The main disadvantages of bottle feeding are that formula milk is expensive and it is not as easily digested as breast milk. Also, unless the bottles are carefully cleaned and sterilised and unless the milk is made with boiled cooled water, microbes can be passed to the baby.

In some parts of the world, bottle feeding is a leading cause of gastrointestinal upset and deficiency disease in babies. There is an ongoing campaign to encourage breast feeding.

Human milk is low in bacteria and contains antimicrobial factors so that breast-fed infants suffer fewer infections, particularly the dangerously dehydrating gastroenteritis (see page 258). Bottle-fed infants in the developing countries may have a 10–15 times greater mortality than breast-fed babies.	**Artificial milk ('formula')** is based on cow's milk, but it must be modified since the gastrointestinal tract and kidneys of the human infant are immature and incapable of dealing with the 'richness' of cow's milk.	

Cow's milk compared with human milk

Fat	High in long-chain, saturated fatty acids	Difficult to digest, inhibits calcium absorption
Protein	Three times higher	Infant kidneys cannot cope, excess amino acids may cause brain damage
	High casein: whey ratio	Causes hard curd in stomach – not easily digested
Minerals	Very high (particularly sodium)	Infant kidney cannot cope – severe (often fatal) dehydration
Lactose (milk sugar)	Very high	Lactose intolerance – may lead to severe disease, the symptoms of which may include brain damage

Human milk is low-cost, is delivered at body temperature, requires no preparation and breast-feeding encourages a social bond between mother and infant. Suckling may have a contraceptive effect, although this is not certain.

Postnatal care of mother and baby

Mother Soon after the baby is born, the mother should start doing regular exercises to strengthen the muscles which have stretched out of shape during birth.

Where the placenta was attached inside the uterus, a wound remains which takes four to six weeks to heal. During this time a substance called lochia is discharged from the wound and passes out of the vulva. This area needs to be kept very clean because, until the uterus heals, the reproductive and urinary passages can easily become infected with microbes. Regular bathing is essential, preferably with a little salt added to the water.

Baby It takes a few weeks before the baby's temperature-regulating mechanism begins to work efficiently and before the baby builds up a layer of fat under its skin. At first, the baby's room needs to be heated to about 20 °C. If a heater is used, the air may become very dry, which can damage the baby's respiratory passages. So it is beneficial to take a baby out of doors in warm clothing for an hour or two of fresh air each day.

A baby should be bathed once a day, ideally before a meal. The mother should wash her hands before and after she feeds her baby. If bottles are used they should be cleaned in hot water and detergent with a bottle brush and placed in sterilising solution. Teats should be washed and boiled after use.

1 Copy and complete the following paragraph about the birth of a human baby.

An expectant mother knows when she is about to give birth because her _____ begins to experience waves of contraction. These contractions are caused by an increased release of the hormone _____ from the pituitary gland, and become more and more powerful as the concentration of the hormone _____ falls. Eventually the contractions are so powerful that the _____ dilates, the _____ bursts and the 'waters' are released. Further powerful contractions push the baby through the _____ or birth canal (usually head first, but occasionally feet or bottom first in what is called a breech birth). Once the baby has been delivered it is important that it takes deep breaths because it may have been deprived of _____ as the _____ cord is compressed during delivery. This cord is clamped and cut, and relatively mild contractions of the uterus cause the _____ to come away from the wall of the uterus and pass out of the vagina as the _____.

Twins

Humans usually give birth to a single baby. Occasionally two embryos develop together, each with its own placenta and umbilical cord, resulting in **twins**. There are two kinds of twins, and they arise in different ways, as shown in the diagram below.

Very occasionally three or more ova are released and fertilised at the same time, resulting in a multiple birth. This is quite common in women who have been treated with a **fertility drug**. The uterus cannot expand enough to contain several fetuses growing and developing at the same time, and the mother often gives birth early, usually around the seventh month of the pregnancy. Increasingly, medical care (including the use of incubators) means that the babies may survive.

The development of twins.

A single ovum is released from the ovary.

The ovum is fertilised by one sperm.

The zygote divides to form an embryo.

The embryo splits into two identical embryos.

Each embryo completes its development.

Twins are **identical** because they each contain copies **of the same set of genes**.

Two ova are released from the ovary at the same time.

Each ovum is fertilised by a different sperm.

Each zygote forms an embryo.

Each embryo completes its development.

Twins are **non-identical** because they each contain different sets of genes.

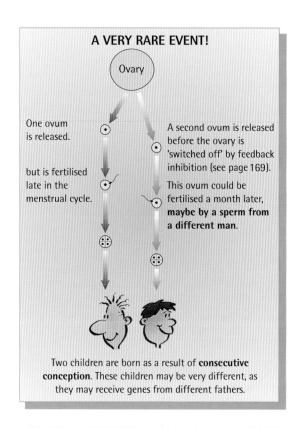

A VERY RARE EVENT!

One ovum is released.

but is fertilised late in the menstrual cycle.

A second ovum is released before the ovary is 'switched off' by feedback inhibition (see page 169).

This ovum could be fertilised a month later, **maybe by a sperm from a different man**.

Two children are born as a result of **consecutive conception**. These children may be very different, as they may receive genes from different fathers.

Identical twins have the same genes.

Non-identical twins are no more alike than any other brothers and sisters.

Multiple births can happen naturally, or following treatment with fertility drugs.

2 Describe the role of hormones in the birth and early growth of a human baby.

3 Consider this list of statements about identical twins, and say whether each is true or false.
   a They each have the same genes.
   b They are formed from two separate ova.
   c They each have their own placenta and umbilical cord.
   d They may be of the same sex or different sexes.
   e They are also known as fraternal twins.
   f They are formed from a single fertilised egg that splits in two.

Development of organisms and the continuity of life

3 9 Sexually transmitted diseases

Objectives

- To understand that disease-causing organisms can be transmitted between partners during sexual activity
- To name some organisms responsible for sexually transmitted diseases

The control of **sexually transmitted diseases** (STDs) requires the interaction of individuals and communities. These diseases, some of which are listed on the right, are most likely to be contracted by sexual contact (the responsibility of the individual) but can only be controlled by a concerted effort both locally and worldwide.

Individuals must take care with sexual habits. A STD can be transmitted quickly through a population, so individuals should:

- know the sexual history of their partners
- use a condom for barrier protection
- have a medical check if any symptoms occur.

Communities must offer testing and treatment, e.g. by family doctors.

- Individuals at greatest risk, (e.g. drug users), can be offered testing for HIV.
- Sexual contacts can be traced to identify sources of infection.

Worldwide involvement can include, for example,

- education programmes to prevent infection
- provision of antibiotics
- development of vaccines and antiviral drugs.

STDs can be caused by bacteria, viruses or fungi.

Gonorrhea is a common STD caused by a bacterium. Bacterial STDs are treated with antibiotics (e.g. penicillin) but resistant strains are developing.

Viral STDs are increasing in frequency. These include AIDS (acquired immune deficiency syndrome).

The causes, effects and treatment for gonorrhea and AIDS are summarised in the table below.

Name of STD and infective organism	Signs and symptoms	Transmission	Treatment
Gonorrhea (caused by bacterium)	1. Pain or burning when passing urine 2. A creamy discharge from the penis or vagina 3. Inflammation of the testicles	Usually by penetrative sex– i.e. when the penis enters the vagina, mouth or anus	Once diagnosed (an easy test in a clinic), treatment is straightforward, involving a course of **antibiotics**
AIDS (caused by virus, HIV–human immunodeficiency virus)	A flu-like illness in the early stages. Many AIDS-related conditions may follow as the immune system begins to fail – e.g. fungal infection of the lungs	1. Unprotected sex with an infected person 2. Contact with an infected person's blood 3. From mother to child, during pregnancy or childbirth 4. Sharing syringes while injecting drugs	**There is no cure.** Antiviral treatment slows down the progression from HIV + status to full-blown AIDS

1 Suggest two steps an individual can take to reduce the risk of named diseases.

2 What are the responsibilities of a community health service?

3 Name one viral and one bacterial sexually transmitted disease (STD).

4 For any one named STD suggest how individuals, local communities and scientists worldwide might be involved in its control.

3·10 Growth

- To understand how growth can be measured
- To understand that there is considerable variation in the rate of human growth
- To understand how a growth curve is constructed
- To appreciate some of the factors that affect growth in humans

How do you know whether you are 'growing up' properly? Schools and medical practices make 'growth measurements' to check that a child or young person is growing. These measurements are compared with the expected growth for a person of the same age and sex. Clearly it is very important to know what the expected measurement should be, and to be certain that all the measurements are taken under the same conditions.

Measurement of growth

Growth curves such as the one shown below are useful for comparing measurements from different people. They are made by measuring some feature of many individuals and plotting the results against time. There are some important points to consider:

- Take **samples** from populations, for example, collect data from every tenth student on a school's alphabetical register.

- Calculate the **mean** to minimise the influence of any one individual result.

- Select the correct **parameter** (feature) to measure. **Standing height** is the most commonly used linear measurement, but does not take account of growth in other directions (such as girth – waist measurement) or of growth in different parts of the body. **Body mass** is better in many ways than a linear measurement since it takes volume into account, and therefore includes growth of all body parts. However, body mass measurements do not distinguish between true tissue growth (such as the addition of protein to muscle) and temporary changes (such as fat deposition or variable water intake).

What is normal growth?

Everybody wants to be normal. Many young people are anxious about their size (Why aren't I as tall as him?) or their development (Shouldn't I be shaving? When will my periods start?). Children and young people grow and develop at different rates, and reach different sizes. Many factors determine size, as illustrated opposite, so it should be no surprise that 'normal' covers a very wide range.

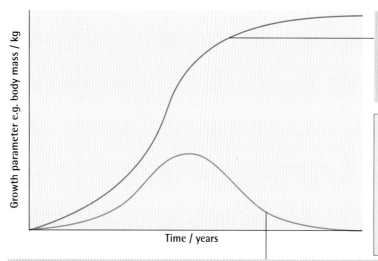

Actual growth curve – this is the **increase** in the measured parameter over a period of time. The general pattern is typically an S-shaped curve – growth starts slowly, speeds up during puberty, then slows and stops altogether when adulthood is reached, typically in the early twenties.

Time / years	Mass / kg	Growth increment / kg
9	32.0	
10	33.0	1.0
11	34.5	1.5
12	36.5	2.0
13	40.0	3.5
14	45.0	5.0
15	48.5	3.5
16	50.5	2.0
17	52.0	1.5
18	53.0	1.0

Rate of growth curve – this is another way of showing the basic growth curve. It describes the **change** in the measured parameter that takes place during successive time intervals – it plots growth increments against time. It is useful for comparing the growth of different parts of the body.

A growth curve is a graph with time on the *x* (horizontal) axis and the measured parameter such as height or body mass on the *y* (vertical) axis.

Genes – many genes on several different chromosomes affect body size.
For example sex-linked genes mean that:
- men are **usually** taller than women
- girls are **rarely** taller than their father.

Hormones – both the **type** of hormone and **when it is secreted** may affect final body size. **Sleep** is vital because growth hormone is secreted faster when the body is at rest.

Growth Hormone

Human growth hormone can be given to children at the lower end of the height range. This hormone is made by genetic engineering.

Racial origins can make great differences to body size – probably both **genes** and **nutrition** are involved.

Nutrition – both **type** and **quantity** of nutrients, and the period of time for which they are available, affect final body size.

Great variation in body size

Many factors affect growth, so there is a wide variation in 'normal' size. Many doctors also believe that psychological well-being can influence growth. A stress-free and caring environment may be very significant in the normal growth and development of a young person.

Growth patterns in humans

Several stages can be recognised during the growth and development of a human from birth to adulthood. These can be simply described on a general growth curve as infancy, childhood, puberty, adolescence and adulthood, as shown opposite. However, a general growth curve for a human does not show:

- ⌐ changes in **growth of individual organs**
- ⌐ changes in **proportions**
- ⌐ effects of **growth spurts**.

These additional factors make it very difficult to say what is 'normal' growth for a human.

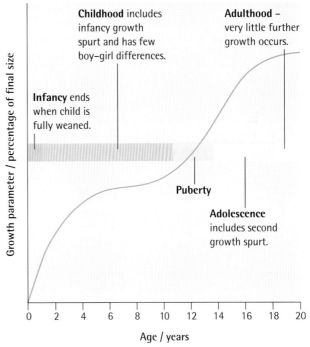

Childhood includes infancy growth spurt and has few boy–girl differences.

Adulthood – very little further growth occurs.

Infancy ends when child is fully weaned.

Puberty

Adolescence includes second growth spurt.

Growth parameter / percentage of final size (y-axis)

Age / years (x-axis)

General growth pattern in humans.

---

1 What are the factors that may affect the growth of an individual?

2 What factors should be considered when producing a growth curve?

3 List the stages, in order, that occur in the growth and development of a human from birth to adulthood.

Development of organisms and the continuity of life

Questions on reproduction and growth

1 The graph below shows the levels of the hormones oestrogen and progesterone in a woman's blood during a month when she becomes pregnant.

Use the information in the graph and your own knowledge to answer the questions below.

Amount of hormone in blood/arbitrary units

Time / days

a When are the levels of oestrogen and progesterone equal?

b Which process occurred between day 0 and day 5?

c Give ONE function of each of these hormones.
  i Oestrogen
  ii Progesterone

d What evidence from the graph shows that an ovum was fertilised?

e Copy the graph. Draw a line between day 16 and day 30 to show a probable level of progesterone which would be found in the woman's blood if she had NOT become pregnant.

f How does the lining of the uterus help in the development of a fertilised ovum?

(Edexcel June 1996)

2 The diagram below shows the reproductive organs of the human male after an operation called a 'vasectomy' has been performed. Following a vasectomy, the man can still ejaculate fluid produced by the prostate and Cowper's glands.

Bladder

Cowper's gland

A

Penis

Prostate gland

Vas deferens (sperm duct)

B

a Name parts A and B.

b Put an 'X' on the diagram to show where sperms are made.

c i In what way are the reproductive organs of the male with the vasectomy different from those of a normal, untreated male?

  ii Explain how this will act as a method of contraception.

d A man infected with the human immuno-deficiency virus (HIV) may transmit AIDS (acquired immuno-deficiency syndrome) to another person. The virus is transmitted in body fluids. Following a vasectomy, is it still possible for an infected man to pass AIDS to another person? Explain your answer.

(SEG June 1991)

3 The following table provides information about the body temperature of a young woman on each day throughout a single menstrual cycle.

a Plot all of this information in the form of a graph.

b i What is the range of the body temperature during the cycle?

Day of menstrual cycle		Body temperature / °C
1		36.5
2		36.2
3	Menstruation	36.2
4		36.2
5		36.2
6		36.2
7		36.3
8		36.2
9		36.4
10		36.3
11		36.2
12		36.1
13		36.2
14	Ovulation	36.2
15		36.5
16		36.7
17		36.8
18		36.7
19		36.7
20		36.8
21		36.7
22		36.6
23		36.6
24		36.7
25		36.6
26		36.6
27		36.7
28		36.6

ii These measurements were made at the same time each day, in the same room and while the woman was wearing the same dressing gown. Why is this important?

c i The times of menstruation and ovulation are shown in the table. What changes in temperature coincide with these events?

ii How could this information be used:
(a) as a method of contraception
(b) to help increase the chance of conception?

d Which other methods of contraception are available to a woman? Why are these methods more successful than the one outlined in part **c**?

4 Below is a diagram of part of a human placenta.

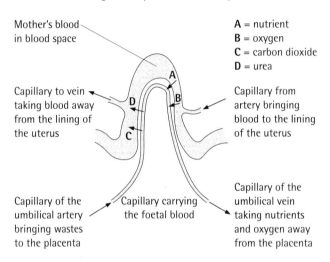

Mother's blood in blood space

A = nutrient
B = oxygen
C = carbon dioxide
D = urea

Capillary to vein taking blood away from the lining of the uterus

Capillary from artery bringing blood to the lining of the uterus

Capillary of the umbilical artery bringing wastes to the placenta

Capillary carrying the foetal blood

Capillary of the umbilical vein taking nutrients and oxygen away from the placenta

Use the information in the diagram to describe the flow of blood and exchange of dissolved nutrients, gases and excretory products which take place in the placenta. Your description should start with blood flowing from the foetus to the placenta.

(MEG June 1994)

5 The temperature of the human fetus whilst in the uterus is about 0.5 °C above that of its mother. At birth it emerges into a relatively cool, dry atmosphere and immediately encounters a problem of temperature control.

a Suggest why the temperature of the fetus is above that of its mother.

b Explain how the following help the newborn baby to control its temperature:
i from about the fifth month of pregnancy onwards a layer of subcutaneous fat is developed by the fetus
ii at birth the blood vessels to the baby's skin constrict very quickly.

c A baby born prematurely is less able to control its body temperature and must be kept in an incubator (see photograph).
i A constant temperature is maintained within the incubator, using a thermostat and an electric heater. Use this example to explain the meaning of the term negative feedback.
ii Suggest two functions of the hood that covers the incubator.

An incubator provides a constant warm environment for a premature baby.

d The premature baby must be fed through a plastic tube going through its nostril into its stomach.
i The food supplied to the baby contains substantial quantities of carbohydrate and protein. Suggest one function of each of these substances in the body of the newborn baby.
ii Name one substance normally supplied across the placenta in the late stages of pregnancy which the artificial diet is unlikely to supply. What problem might this cause for the newborn baby?

6 The table below shows the average height of boys and girls up to the age of 18 years.

a Plot this information as a pair of standard growth curves. Use the same axes for boys and girls.
b On the graph indicate the periods which correspond to weaning, childhood, puberty and adolescence.
c When does the most rapid growth take place?
d At what age are girls generally taller than boys?

Age / years	Average height / cm	
	Boys	Girls
0 (at birth)	52	51
1	76	75
2	88	88
3	97	97
4	103	103
5	110	110
6	118	117
7	125	122
8	131	128
9	135	133
10	141	140
11	145	146
12	150	153
13	156	158
14	164	161
15	169	162
16	172	162
17	174	162
18	175	162

Reproduction in flowering plants: flowers

Objectives

- To understand the part played by flowers in the life of a flowering plant
- To be able to identify the parts of a typical flower
- To be able to state the functions of the parts of a flower

An individual plant, like any other living organism, eventually dies. For a *species* of plant to survive, the *individual* plants must be able to replace themselves. This is the process of **reproduction**, an essential part of the life cycle of the plant.

Sexual reproduction in plants

Flowering plants, as their name suggests, are able to reproduce using highly adapted structures called **flowers**. The life cycle of a flowering plant is outlined below.

Flowering plants reproduce sexually. The following list shows the stages that can be recognised in the reproduction of flowering plants.

1. The young plant develops reproductive organs.
2. Sex cells (gametes) develop inside the reproductive organs.
3. The male sex cells are transferred to the female sex cells.
4. Fusion of male and female sex cells (fertilisation) occurs, and a zygote is produced.
5. The zygote develops into an embryo.
6. The embryo grows into a new young plant, and the cycle starts all over again.

Whereas animals move around freely (they are **motile**), plants live in a fixed position. So, in plants:

- Male gametes may have to be carried some distance to meet female gametes.
- Young plant embryos may have to be carried some distance to get away from their parents!

Most plants are **hermaphrodite**, that is, they have male and female sexual parts on the same individual. This means that the male gametes only have to travel a short distance to the female gametes.

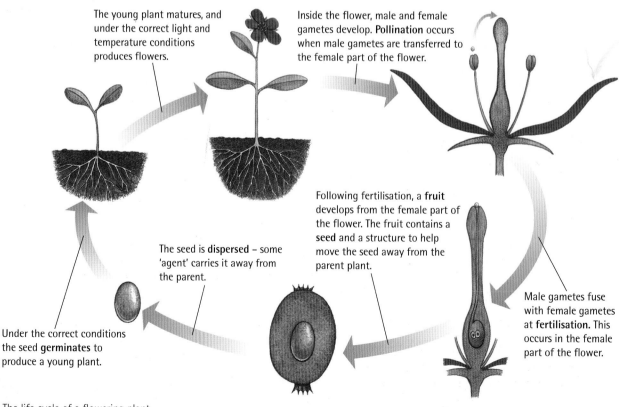

The young plant matures, and under the correct light and temperature conditions produces flowers.

Inside the flower, male and female gametes develop. **Pollination** occurs when male gametes are transferred to the female part of the flower.

Following fertilisation, a **fruit** develops from the female part of the flower. The fruit contains a **seed** and a structure to help move the seed away from the parent plant.

Male gametes fuse with female gametes at **fertilisation**. This occurs in the female part of the flower.

The seed is **dispersed** – some 'agent' carries it away from the parent.

Under the correct conditions the seed **germinates** to produce a young plant.

The life cycle of a flowering plant.

The formation of flowers

A flower is formed from a bud, which is a collection of cells at the end of a flower stalk. The cells receive hormone messages from the main plant body, and gradually develop into four rings of specialised leaves – the flower. These have the sole function of forming sex cells and making sure that fertilisation occurs.

The structure of a typical insect-pollinated flower is shown in the diagram below.

A cross-section (transverse section) of a flower shows that it is made up of four 'rings' of leaves.

Stigma – a 'platform' on which the pollen grains land.

Each plant species has its own uniquely shaped pollen grains. Scientists can find out about the vegetation that once existed in a particular area by collecting and studying pollen grains released thousands of years ago.

Stamens – the male parts of the flower

Carpel – the female part of the flower

Petals – usually brightly coloured and scented. They may produce **nectar**, a sugary solution, from small glands at their bases. Colour, nectar and scent attract pollinating insects.

Sepals are green and protect the flower bud. They usually disappear after pollination.

Flower stalk – swollen tip acts as a base for the four sets of floral leaves.

Anther – contains four **pollen sacs** filled with **pollen grains**. Each pollen grain contains a **male nucleus** (male gamete).

Filament – a long stalk that holds the anther in the best position to release pollen onto a visiting insect

Style – a stalk which holds the stigma in the best position to receive pollen grains

Position of nectary

Ovary – a hollow chamber. The **ovules** develop from the walls of the ovary:

Single ovule

Female nucleus in ovum – the female gamete

Micropyle – entry point for male nucleus at fertilisation

Ovary wall

The structure of a flower: the convolvulus (morning glory). A flower grows from a flower bud and is specialised to produce and release the male and female gametes.

1. Look at the table on the right. Match each part of a flower to its function. Write the letter and number to show your answer, for example, (a)–5.

2. Copy and complete the following paragraph.
The life cycle of a flowering plant has a number of stages. A young plant develops when a seed _____. The plant matures until it produces a _____ which is a collection of leaves specialised for _____. Male gametes are transferred to the female part of the flower by _____ and fuse with female gametes at _____. Following this process the ovary develops into a _____ which contains a _____ and a structure to help move it away from the parent plant. This process, which is called _____, requires some agent or vector to remove the seed from the parent plant.

Flower parts	Functions
(a) pollen	1 to support the anther
(b) flower stalk	2 to secrete a sugary solution
(c) style	3 to contain the female gametes
(d) filament	4 to protect the flower in bud
(e) anther	5 to deliver the male gamete
(f) sepal	6 to form a base for the flower
(g) petal	7 to hold up the stigma
(h) nectary	8 to attract insects
(i) ovary	9 to produce pollen
(j) sepal	10 to receive pollen

Pollination: the transfer of male sex cells to female flower parts

Objectives
- To define the term pollination
- To understand the difference between self-pollination and cross-pollination
- To describe how flowers may be adapted to pollination by insects or wind
- To describe how honey bees are adapted as insect pollinators

In **self-pollination** pollen is transferred from anther to stigma **of the same plant**. This is very efficient (the pollen doesn't have to travel very far) but does not offer much chance of genetic variation (see page 206).

Self-pollination and cross-pollination

For sexual reproduction to occur, the male gametes must be transferred to the female part of the flower – this transfer is the process of **pollination**. The transfer may come about within the same flower (self-pollination) or from one flower to another of the same species (cross-pollination), as shown in the diagram on the right.

Cross-pollination offers many advantages, and some species make sure that it happens.

- Some have special proteins on the surface of the stigma that prevent pollen tubes forming if the pollen comes from the anthers of the same plant. These are **self-sterile** plants.
- In some plants, the anther and the stigma are so far away from one another in the flower that it is not very easy for pollen to travel from the anther to the stigma of the same flower.
- A few plants, such as ash, willow and holly, have separate male and female plants.

In **cross-pollination** pollen is transferred from anther to stigma **of another plant of the same species**. This is risky (pollen may never reach the other plant) but offers a greater chance of genetic variation than self-pollination.

Pollination by wind and insects

Whether self- or cross-pollination occurs, some agent or vector is needed to carry the pollen grains from the anthers to the stigma. This agent is most often an insect or the wind. Flowers show many adaptations to successful **insect pollination** or **wind pollination**. Some of the insects that act as pollinators have also become adapted to make the most of their relationship with flowers. The table on the opposite page shows how some plants are adapted for pollination by insects or plants. The honey bee feeds on nectar and pollen.

Cross-pollination is the only possibility for flowers that are not hermaphrodite. Sometimes a plant has only male or only female flowers. This is **very** risky, since plants of the opposite sex may not be nearby, but offers a very great chance of genetic variation (page 206).

Wind-pollinated flowers such as this grass have small, inconspicuous petals. The anthers and stigmas hang outside the flower.

Wind-pollinated flower e.g. maize

Wind-pollinated flowers are often produced at colder times of the year, when very few insects are flying.

Bract: leaf-like structure which holds the parts of the flower.

Tiny petal: helps to push the bracts apart to expose stigma and stamens.

Pollen: light and produced in huge quantities. Has smooth coat and tiny 'wings' to help transfer by the wind.

Stigma: long and feathery to give a large surface area for pollen to land on. Often hang out into the wind.

No nectar or scent – no need to attract insects.

Anthers are held at the middle so that they can shake to release the pollen.

Filaments: long and flexible so that anthers are held out into the wind.

Part of flower	Insect-pollinated (e.g. convolvulus)	Wind-pollinated (e.g. grass)	Reason
Petals	Usually large, brightly coloured, scented, often with nectaries Guide lines may be present.	Small, green or dull in colour, no scent or nectaries	Insects are attracted to colour and scent. Guide lines direct insects to nectaries, past anthers.
Anthers	Stiff, firmly attached and positioned where insects must brush against them	Hang loosely on long thin filaments	Wind is more likely to dislodge pollen from exposed, dangling anthers than from enclosed ones.
Pollen	Small amounts of large, sticky grains	Enormous quantities of light, smooth pollen grains	Sticky grains attach to hairs on insect's body. Larger amounts from wind-pollinated flowers mean pollination is more likely.
Stigma	Usually flat or lobe-shaped, and positioned where insect must brush against them	Long and feathery, and hanging outside flower	Feathery stigmas form a large network to catch pollen being blown past the flower.

Experimental design: using models

Scientists use **models** of living organisms to study one or two features of the organism. Living organisms may have features that other organisms can detect, but that humans cannot. These might affect the results of an experiment, so a model is easier to study.

Two students were interested in why honey bees visit wallflowers. One of them believed that the *colour* of the flower attracted the bees but the other was convinced that it was the *scent*.

1. Design an experiment to determine whether colour or scent is the more important stimulus to the honey bees. In your design:
   - devise suitable models for the wallflowers
   - clearly state the independent (input) and the dependent (outcome) variables
   - suggest any variables that should be fixed, and say how you would fix them
   - consider whether there are any controls that you might use
   - draw a table that would be suitable for the presentation of your data.

Development of organisms and the continuity of life

3·13 Fertilisation and the formation of seed and fruit

Objectives
- To define the process of fertilisation
- To understand the role of the pollen tube
- To recall which parts of a flower form the fruit
- To understand that a seed contains a food store as well as an embryo

Fertilisation follows pollination

Pollination is complete once the pollen released from an anther has landed on the stigma of the same or another flower. The next step in the plant's reproductive process is **fertilisation**, the fusion of the male and female gametes. The diagram opposite shows how the nucleus from the pollen grain travels down a **pollen tube** to combine with the nucleus of the ovum.

The formation of fruit and seed

After the male nucleus has fused with the ovum, the resulting **zygote** divides many times to produce an **embryo**. The development of a seed and the structure of the embryo are described in the diagram on the opposite page.

Once fertilisation is complete, the developing seed sends hormone messages to the flower, and a number of changes take place:

- The sepals and petals wither away, and may fall off.
- The stamens, stigma and style wither away.

These structures have now completed their function, and would use up valuable food compounds if they remained.

- The wall of the ovary changes. It may become hardened and dry, or fleshy and succulent, and in the wallflower it forms a leathery pouch.

The ovary is now called a **fruit**. A fruit is a fertilised ovary, and has the function of dispersing the seeds away from the parent plant, as we shall see on page 192.

Pollen grain – chemical signals released by the stigma ensure that a pollen tube is only produced when pollen lands on a stigma of the same species.

Pollen tube grows down through the style and acts as a channel to deliver the male gamete from the pollen grain to the female gamete in the ovule.

Ovary wall – ovules are attached to the inside of the ovary wall by a short stalk.

Ovule contains the female gamete, and some other cells which may develop into food reserves.

Stigma

Style

Fertilisation occurs when the haploid male and female gametes fuse to form a diploid zygote.

Fertilisation also triggers some other cells in the ovule to divide rapidly and form a food store inside the seed.

Micropyle – a gap in the covering of the ovule. The tip of the pollen tube locates this gap and the male gamete enters the ovule through it.

Note that only one fertilisation is shown here. Each ovule needs its own pollen grain and pollen tube to be fertilised. A plum has only one ovule in each ovary, a wallflower has a few tens and a poppy may have thousands of ovules in one ovary!

Stages in the development of a fruit

Tomato flowers – the petals are still obvious.

After fertilisation, the petals have fallen off, the stigma and style have withered and the carpel is beginning to swell.

In the ripe fruit, the ovary wall is swollen and succulent. What do you think is the purpose of the bright red colour?

The formation of seed and fruit following fertilisation.

After successful fertilisation the sepals, petals and anthers wither away. The stigma and style also wither so that only the ovary remains on the flower stalk.

Seed coat (testa) prevents drying out of the embryo.

Cotyledons (seed leaves) may form the food store for the embryo. There is **one** seed leaf in monocotyledons such as grasses, or **two** in dicotyledons such as peas and beans.

Endosperm – tissue which forms the food store in cereal crops.

Ovary wall may become dry and hard (in a Brazil nut, for example), very soft and fleshy (in a plum, for example) or form a leathery pouch (as in the wallflower).

Plumule (young shoot)
Radicle (young root)
together with the cotyledons these make up the **embryo**. The embryo develops into a new young plant after germination.

Fertilised ovule develops into a seed, with the zygote forming the embryo.

Micropyle – a small hole in the testa which allows the entry of water and oxygen as the seed germinates.

Remember!
- The **carpel** becomes the **fruit**.
- The **ovule** becomes the **seed**.

Fruit or vegetable?
If it's been formed following Fertilisation it's a Fruit; if there's no sex inVolved it's a Vegetable. Potatoes and carrots are vegetables but tomatoes are fruits.

Not all seeds are edible
Seeds contain stores of carbohydrate, fat, protein, minerals and other food compounds. These are used up by the embryo as it develops into a young plant, but also form an excellent food source for animals (including humans). But note ...
- Uncooked castor oil seeds contain a deadly poison, **ricin**, which was used to kill the Romanian dissident Georgi Markov.
- Almonds contain **cyanide**. Don't eat too much marzipan since this is made from almond paste!

1 In one sentence, explain the difference between pollination and fertilisation.

2 Draw a simple diagram of a typical hermaphrodite flower. On your diagram label:
  a the parts that fall off after fertilisation
  b the parts that develop into a fruit.

3 Define the word 'seed'.

4 Classify each of the following as:
  a fruit b seed or c neither fruit nor seed.
    Tomato, cucumber, Brussels sprout, baked bean, runner bean, celery, pea, grape

5 Two students suggested that the wallflower cannot produce fruits unless pollination has taken place. Their teacher showed them how to prevent bees reaching the flowers by covering the flowers in a fine mesh bag, and how to transfer pollen with a fine paintbrush.

  a Describe how the students could carry out an experiment to test their hypothesis.

  b Suggest how they could modify their experiment to test whether self- or cross-pollination produced more seeds in the wallflower.

In your answer be sure to describe any controls which they could include, and any steps they could take to ensure that their results were valid.

Objectives
- To define the term dispersal
- To describe how fruits and seeds may be adapted for dispersal
- To understand why dispersal is necessary

Dispersal of seeds and fruits.

Remember! Both **pollination** and **dispersal** use animals and/or wind as 'agents'. Make certain that you can distinguish these processes.

An adult plant with well developed root and shoot systems is well adapted to exploit the resources of the environment.

Competition for limited resources is reduced by a range of methods of **seed dispersal**.

By wind

In the **dandelion** a pappus is formed from sepals after fertilisation.

The **sycamore** has two extended wings formed from two fused carpels.

Seed contained in two fused carpels

Seed

By animals

Avens actually produces a **false** fruit because the style (not just the ovary) is involved in dispersal.

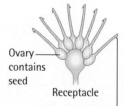

Ovary contains seed

Receptacle

Hooked style is lignified (woody) and attaches to hair or fur of animals.

By water

In the **coconut**, the fibrous ovary wall allows the fruit to float in water.

Seed

By an explosive mechanism
e.g. lupin

In the lupin, the carpel splits and twists, ejecting the seeds.

In the **plum**, succulent flesh offers a food reward to animals.

Pedicel – the stalk which attached the fruit to the adult plant

Seed is resistant to the digestive juices of the animal, and passes out in the faeces.

Coloured skin attracts animals.

Remains of style

Seeds need to be dispersed away from the parent plant

After fertilisation, the seeds are attached to the parent plant. Before it can germinate and develop into a new young plant, the seed (enclosed in the fruit) must be separated from its parent plant. If the young plant remains close to its parent, it would need to **compete** with the parent for resources such as light energy, water and carbon dioxide. The parent plant has some means of **dispersing** the seeds and fruits, that is, separating them from the parent so they are far enough away to avoid competition. Fruits may be adapted in different ways to aid dispersal of the seeds, as shown in the diagrams on the opposite page. Agents that disperse fruits include wind, water and animals.

Lots of fruits increase the chances of success

Any method of seed dispersal is very risky. The seeds may fall beneath the parent plant, and be out-competed for vital resources, or they may land in a place that is entirely unsuitable for germination and growth. Plants produce enormous numbers of fruits, which makes it more likely that at least a few will land in a suitable place for germination and development. A single mature oak tree, for example, might produce a million acorns (oak fruits) in a single year!

The poppy disperses its seeds using the wind. The fruit dries out, and then splits along lines of weakness. The seeds are now exposed to the wind, and blow away from the parent plant.

1 During a class investigation, a group of students measured the time taken for a dropped dandelion fruit to reach the ground, and also the distance travelled by the fruit in that time.

Time taken / s	Distance travelled / cm
6	100
9	140
3	65
14	200
7	105
7	95
9	135
11	170
2	45
8	165

a Plot this information as a scatter graph.

b Is there any relationship between the time spent floating and the efficiency of dispersal of the dandelion fruit?

c Look at the photograph of dandelion fruits. Is there any feature of the fruit that would be likely to increase the length of time it spent floating?

d The teacher insisted that the students dropped all of the fruits from the same height, and in the same corner of the laboratory. Why?

Dandelion fruits are dispersed by wind.

3·15 Germination of seeds

Development of organisms and the continuity of life

Objectives

- To define the term germination
- To understand the conditions required for germination
- To describe the structural changes that accompany germination of the broad bean

Dispersal allows plants to spread their seeds so they can develop without competition from their parents. A seed is made up of an embryo and a food store, all enclosed within a seed coat. If environmental conditions are suitable, the embryo will begin to use the food store in the seed and grow into a new young plant. This development of a seed to a new young plant is called **germination**.

Conditions for germination

A seed needs the following to germinate:

- a **supply of water**
- **oxygen** for **aerobic respiration** (see page 114)
- a **temperature suitable** for the enzymes involved in germination (see page 33).

These requirements are explained more fully in the diagram below.

Some seeds have other requirements as well as the ones shown in the diagram. A few need particular conditions of light (for example, lettuce).

Start here!

Start of germination

Germination proceeds

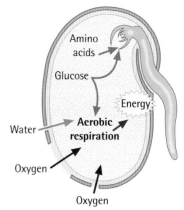

Dormant seed – embryo and food stores are surrounded by an impermeable seed coat. The micropyle is the only gap in the seed coat.

Environmental factors that affect germination are very similar to those that affect enzyme activity. This indicates that **germination is a process controlled by enzymes** (page 32).

Water enters through the micropyle and:
- activates enzymes to convert insoluble stores to soluble foods
- makes tissues swell so that the testa is split open.

Enzymes work at their **optimum temperature**.

Water and oxygen enter through gaps in the testa. Oxygen and glucose enable aerobic respiration, which releases energy. The embryo is able to grow as it receives raw materials and energy.

Dormancy will continue if the embryo in the seed does not experience the right conditions:
- if kept in anaerobic conditions
- if kept dry
- if kept cool.

Oxygen and water cannot reach the embryo if the testa remains impermeable. Some seeds must pass through an animal's gut (where digestive juices are present) before the testa is weakened enough for the seeds to germinate.

Seeds kept dry in a vacuum, as in seed packets, can be stored for long periods

Conditions for germination.

Dormancy

If a seed does not experience ideal conditions for germination immediately, it will not die. Most seeds can survive long periods of poor conditions, only germinating when conditions improve. Seeds survive in a resting state called **dormancy** during which they use hardly any food. The very low water content of seeds allows them to remain dormant, and the availability of water is one of the conditions that allows a seed to escape dormancy and germinate.

Structural changes during germination

Many biochemical processes go on inside the seed during germination. There are also external changes that can easily be seen as a seed begins to develop into a young plant. Different types of seed germinate in different ways. We shall take the broad bean as an example.

The broad bean shows **hypogeal germination**. 'Hypogeal' means 'below the ground' ('hypo' sounds like 'low' and 'geo' refers to 'earth'). The seed remains below the ground throughout the whole process. The stages involved in hypogeal germination are described in the diagram below.

The seedling must start to photosynthesise before all the food stores are used up. For this reason each seed type has an optimum depth for planting. If a seed is planted too deep, the shoot can't get above the ground before all the reserves are used up. Very tiny seeds (lettuce for example) often require a light signal to trigger germination. They will not germinate unless they are close to the surface of the soil, where they are in less danger of using up their food stores too quickly.

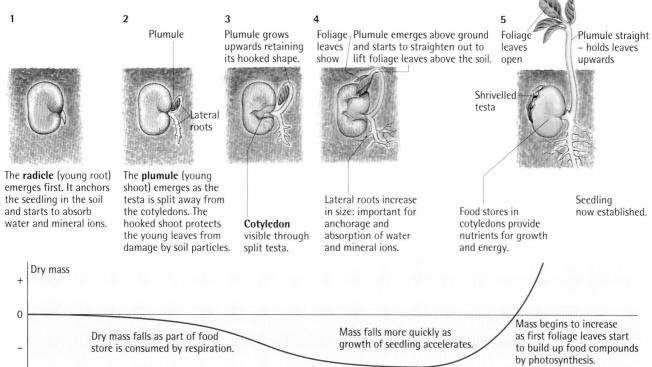

1
The **radicle** (young root) emerges first. It anchors the seedling in the soil and starts to absorb water and mineral ions.

2
Plumule
The **plumule** (young shoot) emerges as the testa is split away from the cotyledons. The hooked shoot protects the young leaves from damage by soil particles.
Lateral roots

3
Plumule grows upwards retaining its hooked shape.
Cotyledon visible through split testa.

4
Foliage leaves show | Plumule emerges above ground and starts to straighten out to lift foliage leaves above the soil.
Lateral roots increase in size: important for anchorage and absorption of water and mineral ions.

5
Foliage leaves open
Plumule straight – holds leaves upwards
Shrivelled testa
Food stores in cotyledons provide nutrients for growth and energy.
Seedling now established.

Dry mass
+
0
–
Dry mass falls as part of food store is consumed by respiration.
Mass falls more quickly as growth of seedling accelerates.
Mass begins to increase as first foliage leaves start to build up food compounds by photosynthesis.

Germination of the broad bean. Dry mass is used as a measure of the food stores because wet mass would include water absorbed from the soil, and the amount of water absorbed and lost can vary greatly.

1 Copy and complete the following paragraph.
Before germination, a seed must absorb _____ from the soil. The seed coat is impermeable to this substance, and it enters through a hole called the _____. This absorption causes the seed to _____ and split the _____. The gas _____ can now enter, which is necessary for _____. The energy from this process, together with soluble food compounds, allows the _____ to grow. The young root or _____ appears first and grows downwards by _____, providing _____ and absorbing water and minerals for the seedling. The young shoot or _____ appears next. This grows upwards and eventually bursts through the soil. The first _____ leaves develop and the seedling is able to produce its own food by _____.

2 How would you attempt to prove that germination is controlled by enzymes?

3·16 Vegetative propagation

Objectives

▢ To understand that plants can reproduce asexually

▢ To understand some of the benefits of vegetative propagation

▢ To describe examples of vegetative propagation

Sexual reproduction provides variation

The plant life cycle shown on page 186 shows sexual reproduction, which depends on the fusion of male and female **gametes**. Sexual reproduction consumes energy that otherwise could be used by the parent plant. However, it also leads to **variation** (see page 218). Sexual reproduction occurs in all advanced organisms.

Asexual reproduction can be advantageous

Plants arrive in new locations by the dispersal of seeds. There are occasions, however, when a plant would benefit from simply producing many copies of itself. For example:

▢ When a single plant arrives in a new habitat it can occupy this habitat if many copies can be produced quickly.

▢ When a plant is well suited to its habitat, any variation might be a disadvantage.

Many plants are able to reproduce **asexually** – without gametes, pollination, fertilisation and dispersal. This form of asexual reproduction, also known as **vegetative propagation**, is outlined in the diagram below.

Vegetative propagation has certain features.

▢ The new miniature plant is formed by copying cells from the parent plant (by **mitosis**, page 204), and has characteristics identical to its parent.

▢ The miniature plant can be nourished by the parent plant until it is established enough to live independently.

▢ The plant does not need to produce any flowers.

Many different methods of vegetative propagation happen naturally. Two common examples are described in the diagrams opposite – the formation of **runners** and **stem tubers**. As well as being organs of vegetative propagation, tubers also store food when photosynthesis is easy. The food can then be used for growth at the beginning of the following year when photosynthesis might be slower. This allows the plant to **perennate**, or live on from year to year. For this reason, tubers are also known as **organs of perennation**.

Vegetative propagation does not depend on any external agent for pollination or dispersal.

No need for complex germination process. All new plants are in a habitat which should provide good growing conditions. Plant does not need to produce large numbers of seeds, many of which would be wasted.

Energy and raw materials are not used to produce special reproductive structures (i.e. flowers). Vegetative propagation is like an extension of normal growth.

Young plant must compete with parent for light, water and nutrients. This may not be a problem if the parent plant dies after.

Bud grows from parent plant, often at ground level.

Bud develops into complete miniature plant – leaves, stem and roots are all present.

Young plant breaks away from parent and can live an independent life.

The principles of vegetative propagation.

Tuber in winter

Scar where potato was attached to shoot

New shoot beginning to develop – these make the 'eyes' on the potato.

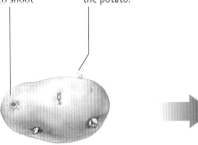

These 'seed' potatoes are allowed to produce short shoots, then planted to produce a new potato crop. They are not true 'seeds' as they were not formed by fertilisation.

Plant in summer

The shoots have developed enough to photosynthesise. They send food compounds along underground shoots, the tips of which swell to form 'new' potatoes.

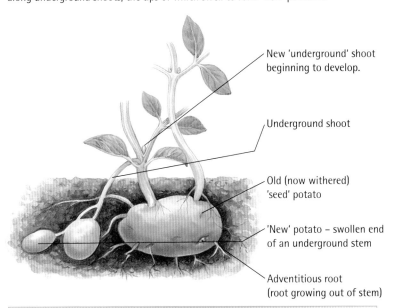

New 'underground' shoot beginning to develop.

Underground shoot

Old (now withered) 'seed' potato

'New' potato – swollen end of an underground stem

Adventitious root (root growing out of stem)

The 'new' potatoes are identical to the parent and to one another so they are all susceptible to the same diseases. The Irish famines of the nineteenth century resulted from blight fungus infecting almost all of the potato crop.

Bud on strawberry runner – can develop into another plant if it touches the ground and forms roots.

Plants are smaller the further they are from the parent plant since:
- they are younger
- they are 'last in line' for food compounds transported along the runner.

Terminal (end) bud on runner

Each parent plant produces runners so a dense patch of plants forms, crowding out other competitor species. Once the plants are established some vertical shoots produce flowers and, eventually, fruits.

Lateral (sideways) shoot is called a runner. Eventually the runner rots away, and the new plant exists independently.

Where the runner touches the ground it forms **adventitious roots**. Soon normal leafy shoots develop from the rooted runner.

Vegetative propagation. Potatoes reproduce using tubers; strawberries use lateral shoots called runners.

Sexual and asexual reproduction compared

Sexual reproduction and vegetative propagation both have advantages and disadvantages. Many plants make the best of both worlds, and reproduce both sexually and asexually.

1 Name two food compounds that could be detected in the transport system of a strawberry runner.

2 Suggest two storage compounds that would be present in a potato tuber. Describe simple chemical tests that would allow you to confirm their presence.

3 The two examples of vegetative propagation shown above both rely on shoots growing away from the parent plant. Given a razor blade, a red water-soluble dye and a microscope, describe how you would show that these underground or sideways-growing structures are in fact shoots and not roots.

3·17 Artificial propagation

- To understand some of the benefits of vegetative propagation
- To appreciate how humans have exploited vegetative propagation

People use their knowledge of vegetative propagation to increase stocks of plants. Sometimes they use natural methods, for example by dividing up clumps of bulbs, or sometimes they carry out a process that would not happen in nature, such as taking cuttings from a particularly desirable plant. **Artificial propagation** is a form of plant propagation that would not occur naturally (in plants living in the wild). Stem cuttings and tissue culture are both examples of artificial propagation. These techniques are outlined in the diagrams below and opposite.

Clones and cloning

The most obvious feature of vegetative propagation is that there is no mixing of genetic material from different parents. The offspring are therefore identical to one another. A population of genetically identical individuals produced from a single parent is called a **clone**. Members of the clone have the same characteristics as the parent, which is very useful if the parent plant is well suited to particular environments, or is desirable to consumers. In natural conditions a clone may be at a disadvantage since any environmental change – a disease for example – could eliminate *all* members of the clone if the parent had no resistance to this change. Despite these disadvantages, artificial propagation and the production of clones is a very widely used practice in modern agriculture and horticulture.

A **cutting** is produced by cutting off a short piece of stem just below a point where a leaf joins the stem. The cutting is trimmed so that only two or three leaves remain.

Many ornamental house plants are produced using stem or leaf cuttings. The compost is usually replaced with a jelly containing minerals, hormones to stimulate rooting and growth, and sometimes glucose to provide an energy source for the developing roots.

The cuttings are put into a rooting compost, and then covered with a clear polythene cover. This:
- prevents excessive loss of water (which cannot be replaced without roots)
- prevents entry of fungal spores which might infect the cuttings.

The cut end of the stem is dipped into **hormone rooting powder.** This promotes the growth of new cells into roots.

New leaves begin to develop where old leaves used to be.

Roots develop from cut end of stem.

Geraniums can be artificially propagated by stem cuttings.

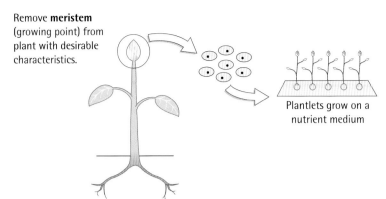

Remove **meristem** (growing point) from plant with desirable characteristics.

The tissue is sterilised (with bleach solution) and broken up into cells. The cell walls are removed (using the enzyme cellulase) to produce **protoplasts** (plant cells without cell walls). These can be treated with plant hormones to make them divide.

Plantlets grow on a nutrient medium

This method is ideal for plants that are to be transported. For example, rubber 'trees' can be started in Britain then transferred to Malaysia for planting.

Tissue culture allows many individuals to be grown in a small space.

Auxin concentration / parts per million	Initial length of stem piece / mm	Final length of stem piece / mm	Change of length / mm	Percentage change in length
0	20	21		
1	20	22		
2	20	23		
5	20	25		
0	20	26		

A group of students used some geranium stems for an experiment on auxins. If a section of stem is placed in auxin solution, the effect of this plant hormone can be detected by measuring the change in length of the stem.

1 **a** Why is it important to measure the pieces of stem before they are placed in the auxin solution?

b It is not important that the pieces of stem were removed from the solution after *exactly* 24 hours, but it is important that they each spent *exactly* the same amount of time in the solution. Why?

The results obtained are given in the table above.

c **i** Copy the table and complete the final two columns.

ii Plot a graph to illustrate the effect of auxin concentration on stem length.

iii The diagrams show a piece of stem before and after floating in another auxin solution.

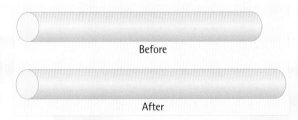

Before

After

Use the diagram and your graph to calculate the concentration of this auxin solution.

2 Auxins can be used in rooting powders. The diagrams on the right show the stages of an investigation using rooting powder.

a Suggest why the piece of plant stem was split before it was placed in rooting powder (stage 2).

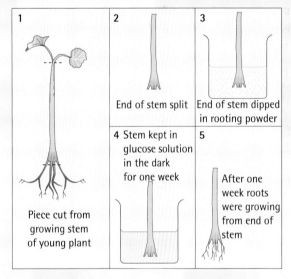

1 Piece cut from growing stem of young plant

2 End of stem split

3 End of stem dipped in rooting powder

4 Stem kept in glucose solution in the dark for one week

5 After one week roots were growing from end of stem

b Suggest why the piece of plant stem needed to be kept in glucose solution in stage 4.

c Redraw stage 1 to suggest how the students could have modified their technique if they wished to demonstrate the process of artificial propagation.

d Suggest one advantage and one disadvantage of an artificial propagation technique such as this one.

e When stem sections like these are placed in growing solution, they are usually surrounded by a clear plastic container. Why are they enclosed in this way? Why is it important that the container is clear?

3·18 Variation and inheritance

Objectives

- To know that there is variation between individuals of the same species
- To appreciate that some differences are inherited whereas others are acquired during the life of the individual
- To understand that genetics has a major impact on the lives of humans
- To understand that chromosomes, located in the nucleus, carry information about inherited characteristics

Inherited and acquired characteristics

Living organisms vary in many ways. For example, humans all have the same general shape and the same set of body organs, but some features differ from one person to the next, such as height, weight, eye and hair colour, shape of nose, language, knowledge and skills. These are examples of **individual variation**.

Some of these features that vary from person to person may be inherited from the parents. Examples of these **inherited** (or **hereditary**) **characteristics** include the tendency to develop some diseases, such as cystic fibrosis, and the permanent colour of the skin. Some, such as a temporary suntan or a scar, cannot be inherited – these are called **acquired characteristics**. Many acquired characteristics can be changed (for example, body mass can be changed by an adjustment to the diet). Inherited characteristics cannot usually be altered (except temporarily).

Genetics

The study of inherited characteristics, and the way they are passed on from one generation to another, is called **genetics**. Our knowledge of the subject of genetics is expanding extremely rapidly, and this knowledge depends upon our understanding of the molecule DNA (see page 202).

When we study inheritance we are looking for answers to several important questions:

- What is a characteristic? Why does a cell or organism develop a certain characteristic?

- How can characteristics be passed on accurately from one cell to another?
- How are the characteristics of two different organisms combined at fertilisation?
- How do characteristics vary from one organism to another and from one generation to another?

Answers to questions such as these help us in many ways, for example to increase our understanding about genetic diseases, and to develop techniques to 'add' desirable characteristics to our domestic animals and plants.

Sexual reproduction and inheritance

The production of offspring by sexual reproduction always involves the **production of gametes** and **fertilisation** (see page 165). In sexual reproduction:

- The only part of the male gamete (sperm in mammals) that goes to form the zygote is the **nucleus**.
- The gametes are formed by **cell division**.
- The young organism develops from a single fertilised egg by **cell division**.

So, if we are to understand how characteristics are passed on during reproduction, we should look carefully at the structure of the nucleus, and how the nucleus behaves during cell division.

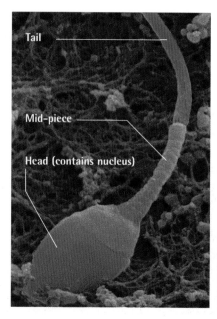

Tail

Mid-piece

Head (contains nucleus)

Human sperm × 1000. Only the 'head' (containing the nucleus) enters the egg at the time of fertilisation.

The contents of the nucleus

Special stains can be used to show up the contents of the nucleus. If the cell is not actually dividing, these contents are rather unclear but as the cell begins to divide the contents show up as a series of thread-like structures. As the threads shorten they take up the stain. For this reason they were called **chromosomes** (literally 'coloured bodies'). The structure of a chromosome is outlined below.

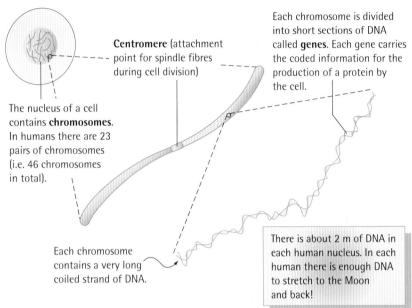

Centromere (attachment point for spindle fibres during cell division)

Each chromosome is divided into short sections of DNA called **genes**. Each gene carries the coded information for the production of a protein by the cell.

The nucleus of a cell contains **chromosomes**. In humans there are 23 pairs of chromosomes (i.e. 46 chromosomes in total).

Each chromosome contains a very long coiled strand of DNA.

There is about 2 m of DNA in each human nucleus. In each human there is enough DNA to stretch to the Moon and back!

The structure of a chromosome.

A great deal of evidence suggests that the chromosomes carry **genetic information** – the information that gives the particular characteristics to a cell:

- If sections of chromosome are transferred from one cell to another, the characteristics of the recipient cell change.
- If chromosomes are deliberately damaged, the characteristics of the cell change.
- In some cells, the chromosomes are seen to swell when proteins are being manufactured in the cell.
- The only difference between the nuclei of male and female cells is the presence of one particular chromosome (see page 216). (Males and females certainly have different characteristics!)

1 Look around your class. This group of humans shows many variations between individuals. Suggest one variation that is inherited and one that is acquired.

2 Find three newspaper articles that include the words 'gene', 'genetic' or 'inheritance' in their headings. Summarise one of the articles in three or four sentences.

3 a What is a chromosome? What evidence is there that chromosomes carry genetic information?

   b When can chromosomes be observed? Explain why this is possible.

A **karyotype** – a photograph of human chromosomes arranged in pairs. The 23rd pair is an X and a Y chromosome – this cell comes from a male.

3·19 DNA, proteins and the characteristics of organisms

Objectives
▶ To know that cell characteristics depend on proteins
▶ To understand the principle of the genetic code
▶ To be able to describe the replication of DNA

Characteristics depend on proteins

It has been discovered that the characteristics that a cell or organism possesses depend on the **proteins** that the cell can manufacture.

For cells to specialise in the many different ways that they do, they must make different proteins. The instructions as to which proteins should be manufactured at any one time in a cell are carried as **genes** on the **chromosomes**. Chemical tests have shown that chromosomes are largely composed of the enormous molecule called **deoxyribonucleic acid** or DNA for short. In other words:

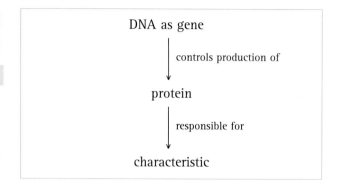

DNA as gene

↓ controls production of

protein

↓ responsible for

characteristic

DNA carries its instructions as coded messages using just four different chemical compounds called **nucleotide bases** or organic bases (see page 39). The names of the bases are shown in the diagram below, but you only need to remember their initial letters (A, T, G and C) to understand how the code works.

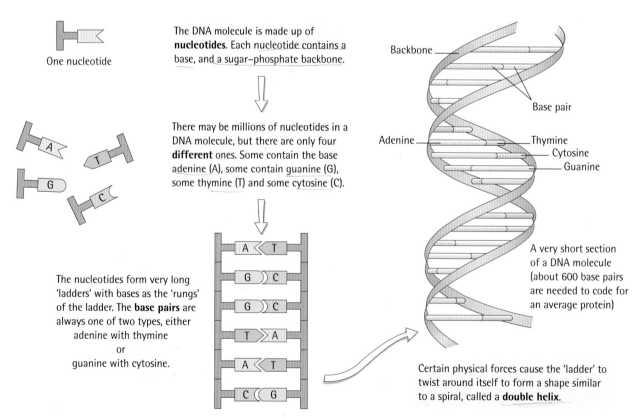

One nucleotide

The DNA molecule is made up of **nucleotides**. Each nucleotide contains a base, and a sugar–phosphate backbone.

There may be millions of nucleotides in a DNA molecule, but there are only four **different** ones. Some contain the base adenine (A), some contain guanine (G), some thymine (T) and some cytosine (C).

The nucleotides form very long 'ladders' with bases as the 'rungs' of the ladder. The **base pairs** are always one of two types, either adenine with thymine
or
guanine with cytosine.

Backbone

Base pair

Adenine

Thymine
Cytosine
Guanine

A very short section of a DNA molecule (about 600 base pairs are needed to code for an average protein)

Certain physical forces cause the 'ladder' to twist around itself to form a shape similar to a spiral, called a **double helix**.

The structure of DNA. The exact length of the DNA molecule is known only for the simplest of organisms, such as bacteria. It is very important to remember that: **adenine** always pairs with **thymine**, and **guanine** always pairs with **cytosine**.

Passing the messages to the ribosomes

This coded information in the genes is located on the chromosomes, which are in the nucleus. You may remember that the protein-manufacturing stations, called **ribosomes**, are found outside the nucleus, in the cytoplasm. How does the code pass from the nucleus to the ribosomes in the cytoplasm? It is carried by another type of nucleic acid, called **messenger RNA (mRNA)**.

Transcription and translation

The mRNA is made by a process called **transcription**, which literally means 'cross writing'. The base sequence in the DNA is **transcribed** into another base sequence in the mRNA, using very similar base pairing rules to those used in the replication of DNA. There is one important difference – RNA never contains the base thymine (T). Thymine is replaced by a fifth base called **uracil (U)** so instead of the base pair A–T used in DNA replication, in transcription we have the base pair A–U.

Once it has been made, the mRNA leaves the nucleus and travels to the ribosomes. The sequence of bases in the mRNA is used to build up a sequence of amino acids into a protein in the ribosome. This process is called **translation** – it involves rewriting the language of bases into a language of amino acids. The processes of transcription and translation are outlined in the diagram below.

Summary of replication, transcription and translation

It is quite easy to confuse the various processes involving nucleic acids. Remember:

- Replication makes a DNA copy, using DNA.
- Transcription makes mRNA, using DNA.
- Translation makes protein, using mRNA.

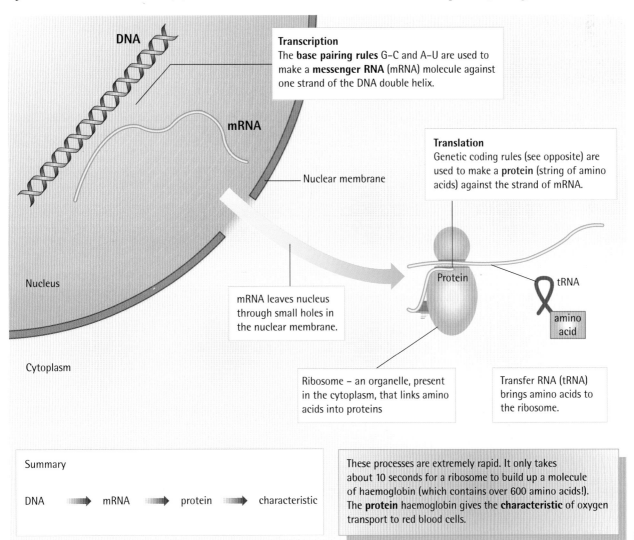

DNA

Transcription
The **base pairing rules** G–C and A–U are used to make a **messenger RNA** (mRNA) molecule against one strand of the DNA double helix.

mRNA

Translation
Genetic coding rules (see opposite) are used to make a **protein** (string of amino acids) against the strand of mRNA.

Nuclear membrane

Nucleus

mRNA leaves nucleus through small holes in the nuclear membrane.

Cytoplasm

Protein

tRNA

amino acid

Ribosome – an organelle, present in the cytoplasm, that links amino acids into proteins

Transfer RNA (tRNA) brings amino acids to the ribosome.

Summary

DNA ➡ mRNA ➡ protein ➡ characteristic

These processes are extremely rapid. It only takes about 10 seconds for a ribosome to build up a molecule of haemoglobin (which contains over 600 amino acids!). The **protein** haemoglobin gives the **characteristic** of oxygen transport to red blood cells.

How information in DNA codes for characteristics in cells.

3·20 Cell division

Objectives

- To understand why it is necessary to copy genetic material accurately
- To know that copying division is called mitosis, and results in cells with an identical number and type of chromosomes as their parent cells
- To know how chromosomes behave during mitosis
- To know where mitosis takes place in the bodies of mammals and flowering plants
- To understand the need for a special cell division in the formation of haploid gametes

Mitosis is copying division

Characteristics are transmitted from one generation of cells to the next. For this to happen, the chromosomes must be accurately copied and passed on when cells divide. Each chromosome has a partner, forming **homologous pairs**. Both chromosomes in an homologous pair have the same genes in the same positions. The diagram below shows cell division in which the new cells are copies of the parent cell – **mitosis**.

Mitosis is for growth

Both plants and animals grow by mitosis.

- In animals each tissue provides its own new cells when they are needed, e.g. liver produces liver cells.
- In plants cell division in the **cambium** increases the plant girth (the plant gets thicker), and cell division in the **meristems** at the tips of the roots and shoots leads to an increase in length (see page 88).

A **zygote** results from the fusion of egg and sperm.

All cells contain two sets of chromosomes e.g. human body cells have two sets of 23, a total of 46 chromosomes.

DNA is replicated exactly.

For simplicity, only one homologous pair of chromosomes is shown here.

Each **chromosome** now becomes two identical **chromatids** joined at the **centromere**.

Centromere

Chromosomes become attached to a **spindle** (fibres which run from one **pole** to the other).

The individual chromosomes line up at the **equator** (midline) of the cell.

Mitosis – copying division which produces identical daughter cells

The centromere divides and spindle fibres shorten so that the two chromatids in each chromosome separate. They move to opposite ends of the cell.

An adult human has about 50 billion cells, all containing the same genetic information as the zygote.

The original cell has now become two daughter cells:
- identical to one another
- identical to parent cell
- same number of chromosomes as parent cell.

The cell membrane 'pinches in' to separate the two sets of chromatids into two cells.

Mitosis – copying division. Note that cell division is a continuous process. Although the diagram shows mitosis in a series of stages, in reality each stage merges into the next one.

Development of organisms and the continuity of life

Meiosis is reduction division

During sexual reproduction (see page 165) two gametes fuse to form the zygote. The gametes must contain only one set of chromosomes, otherwise the zygote would have twice as many chromosomes as it needed! This principle is outlined in the diagram on the right.

Each cell of an organism has a fixed number of chromosomes within the nucleus. The number of chromosomes in a normal body cell is the **diploid number** (or $2n$); the number of chromosomes in a gamete is the **haploid number** (or n). Fertilisation is the **fusion of haploid gametes to restore the diploid number in the zygote**. Gametes are formed by a type of cell division called **meiosis** or **reduction division**, shown in the diagram below.

Meiosis only happens in the gamete-producing organs: the testes and the ovaries in animals, and the pollen sacs of the stamens and the ovules in the ovary in plants.

Reduction division ensures that the number of chromosomes in sexually reproducing organisms is kept constant.

Adult cells contain chromosomes in **homologous pairs**.

($2n$)

Gametes must contain single chromosomes, **one** from each homologous pair.

(n) (n)

Offspring's cells contain chromosomes in homologous pairs. Each pair contains one chromosome from the mother and one from the father.

($2n$)

Meiosis is called reduction division because it halves the number of chromosomes in cells.

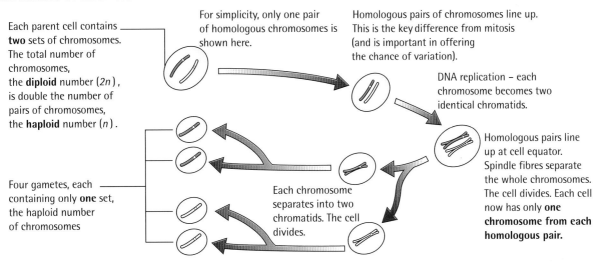

Each parent cell contains **two** sets of chromosomes. The total number of chromosomes, the **diploid** number ($2n$), is double the number of pairs of chromosomes, the **haploid** number (n).

For simplicity, only one pair of homologous chromosomes is shown here.

Homologous pairs of chromosomes line up. This is the key difference from mitosis (and is important in offering the chance of variation).

DNA replication – each chromosome becomes two identical chromatids.

Homologous pairs line up at cell equator. Spindle fibres separate the whole chromosomes. The cell divides. Each cell now has only **one chromosome from each homologous pair.**

Each chromosome separates into two chromatids. The cell divides.

Four gametes, each containing only **one** set, the haploid number of chromosomes

1 Cells in bone marrow undergo mitosis. Some of these cells become red blood cells, to replace those lost as they wear out. A typical red blood cell lasts for 120 days before it is removed from the circulation.
   a Suggest why red blood cells last for a short time.
   b Which organ removes red blood cells from blood?
   c This organ stores the main metal ion that forms part of the red blood cell. Which ion is this, and what molecule is it a part of inside the red blood cell?

   d The human circulation contains about 5 dm^3 of blood. Each dm^3 of blood contains 5 000 000 red blood cells. (1 dm^3 = 1 000 000 mm^3.)
   i Calculate how many red blood cells there are in the human circulation.
   ii The total number of red blood cells is replaced every 120 days. Calculate how many cells are replaced each day. How many are replaced each second?

Development of organisms and the continuity of life

Objectives
- To recall that living organisms differ from one another
- To distinguish between continuous and discontinuous variation

Living organisms differ from one another. Even members of the same species have slightly different sets of characteristics. Some of these differences are inherited from their parents, and others are the result of the environment. Scientists who study variation are interested in questions such as:

- Are all of the variations of the same type?
- How do the variations come about?
- How are the variations in characteristics passed on from parents to offspring?
- What is the importance of these variations?

There are two types of variation – **discontinuous variation** and **continuous variation**.

Discontinuous variation
Characteristics that show discontinuous variation have several features:

- An organism either has the characteristic or it doesn't have it. There is no range of these characteristics between extremes. An organism can easily be placed into definite categories, and there is no disagreement about the categories.
- These characteristics are usually **qualitative** – they cannot be measured.
- They are the result of genes only – they are not affected by the environment.

An example of discontinuous variation is shown in the diagram above right.

Continuous variation
Characteristics that show continuous variation have different features:

- Every organism within one species shows the characteristic, but to a different extent. The characteristic can have any value within a range. Different scientists might well disagree about which category any single organism falls into.

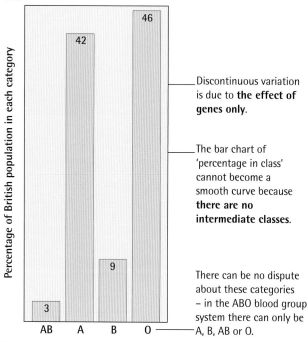

Discontinuous variation is due to **the effect of genes only**.

The bar chart of 'percentage in class' cannot become a smooth curve because **there are no intermediate classes**.

There can be no dispute about these categories – in the ABO blood group system there can only be A, B, AB or O.

Human blood groups are an example of discontinuous variation. Another example is gender – you are either male or female.

- These characteristics are usually **quantitative** – they can be measured.
- They result from several genes acting together, or from both genes and the environment.

An example of continuous variation is shown in the diagram at the top of the opposite page.

Characteristics can be both discontinuous and continuous
Some characteristics are difficult to classify as either discontinuous or continuous variation. Human hair colour, for example, appears in a range from black to blond with many intermediate colours (it shows continuous variation as a result of the involvement of many genes). However, the gene for red hair is masked by every other hair colour gene (which gives a discontinuous situation – hair is either red or not red). Eye colour can be identified as brown or not brown, which would classify it as a discontinuous variation, or it can be put into a range of many intermediate classes, which would make it a continuous variation. A simple guideline is: 'if it can be measured and given a numerical value, it is a continuous variation'.

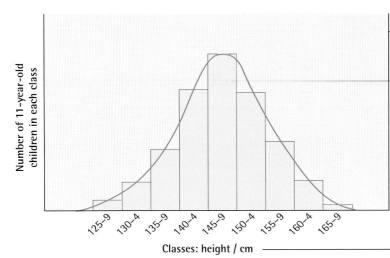

Number of 11-year-old children in each class

Classes: height / cm

125–9 130–4 135–9 140–4 145–9 150–4 155–9 160–4 165–9

Continuous variation is due to the combined effects of **genes** and the **environment**.

The bar chart of 'number in class' can be redrawn as a smooth curve because there are **many possible intermediate classes between the two extremes** (the curve becomes smoother if the classes become smaller, e.g. 1 cm rather than 5 cm).

There could be a dispute about the boundary of these classes. One observer might use, for example, 127–31, 132–6, etc. rather than the boundaries shown.

Human height is an example of continuous variation. Other examples include quantitative characteristics such as chest circumference, body mass and hand span.

Francis Galton was a cousin of Charles Darwin. He investigated intelligence as an example of phenotype, and believed that 'nature' (genotype) was much more important than 'nurture' (environment). He suggested that:

a children from families where the parents were uneducated would always have low intelligence

b females were less intelligent than males – he suggested the 'ideal' child would be born to 'a man of genius and a woman of wealth'.

His ideas have rightly been updated, but he does deserve some credit – his studies showed that identical twins were genetically the same.

Phenotype and genotype

Variations in characteristics allow us to recognise different organisms, and to place them in different categories. The overall appearance of an organism is a result of the characteristics that it has inherited from its parents and the characteristics that result from the effects of the environment. The following equation summarises this:

Phenotype	=	**genotype**	+	**effects of the environment**
the observable characteristics of an organism		the full set of genes it possesses		

Some characteristics result from both genes and environment. For example, a bean seedling has the genes to develop chlorophyll (and turn green) but it won't do so unless it receives enough light. A young mammal has the genes to develop a rigid bony skeleton, but it won't do so unless it receives calcium in its diet.

1 Copy and complete the following paragraph.
Variation occurs in two forms, _____, which shows clear-cut separation between groups showing this variation, and _____, in which there are many intermediate forms between the extremes of the characteristic. The first of these is the result of _____ alone, whilst the second is also affected by _____ factors. The sum of the genes that an organism contains is called its _____ and the total of all its observable characteristics is called the _____.
The two are related in a simple equation: _____ equals _____ plus _____.

2 Which of the following is an example of discontinuous variation?
Body mass, chest circumference, blood group, hairstyle, height
Explain:
a why you chose one of these characteristics
b why you rejected the others.

3 Two students in the first year of secondary school were carrying out a mathematical investigation. They decided to measure the heights of all of the other students in their class. The results are shown in the table below.

a Plot these results as a bar chart.
b Does this illustrate continuous or discontinuous variation? Explain your answer.
c Suggest one characteristic that the students could have recorded to illustrate the other kind of variation.

Height category / cm	Number in category
121–125	2
126–130	4
131–135	9
136–140	6
141–145	4
146–150	1

3·22 Causes of variation

Objectives

- To identify mutation and sexual reproduction as sources of variation
- To understand that mutations may involve whole chromosomes or genes within them
- To recognise that environmental factors may increase the likelihood of mutation

Permanent changes to the phenotype

Permanent characteristics that can be inherited are due to the genetic make-up of an organism. This may be altered, thereby increasing variation, as a result of **mutation** or of **sexual reproduction**.

Mutation

A **mutation** is a change in the type or amount of DNA and can arise because of:

- mistakes in the copying of DNA as cells get ready to divide – pairing with the 'incorrect' base
- damage to the DNA – some environmental factor might alter the bases present in the DNA
- uneven distribution of chromosomes during the division of cells.

Chromosome mutations occur when cell division fails to work with complete accuracy. For example, when human gametes are formed each gamete should receive 23 chromosomes. Occasionally an error occurs. The consequences of chromosome mutations are often serious. One example is outlined in the diagram below.

Gene mutations occur when part of the DNA on a single chromosome is changed. As a result a defective protein may be produced, or no protein at all. This can lead to a considerable change in a characteristic. There are many examples, including **sickle cell anaemia**, shown opposite.

Beneficial mutations

Not all mutations are harmful. Many of them give benefits to the organisms that have them, and aid adaptation to the environment (see page 220). Some may cause harm in one environment but be a benefit in another! Sickle cell anaemia is an example of this (see page 215).

Development of organisms and the continuity of life

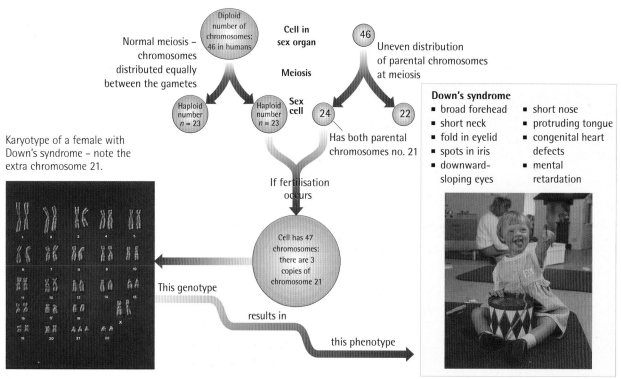

Karyotype of a female with Down's syndrome – note the extra chromosome 21.

Chromosome mutation and Down's syndrome

208

Normal gene for haemoglobin

Normal mRNA made by transcription

Normal haemoglobin made by translation

Haemoglobin gene has mutated – one base has changed

Faulty mRNA made by transcription

Faulty haemoglobin made by translation

Weakness
Aching joints
Poor circulation

Sickle cell anaemia (A sickle has a curved blade for cutting grass.)

Radiation can increase mutation rates

Mutations occur spontaneously (for no apparent reason), though they are very rare events. However, a number of factors (called **mutagens**) can increase the rate of mutation. Important mutagens are:

- **radiation** – gamma, ultraviolet and X-radiation can all damage DNA and so cause mutations
- **chemicals** – tars in tobacco smoke, high concentrations of some preservatives and some plant control hormones can cause mutation.

Mutations may be linked with cancer. A mutagen that causes uncontrolled cell division is called a **carcinogen** ('cancer maker').

Sexual reproduction leads to variation

Sexual reproduction mixes up genetic material in three ways, as shown below, producing new genotypes and so variations in phenotype.

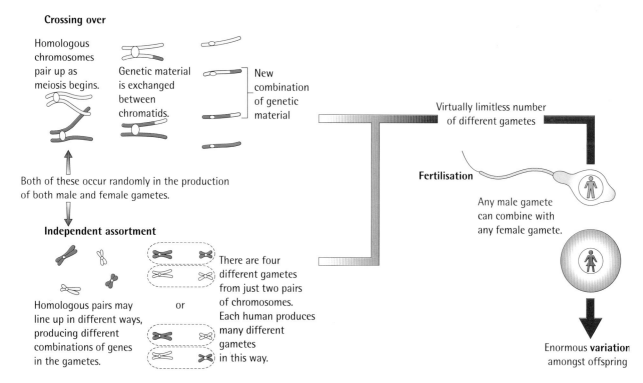

Crossing over

Homologous chromosomes pair up as meiosis begins.

Genetic material is exchanged between chromatids.

New combination of genetic material

Both of these occur randomly in the production of both male and female gametes.

Independent assortment

Homologous pairs may line up in different ways, producing different combinations of genes in the gametes.

or

There are four different gametes from just two pairs of chromosomes. Each human produces many different gametes in this way.

Virtually limitless number of different gametes

Fertilisation

Any male gamete can combine with any female gamete.

Enormous **variation** amongst offspring

Crossing over, **independent assortment** and **fertilisation** all lead to variation. There is very little chance that any two gametes from one individual will be identical. The combined effects of mutation and sexual reproduction lead to enormous variation between individuals.

1 What is a gene mutation? Give an example of:
   a a harmful
   b a beneficial
   gene mutation.

2 What is a carcinogen?
   Give two examples of carcinogens.

3 How does sexual reproduction lead to variation amongst members of a population?

Development of organisms and the continuity of life

Inheritance

Objectives

☞ To recall the features of sexual and asexual reproduction

☞ To be able to define the terms gene and allele, homozygous and heterozygous, dominant and recessive

Reproduction: a reminder

Living organisms can pass on their characteristics to the next generation (**reproduce**) in two ways (p. 164).

Asexual reproduction:

☞ involves only one parent organism

☞ all the characteristics of this one parent are passed on to all of the offspring

☞ many organisms reproduce asexually when conditions are favourable (e.g. when there is plenty of food), and build up their numbers quickly.

Sexual reproduction:

☞ requires two organisms of the same species, one male and one female

☞ each individual produces sex cells (**gametes**)

☞ sexual reproduction always involves **fertilisation** – the fusion of the gametes

☞ offspring receives some genes from each parent, so shows a mixture of parental characteristics.

In sexual reproduction, a mixture of genes is passed from parents to offspring. This handing down of genes is not random, and there are certain rules that govern how genes will be passed on and which ones will show up in the offspring.

The inheritance of characteristics

Chromosomes carry genetic information as a series of **genes**, such as the gene for eye colour, the gene for earlobe shape and the gene for hair texture. Each chromosome in the nucleus of a diploid organism has a partner that carries the same genes. Such a pair of chromosomes is called an **homologous pair**.

Each chromosome in a pair may carry alternative forms of the same gene. These alternative forms are called **alleles**. For example, the gene for eye colour has alleles that code for blue or brown. If both alternative alleles are present in a particular cell nucleus, then the cell is **heterozygous** for that characteristic. On the other hand, if the nucleus carries the same allele on both members of the homologous pair, then the cell is **homozygous**. The meaning of these genetic terms is outlined in the diagram at the top of the next page.

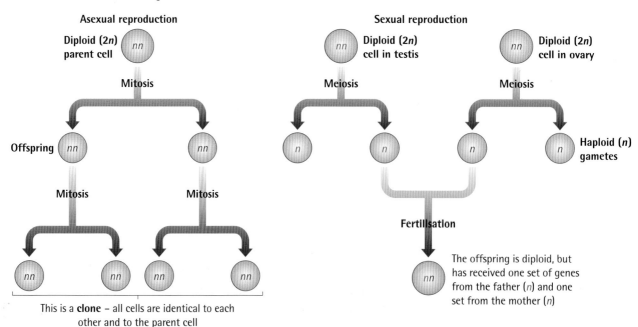

Organisms can reproduce asexually or sexually.

210

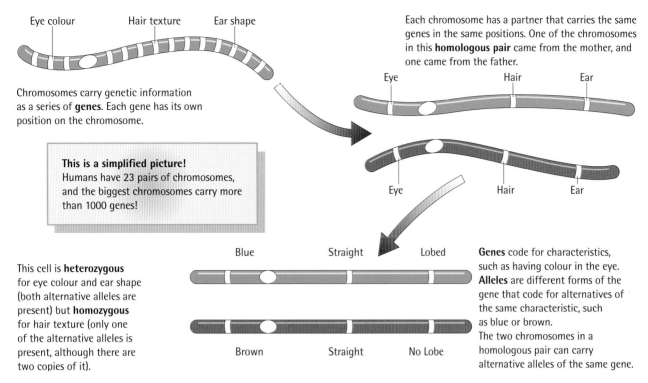

Eye colour   Hair texture   Ear shape

Chromosomes carry genetic information as a series of **genes**. Each gene has its own position on the chromosome.

This is a simplified picture!
Humans have 23 pairs of chromosomes, and the biggest chromosomes carry more than 1000 genes!

Each chromosome has a partner that carries the same genes in the same positions. One of the chromosomes in this **homologous pair** came from the mother, and one came from the father.

Eye   Hair   Ear

Eye   Hair   Ear

Blue   Straight   Lobed

Brown   Straight   No Lobe

This cell is **heterozygous** for eye colour and ear shape (both alternative alleles are present) but **homozygous** for hair texture (only one of the alternative alleles is present, although there are two copies of it).

Diploid organisms have homologous pairs of chromosomes in the nucleus.

Genes code for characteristics, such as having colour in the eye. **Alleles** are different forms of the gene that code for alternatives of the same characteristic, such as blue or brown.
The two chromosomes in a homologous pair can carry alternative alleles of the same gene.

In a heterozygous cell, when the members of the homologous pair separate during meiosis the gametes will contain different alleles. This means that when gametes fuse at fertilisation, the resulting zygote may have a number of different possible allele combinations. The production of gametes and the formation of different zygotes in this way are explained in the diagram below.

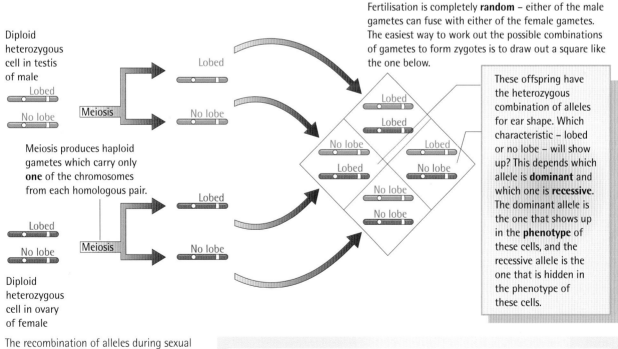

Diploid heterozygous cell in testis of male

Lobed
No lobe

Meiosis

Lobed
No lobe

Meiosis produces haploid gametes which carry only **one** of the chromosomes from each homologous pair.

Lobed
No lobe

Meiosis

Lobed
No lobe

Diploid heterozygous cell in ovary of female

Fertilisation is completely **random** – either of the male gametes can fuse with either of the female gametes. The easiest way to work out the possible combinations of gametes to form zygotes is to draw out a square like the one below.

Lobed
Lobed
No lobe   Lobed
Lobed   No lobe
No lobe
No lobe

These offspring have the heterozygous combination of alleles for ear shape. Which characteristic – lobed or no lobe – will show up? This depends which allele is **dominant** and which one is **recessive**. The dominant allele is the one that shows up in the **phenotype** of these cells, and the recessive allele is the one that is hidden in the phenotype of these cells.

The recombination of alleles during sexual reproduction gives rise to a great variation among offspring. This leads to the evolution of new strains, races and, eventually, new species.

1 Define the terms homologous pair, heterozygous and homozygous.

2 What is the difference between a gene and an allele?

3 What is a meant by a dominant allele?

3·24 Studying patterns of inheritance

Objectives

- To understand the method for describing genetic crosses
- To know the result of crosses involving two heterozygous parents
- To understand the principle of the test cross

Scientists called **geneticists** study the inheritance of characteristics by carrying out breeding experiments. There is a conventional pattern for describing the results of such experiments – a sort of genetic shorthand, shown in the example below.

At fertilisation, any male gamete can fuse with any female gamete

Drawing out chromosomes carrying alleles of genes is very time-consuming. Geneticists write out the stages of crosses using symbols to replace the chromosomes and genes. These symbols should always be identified at the start of a cross.

> Let **B** = brown and **b** = blue.

The **capital** letter is used for the **dominant** allele.

Brown (**B**) and blue (**b**) are **alleles** of the **gene** for eye colour.

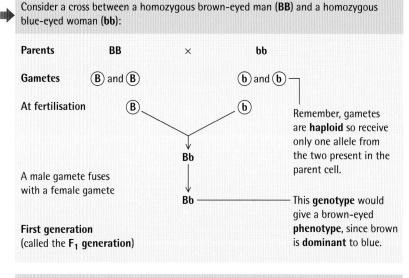

Consider a cross between a homozygous brown-eyed man (**BB**) and a homozygous blue-eyed woman (**bb**):

| Parents | BB | × | bb |

Gametes — B and B ... b and b

At fertilisation — B ... b

Remember, gametes are **haploid** so receive only one allele from the two present in the parent cell.

A male gamete fuses with a female gamete

Bb

Bb — This **genotype** would give a brown-eyed **phenotype**, since brown is **dominant** to blue.

First generation (called the **F₁ generation**)

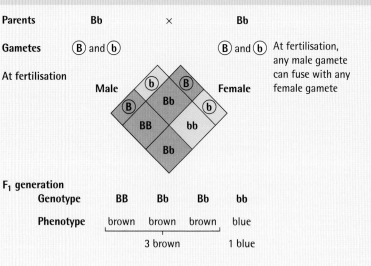

Now consider a cross between two heterozygous parents (**Bb**), i.e. with the same genotype as the F₁ above:

| Parents | Bb | × | Bb |

Gametes — B and b ... B and b

At fertilisation, any male gamete can fuse with any female gamete

F₁ generation

| | Genotype | BB | Bb | Bb | bb |
| Phenotype | brown | brown | brown | blue |

3 brown : 1 blue

The inheritance of eye colour. There are two important points about this cross.

(1) These results are **probabilities**. The offspring *should* be in the 3:1 ratio shown, but each fertilisation is random so they may not be. This ratio is more likely to be seen in very large numbers of offspring. For human families a 3:1 ratio is unlikely since very few mothers give birth to four children at one time.

(2) Every cross between the same two parents is a different event. If two heterozygous parents produce a child with blue eyes (a 1/4 probability) there is still a 1/4 probability that their next child will have blue eyes.

In theory a cross between two heterozygous parents should produce offspring in the ratio of 3 showing dominant to 1 showing recessive. This can be restated as: 'The probability of any offspring showing dominant is 3/4 or 75%; the probability of it showing recessive is 1/4 or 25%'.

Development of organisms and the continuity of life

Test cross

In the eye colour example, both of the genotypes BB and Bb give the same phenotype – brown eyes. It might be important to know whether a particular organism is homozygous or heterozygous, particularly in the breeding of domestic animals. To do this, geneticists use a **test cross** (often called a **back cross to the recessive**). The principle is outlined on the right.

The brown-eyed **phenotype** could have two different **genotypes**.

BB   To distinguish homozygous brown   Bb
from heterozygous brown, they
are each crossed to **blue**.

BB × bb	**Parents**	Bb × bb
Ⓑ or Ⓑ ⓑ or ⓑ	**Gametes**	Ⓑ or ⓑ* ⓑ or ⓑ
All **Bb**	**At fertilisation**	**Bb** or **bb**
All brown eyed	**F₁ generation**	1 brown eyed: 1 blue eyed

*The heterozygous brown can supply the **b** allele for a gamete even though it is 'hidden' in the phenotype of the diploid parent.

If **any** offspring showing the recessive characteristic result from a test cross, the parent **must** have been heterozygous.

A test cross can distinguish different genotypes with the same phenotype.

Reminder!

Ratio: dominant to recessive	Phenotypes of parents
3:1	Both heterozygous
1:1	One heterozygous, one homozygous recessive.

The results of genetic crosses are sometimes shown as a **pedigree**.

Rules for showing a pedigree ('family tree')

This line links the father and the mother

This line links the parents to their offspring

This shows the offspring from the same mother and father.

A key is used to identify different phenotypes:

○ = 'normal' female
◍ = 'affected' female
□ = 'normal' male
▨ = 'affected' male

Solving pedigrees – an example

This family tree ('pedigree') refers to the inheritance of fur colour in rabbits. Brown fur is dominant to white fur. What can you deduce about the genotype of individuals A, B and C?

- Let B = brown and b = white
- ◍ and ▨ must be bb, this is the starting point since the only certainly is that animals with the 'recessive' phenotype must have the homozygous recessive genotype.
- A must be Bb because he has brown fur but can pass on the b allele to one of his daughters (his partner must be Bb too!).
- B must be Bb for the same reason as A is.
- C must be Bb because he has brown fur but must have received the b allele from his mother.

---

1. Draw a diagram to explain how two brown-eyed parents can have a blue-eyed child.

2. Gregor Mendel suggested that a cross between two heterozygous individuals produces offspring in a ratio of 3 showing the dominant characteristic to 1 showing the recessive characteristic. Explain why such crosses rarely give an exact 3:1 ratio.

3. Use a suitable example to explain the value of a test cross.

Inherited medical conditions

There are several important medical examples of monohybrid inheritance, including albinism, Huntington's disease and sickle cell anaemia.

- **Albinism** is caused by a recessive allele. Heterozygous individuals are not affected by the condition, but they are **carriers** of the mutant, recessive allele.

  People with albinism do not produce the pigment **melanin**. This pigment normally makes skin, the iris of the eye and hair a dark colour. These people have pale skin, light hair and pink eyes (the pink is actually the blood in the retina showing up). They are very sensitive to bright light and the skin burns very easily in sunlight.

- **Huntington's disease** is caused by a **dominant** allele so that heterozygous individuals are affected by the condition. The disease affects the central nervous system. There are no symptoms until middle age, but then there is a rapid loss of coordination, leading to death.

- **Sickle cell anaemia** is a condition in which a homozygote has the disease, but a heterozygous individual may gain some benefit in certain environments (see also page 209).

Albinism is caused by a recessive allele.

Let **A** = normal allele and **a** = mutant (albino) allele.

If both parents are heterozygous (ie Aa)

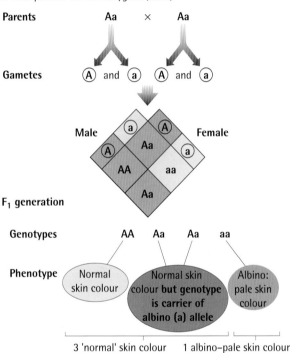

3 'normal' skin colour   1 albino–pale skin colour

Huntington's disease is caused by a dominant allele.

This condition is caused by a **dominant** allele, so a heterozygote will develop the disease.

Let **H** = allele for disease (Huntington's disease) and **h** = normal allele.

If one parent is heterozygous, and the other is homozygous normal:

Because no symptoms are shown until middle age, people with Huntington's disease may already have passed on the mutant allele to their children before knowing they have the disease.

Polydactyly (a condition in which a person has more than five fingers and toes on each hand or foot) is another example of an inherited disease caused by dominant allele. This condition is inherited in the same way as Huntington's disease, but does not have the same lethal results.

Homozygous dominant individuals are very rare. These people **do** show early symptoms, and die very young (or may be spontaneously aborted).

Sickle cell anaemia – carriers are anaemic but are resistant to malaria.

Sickle cell anaemia is caused by a recessive allele.
Let **S** = normal allele and **s** = sickle cell allele.
Consider a cross between two heterozygous parents:

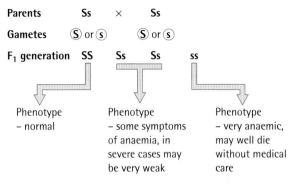

| Parents | Ss | × | Ss |

Gametes: (S) or (s)   (S) or (s)

F₁ generation: SS   Ss   Ss   ss

Phenotype – normal

Phenotype – some symptoms of anaemia, in severe cases may be very weak

Phenotype – very anaemic, may well die without medical care

But ... the **s** allele gives some resistance to malaria so in parts of the world where malaria occurs, for example equatorial Africa:

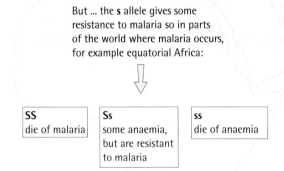

| SS | Ss | ss |
| die of malaria | some anaemia, but are resistant to malaria | die of anaemia |

The inheritance of these three conditions is described on these two pages.

Codominance

Some genes have more than two alleles. For example, the gene controlling the human ABO blood groups has three alleles, given the symbols I^A, I^B and I^O. Neither of the I^A and I^B alleles is dominant to the other, although they are both dominant to I^O. This is called **codominance**. It results in an extra phenotype when both alleles are present together. The genotypes and phenotypes are shown in the table.

Genotype	Phenotype
I^AI^A or I^AI^O	Blood group A
I^BI^B or I^BI^O	Blood group B
I^AI^B	Blood group AB
I^OI^O	Blood group O

The human blood groups are easily detected by a simple test on a blood sample.

---

1 Cystic fibrosis is a common inherited disease caused by a recessive allele. A blood test can detect this allele. A man and his wife were both found to be carriers of the cystic fibrosis allele.

a What is meant by a carrier of the allele?

b Draw a genetic diagram to show the inheritance of cystic fibrosis in any children of this couple. What is the chance that a child will have cystic fibrosis?

2 Huntington's disease (HD) is caused by a dominant allele (**H**) – the other allele (**h**) results in normal working of the central nervous system. This diagram shows how one family is affected by HD.

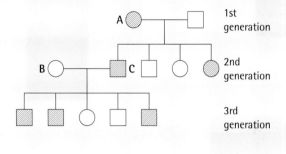

A — 1st generation

B — C — 2nd generation

3rd generation

Key

◯ = Normal female

☐ = Normal male

◉ = Affected female

▨ = Affected male

a What was the genotype of the grandmother, **A**? Explain your reasoning.

b Draw a genetic diagram to show how parents **B** and **C** passed on HD to their children.

c If parents **B** and **C** have a sixth child, what are the chances that it will have HD?

d Most serious genetic diseases are caused by recessive alleles. Explain why a dominant allele that causes a serious disease may quickly disappear from a population.

3 a Draw a genetic diagram to explain the inheritance of blood group in the Wilson family. Mr Wilson has the genotype I^AI^B and Mrs Wilson has the genotype I^OI^O.

b What is the probability of the Wilsons' first child being female?

c What is the probability of this child being female and having blood group A?

d A person with alleles I^A and I^B shows the effect of both alleles in the phenotype. What term is used to describe this?

Development of organisms and the continuity of life

3·26 Sex is determined by X and Y chromosomes

- To understand how sex is determined and inherited in humans
- To know that some genes are sex linked
- To understand the pattern of inheritance of sex-linked genes

The photograph on page 201 shows a complete set of human chromosomes (a karyotype). When all of the chromosomes are arranged in pairs, there may be two left over which differ in size and do not form an homologous pair. These are the **sex chromosomes**. The importance of these sex chromosomes is outlined below.

Note that:

- The man's sperm determines the sex of his children since the woman can only produce gametes with an X chromosome.
- The sex chromosomes carry genes concerned with sexual development, such as development of the sex organs and position of fat stores.
- The sex chromosomes also carry a few genes that code for characteristics that are not concerned with sex. Since these genes are carried on the sex chromosomes, they may show their characteristics only in one sex.

For example the gene for **colour blindness** is carried on the X chromosome. We say that colour blindness is **sex linked**.

The inheritance of sex

Each human body cell has 46 chromosomes. There are 22 **pairs** of chromosomes plus another two chromosomes which may not look alike. These are the **sex chromosomes**. Female cells have two sex chromosomes that are alike (called XX) and male cells have two sex chromosomes that are not alike (XY).

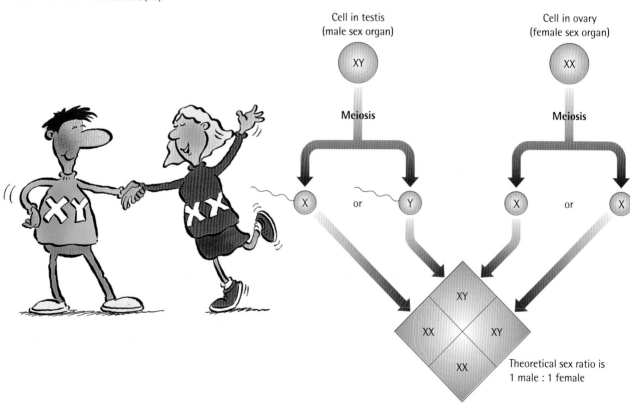

Cell in testis (male sex organ) — XY — Meiosis → X or Y

Cell in ovary (female sex organ) — XX — Meiosis → X or X

XY
XX   XY
XX

Theoretical sex ratio is 1 male : 1 female

The inheritance of sex-linked characteristics

One well-known sex-linked characteristic is **haemophilia** This is a disease in which the blood fails to clot properly. It is an X-linked condition. The inheritance of this disease is shown below. Red–green colour blindness is inherited in a similar way – there are many more males than females who cannot distinguish red from green.

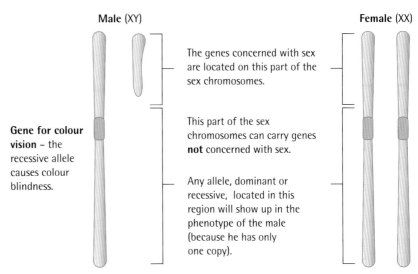

Gene for colour vision – the recessive allele causes colour blindness.

The genes concerned with sex are located on this part of the sex chromosomes.

This part of the sex chromosomes can carry genes **not** concerned with sex.

Any allele, dominant or recessive, located in this region will show up in the phenotype of the male (because he has only one copy).

Any gene carried on the sex chromosomes is sex linked.

The inheritance of haemophilia

Let **H** = normal allele and
h = mutant allele.

Because these alleles are carried on the X chromosome, it is necessary to show the sex chromosomes in the pattern of inheritance. For example,

Female

Female, so two X chromosomes

Heterozygous for haemophilia gene

Male

$X^H Y$

Male, so only **one** X chromosome

Remember – no 'haemophilia' gene on the Y chromosome.

Two unaffected parents can produce a son with haemophilia.

Note that a daughter with haemophilia ($X^h X^h$) could only be produced if **both** parents contributed X^h gametes – if the father had haemophilia. In this case his condition would be known and the daughter's condition might be expected.

Consider a cross between a carrier woman and a normal man:

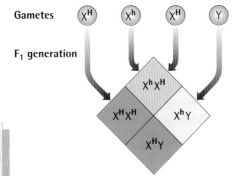

Parents $X^H X^h$ × $X^H Y$

Female – normal phenotype but a carrier of the mutant allele

Male – normal phenotype

Gametes X^H X^h X^H Y

F$_1$ generation

$X^h X^H$
$X^H X^H$ $X^h Y$
$X^H Y$

Key

Carrier female

Normal male/female

Male with haemophilia

Colour blindness

Parents $X^C X$ × $X^C X^c$

Male: not colour blind

Female: carrier

Gametes X^C Y X^C X^c

F$_1$ generation

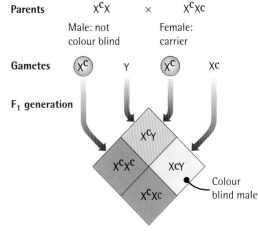

$X^C Y$
$X^C X^C$ $X^c Y$
$X^c X^c$

Colour blind male

---

1 Use a simple genetic diagram to explain why there are approximately equal numbers of male and female babies.

2 Why are males more likely to have red–green colour blindness than females? How could you explain, genetically, a colour-blind female?

3 Haemophilia is a sex-linked characteristic. The diagram above shows how the allele for haemophilia is inherited.

a Explain why the mother is described as a carrier of this condition.

b If she has one child, what is the probability of her having a haemophiliac son?

3·27 Variation and natural selection: the evolution of species

Objectives
- ☐ To understand the meaning of adaptation, and to provide examples of this
- ☐ To realise that Darwin's theory benefited from the ideas of other scientists

Adaptation

As we have seen, living organisms differ from one another. Some of these variations make an organism well suited to its environment, some make no difference, and others make the organism *less* well suited to its environment. An organism that is well suited to make the most of the limited resources within its environment is said to show **adaptation** to its environment, as shown opposite. The cactus (see page 93), polar bear and camel are all well adapted to their environments.

A lion has adaptations that enable it to capture prey efficiently. These are:
- ☐ structural (e.g. teeth and claws)
- ☐ biochemical (e.g. extra protein-digesting enzymes)
- ☐ behavioural (e.g. hunting in groups).

The work of Charles Darwin

Charles Darwin (1809–82) was a British naturalist who took part in a world voyage on a ship called HMS *Beagle*. The voyage, which began in 1831 and lasted for five years, allowed Darwin to see many examples of adaptations. His most famous observations were made on the Galapagos Islands off the west coast of South America. Some species seemed to have adaptations to life on particular islands, but had similarities, and Darwin suspected that they all originated from a single species. An example is shown above right.

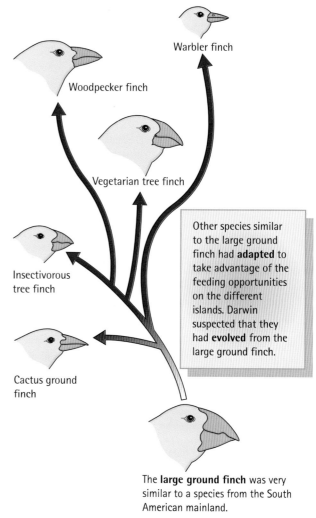

Warbler finch

Woodpecker finch

Vegetarian tree finch

Insectivorous tree finch

Cactus ground finch

Other species similar to the large ground finch had **adapted** to take advantage of the feeding opportunities on the different islands. Darwin suspected that they had **evolved** from the large ground finch.

The **large ground finch** was very similar to a species from the South American mainland.

Finches of the Galapagos islands show adaptations to the food resources on the different islands.

Evolution by natural selection

At the time that Darwin lived, most people believed that each species was fixed, and had been put on Earth in its current form by a creator – God. Darwin thought that species were not fixed, and that they changed through time to produce new species. He called this changing through time **evolution**. At first he was unable to convince other scientists because he could not suggest a **mechanism for evolution**. However, he eventually published his ideas in a famous book, *The Origin of Species by Means of Natural Selection*. An outline of the events leading to this publication is shown on the opposite page.

As a result of many observations made during his voyage on HMS *Beagle*, Charles Darwin began to think that living organisms could change in structure. Darwin suggested that species became adapted to meet the challenges of their environment.

The Rev. Thomas Malthus was a mathematician who showed that populations of living organisms would increase indefinitely unless they were kept in check by limited resources.

Charles Lyell was a geologist who showed that the Earth's rocks were very old. He pointed out that rocks of different ages contained the fossilised remains of different animals and plants.

Darwin proposed a mechanism of evolution by natural selection

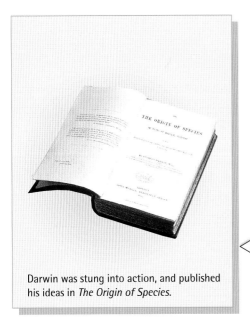

Darwin was stung into action, and published his ideas in *The Origin of Species*.

Darwin and *The Origin of Species*

Alfred Russell Wallace was a professional animal collector working in Malaysia. He wrote to Darwin, and Darwin realised that Wallace had reached the same conclusions about natural selection.

1 What is meant by the term adaptation?

2 Name one animal and one plant with which you are familiar, and describe how each is adapted to its environment.

Development of organisms and the continuity of life

Objective
▐ To understand how adaptation leads to natural selection

Darwin's ideas about natural selection can be summarised under a number of headings, as shown in the diagram below.

Natural selection may lead to new species

Some organisms are better suited to their environment than others. These organisms will be more likely to survive and breed than some of their competitors. Because of this, the characteristics they possess will become more common in the species over successive generations. If we consider one such characteristic, for example neck length in antelopes, we should be able to draw a graph showing how this characteristic is distributed in the population (see page 206). If the environment applies a **selection pressure** such as a limited availability of leaves for food, one part of the population may be favoured. In a few generations' time the graph may look rather different, as shown on the opposite page. If two populations of this antelope were separated from one another, natural selection might favour different adaptations in the two environments. Eventually the two different populations of antelope could have so many different adaptations that they can no longer interbreed – they are said to be different **species**.

Alternative theories of evolution

Early scientists and religious leaders believed that a creator had placed all living organisms on the Earth in their present-day forms. Even once the evidence for evolution had been accepted, not everyone agreed with Darwin's idea of natural selection. Jean Baptiste Lamarck was a Frenchman who lived about 70 years before Darwin. He believed that organisms adapted to their environment by 'use and disuse', that is, a giraffe might gain a long neck by stretching up for food in a tall tree. However, Lamarck was never able to show how these acquired characteristics could be passed on from one generation to another. The major difference between the theories of Darwin and Lamarck was that:

▐ **Lamarck** suggested that the environment *caused* the variations

▐ **Darwin** suggested that the environment *selected* the variations, which had arisen purely by chance.

Over-production – all organisms produce more offspring than can possibly survive, and yet populations remain relatively stable. e.g. a female peppered moth may lay 500 eggs, but the moth population does not increase by the same proportion!

Struggle for existence – organisms experience environmental resistance i.e. they compete for the limited resources within the environment. e.g. several moths may try to feed on the same nectar-producing flower.

Variation – within the population there may be some characteristics that make the organisms that have them more suited for this severe competition. e.g. some moths might be stronger fliers, have better feeding mouthparts, be better camouflaged while resting or be less affected by rain.

Survival of the fittest – individuals that are most successful in the struggle for existence (i.e. that are the best suited/adapted to their environment) are more likely to survive than those without these advantages. e.g. peppered moths: dark-coloured moths resting on soot-covered tree trunks will be less likely to be captured by predators than light-coloured moths.

Advantageous characteristics are passed on to offspring – the well-adapted individuals are more likely to breed than those that are less well-adapted – they pass on their genes to the next generation. This process is called **natural selection**. e.g. dark-coloured moth parents will produce dark-coloured offspring.

Evolution by means of natural selection

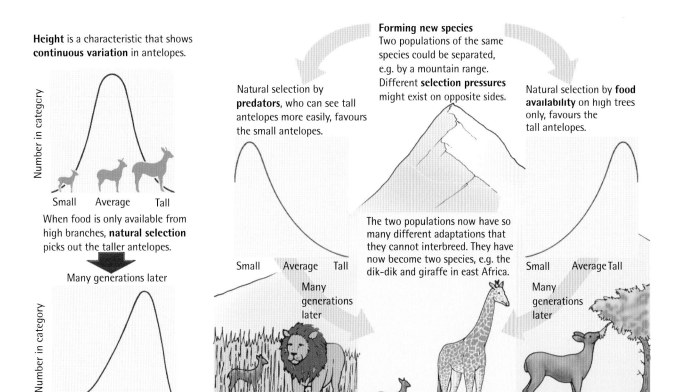

Height is a characteristic that shows **continuous variation** in antelopes.

(left graph: Number in category vs Small, Average, Tall)

When food is only available from high branches, **natural selection** picks out the taller antelopes.

Many generations later

(lower left graph: Number in category vs Small, Average, Tall)

The formation of new species

Natural selection by **predators**, who can see tall antelopes more easily, favours the small antelopes.

(centre-left graph: Small, Average, Tall)

Many generations later

Forming new species
Two populations of the same species could be separated, e.g. by a mountain range. Different **selection pressures** might exist on opposite sides.

The two populations now have so many different adaptations that they cannot interbreed. They have now become two species, e.g. the dik-dik and giraffe in east Africa.

Natural selection by **food availability** on high trees only, favours the tall antelopes.

(centre-right graph: Small, Average Tall)

Many generations later

The development of antibiotic-resistant strains of bacteria (see page 272) is a well-known example of natural selection.

---

1 Using only the following information, answer questions **a** to **d**.

Cepaea is a type of snail which shows considerable variation in its shell colour. The basic colour can be yellow, brown, fawn, pink, orange or red. Over the top of this basic colour up to five bands of a darker colour may occur, around the shell. Colour of shell provides camouflage for the snail because some colours are more difficult to see than others against the background.

Cepaea is an important part of the diet of thrushes. These birds collect snails and break open their shells by banging them on a stone. Thrushes tend to use the same stone, called an 'anvil', whenever feeding in a particular area.

It is possible to collect the remains of the shells and count the number of each shell type. It is also possible to collect the live snails in the same area and count the numbers of each shell type.

Collections of both live snails and broken shells were made in an area where the ground layer plants gave a fairly evenly coloured background. The results are shown in the table.

a How many more live, unbanded *Cepaea* were collected than banded?

b Suggest an explanation for thrushes taking more banded snails even where there appear to be more unbanded snails in the live populations.

	Number of snails			
	Banded	Unbanded	Total	% Banded
Live snails	264	296	560	47.0
Shell remains from 'anvils' in the area	486	377	863	56.0

c Which type of shell, banded or unbanded, would you expect to occur most frequently in a live snail population
  i amongst dead leaves in a wood?
  ii amongst grasses growing on a sand dune?

d The main points of the theory of evolution by natural selection are listed below.
  A The number of offspring is far greater than the number surviving to adult stage.
  B Variation exists among the offspring.
  C Some variations are useful and help the organisms to survive.
  D Competition occurs between the offspring.
  E Only those surviving can breed.
  Natural selection can change the proportions of the different colours in a snail population. Use the five points **A** to **E** above to describe how this change might come about.

(MEG June 1992)

Objective
▸ To understand the process of artificial selection

Making organisms useful to humans

Variation occurs naturally and randomly in all living organisms, but the natural environment is not the only agent of selection. Ever since early humans began to domesticate animals and plants, they have been trying to improve them. This improvement is brought about by selecting those individuals that have the most useful characteristics and allowing only these individuals to breed. This process is called **artificial selection**. Humans have replaced the environment as the agents of selection. There are many important examples of selective breeding:

▸ **Jersey cattle** have been bred to produce milk with a very high cream content.

▸ All domestic **dogs** are the same species, but some have been bred for appearance (e.g. Pekinese), some for hunting (springer spaniels) and some as aggressive guards (Rottweilers).

▸ **Wheat** has been bred so that all the stems are the same height (making harvesting easier) and the ears separate easily from the stalk (making collection of the grain easier).

Some examples of artificial selection are shown below and opposite. The same species can be bred in different ways for different purposes. Early horses have become specialised as carthorses or for racing, for example.

Maintaining variation

What appears to humans as a valuable characteristic might not always be valuable in a natural situation. For example, a Chihuahua dog would probably not survive in the wild because its hunting instincts have been bred out to make it more suitable as a pet. It is very important that humans preserve animal and plant genes for characteristics that do not offer any advantage to us at the moment. A cow with a limited milk yield may carry a gene that makes it resistant to a disease which is not yet a problem in domestic herds, for example. This resistance gene might be extremely valuable if ever such a disease did become established. For this reason many varieties of animals and plants are kept in small numbers in rare-breed centres up and down the country. Plant genes may be conserved as seeds, which are easy to store, and some animal genes may be kept as frozen eggs, sperm or embryos.

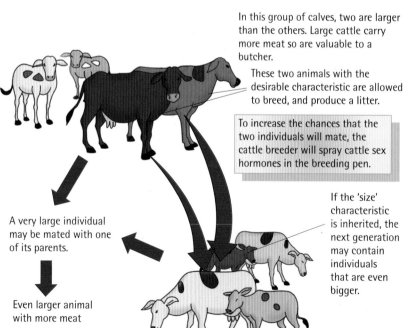

In this group of calves, two are larger than the others. Large cattle carry more meat so are valuable to a butcher.

These two animals with the desirable characteristic are allowed to breed, and produce a litter.

To increase the chances that the two individuals will mate, the cattle breeder will spray cattle sex hormones in the breeding pen.

A very large individual may be mated with one of its parents.

Even larger animal with more meat

If the 'size' characteristic is inherited, the next generation may contain individuals that are even bigger.

Artificial insemination

Male animals, no matter how many useful characteristics they have, **cannot give birth to young animals!** So:

▪ Most male offspring will be fattened up for selling as meat.

▪ 'Desirable' males may be electrically stimulated to ejaculate – the sperm is collected and frozen. One male can easily produce several hundred samples.

▪ The sperm can be taken to a cattle breeding farm and used to inseminate many females.

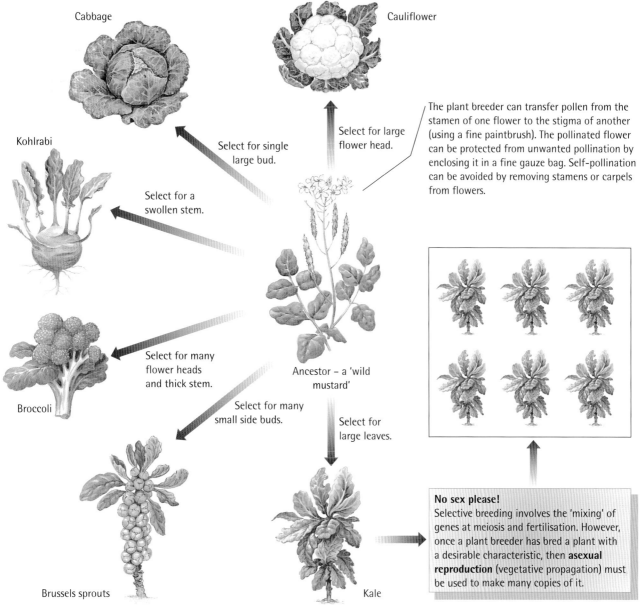

Cabbage

Cauliflower

Kohlrabi

Select for single
large bud.

Select for large
flower head.

Select for a
swollen stem.

The plant breeder can transfer pollen from the
stamen of one flower to the stigma of another
(using a fine paintbrush). The pollinated flower
can be protected from unwanted pollination by
enclosing it in a fine gauze bag. Self-pollination
can be avoided by removing stamens or carpels
from flowers.

Select for many
flower heads
and thick stem.

Broccoli

Ancestor – a 'wild
mustard'

Select for many
small side buds.

Select for
large leaves.

No sex please!
Selective breeding involves the 'mixing' of
genes at meiosis and fertilisation. However,
once a plant breeder has bred a plant with
a desirable characteristic, then **asexual
reproduction** (vegetative propagation) must
be used to make many copies of it.

Brussels sprouts

Kale

Artificial selection has produced many vegetables
from one ancestor species.

Three major differences between artificial and natural selection

- In artificial selection, humans are the agents of selection, while natural selection depends upon the natural environment.

- Artificial selection is much quicker than natural selection.

- Artificial selection offers no advantage to the animal or plant in its natural environment.

It is likely that selective breeding will be replaced by genetic engineering in the future. This technique, explained on page 224, is much more predictable than selective breeding and produces useful results more quickly.

1 A potato grower wanted to produce a new
variety of potato which grows quickly and makes
good chips. She has one variety which grows
quickly but makes poor chips, and another which
grows more slowly but makes good chips.
When plants of these two varieties produce
flowers she crosses the two varieties. Later she
collects the seeds and plants them.

a To cross the two varieties, the grower pollinates
a flower of one variety with pollen from the
other.
Describe how the grower should do this.

b From the seeds she collects, she finds that one
of the new plants grows very quickly and
produces potatoes which make good chips.
How would she produce a crop of potatoes
which are exactly the same?

(NEAB June 1992)

Development of organisms and the continuity of life

223

3·30 Genetic engineering

Objectives

- To understand the term genetic engineering
- To understand the value of enzymes in genetic engineering
- To be able to describe a technique in genetic engineering
- To list some products of genetic engineering that are of value to humans

What is genetic engineering?

The examples of selective breeding described on page 222 are a form of genetic engineering, since humans are interfering with the natural flow of genetic material from one generation to the next when they choose the animals or plants that will be allowed to reproduce (and pass on their genes). However, what we now call genetic engineering is a much more predictable and refined process than selective breeding. In this process:

- Genes that code for characteristics valuable to humans are identified.
- These genes are removed from the animal or plant that normally shows this characteristic.
- The genes are transferred to another organism, usually one that grows very quickly.
- This organism 'reads' the gene it has received, and shows the characteristic that is valuable to humans.

Recombinant DNA technology

In many cases the characteristic is the ability to manufacture a product that has some medical or industrial value. Because DNA (a gene) from one organism is being transferred to the DNA of another organism to make a new combination of DNA, this 'modern' genetic engineering is often referred to as **recombinant DNA technology**. The principle of this technique sounds very straightforward, but in practice it is extremely difficult.

- The genetic material is microscopic in size. A technician can't use a pair of scissors to cut out a gene!
- The **host** organism, that is, the one that will receive the valuable gene, would not normally take in DNA from another organism.

- The host organism might not show the valuable characteristic, for example it may not make a particular protein, even though it now has the DNA that codes for the protein.

Technological advances have overcome these potential problems. Key to success has been the discovery of:

- **enzymes** that can cut DNA from one chromosome and paste it into another, acting like scissors and glue
- **vectors** that can carry the gene from one organism to another
- **culture techniques** that allow large quantities of the valuable product to be produced and collected, even if the host organism would not normally produce it.

Many compounds can be manufactured by genetically engineered bacteria, including insulin and other products which are used directly by humans. These products are otherwise often taken from animals. For example, insulin can be isolated from the pancreas of a pig.

Recombinant DNA technology has several advantages:

- The product is very pure, and can be the human version of a protein rather than a version produced by another animal. The human protein is likely to work more efficiently in a person, and is less likely to be rejected by the body's defences.
- The product can be made in large quantities, making it less expensive and more readily available. Insulin produced in this way costs about 1% as much as insulin produced from pig pancreas.
- The process can be switched on or off easily as the bacteria can be stored until needed again. The product can be made as required rather than just when animal carcasses are available.

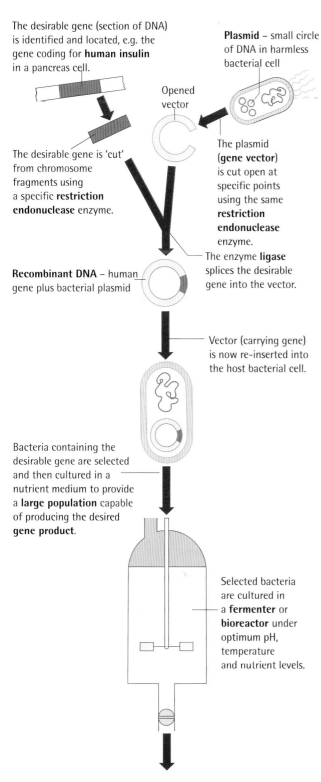

The desirable gene (section of DNA) is identified and located, e.g. the gene coding for **human insulin** in a pancreas cell.

Plasmid – small circle of DNA in harmless bacterial cell

Opened vector

The desirable gene is 'cut' from chromosome fragments using a specific **restriction endonuclease** enzyme.

The plasmid (**gene vector**) is cut open at specific points using the same **restriction endonuclease** enzyme.

Recombinant DNA – human gene plus bacterial plasmid

The enzyme **ligase** splices the desirable gene into the vector.

Vector (carrying gene) is now re-inserted into the host bacterial cell.

Bacteria containing the desirable gene are selected and then cultured in a nutrient medium to provide a **large population** capable of producing the desired **gene product**.

Selected bacteria are cultured in a **fermenter** or **bioreactor** under optimum pH, temperature and nutrient levels.

Product

After some processing, for example to remove the bacterial cells for recycling, the product is extremely pure and relatively inexpensive. Important examples of such gene products are:

- **insulin** (required for the treatment of diabetes)
- **human growth hormone**
- **factor VIII** (blood clotting factor for haemophilia)
- **BST** is an important animal hormone used to speed up the growth of beef cattle.

Genetic engineering (recombinant DNA technology) depends on enzymes and the culture of microorganisms.

A plasmid of bacterial DNA

1 The following table lists events from the identification of a human gene coding for a hormone "X" to the commercial production of hormone "X".

Genes can be transferred into plasmids, tiny circles of DNA which are found in bacteria.

Show the correct sequence of events 1 to 8 by copying the table below and writing the appropriate number in each box provided. The first (number 1) and last (number 8) have been completed for you.

Event	Number
Cutting of a bacterial plasmid using restriction endonuclease	
Cutting of human DNA with restriction endonuclease	
Identification of the human DNA which codes for hormone "X"	1
Many identical plasmids, complete with human gene, are produced inside the bacterium.	
Mixing together human gene and "cut" plasmids to splice the human gene into the plasmid	
Some of the cloned bacteria are put into an industrial fermenter where they breed and secrete the hormone.	8
The bacterium is cloned.	
Using the plasmid as a vector, inserting it, complete with human gene, into a bacterium	

(Edexcel Nov. 1994 [part])

Development of organisms and the continuity of life

Objectives

▢ To describe how organisms other than bacteria may be altered by genetic engineering

▢ To appreciate that there are moral and environmental problems associated with the use of genetic engineering

Transgenic organisms

Bacteria are not the only organisms that can be modified by gene transfer. Genetic engineers have been able to transfer genes into flowering plants, fungi and mammals and thus alter the characteristics of these higher organisms. An organism that has received genes from a different species is called a **transgenic** organism. The major problem is finding a vector that can carry the gene into the new host. Different vectors have been used for different hosts, as described opposite.

Genetic modification of plants

The bacterium *Agrobacterium tumefaciens* has proved to be a very useful organism in gene transfer work, for two reasons:

▢ It carries plasmids, and using the techniques described on page 225 these plasmids can be recombined with a useful gene.

▢ The plasmid in this organism is called the **Ti plasmid**. It has the ability to force cells infected with it to divide very rapidly to form a tumour (called a **crown gall** in plants). Each cell in the tumour will then contain the 'useful' gene.

Gene transfer in animals

Scientists can keep ova alive in a Petri dish. Transgenic animals are produced by introducing a desirable gene into the nucleus of a fertilised ovum using a fine pipette. When the fertilised ova containing the transferred gene have divided a few times, the ball of cells is implanted into a female animal and grows into a transgenic animal. This animal will be able to manufacture the protein coded for by the desirable gene.

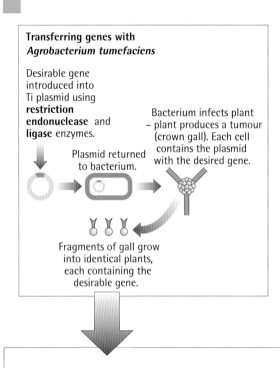

Transferring genes with *Agrobacterium tumefaciens*

Desirable gene introduced into Ti plasmid using **restriction endonuclease** and **ligase** enzymes.

Plasmid returned to bacterium.

Bacterium infects plant – plant produces a tumour (crown gall). Each cell contains the plasmid with the desired gene.

Fragments of gall grow into identical plants, each containing the desirable gene.

Important examples include

- plants that produce a natural pesticide

- tomato plants which 'rot' very slowly

- plants which make a thicker cuticle so are drought-resistant

Nuclear transfer

Scientists arrange for the transferred gene to be 'read' in the cells of the mammary glands, so that the desirable product is released in the milk. The product, for example **factor VIII** which is used to treat haemophilia or **α-antitrypsin** which is used to treat inefficient immune systems, can then be purified from the milk.

A transgenic animal which produces such a protein may be extremely valuable – the market for factor VIII, for example, is probably worth hundreds of millions of dollars worldwide. The techniques involved in producing these animals are very complex and for every success there are many failures. For this reason scientists are anxious to keep such transgenic organisms for as long as possible, and are unwilling to risk 'losing' the gene in offspring produced by traditional sexual reproduction. Such transgenic animals may be cloned as the techniques of cloning animals from small pieces of tissue are quite well understood. 'Dolly' the sheep is an animal cloned from a piece of mammary gland tissue (she was allegedly named Dolly after the American singer, Dolly Parton!).

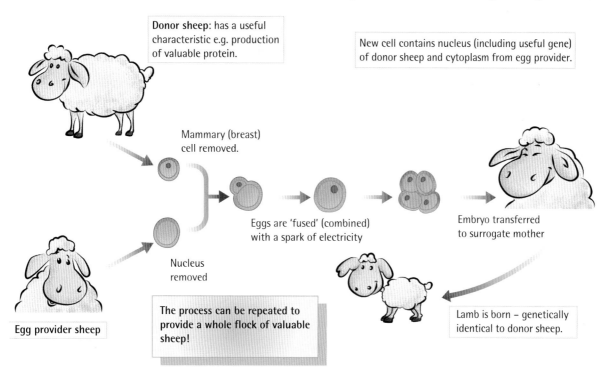

Donor sheep: has a useful characteristic e.g. production of valuable protein.

New cell contains nucleus (including useful gene) of donor sheep and cytoplasm from egg provider.

Mammary (breast) cell removed.

Eggs are 'fused' (combined) with a spark of electricity

Embryo transferred to surrogate mother

Nucleus removed

Egg provider sheep

The process can be repeated to provide a whole flock of valuable sheep!

Lamb is born – genetically identical to donor sheep.

Nuclear transfer and cloning of 'Dolly'.

If transgenic animals can be cloned in the same way the cost of these valuable protein products should go down and their availability to sufferers of potentially fatal conditions should increase.

This use of cloning is very similar to the vegetative propagation techniques used to make many copies of a plant with desirable characteristics (see page 198).

Embryo splitting is another form of cloning
Embryo splitting has been known about for more than 20 years. In this method of cloning an early embryo is split into individual cells or small groups of cells – this happens naturally with twins (see page 180). Each cell or group of cells develops into a new embryo. Tetra, a rhesus monkey, was the first primate to be produced by cloning – in her case the embryo was split at the eight-cell stage into four identical embryos ('tetra' means 'four' in Greek). Although not strictly genetic engineering, this technique of cloning animals has a number of other uses (see figure on next page).

▶ Cloned laboratory animals are used in medical research – as they are all identical the experimenter can be sure that the results obtained from experiments on these animals are due to the treatment given to them and *not* to any genetic difference between the animals.

- The zygotes of rare animals can be divided and transplanted into the wombs of common species to maximise the production of the rarer species. This use of a 'substitute mother' is called surrogacy.
- A human embryo can be produced by *in vitro* fertilisation (see page 171). If the parents are known to be carriers of a genetic disease the embryo can be divided into several clones. Some of the clones can be used for testing for the presence of the gene causing the disease – if they are found to be disease-free one or more of the other clones can be returned to the mother's uterus to develop into a fetus.

Embryo-splitting and cloning of Tetra

The value of embryo-splitting

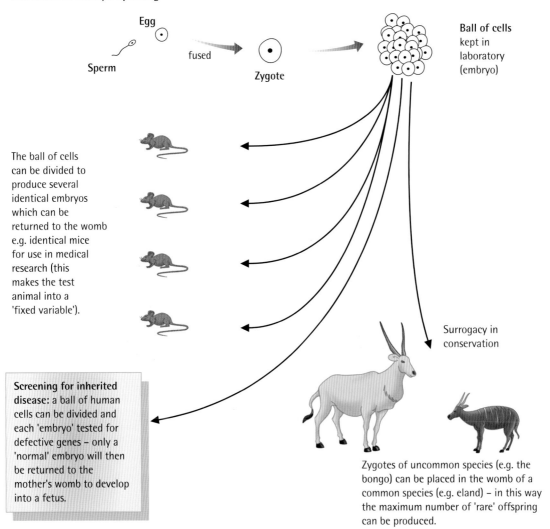

The ball of cells can be divided to produce several identical embryos which can be returned to the womb e.g. identical mice for use in medical research (this makes the test animal into a 'fixed variable').

Screening for inherited disease: a ball of human cells can be divided and each 'embryo' tested for defective genes – only a 'normal' embryo will then be returned to the mother's womb to develop into a fetus.

Surrogacy in conservation

Zygotes of uncommon species (e.g. the bongo) can be placed in the womb of a common species (e.g. eland) – in this way the maximum number of 'rare' offspring can be produced.

Moral and environmental concerns about genetic modification

The benefits claimed for genetically modified products, and potential problems, are shown in the table below.

Benefits	Problems
Engineered organisms can offer higher yields from fewer resources. With plants, for example, this might reduce the need for pesticides and fertilisers	Plants engineered for pesticide resistance could cross-pollinate with wild relatives, creating 'superweeds'
Crops engineered to cope with extreme environmental conditions will open up new areas for cultivation, and reduce the risk of famine	Engineered bacteria may escape from the laboratory or the factory, with unpredictable consequences
Genetic engineering gives much more predictable results than selective breeding	'New' organisms might be patented. A company that has spent a lot of money on developing such an organism might refuse to share its benefits with other consumers, making the company very powerful
Foods can be engineered to be more convenient, such as potatoes which absorb less fat when crisps are made, or even to contain medicinal products such as vaccines	How far should we allow research into human gene transfer to go? Will we allow the production of 'perfect' children, with characteristics seen to be desirable by parents?

Gene therapy

Gene therapy is the transfer of healthy human genes into a person's cells that contain mutant alleles which cause disease. The principle of gene therapy is outlined below.

Gene therapy may be able to repair diseased human cells.

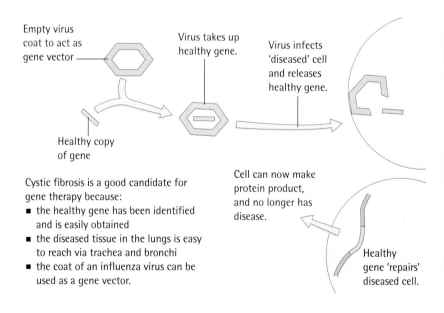

Cystic fibrosis is a good candidate for gene therapy because:
- the healthy gene has been identified and is easily obtained
- the diseased tissue in the lungs is easy to reach via trachea and bronchi
- the coat of an influenza virus can be used as a gene vector.

1 Why is *Agrobacterium tumefaciens* a useful organism to genetic engineers?

2 What might be the benefits of transferring nitrogen-fixing genes from bacteria to other organisms?

3 Describe one example of gene therapy. Explain why this form of treatment is thought likely to be successful in the example which you describe.

4.1 Ecology and ecosystems

Environmental survival kit

All living organisms depend upon their environment for three 'survival essentials'. These are a **supply of food**, **shelter** from undesirable physical conditions and a **breeding site**. The living organism **interacts** with its environment – for example, a living plant:

- removes carbon dioxide, water and light energy from its habitat
- may be eaten by an animal or a parasite
- depends upon soil for support.

Factors in the environment affect the growth of the plant. Some of these factors are **biotic** – other living organisms – and some are **abiotic** – the non-living components of the habitat. **Ecology** is the study of living organisms in relation to their environment. The interactions between the organism and its environment are summarised below.

Changing with the seasons

The ability of the habitat to supply living organisms with their requirements may vary at different times of year. The ecosystem in the photograph opposite will only exist for a certain period of time – as food or water becomes exhausted some animals may leave. These will then be followed by the predators which feed on them. The great animal **migrations** seen in East Africa result from the changing conditions in the animals' environment, for example:

- poor rain means little growth of grass
- herbivores leave for areas of fresh growth
- carnivores follow herbivores
- (then scavengers follow carnivores!).

Living together

Living organisms normally exist in groups. The names given to these groups, and the way they interact with the abiotic environment, are explained opposite.

Carbon dioxide

'Fertiliser' in faeces

Food

Water and mineral ions from soil

A giraffe feeds on a thorn tree. The tree requires water, mineral ions, carbon dioxide and light to grow. The giraffe may provide carbon dioxide from respiration, and ions from decomposition of its faeces.

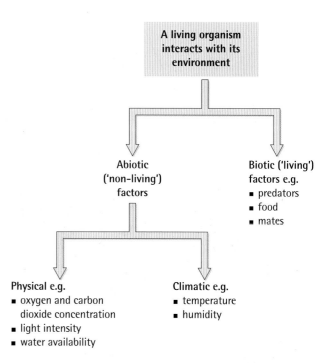

A living organism interacts with its environment

Abiotic ('non-living') factors

Biotic ('living') factors e.g.
- predators
- food
- mates

Physical e.g.
- oxygen and carbon dioxide concentration
- light intensity
- water availability

Climatic e.g.
- temperature
- humidity

Organisms and their environment

230

A **population** is all of the members of the same species (e.g. flamingoes) in a particular area.

A **community** is all of the populations of living organisms in one area (e.g. flamingoes, zebra, wildebeest and grass). The community is the **biotic environment**.

Air, water and soil make up the **abiotic environment**.

An **ecosystem** is all the living organisms and the non-living factors in a particular part of the environment.

A **habitat** is a part of the environment that can provide food, shelter and a breeding site for a living organism (e.g. a patch of grassland).

Organisms exist in groups within an ecosystem.

1. Define the terms population, community and ecosystem.

2. Name two abiotic factors that might determine whether or not a habitat is suitable for a living organism.

3. Suggest two ways in which a plant and an animal in the same habitat may interact.

4. What must a habitat provide?

5. How are the following observations related?
   - Very few flying insects are found in Britain during the winter.
   - Swallows migrate to Africa during the winter.
   - Hobbies (small bird-eating falcons) leave Britain in late autumn.

6. What is meant by the term ecology?

7. a A group of pupils were studying a forest. They noticed that the plants grew in two main layers. They called these the tree layer and the ground layer.

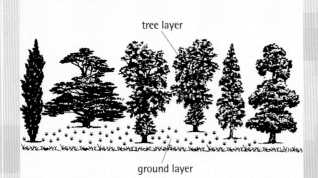

tree layer

ground layer

The pupils measured the amount of sunlight reaching each layer at different times in the year. Their results are shown on the graph.

i During which month did most light reach the tree layer?

ii During which month did most light reach the ground layer?

iii Suggest why the amount of sunlight reaching the ground layer is lower in mid-summer than in the spring.

b The pupils found bluebells growing in the ground layer. Bluebells grow rapidly from bulbs. They flower in April and by June their leaves have died.

   i Suggest why bluebells grow rapidly in April.

   ii Suggest why the bluebell leaves have died by June.

(MEG June 1998 [part])

4.2 Feeding relationships: food chains and food webs

Objectives
- To know that the feeding relationships in an ecosystem can be expressed as food chains
- To understand why energy transfer through an ecosystem is inefficient
- To understand why complex food webs are the most stable

Food chains

The most obvious interaction between different organisms in an ecosystem is feeding. During feeding, one organism is obtaining food – energy and raw materials – from another one. Usually one organism eats another, but then may itself be food for a third species. The feeding relationships of the different organisms in the ecosystem can be shown in a **food chain**, as in the diagram below.

Energy transfer is inefficient

The amount of energy that is passed on in a food chain is reduced at every step. Since energy can be neither created nor destroyed, it is not lost but is converted into some other form. During respiration, some energy is transferred to the environment as heat. The flow of energy through a food chain, and the heat losses to the environment, are illustrated in the diagram opposite.

Food webs

Since so little energy is transferred from the base to the top of a food chain, a top carnivore must eat many herbivores. These herbivores are probably not all of the same species. In turn, each herbivore is likely to feed on many different plant species. All these different feeding relationships can be shown in a **food web**.

The more complicated a food web, the more stable the community is. For example, in the forest food web shown opposite, if the number of squirrels fell, the owls could eat more worms, mice and rats. The mice and rats would have less competition for food from squirrels, and so might reproduce more successfully.

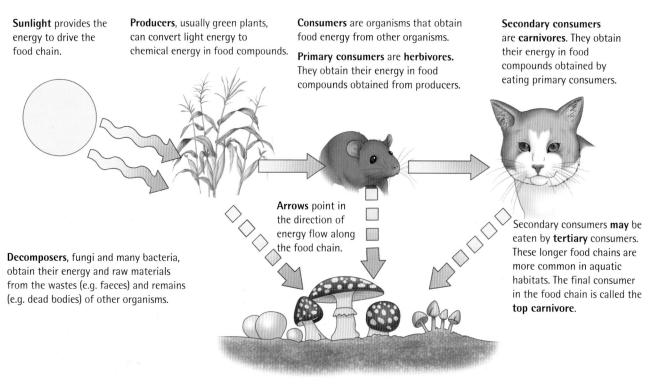

Sunlight provides the energy to drive the food chain.

Producers, usually green plants, can convert light energy to chemical energy in food compounds.

Consumers are organisms that obtain food energy from other organisms.

Primary consumers are **herbivores.** They obtain their energy in food compounds obtained from producers.

Secondary consumers are **carnivores**. They obtain their energy in food compounds obtained by eating primary consumers.

Arrows point in the direction of energy flow along the food chain.

Decomposers, fungi and many bacteria, obtain their energy and raw materials from the wastes (e.g. faeces) and remains (e.g. dead bodies) of other organisms.

Secondary consumers **may** be eaten by **tertiary** consumers. These longer food chains are more common in aquatic habitats. The final consumer in the food chain is called the **top carnivore**.

Food chains show energy flow through an ecosystem. Each organism in the food chain represents a different **trophic** (feeding) **level**.

Organisms and their environment

Energy transfer

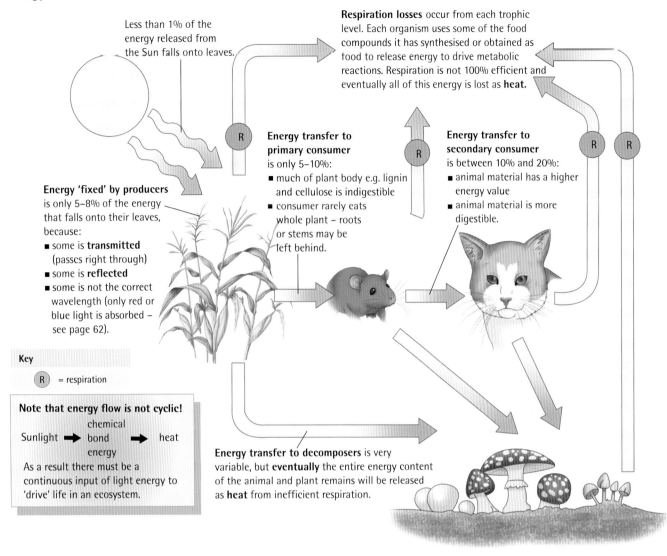

Less than 1% of the energy released from the Sun falls onto leaves.

Respiration losses occur from each trophic level. Each organism uses some of the food compounds it has synthesised or obtained as food to release energy to drive metabolic reactions. Respiration is not 100% efficient and eventually all of this energy is lost as **heat.**

Energy 'fixed' by producers is only 5–8% of the energy that falls onto their leaves, because:
- some is **transmitted** (passes right through)
- some is **reflected**
- some is not the correct wavelength (only red or blue light is absorbed – see page 62).

Energy transfer to primary consumer is only 5–10%:
- much of plant body e.g. lignin and cellulose is indigestible
- consumer rarely eats whole plant – roots or stems may be left behind.

Energy transfer to secondary consumer is between 10% and 20%:
- animal material has a higher energy value
- animal material is more digestible.

Key

(R) = respiration

Note that energy flow is not cyclic!

Sunlight → chemical bond energy → heat

As a result there must be a continuous input of light energy to 'drive' life in an ecosystem.

Energy transfer to decomposers is very variable, but **eventually** the entire energy content of the animal and plant remains will be released as **heat** from inefficient respiration.

A simple forest food web

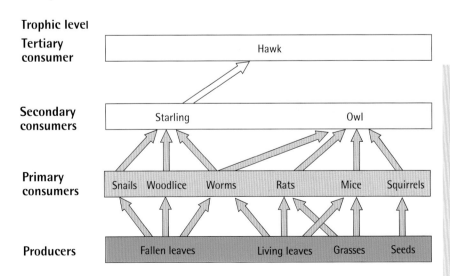

Trophic level

Tertiary consumer — Hawk

Secondary consumers — Starling, Owl

Primary consumers — Snails, Woodlice, Worms, Rats, Mice, Squirrels

Producers — Fallen leaves, Living leaves, Grasses, Seeds

1. Define the terms producer, consumer and decomposer. Which of these could be omitted from an ecosystem? Explain your answer.
2. Write out a food chain from a named ecosystem which you have studied.
3. Why are food chains usually restricted to three or four trophic levels?

More examples of feeding relationships

Food chains and food webs in aquatic (watery) environments can be longer than those on the land. This is because this type of environment has space and ideal growth conditions for many producers. Even with energy losses at every stage there is enough 'trapped' energy for more steps in the chain. Many of these food chains begin with phytoplankton (tiny green plants) or algae.

A freshwater food chain

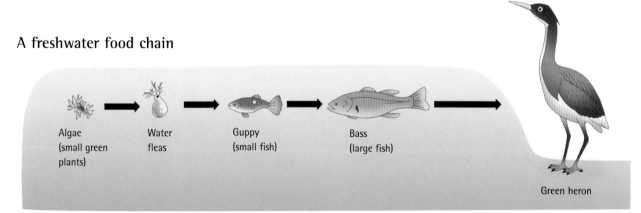

Algae (small green plants) → Water fleas → Guppy (small fish) → Bass (large fish) → Green heron

A seashore food chain

Algae on rocks (seaweed) → Limpets → Crabs → Gull

The seashore is an excellent environment for animals, at least as far as food is concerned, because fresh supplies are delivered with every tide!

Some of the top predators on seashores need so much food that they need to travel between different parts of the habitat. A gull, for example, might have to fly to several different parts of the same shore.

1 Look at the three aquatic feeding relationships shown on this page and the next. Make a table like this one:

Producers	Herbivores	Carnivores	Top carnivores

2 Shark fishing is a popular sport. Explain what might happen if all of the sharks living around a section of reef were captured by fishermen.

Coral reef food web

The most complex food webs are found in the ocean.

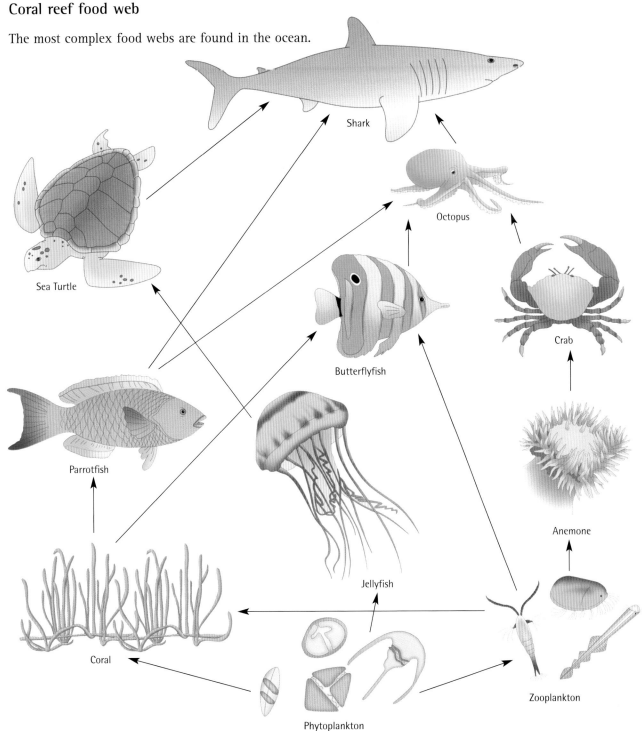

Shark

Sea Turtle

Octopus

Crab

Parrotfish

Butterflyfish

Anemone

Jellyfish

Coral

Zooplankton

Phytoplankton

3 Use words from the following list to complete the paragraph about ecosystems. You may use each word once, more than once or not at all.

decomposition, producer, chemical, carnivore, consumer, photosynthesis, energy, light, elements, decomposers, herbivore.

In each ecosystem there are many feeding relationships. A food chain represents a flow of _____ through an ecosystem, and always begins with an organism called a _____ which is able to trap _____ energy and convert it to _____ energy. An organism of this type is eaten by a _____, which is a kind of _____ that feeds only on plant material. This type of organism is, in turn, eaten by a ——— (an organism that consumes other animals).

4.3 Feeding relationships: pyramids of numbers, biomass and energy

Pyramids of numbers

Look at the food chain on page 232. Two things should be clear:

- The organisms tend to get bigger moving along the food chain. Predators, such as the cat, need to be large enough to overcome their prey, such as the mouse.

- Energy is 'lost' as heat on moving from one trophic level to the next, so an animal to the right of a food chain needs to eat several organisms 'below' it in order to obtain enough energy. For example, a rabbit eats many blades of grass.

Food chains and food webs provide **qualitative** information about an ecosystem – they show which organism feeds on which other organism. How do we show **quantitative** information, for example how many predators can be supported by a certain number of plants at the start of the chain? We can use a **pyramid of numbers** or a **pyramid of biomass**, as shown in the diagram below.

Pyramids of energy

A pyramid of biomass describes how much biomass is present in a habitat *at the time the sample is taken*. This can be misleading, because different feeding levels may contain organisms that reproduce, and so replace themselves, at different rates. For example, grass in a field would replace itself more quickly than cattle feeding on the grass, so when the pyramid of biomass is constructed there would be more 'cattle biomass' than 'grass

Pyramid of numbers – a diagrammatic representation of the number of different organisms at each trophic level in an ecosystem **at any one time**

Note

1 The number of organisms at any trophic level is represented by the length (or the area) of a rectangle.
2 Moving up the pyramid, the **number** of organisms generally **decreases**, but the **size** of each individual **increases**.

Problems

a The range of numbers may be enormous – 500 000 grass plants may only support a single top carnivore – so that drawing the pyramid to scale may be very difficult
b Pyramids may be **inverted**, particularly if the **producer is very large** (e.g. an oak tree) or **parasites feed on the consumers** (e.g. bird lice on an owl).

Pyramid of biomass – which represents the **biomass** (number of individuals × mass of each individual) at each trophic level **at any one time**. This should solve the scale and inversion problems of the pyramid of numbers.

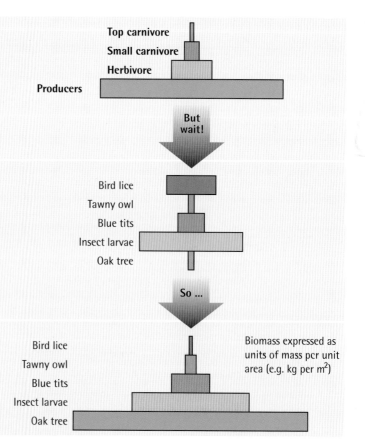

Top carnivore
Small carnivore
Herbivore
Producers

But wait!

Bird lice
Tawny owl
Blue tits
Insect larvae
Oak tree

So ...

Bird lice
Tawny owl
Blue tits
Insect larvae
Oak tree

Biomass expressed as units of mass per unit area (e.g. kg per m^2)

Ecological pyramids represent numerical relationships between successive trophic levels. The pyramid of biomass is useful because the biomass gives a good idea of how much energy is passed on to the next trophic level.

biomass' and the pyramid would be inverted. To overcome this difficulty a **pyramid of energy** can be constructed. This measures the amount of energy flowing through an ecosystem *over a period of time*. The time period is usually a year, since this takes into account the changing rates of growth and reproduction in different seasons. It is even possible to add an extra base layer to the pyramid of energy representing the solar energy entering that particular ecosystem.

Pyramid of energy: energy values are expressed as units of energy per unit area per unit time (e.g. kJ per m² per year).

Gathering data for ecological pyramids

To construct a pyramid of numbers or of biomass, organisms must be captured, counted and (perhaps) weighed. This is done on a **sample** (a small number) of the organisms in an ecosystem. Counting every individual organism in a habitat would be extremely time-consuming and could considerably damage the environment.

The sample should give an accurate estimate of the total population size. To do this:

- The sampling must be **random** to avoid any bias. For example, it is tempting to collect a large number of organisms, by looking for the areas where they are most common. To avoid this, the possible sampling sites can each be given a number and then chosen using random number generators on a computer.

- The sample must be the **right size** so that any 'rogue' results can be eliminated. For example, a single sample might be taken from a bare patch of earth, whereas all other sites are covered with vegetation. The single sample from the bare patch should not be ignored, but its effects on the results will be lessened if another nine samples are taken. A **mean value** can then be used.

Sampling plants and sessile animals

Once the organisms in a sample have been identified and counted, the population size can be estimated. For example, if 10 quadrats gave a mean of 8 plants per quadrat, and each quadrat is one-hundredth of the area of the total site, then the total plant population in that area is $8 \times 100 = 800$.

A quadrat is a square frame made of wood or metal. It is simply laid on the ground and the number of organisms inside it is counted.

A quadrat is used most commonly for estimating the size of plant populations, but may also be valuable for the study of populations of sessile or slow-moving animals (e.g. limpets).

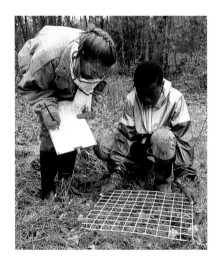

4.4 Decay is a natural process

Objectives

- To understand that nutrients in dead organisms are recycled
- To know that the process of decay often begins with the activities of scavengers
- To know how saprotrophic nutrition is responsible for decomposition

Recycling nutrients

Humans have an unusual skill – they can modify their environment to suit themselves. For example, we cut down forests and plant crops, and we build houses. Many building materials are natural, such as wood and straw, and the environment treats these materials as the dead remains of once-living organisms – the environment reclaims the nutrients and returns them to the ecosystem.

Starting with scavengers

When an organism dies, the nutrients in its body are returned to the environment to be reused. The nutrients are recycled by a series of processes carried out by other living organisms. The first ones to appear are usually the **scavengers** which break up the dead bodies into more manageable pieces. Scavengers eat some of the dead body, but leave behind blood or small pieces of tissue.

Scavengers such as the vulture feed on dead bodies.

Decomposition by microorganisms

The remains that are left are **decomposed** by the feeding activities of microorganisms. These fungi and bacteria feed by secreting enzymes onto the remains and absorbing the digested products. This form of nutrition is called saprotrophic feeding (see page 12).

The diagram on the opposite page illustrates some of the features of the decomposition process. The decay process provides energy and raw materials for the decomposers. It also releases nutrients from the bodies of dead animals and plants, which can then be reused by other organisms, for example:

$$\textbf{Sugar} \text{ in dead rabbit}$$
$$\downarrow \text{respiration by microorganisms}$$
$$\textbf{carbon dioxide}$$
$$\downarrow \text{photosynthesis in plant}$$
$$\text{sugar in plant}$$

In this way substances pass through **nutrient cycles** as microbes convert them from large, complex molecules in animal and plant remains to simpler compounds in the soil and the atmosphere. The next sections describe the recycling of the elements carbon and nitrogen.

Importance of decomposition processes to humans

- Organic waste in sewage is decomposed and made 'safe' in water treatment plants (see page 259).
- Organic pollutants such as spilled oil may be removed from the environment by decomposing bacteria (see page 11).
- Food is spoiled due to decomposition by fungi and bacteria. Many food treatments alter physical conditions to inhibit enzyme activity.
- Wounds may become infected by saprotrophs, leading to tissue loss or even to death. Many medical treatments inhibit the multiplication or metabolism of saprotrophs.

Saprotrophs cause decay.

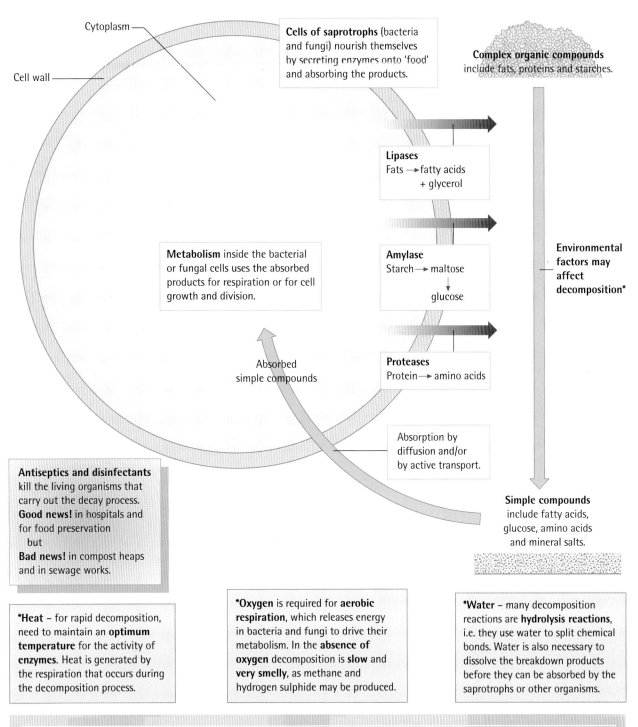

Cytoplasm

Cell wall

Cells of saprotrophs (bacteria and fungi) nourish themselves by secreting enzymes onto 'food' and absorbing the products.

Complex organic compounds include fats, proteins and starches.

Lipases
Fats → fatty acids + glycerol

Amylase
Starch → maltose
↓
glucose

Proteases
Protein → amino acids

Metabolism inside the bacterial or fungal cells uses the absorbed products for respiration or for cell growth and division.

Absorbed simple compounds

Absorption by diffusion and/or by active transport.

Environmental factors may affect decomposition*

Simple compounds include fatty acids, glucose, amino acids and mineral salts.

Antiseptics and disinfectants kill the living organisms that carry out the decay process.
Good news! in hospitals and for food preservation but
Bad news! in compost heaps and in sewage works.

***Heat** – for rapid decomposition, need to maintain an **optimum temperature** for the activity of **enzymes**. Heat is generated by the respiration that occurs during the decomposition process.

***Oxygen** is required for **aerobic respiration**, which releases energy in bacteria and fungi to drive their metabolism. In the **absence of oxygen** decomposition is **slow** and **very smelly**, as methane and hydrogen sulphide may be produced.

***Water** – many decomposition reactions are **hydrolysis reactions**, i.e. they use water to split chemical bonds. Water is also necessary to dissolve the breakdown products before they can be absorbed by the saprotrophs or other organisms.

---

1 Copy and complete the following paragraph.
During the process of decay, _____ and _____ convert complex chemicals into _____ ones. For example, proteins are converted to _____ , and _____ to fatty acids and glycerol. These decay processes involve the biological catalysts called _____ , and so the processes are affected by changes in _____ and _____ . Humans exploit decay, for example in the treatment of _____ to provide drinking water, and may deliberately limit decay, for example in the preservation of _____ .

2 Gardeners often place vegetable waste on a compost heap. Over the course of time the waste will be decomposed.
a What do gardeners gain from the decomposed waste?
b Why do gardeners sometimes spray water over the heap in warm summer weather?
c Why do gardeners often build compost heaps on a pile of loose-fitting sticks or bricks?

4.5 The carbon cycle

Objectives
- To recall why living organisms need carbon-containing compounds
- To appreciate that carbon is cycled between complex and simple forms by the biochemical processes of photosynthesis and respiration
- To understand that formation and combustion of fossil fuels may distort the pattern of the carbon cycle

Carbon-containing nutrients – a reminder

The Sun keeps supplying *energy* to food chains. However, the supply of *chemical elements* to living organisms is limited, and these elements must be recycled. The nutrient elements are cycled between simple forms in the non-living (abiotic) environment and more complex forms in the bodies of living organisms (the biotic component of an ecosystem). Living organisms require carbon-containing compounds as:

- a source of energy, released when carbon-containing compounds are oxidised during respiration (particularly carbohydrates and fats)
- **raw materials** for the growth of cells (particularly fats and proteins).

Recycling carbon compounds

Plants, and some bacteria, manufacture these compounds from carbon dioxide during the process of photosynthesis (see page 60). Animals obtain them in a ready-made form by feeding on other living organisms (see page 52), and decomposers obtain them as they break down the dead bodies or wastes of other living organisms. These processes of feeding, respiration, photosynthesis and decomposition **recycle** the carbon over and over again. Theoretically, the amount of carbon dioxide fixed by photosynthesis should equal the amount released by respiration. As a result the most accessible form of carbon in the non-living environment, that is **carbon dioxide**, remains at about the same concentration year after year after year (about 0.03% of the atmosphere). Other processes may affect this regular cycling of carbon.

- Sometimes conditions are not suitable for respiration by decomposers, and carbon dioxide remains 'locked up' in complex carbon compounds in the bodies of organisms. For example, anaerobic, low pH or extreme temperature conditions will inhibit decomposition – this is how fossil fuels have been laid down in environments where decomposition is not favoured.

- Over millions of years the formation of fossil fuels has removed carbon dioxide from the environment. Humans have exploited fossil fuels as a source of energy over a relatively short time, and the **combustion** of oil, gas, coal and peat has returned enormous volumes of carbon dioxide to the atmosphere. As a result carbon dioxide concentrations are increasing (see page 251).

- The burning of biomass fuels such as wood and alcohol also returns carbon dioxide to the atmosphere, and can have a very severe local effect although worldwide it is less significant than the combustion of fossil fuels.

The way in which these different processes contribute to the cycling of carbon is illustrated opposite.

---

1 Refer to the carbon cycle opposite.
   a Name the simple carbon compound present in the abiotic part of the ecosystem.
   b Name two compounds present in the biotic part of the ecosystem.
   c Which processes raise the concentration of carbon dioxide in the atmosphere?
   d Which process reduces carbon dioxide concentration in the atmosphere?
   e Name the process that distributes carbon dioxide throughout the atmosphere from places where it is released.
   f Suggest a reason why some fossil fuels were formed as sediments at the bottom of ancient seas.

The processes of photosynthesis, feeding, death, excretion and respiration lead to the cycling of carbon between living organisms and their environment. Fossil fuel formation and combustion affect the concentration of carbon dioxide in the atmosphere.

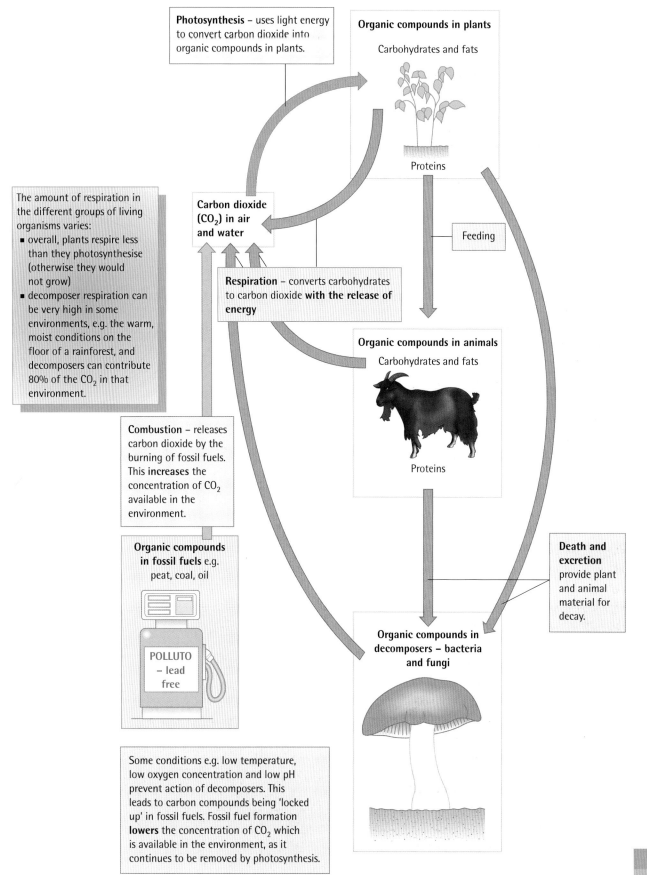

Photosynthesis – uses light energy to convert carbon dioxide into organic compounds in plants.

Organic compounds in plants

Carbohydrates and fats

Proteins

Carbon dioxide (CO_2) in air and water

The amount of respiration in the different groups of living organisms varies:
- overall, plants respire less than they photosynthesise (otherwise they would not grow)
- decomposer respiration can be very high in some environments, e.g. the warm, moist conditions on the floor of a rainforest, and decomposers can contribute 80% of the CO_2 in that environment.

Feeding

Respiration – converts carbohydrates to carbon dioxide **with the release of energy**

Organic compounds in animals

Carbohydrates and fats

Proteins

Combustion – releases carbon dioxide by the burning of fossil fuels. This **increases** the concentration of CO_2 available in the environment.

Organic compounds in fossil fuels e.g. peat, coal, oil

POLLUTO – lead free

Death and excretion provide plant and animal material for decay.

Organic compounds in decomposers – bacteria and fungi

Some conditions e.g. low temperature, low oxygen concentration and low pH prevent action of decomposers. This leads to carbon compounds being 'locked up' in fossil fuels. Fossil fuel formation **lowers** the concentration of CO_2 which is available in the environment, as it continues to be removed by photosynthesis.

The carbon cycle

4.6 The nitrogen cycle

Plants need nitrate

Plants need nitrogen for the synthesis of proteins and other compounds, including DNA and vitamins. Nitrogen gas makes up about 80% of the Earth's atmosphere, but plants do not have the enzymes necessary to use the nitrogen directly – instead they must absorb it as **nitrate**. Nitrate is formed by two sets of processes carried out by microorganisms – **nitrogen fixation** and **nitrification**.

Nitrogen fixation

In **nitrogen fixation**, nitrogen and hydrogen are combined to form ammonium ions and then nitrate. The process depends upon enzymes that are only possessed by certain bacteria called **nitrogen-fixing bacteria**. Some of these bacteria live free in the soil, but a very important species called *Rhizobium leguminosarum* lives in swellings called **nodules** on the roots of leguminous plants such as peas, beans and clover. Nitrogen fixation only happens if oxygen is present. It also occurs naturally in the atmosphere when the energy from lightning combines nitrogen directly with oxygen. Farmers can plant legumes in a crop rotation scheme to avoid having to use so much nitrogen-containing fertiliser. This saves money, and also limits pollution of water (see page 254).

Nitrification

In **nitrification**, ammonium ions produced by the decomposition of amino acids and proteins are oxidised, first to **nitrite** and then to nitrate. The process is carried out by **nitrifying bacteria** which live in the soil. Nitrification only happens if oxygen is present. In the absence of oxygen the process is reversed, and **denitrifying bacteria** obtain their energy by converting nitrate to nitrogen gas. This is why waterlogged soils, for example, tend to lose nitrate as nitrogen gas.

Recycling nitrogen

Once nitrate has been formed by either nitrogen fixation or nitrification, it can be absorbed by plants through their roots. Eventually the plant dies, and its body is added to the animal wastes and remains in the soil. Decomposers break down the nitrogen compounds in these wastes and remains and the formation of nitrate can begin again.

In a typical ecosystem the processes shown opposite recycle nitrogen between living organisms and the environment. However, some processes cause the loss of nitrate from the environment. This happens naturally as a result of **denitrification** (see above), and less naturally when crops are **harvested** and removed from the site where they have grown. These losses of nitrate can be made up either by nitrogen fixation or by adding nitrate in the form of fertilisers.

1. Use your knowledge of the nitrogen cycle to explain how the following farming practices might improve soil fertility.
   a ploughing in stubble rather than burning it
   b draining waterlogged fields
   c planting peas or beans every third year
   d adding NPK fertiliser
   e adding well-rotted compost
2. Explain why farmers drain waterlogged fields.

The nitrogen cycle

The processes of nitrification, absorption, feeding, death, excretion and decay lead to the cycling of nitrogen between living organisms and their environment. In a natural ecosystem nitrogen fixation can 'top up' the cycle and make up for losses by denitrification.

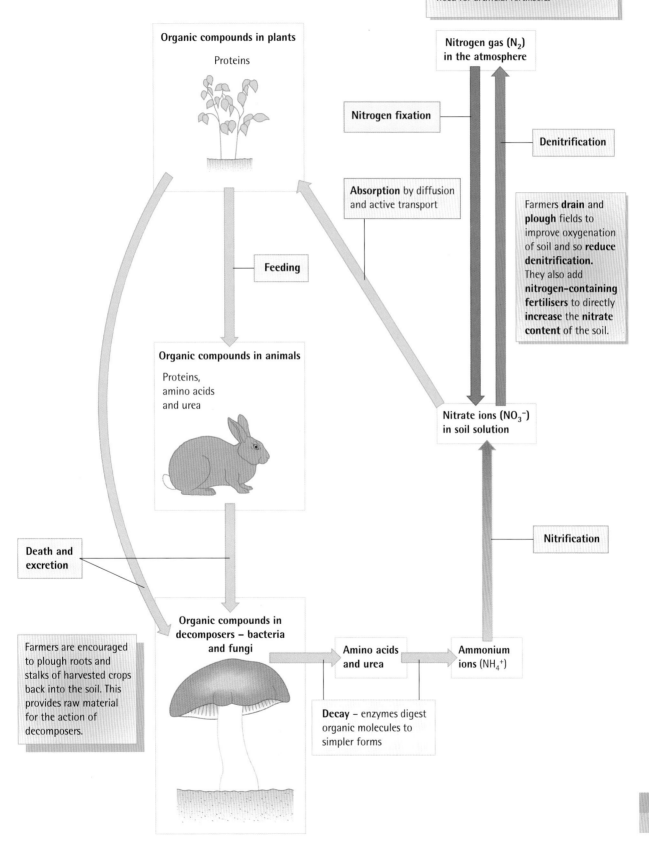

Some plants, called **legumes** (beans and peanuts are examples), have swelling on their roots. These **root nodules** contain bacteria, which can convert nitrogen gas to nitrate ions. These plants reduce the need for artificial fertilisers.

Organic compounds in plants

Proteins

Nitrogen gas (N_2) in the atmosphere

Nitrogen fixation

Denitrification

Absorption by diffusion and active transport

Feeding

Farmers **drain** and **plough** fields to improve oxygenation of soil and so **reduce denitrification.** They also add **nitrogen-containing fertilisers** to directly **increase** the **nitrate content** of the soil.

Organic compounds in animals

Proteins, amino acids and urea

Nitrate ions (NO_3^-) in soil solution

Death and excretion

Nitrification

Farmers are encouraged to plough roots and stalks of harvested crops back into the soil. This provides raw material for the action of decomposers.

Organic compounds in decomposers – bacteria and fungi

Amino acids and urea

Ammonium ions (NH_4^+)

Decay – enzymes digest organic molecules to simpler forms

4.7 Water is recycled too!

Water and life
Life first evolved in water for a number of reasons:

- The molecules that were used by living organisms, and that made up their structure, were dissolved in the first seas.
- In the muddy estuaries and shallow seas of the primitive Earth, the molecules could become concentrated enough to react together.
- Water acted as a protective shield for the first living organisms against the damaging ultraviolet rays from the Sun.

Recycling water
Life continues on this planet because water has special properties. In particular, all three states of water – solid ice, liquid water and gaseous water vapour – exist at the temperatures found on the Earth's surface. The temperature varies at different times and at different places on the planet, but the average temperature over the Earth's surface is about 16.5 °C. This means that ice, liquid water and water vapour are all present and are continually interchanging. Water is recycled between different parts of the environment, as shown in the water cycle below.

The water cycle
All of the elements that make up living organisms, not just carbon and nitrogen, are recycled. The water cycle is different to the cycles of carbon and nitrogen because:

- only a tiny proportion of the water which is recycled passes through living organisms

- the most important factor in water recycling is heat energy from the Sun. This evaporates water, and also creates the temperature gradients which lead to winds.

The steps involved in the water cycle are shown in the diagram opposite.

The special properties of water
The picture of the kangaroo shows the importance of the properties of water to living things.

The **high specific heat capacity** of water means that cells or bodies with a high water content tend to resist heating up or cooling down, even when the temperature of their environment changes.

Evaporation of water from a surface allows loss of heat. Water has a **high latent heat of vaporisation**.

Because water is **incompressible**, it provides excellent support. Water helps support a whole organism (e.g. a fish), or part of an organism (e.g. the eyeball, or the erect penis of a mammal).

Water is an excellent **transport medium** for many biological molecules, such as oxygen, glucose, amino acids, sodium ions and urea.

Water is an excellent **lubricant**, for example in saliva or in the synovial fluid of movable joints.

Water can be a **biological reagent**, for example in the processes of photosynthesis and digestion.

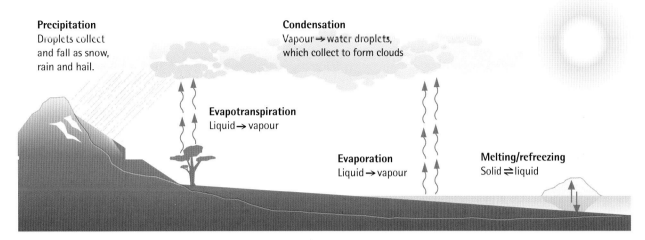

Precipitation
Droplets collect and fall as snow, rain and hail.

Condensation
Vapour → water droplets, which collect to form clouds

Evapotranspiration
Liquid → vapour

Evaporation
Liquid → vapour

Melting/refreezing
Solid ⇌ liquid

The water cycle is maintained by heat energy from the Sun.

1 a Explain how nitrogen in the muscle protein of a herbivore may be recycled to form protein in another herbivore some years later.

b Explain how the activities of some bacteria form a part of both the carbon and nitrogen cycles.

(CIE 'O' level May-June 2004)

2 Use words from the following list to complete the paragraphs about ecosystems. You may use each word once, more than once or not at all.

respiration, decomposition, producer, chemical, carnivore, consumer, photosynthesis, energy, light, elements, decomposers, herbivore

In each ecosystem there are many feeding relationships. A food chain represents a flow of _____ through an ecosystem, and always begins with an organism called a _____ which is able to trap _____ energy and convert it to _____ energy. An organism of this type is eaten by a _____, which is a kind of _____ that feeds only on plant material. This type of organism is, in turn, eaten by a _____ (an organism that consumes other animals).

The process in which light energy is transferred into a chemical form is called _____ – eventually the energy is released from its chemical form during the process of _____ This process provides energy for all living organisms, including _____ which are microbes that feed on the remains of animals and plants.

3 In Africa, mammals called jackals are quite common. They feed on small herbivores such as young springboks and dik-diks, hunting in packs to catch their prey. They will also eat larger herbivores such as kudu that have been killed by larger predators such as lions.

A farmer in South Africa found that a number of his sheep, while feeding on grassland, were being killed by jackals. He noted that jackals always kill sheep by attacking their necks. He designed a plastic collar for the sheep that covered their necks. None of his sheep have been killed since fitting these collars. Other farmers are now buying the collars to protect their sheep from jackal attack.

a The prey species of the jackal are usually primary consumers. State the type of food that all primary consumers eat.

b Name the two carnivores identified in the text.

c Construct a food chain for the jackal to show its relationship with sheep.

d Suggest a reason why jackals survive better when they hunt in packs.

e When the farmer started to use collars on his sheep, although none of his sheep were being killed, the population of jackals did not decrease. Suggest why the number of jackals did not decrease.

f Name two structures, found in the neck of a sheep, that could be damaged when jackals attack it.

g Some of the protected sheep die of old age and their remains are eaten by other animals. Suggest and explain why the collars of the dead sheep could create an environmental problem.

(IGCSE May-June 2004)

Organisms and their environment

Questions on decay and cycles

1. The diagram on the right represents a food web in the Southern Ocean.
   a i From the diagram, identify an example of each of the following
      a carnivore   *a decomposer*
      a herbivore   *a producer*
      ii Draw a food chain of **five** organisms selected from the food web.
   b In most food chains, the number of individuals decreases at each stage in the chain whilst the size of individuals increases. State the stage in the diagram at which this rule does **not** apply. Explain your answer.
   c Explain, with reference to the transfer of energy in food chains, why it might be more efficient for humans to eat herbivores rather than to eat carnivores.

   (IGCSE June 1997)

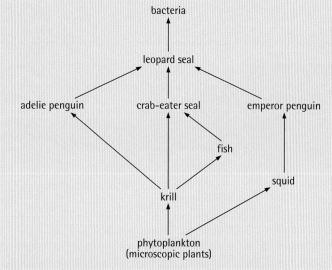

2. The diagram on the right shows part of the nitrogen cycle.
   a i Name the gas **A**.
      ii Copy the diagram and write the letter **B** next to **two** of the arrows in the cycle which represent stages involving bacteria.
      iii On your copy, label with an **X** the arrow which represents the process of denitrification.
   b i Name a chemical which is made by plants from the nitrates they absorb from the soil.
      ii Name an excretory product containing nitrogen, which is produced by animals.

   (IGCSE Nov. 1997)

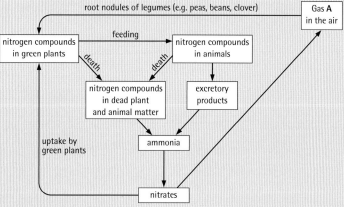

3. The drawings on the right show some of the changes which can take place in a tropical rain forest because of human activity.
   a Give TWO reasons why rain forests have been cut down.
   b The amount of rain falling on the forest area decreases after the trees have been cut down. Suggest the possible reason for this.
   c Describe the effects that removing the trees has on the animal life in the area.
   d Why do the crops fail after a few years?
   e Some of the world's mixed forests have been cut down and the area replanted with only one or two species of tree.
   Explain the disadvantage of this compared with allowing the forest to regrow naturally with many species of tree.

   (Edexcel June 1997)

4 a Explain why food webs can be considered large
      recycling systems.
   b Farming practices disrupt food webs. To what extent
      do you agree or disagree with this statement?
   c Using your knowledge of food webs describe a food
      web which exists on a farm located in your area. Give
      reasons for your answer.
   d At a campsite in the Caribbean countryside, food is
      cooked using gas from a biodigester, which utilises
      unwanted plant and animal material from the camp.
      Explain why this is possible.

5 Caribbean farmers sometimes:

   a Plant peas and corn together to ensure that the corn
      plants could grow well. Use your knowledge of the
      nitrogen cycle to explain this practice.
   b Use manure from farm animals as fertiliser for their
      crops, which are sold in the organic produce section at
      the greengrocer's store. Comment on this practice.

6 Read the following passage.

   In any ecosystem there is a *flow* of energy along food
   chains but a *cycling* of elements such as carbon and
   nitrogen. Carbon is an important element since it is
   found in all organic molecules – it is circulated between
   living organisms and their environment through the
   processes of respiration and photosynthesis.

   The atmosphere contains about 0.03% carbon dioxide
   but this is increasing. It is believed that the cutting
   down of forests reduces the amount of carbon dioxide
   removed by photosynthesis, and the burning of wood
   and fossil fuels increases the atmospheric concentration
   of this gas. Most fossil fuels – such as oil, coal, peat and
   gas – were made from the bodies of dead organisms
   during the Carboniferous period about 350 million years
   ago. The bodies of these organisms did not decay
   because of the conditions surrounding them after death
   – very damp, anaerobic conditions do not allow decay to
   occur, for example. Later, the remains of these organisms
   were heated and subjected to pressure by Earth
   movements and the fossil fuels were formed.

   When fossil fuels are burned both energy and carbon
   dioxide are released. It is thought that both heat energy
   and the carbon dioxide contribute to Global Warming.
   Global Warming may be responsible for changing
   weather patterns, such as severe rainstorms and high
   winds. These may dramatically affect ecosystems, by
   flooding for example.

   Remind yourself of the carbon cycle on page 241.

   a Write an equation for photosynthesis.

   b Name the pigment required for trapping of light
      energy in photosynthesis.

   c What effect does cutting down forests have on
      atmospheric carbon dioxide levels?

   d Forest waste is often burned to clear land for farming.
      How does this burning affect the carbon dioxide
      content of the atmosphere?

   e Name the two main groups of organisms responsible
      for decay and decomposition.

   f State two benefits to plants of decomposition in an
      ecosystem.

   g Suggest one effect on the environment of the burning
      of fossil fuels, apart from affecting the composition of
      the atmosphere.

4.8 Factors affecting population size

Environmental resistance

By taking samples and counting the numbers of organisms in a particular habitat, an ecologist can study how any factor affects the size of a population. For example, a woodland manager might wish to know whether thinning the trees in the wood affects the population of low-growing plants, or a farmer might wish to know whether the time of grass-cutting affects the population of bank voles. These factors may be **living (biotic)** or **non-living (abiotic)**. Together they affect the rate at which a population grows, and also its final size. All the factors that affect population growth and size together make up the **environmental resistance**.

Some significant **biotic** factors that affect population growth include:

- **Food** – both the quantity and the quality of food are important. Snails, for example, cannot reproduce successfully in an environment low in calcium, no matter how much food there is, because they need this mineral for shell growth.
- **Predators** – as a prey population becomes larger, it becomes easier for predators to find the prey. If the number of predators suddenly falls, the prey species might increase in number extremely quickly.
- **Competitors** – other organisms may require the same resources from the environment, and so reduce the growth of a population. For example, all plants compete for light. Competition for territory and for mates can drastically reduce the growth of individual organisms.
- **Parasites** – these may cause disease, and slow down the growth and reproductive rate of organisms within a population.

Important **abiotic** factors affecting population growth include:

- **Temperature** – higher temperatures speed up enzyme-catalysed reactions and increase growth.
- **Oxygen availability** – affects the rate of energy production by respiration.
- **Light availability** – for photosynthesis. Light may also control breeding cycles in animals and plants.
- **Toxins and pollutants** – tissue growth can be reduced by the presence of, for example, sulphur dioxide (see page 251), and reproductive success may be affected by pollutants such as oestrogen-like substances.

Growth curves and carrying capacity

When a small population begins to grow in a particular environment, the environmental resistance is almost non-existent – there may be plenty of food and no accumulation of poisonous wastes. The diagram opposite shows how environmental resistance eventually limits population growth, and the environment reaches its **carrying capacity**. Unless the environmental resistance is changed, perhaps by a new disease organism, the size of the population will only fluctuate slightly. Organisms that are able to maintain their population, or even increase it, must be well adapted to their particular environment.

Humans exploit environmental resistance

People use their understanding of environmental resistance to manage populations. For example:

- Predators are eliminated from farm situations.
- More food is made available to domestic animals.
- Nitrogen fertilisers and artificial light are used to boost plant growth.
- Predators may be used to control pests.
- Anaerobic conditions or low temperatures are used to prevent populations of microbes from consuming our food.
- Competitors are eliminated from crops using pesticides.

Examples can be found on pages 268 and 272.

Organisms and their environment

248

Factors affecting population growth

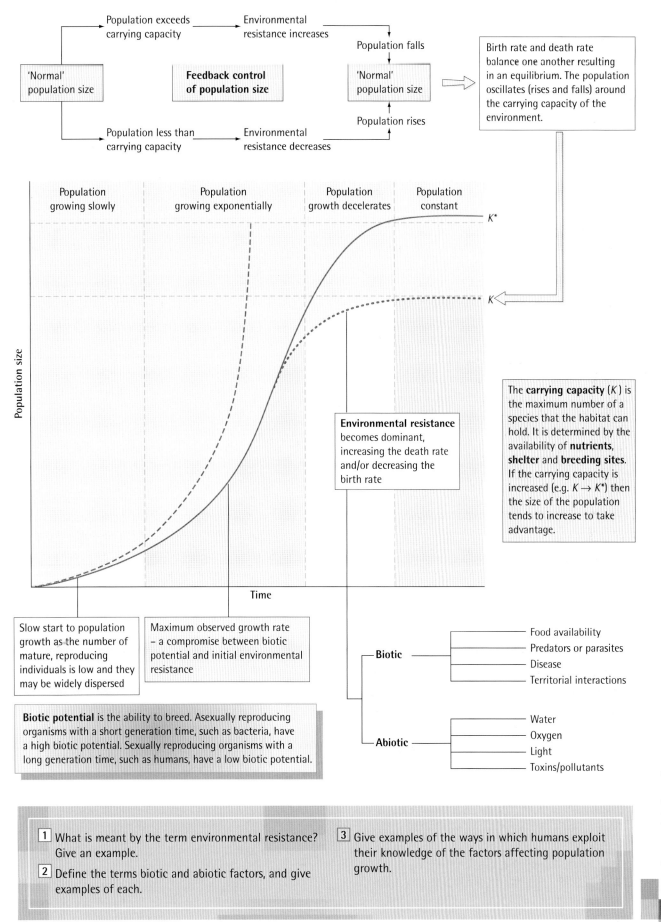

Population exceeds carrying capacity → Environmental resistance increases → Population falls

'Normal' population size

Feedback control of population size

'Normal' population size

Birth rate and death rate balance one another resulting in an equilibrium. The population oscillates (rises and falls) around the carrying capacity of the environment.

Population less than carrying capacity → Environmental resistance decreases → Population rises

Population growing slowly | Population growing exponentially | Population growth decelerates | Population constant

K^*

K

Population size

Time

Environmental resistance becomes dominant, increasing the death rate and/or decreasing the birth rate

The **carrying capacity** (K) is the maximum number of a species that the habitat can hold. It is determined by the availability of **nutrients**, **shelter** and **breeding sites**. If the carrying capacity is increased (e.g. $K \rightarrow K^*$) then the size of the population tends to increase to take advantage.

Slow start to population growth as the number of mature, reproducing individuals is low and they may be widely dispersed

Maximum observed growth rate – a compromise between biotic potential and initial environmental resistance

Biotic
- Food availability
- Predators or parasites
- Disease
- Territorial interactions

Abiotic
- Water
- Oxygen
- Light
- Toxins/pollutants

Biotic potential is the ability to breed. Asexually reproducing organisms with a short generation time, such as bacteria, have a high biotic potential. Sexually reproducing organisms with a long generation time, such as humans, have a low biotic potential.

1 What is meant by the term environmental resistance? Give an example.

2 Define the terms biotic and abiotic factors, and give examples of each.

3 Give examples of the ways in which humans exploit their knowledge of the factors affecting population growth.

4.9 Human population growth

Objectives
- To know that the evolution of humans from hunter-gatherers to permanent settlers caused changes in the environment
- To understand the form of a human population growth curve

Humans, like other organisms, must find **food**, **shelter** and a **place to breed**. The first humans were hunter-gatherers who moved from place to place, taking what they needed to satisfy these requirements (but allowing the environment to recover once they moved on). After the most recent Ice Age this method of living became more difficult and humans began to settle in the most suitable areas. This meant that the environment did not have time to recover.

Growth of the human population

As with other organisms, the growth of the human population can be presented as a population growth curve. The number of humans increases, by reproduction, until the carrying capacity of the environment has been reached. Humans have the ability to alter their environment to raise the carrying capacity. Three major changes in human activities led to significant surges in the world population, as shown below.

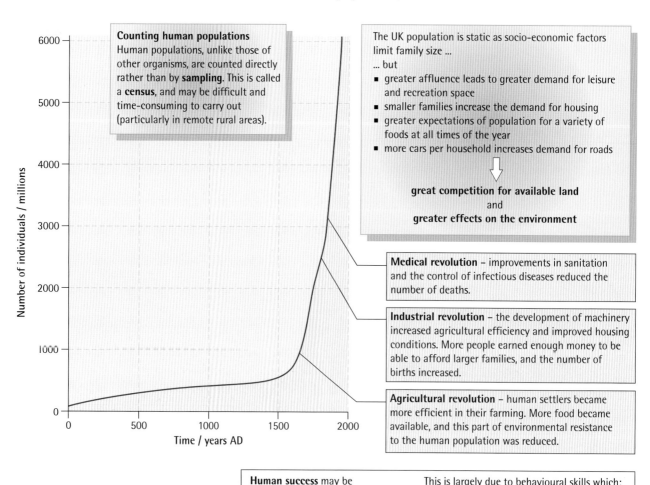

Counting human populations
Human populations, unlike those of other organisms, are counted directly rather than by **sampling**. This is called a **census**, and may be difficult and time-consuming to carry out (particularly in remote rural areas).

The UK population is static as socio-economic factors limit family size ...
... but
- greater affluence leads to greater demand for leisure and recreation space
- smaller families increase the demand for housing
- greater expectations of population for a variety of foods at all times of the year
- more cars per household increases demand for roads

great competition for available land
and
greater effects on the environment

Medical revolution – improvements in sanitation and the control of infectious diseases reduced the number of deaths.

Industrial revolution – the development of machinery increased agricultural efficiency and improved housing conditions. More people earned enough money to be able to afford larger families, and the number of births increased.

Agricultural revolution – human settlers became more efficient in their farming. More food became available, and this part of environmental resistance to the human population was reduced.

Human success may be measured as:
- worldwide distribution
- large number of individuals
- dominance over other species.

This is largely due to behavioural skills which:
- allow solution of complex problems
- allow control/modification of environment leading to **changes in carrying capacity** of the environment.

Human population of the world

Organisms and their environment

4.10 Human impacts on the environment: pollution of the atmosphere

Objectives

- To understand that humans can alter their environment
- To understand how changes in human population have altered our impact on the environment
- To consider human effects in terms of cause, effect and possible remedies

Humans already are, or could easily become, the most significant biotic factor in every environment. Primitive humans had a *temporary* effect on the environment – hunting, fishing and burning wood – because they were **nomadic** and allowed the environment periods of time to recover. After humans became **cultivators** and **settlers** (thousands of years ago) the following 'effects' on the environment gradually became noticeable:

- The use of tools and the domestication of animals meant a more efficient **agriculture**.
- The greater need for shelter, agricultural land and fuel meant a greater rate of **deforestation** and **desertification**.
- The careless use of pesticides and fertilisers, together with increasing consumption of fossil fuels, produced problems of **pollution**. These have been added to by the development of nuclear energy sources.

Humans may also have positive effects – we are able to use our skills and knowledge in **conservation**.

Our demands on the environment

Human success, measured as an increase in population size, is largely due to our ability to solve complex problems and modify the environment for our benefit. This places great demands on the environment causing changes in **the atmosphere, the aquatic environment** and **the land**.

Humans have also, intentionally or otherwise, seriously upset the balance of populations of other living organisms.

Causes, effects and remedies for pollution

Pollution is any effect of human activities upon the environment, and a **pollutant** is any product of human activities that has a harmful effect on the environment. When looking at pollution, we shall consider three key points:

- What is the **cause**?
- What are the **effects**?
- What are the **solutions**?

---

1. The following table contains information on human population changes since the year 1700.

Year	Population/millions
1700	700
1750	800
1800	900
1850	1200
1900	1600
1950	2500
1980	4450
1990	5300

a Plot these data in the form of a graph.

b Calculate the likely world population in the year 2050 if the growth rate shown between 1700 and 1800 had remained constant.

c Calculate the likely world population in the year 2050 if the trend in your graph continues.

d Explain the difference between your answers to **b** and **c**.

Organisms and their environment

Pollution of the atmosphere

There are three main problems with the Earth's atmosphere:

- the **greenhouse effect**
- changes to the **ozone layer**
- production of **acid rain.**

Burning of fossil fuels has a major effect on the atmosphere. The combustion process oxidises elements and compounds in the fuel, as shown in the equations on the right.

These oxides affect the atmosphere – carbon dioxide is a greenhouse gas, sulphur dioxide contributes to acid rain, and the oxides of nitrogen increase

amounts of both low-level ozone and acid rain. The other major pollutants of the atmosphere are the chlorofluorocarbons (CFCs).

There are also localised problems with lead compounds, and with smoke. The causes and effects of, and possible solutions to, each of these problems are outlined in the diagrams here and on page 253.

$$\text{Carbon} + \text{oxygen} \longrightarrow \text{carbon monoxide (CO)} \text{ and carbon dioxide (CO}_2\text{)}$$

$$\text{Sulphur} + \text{oxygen} \longrightarrow \text{sulphur dioxide (SO}_2\text{)}$$

$$\text{Nitrogen} + \text{oxygen} \longrightarrow \text{nitrogen monoxide (NO)} \text{ and nitrogen dioxide (NO}_2\text{)}$$

Solar radiation

Causes of the increased greenhouse effect

Greenhouse gases trap infrared radiation ('heat') close to the Earth's surface. Solar radiation is allowed to enter the lower atmosphere but is not allowed to escape. The greenhouse effect is increasing because of raised levels of these greenhouse gases:

- **carbon dioxide** released by combustion of fossil fuels in power stations and internal combustion engines (in cars and lorries, for example)
- **methane** produced in the guts of ruminants such as cows, and in the waterlogged conditions of swamps and rice fields
- **CFCs (chlorofluorocarbons)** from aerosol propellants and refrigerator coolants.

More methane is produced by **termites** than by all the ruminant mammals on the Earth!

Effects

Good and bad results
Global warming (raised temperatures close to the Earth's surface) causes:

- greater climatic extremes – strong winds, heavier rainfall and unseasonal weather ⎫
- melting of polar ice and changes in density of sea water – rising sea levels and flooding ⎬ all may cause loss of crops
- evaporation of water from fertile areas – deserts form ⎭
- pests may spread to new areas

But

- higher temperatures and more carbon dioxide mean **more photosynthesis** and **more food production.**

Solutions

To limit the effects of greenhouse gases, humans should:

- reduce burning of fossil fuels – explore alternative energy sources
- reduce cutting of forests for cattle ranching or rice growing
- replant forests.

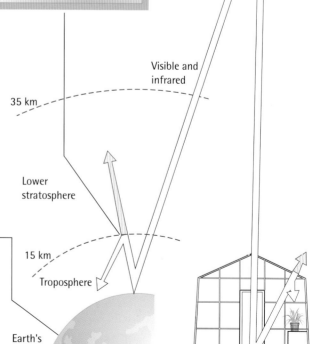

Visible and infrared

35 km

Lower stratosphere

15 km

Troposphere

Earth's surface

Some gases added to the atmosphere act like the panes of glass in a greenhouse and raise the temperature close to the Earth's surface.

Acid rain

Causes

Human activities release acidic gases
- Sulphur and nitrogen in fossil fuels are converted to oxides during combustion.
- More oxidation occurs in the clouds. Oxidation is catalysed by ozone and by unburnt hydrocarbon fuels.
- The oxides dissolve in water, and fall as **acid rain**.

Sulphur dioxide and nitrogen oxides $\xrightarrow{H_2O}$ sulphuric and nitric acids

Effects

Acid rain causes problems
- **Soils** become very acidic. This causes **leaching of minerals** and **inhibition of decomposition**.
- **Water in lakes and rivers** collects excess minerals. This causes **death of fish and invertebrates** so that food chains are disrupted.
- **Forest trees** suffer **starvation** because of leaching of ions and destruction of photosynthetic tissue.

1	2	3	4	5	6	7	8	9	11	12

'Acid' rain   'Pure' rain

Rain of pH 4 is 100 times more acidic than rain of pH 6.

Solutions

Acid rain can be reduced
- Clean up emissions from power stations with **scrubbers**.
- Clean up emissions from car exhausts with **catalytic converters**.

Scrubber

'Clean' gases

Polluted gases → Water spray

Water and dissolved pollutants

Catalytic converters clean up exhaust emissions by encouraging several pollutants to react together to give less harmful products:

From engine

NO, NO_2, CO_2, unburnt fuel

Metal catalysts

CO_2, H_2O, and N_2

To exhaust

'Acid' lakes and fields can be improved by the addition of crushed limestone ($CaCO_3$) – this is very expensive and time consuming.

Acid rain damages both living organisms and buildings made by humans.

Radioactive pollution

The Earth's environment is naturally radioactive due to cosmic radiation emitted from space, and terrestrial radiation emitted from the Earth's crust. However, this background level of radiation is exceeded in many parts of the world by contamination from man-made sources of radioactivity.

'Radiation' here means ionising radiation (as opposed to other non-ionising radiation, e.g. UV, infra-red, microwave). Radiation is emitted from radioactive substances as they spontaneously decay and takes several forms. The types of most concern are:

- alpha particles (α)
- beta particles (β)
- gamma rays (γ)

Each type of radiation has different properties and different penetrating power; e.g. alpha particles can be stopped by a few centimetres of air or a sheet of paper, however they are intensely ionising in the matter they pass through and can cause more damage to living tissue than particles with a longer path. Like alpha particles, beta particles lose their energy within a short distance and their biological significance is greatest if a beta emitter is taken into the body. Gamma radiation particles are similar to x-rays – they are deeply penetrating and strongly ionising; gamma rays can only be stopped by thick layers of concrete, lead or steel.

The decay of radioactive wastes takes a very long time. Some radioactive substances have a half-life of more than 10 000 years, which means they are dangerous for a very long time. (The half-life is the 'period of time required for the disintegration of half of the atoms in a sample of a radioactive substance'.)

Organisms and their environment

There are two major ways in which the atmosphere can become polluted by radiation:

Nuclear power plants

Nuclear power plant accidents can endanger life and the surrounding environment if the radioactive core is exposed and meltdown is occurring and releasing large amounts of radioactivity. This happened at Chernobyl, a nuclear power station in the Ukraine: an accident here destroyed the Chernobyl-4 reactor and killed 30 people, including 28 from radiation exposure. A further 209 on site and involved with the clean-up were treated for acute radiation poisoning and, among these, 134 cases were confirmed (all of whom apparently recovered). Nevertheless 19 of these subsequently died from effects attributable to the accident. Nobody off-site suffered from acute radiation effects. However, large areas of Belarus, Ukraine, Russia and beyond were contaminated in varying degrees.

Nuclear weapons

Nuclear weapon tests that are conducted above ground or under water can release radiation into the atmosphere. A nuclear test is the explosive test of a complete nuclear warhead – some tests in the twentieth century were conducted in areas occupied by soldiers. Most of the troops ordered to take part in the testing programme were not equipped with any specialised protective clothing. They were simply ordered to turn their backs or cover their eyes to avoid being blinded by the flash of the explosion. One former soldier remembers having his hands over his eyes but the flash was so bright that it acted like an x-ray and he could see all the bones in his hands.

Exposure to radioactivity frequently leads to various forms of cancer, including leukaemia. The troops involved have suffered much higher cancer rates than normal. However since cancer may take years to develop, it is difficult to prove that a particular case is linked to a particular cause.

4.11   Pollution of water

Objectives
- To recall why water is important to living organisms
- To understand that water supplies oxygen to living organisms
- To know how excess nutrients in water lead to depletion of oxygen levels
- To recall other aspects of water pollution

The causes of oxygen depletion

All living organisms depend on a supply of water, as we saw on page 244. Many organisms actually live in water. Most of these **aquatic** organisms respire aerobically and so require oxygen from their environment. Any change that alters the amount of oxygen in the water can seriously affect the suitability of the water as a habitat. The two pollutants that most often reduce oxygen in water are:

- **fertilisers** – nitrates and phosphates are added to soil by farmers (see page 256). Some of the fertiliser is washed from the soil by rain into the nearest pond, lake or river. This process is called **leaching**.

- **sewage** – this contains an excellent source of organic food for bacteria, and also contains phosphates from detergents.

How fertilisers and sewage affect the oxygen concentration

Water that contains few nutrients is rich in oxygen and supports a wide variety of living organisms. The oxygen enters the water from the atmosphere by diffusion and from photosynthesising aquatic plants. Simpler forms of life, such as algae and bacteria, are controlled because the low concentration of nutrients such as nitrate is a limiting factor for their growth. If more nutrients are made available, from fertiliser runoff or from sewage, then:

- Algae and other surface plants grow very rapidly, and block out light to plants rooted on the bottom of the river or pond.

- The rooted plants die, and their bodies provide even more nutrients.

- The population of bacteria increases rapidly. As they multiply, the bacteria consume oxygen for aerobic respiration. There is now a biological oxygen demand (or BOD) in the water because of oxygen consumed by these microbes.

- Other living creatures cannot obtain enough oxygen. They must leave the area, if they can, or they will die. Their bodies provide even more food for bacteria, and the situation becomes even worse. This is an example of **positive feedback** – the change from ideal conditions causes an even greater change from ideal conditions.

The lower diagram overleaf shows what happens if a pond or river receives too many nutrients. The process is called **eutrophication**. The pond or river soon becomes depleted of living organisms. Only a few animals, such as *Tubifex* (sewage worms), can respire at the very low oxygen concentrations that are available. The solution to this problem is straightforward – **do not allow excess nutrients into the water**.

A well-balanced natural pond or river

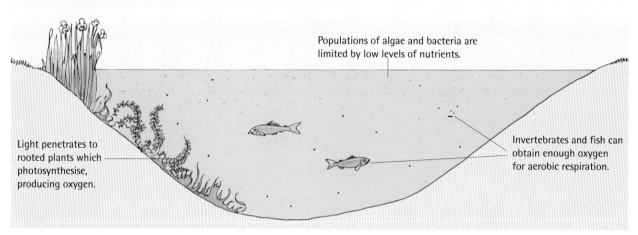

Populations of algae and bacteria are limited by low levels of nutrients.

Light penetrates to rooted plants which photosynthesise, producing oxygen.

Invertebrates and fish can obtain enough oxygen for aerobic respiration.

A nutrient-enriched pond or river

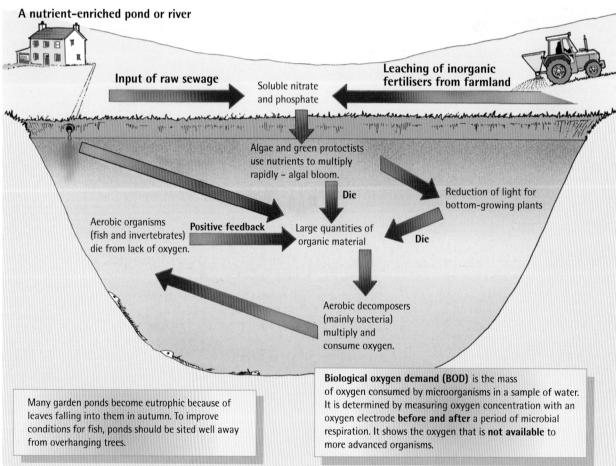

Input of raw sewage

Soluble nitrate and phosphate

Leaching of inorganic fertilisers from farmland

Algae and green protoctists use nutrients to multiply rapidly – algal bloom.

Die

Reduction of light for bottom-growing plants

Aerobic organisms (fish and invertebrates) die from lack of oxygen.

Positive feedback

Large quantities of organic material

Die

Aerobic decomposers (mainly bacteria) multiply and consume oxygen.

Many garden ponds become eutrophic because of leaves falling into them in autumn. To improve conditions for fish, ponds should be sited well away from overhanging trees.

Biological oxygen demand (BOD) is the mass of oxygen consumed by microorganisms in a sample of water. It is determined by measuring oxygen concentration with an oxygen electrode **before and after** a period of microbial respiration. It shows the oxygen that is **not available** to more advanced organisms.

Causes of eutrophication	Effects	Solutions

Unnaturally high levels of nutrients:
■ from leaching of fertilisers
■ from input of raw sewage
■ from liquid manure (slurry) washed out of farmyards.
	Depleted oxygen levels in water cause death of fish and most invertebrates. High nitrate levels can be dangerous to human babies.	■ Treat sewage before it enters rivers (see page 258).
		■ Prevent farmyard drainage entering rivers and ponds.
		■ Control use of fertilisers:
		  – apply only when crops are growing
		  – never apply to bare fields
		  – do not apply when rain is forecast
		  – do not dispose of waste fertiliser into rivers and ponds.
		■ Bubble a stream of air through badly polluted ponds.

Pesticides

Causes

Over-use of pesticides on agricultural land (e.g. to protect a crop from insects) or directly on water (e.g. to kill an aquatic stage of an insect) can raise pesticide levels in water. The pesticide levels are then **amplified** as they pass through food chains. For example, one stickleback may consume 500 *Daphnia*. The living matter in the *Daphnia* will be used for raw materials or lost as heat but the pesticide remains **concentrated in the tissues** of the stickleback.

DDT concentration in parts per million:

Water	Plankton	*Daphnia*	Stickleback	Grebe
0.02	5	50	250	1500

Effects

High concentrations of pesticides may accumulate in the tissues of top carnivores. The pesticide may be toxic (and kill the carnivore) or may affect its metabolism. DDT, used to control mosquitoes in malarial zones, severely reduced breeding success in birds of prey.

Solutions

- Use degradable pesticides – DDT, for example, lasts for a long time and so its use is banned in the UK.
- Explore alternative methods, such as biological pest control.
- Crops that are **genetically modified** to resist attack by insects may reduce the need to use insecticides.

Acid rain (see page 253) also causes significant pollution of water. Some lakes are almost empty of life as a result of pH levels as low as 4 or 5.

1 Sea otters eat fish, and fish eat small crustaceans such as shrimps. The shrimps feed by filtering algae from the water.
   a Write out a food chain that links these organisms.
   b Pesticides are washed from nearby farmland into rivers and then into the sea. Farmers say that the concentration of the pesticides is too low to directly affect the otters. Explain how the pesticides might still cause the death of the otters.

2 Untreated human sewage should not enter river water, but occasionally an overflow from a water treatment plant occurs. The tables below contain information on the changes that occurred in river water downstream from a sewage overflow.

a Plot these data in the form of a line graph. Choose axes to display the information in the way that best relates the abiotic factor to the biotic factors.
b Suggest why the number of bacteria was high at 0 m.
c Explain the shape of the curve for algae.
d How is it possible for fish numbers to fall to zero and then recover?
e Describe the changes in the concentration of oxygen dissolved in the water downstream from the point of sewage entry.
f Explain what might have caused these changes in oxygen concentration.

Distance downstream / m	Concentration of dissolved oxygen / percentage of maximum
0 (point of sewage entry)	95
100	30
200	20
300	28
400	42
500	58
600	70
700	80
800	89
900	95
1000	100

Table 1

Distance downstream / m	Number / arbitrary units of		
	bacteria	algae	fish
0 (point of sewage entry)	88	20	20
100	79	8	6
200	74	7	1
300	60	21	0
400	51	40	0
500	48	70	0
600	44	83	0
700	42	90	0
800	39	84	0
900	36	68	4
1000	35	55	20

Table 2

Objectives

- To recall that pathogens cause disease only when they gain access to body tissues
- To recognise that food and water are possible means of entry to body tissues
- To understand the processes involved in the provision of a safe water supply

Limiting the spread of diseases

Pathogenic microbes can only cause disease if they are able to enter the body and invade the tissues. The body has defences against disease, but there are a number of weaknesses (see page 98). For example, food and water may contain pathogenic microbes. *Salmonella* and *Escherichia coli* (*E. coli*), which cause food poisoning, enter the body in this way, and so do *Cholera vibrio* and *Amoeba* which are waterborne organisms causing cholera and dysentery, respectively. We try to protect ourselves from these diseases by making sure our drinking water, milk and foods are pathogen free.

Safe water: sanitation and water treatment

Living organisms need water for a number of reasons (see page 244). Water can be lost very rapidly from the human body and we need access to a supply of drinking water. Water supplies are kept **potable** (pathogen-free and drinkable) by both **sanitation** and by **sewage treatment**.

Sanitation is the removal of faeces from waste water so that any pathogens they contain cannot infect drinking water.

Pit latrine

In camps and in isolated houses sewage can be disposed of in a hole. The hole is dug deep enough to accept a large quantity of sewage (ideally several metres deep), and then filled in with soil to keep away flies and rats. This type of disposal system – called a 'long drop' or **pit latrine** - is cheap to produce and does not depend on running water, but has several disadvantages:

- The smell can be extremely unpleasant, especially in tropical areas.

- The sewage can overflow, especially during rainy periods. This allows faeces, perhaps contaminated with human pathogens, to reach water supplies and agricultural land. The sewage (and pathogens) can be washed down through the soil and contaminate nearby water supplies.

Where a good water supply is available, a flush WC is connected to the water carriage system and a flow of water carries the waste away.

Diagram of a lavatory pan or water closet (W.C.). Water is flushed around the rim, down the sides, and through the U-bend. Water retained in the U-bend seals off smells from the sewer.

The waste is then treated at a **sewage treatment plant** so that the valuable water can be recycled. The page opposite shows one type of sewage treatment plant called the **activated sludge** system.

The treatment of the sewage has two functions:

- to destroy or eliminate potential pathogens – either by the high temperature in the anaerobic digestion tank, or by chlorination of the water before it is discharged

- to remove organic compounds (mainly in faeces and urine). These might otherwise contribute to the **biological oxygen demand** (BOD – see page 256) of the water into which the treated sewage is discharged. Organic compounds are digested by fungi and bacteria.

In the activated sludge chamber, powerful jets of air keep the sludge aerated so that the processes of decomposition and nitrification (see page 242) can be completed in 8–12 hours. This means that large quantities of sewage can be processed very quickly.

Sewage treatment provides clean water by a combination of physical and biological methods

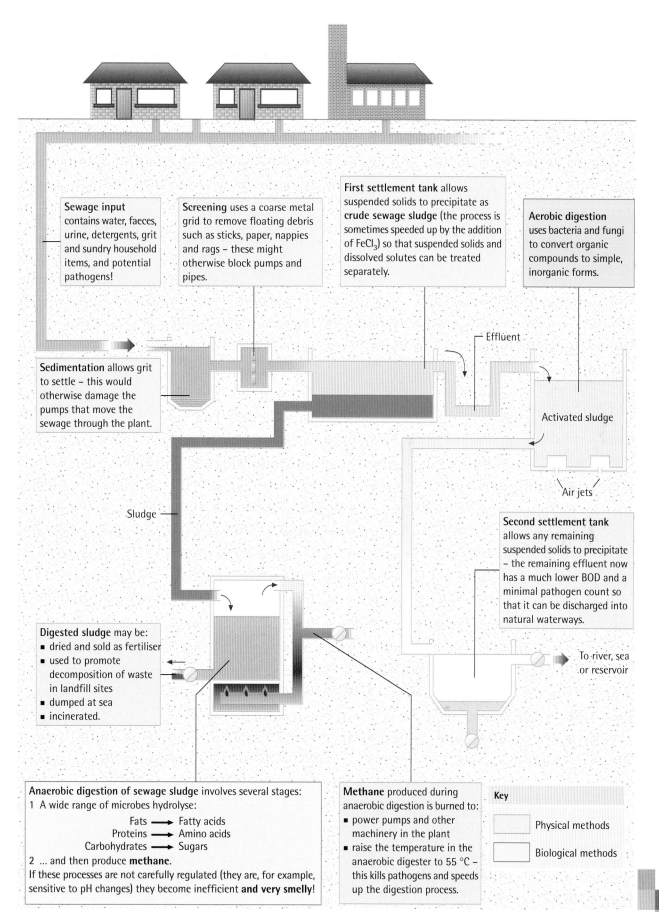

Sewage input contains water, faeces, urine, detergents, grit and sundry household items, and potential pathogens!

Screening uses a coarse metal grid to remove floating debris such as sticks, paper, nappies and rags – these might otherwise block pumps and pipes.

First settlement tank allows suspended solids to precipitate as **crude sewage sludge** (the process is sometimes speeded up by the addition of $FeCl_3$) so that suspended solids and dissolved solutes can be treated separately.

Aerobic digestion uses bacteria and fungi to convert organic compounds to simple, inorganic forms.

Sedimentation allows grit to settle – this would otherwise damage the pumps that move the sewage through the plant.

Effluent

Activated sludge

Air jets

Sludge

Second settlement tank allows any remaining suspended solids to precipitate – the remaining effluent now has a much lower BOD and a minimal pathogen count so that it can be discharged into natural waterways.

To river, sea or reservoir

Digested sludge may be:
- dried and sold as fertiliser
- used to promote decomposition of waste in landfill sites
- dumped at sea
- incinerated.

Anaerobic digestion of sewage sludge involves several stages:

1 A wide range of microbes hydrolyse:

Fats $\longrightarrow$ Fatty acids
Proteins $\longrightarrow$ Amino acids
Carbohydrates $\longrightarrow$ Sugars

2 ... and then produce **methane**.

If these processes are not carefully regulated (they are, for example, sensitive to pH changes) they become inefficient **and very smelly**!

Methane produced during anaerobic digestion is burned to:
- power pumps and other machinery in the plant
- raise the temperature in the anaerobic digester to 55 °C – this kills pathogens and speeds up the digestion process.

Key

☐ Physical methods

☐ Biological methods

Organisms and their environment

4.13 Humans, agriculture and conservation

Around the world, agriculture presents a serious threat to conservation of existing habitats. Although 75% of England is designated as farmland, only 2% of the UK population is involved in farming. In 1850, one farm worker produced enough food for about 4 people; now in advanced agricultural countries the same worker produces enough for 60 people. The enormous rise in productivity of land is due to many factors. These include:

- **increased and more efficient use of machinery** has resulted in increased field sizes and the removal of hedges (see page 262)
- **use of pesticides** to eliminate competitors for crop species has caused the reduction in population of many native wildflowers and some non-target insects and birds by direct toxicity or, more often, by removal of their food sources
- **increased use of inorganic fertilisers** affects plant diversity dramatically and can result in excessive nitrate levels in rivers, leading to eutrophication (page 256)
- the tendency towards **monoculture**.

All of these can have negative effects on the environment.

Currently, there are many people who are very unhappy about agricultural surpluses within the EU and the cost of the Common Agricultural Policy (CAP). After the Second World War, during which Britain had almost been starved into submission, successive governments encouraged farmers to maximise food production with subsidies as well as exhortation. Farmers in the EU and in Britain particularly have responded magnificently to that challenge; British farmers are the most efficient in the world. Unfortunately, very high efficiency usually also has some negative aspects and we are now asking whether these are acceptable.

It all boils down to monoculture!
We have noted above that farms used to be small and mixed but now tend to be large and specialised. Growing a single crop in this way is called **mono-culture** and, as ever, there are pluses and minuses.

Monoculture

⊕ (Good points)

Specialised harvesting techniques: one type of machine can collect all of the crop.

Highly selected strains: varieties of plants with desirable characteristics (see p. 222) can be 'matched' to the conditions.

Mineral/water requirement: scientists can work out exactly what the crop needs, and farmers can make sure they use it.

⊖ (Bad points)

Poor wildlife foods: very little variety of 'weeds' for insects and birds.

Spread of disease: plant pathogens, such as potato blight fungus and tobacco mosaic virus, spread easily: it's not very far to the next ideal food plant!

Loss of genetic variety: may mean that any change in environmental resistance (see p. 248) could damage or kill all of the plants.

Damage to soil: the same minerals will be 'drained' away by many copies of the same plant. As the crop is harvested and taken away the minerals will be lost from the soil.

Organisms and their environment

Loss of amenity value!

Monocultures are boring to look at, and few people enjoy walking in such a monotonous environment.

Some farmers are returning to traditional **crop rotations**, which has several benefits:

Crop rotations

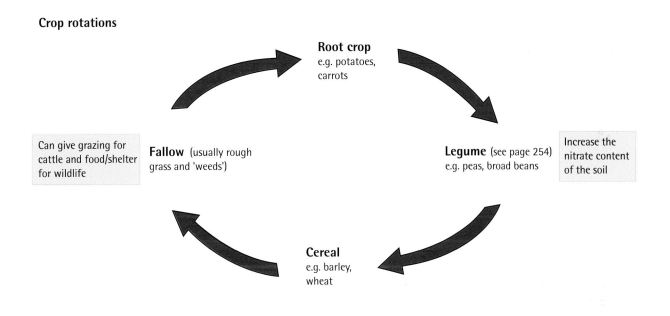

Root crop e.g. potatoes, carrots

Legume (see page 254) e.g. peas, broad beans

Increase the nitrate content of the soil

Cereal e.g. barley, wheat

Fallow (usually rough grass and 'weeds')

Can give grazing for cattle and food/shelter for wildlife

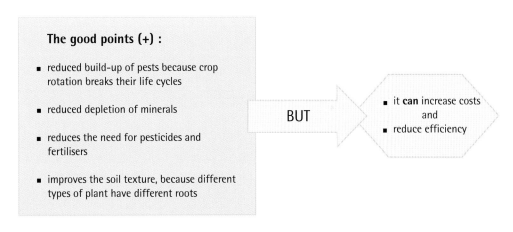

The good points (+) :

- reduced build-up of pests because crop rotation breaks their life cycles

- reduced depletion of minerals

- reduces the need for pesticides and fertilisers

- improves the soil texture, because different types of plant have different roots

BUT

- it **can** increase costs and
- reduce efficiency

The problem for the world is how to balance productivity (more food for humans) and biodiversity (keeping the wide range of wildlife).

Organisms and their environment

4.14 Pollution of the land

Objectives
- To understand that chemical discharges may pollute land as well as air and water
- To understand that many human effects on the land involve loss of wildlife habitat
- To know that there are ways to reverse loss of wildlife habitat

Many of the pollutants already described have an effect on land, as well as on the air or water, for example:

- lead and mercury compounds may poison areas of land
- pesticides may enter land-based food chains
- acid rain can affect the availability of minerals in the soil.

Pollution also includes the loss of wildlife habitat that results from human competition for land.

Removal of hedges
Farmers remove hedges to increase the area where they can grow crops. The benefits of hedgerows as habitats, and the reasons why farmers feel justified in removing them, are outlined below.

Deforestation
The removal of woodland provides firewood, building materials, cleared land for crops or for grazing of cattle. For our first settler ancestors, it also removed the habitat of predators of domestic animals.

The technique used to clear forest today is often called **slash and burn**. The largest trees may be removed for sale as timber for furnishings but the less valuable woods are simply chopped down (slashed) and then burned. The humans using the land gain a short-term benefit, but the damage to

Advantages

Hedges act as **windbreaks** which provide shelter for domestic animals, protect fragile crops, limit soil erosion and reduce water losses by evaporation from soil. A hedge 1 m in height provides these benefits for approximately 2 m to its sheltered side.

Taller hedges offer secure nesting sites for up to 65 **bird species**. These species may be important predators on pest species on local crops.

Fallen leaves and fruits provide **nutrient enrichment** for soil.

Grassy strip provides **shelter** for game birds and overwintering insects, and **nesting sites** for small animals (e.g. voles).

Hedges and associated herbs provide **feeding and breeding** opportunities for **pollinating insects** (including 23 species of butterfly).

Roots improve **soil stability** and limit both wind and water erosion.

Disadvantages

A hedge takes up spaces that could be occupied by crops and reduces economic use of modern agricultural machinery.

Hedge may shade crop species (compete with them for light).

May be a source of insects, and viral and fungal pests (although such species are often specific and are therefore unlikely to be pests of local crop species).

May act as a reservoir of weed species which then invade and compete with crops.

Hedge banks offer burrowing opportunities to rabbits which may then consume crops, especially in the young stages.

Roots may consume water and nutrients which otherwise would be available to crop plants.

Maintenance of hedges is **labour intensive** compared with barbed-wire boundaries.

The removal of hedgerows in Britain has averaged 8000 km per year in the twentieth century. This represents a disaster for wildlife.

wildlife habitats is immediate and humans also suffer in the long term. Newspaper and television headlines emphasise the loss of forest in tropical areas of the world, but it should be remembered that most of the UK was once forested! Some of the penalties of large-scale deforestation are illustrated below.

Urbanisation

The concentration of humans and their machines into small areas creates disturbance so that animals may stop breeding. In addition, roads separate one area of suitable habitat from another, and wildlife areas become fragmented into pieces that are too small to support stable populations of animals and plants. In order to construct roads and buildings, materials must be extracted from the land. The effects of quarrying to extract building materials can be devastating to wildlife.

1 It has been estimated that 100 000 miles of hedgerow have been removed from around Britain's fields since the Second World War. Why has this been done? What are the possible effects on wildlife?

2 What is deforestation? Give reasons why humans should be anxious about this process.

3 Why has urbanisation occurred? List the ways in which urbanisation:

a benefits humans

b is harmful to wildlife.

Suggest one way in which the effects of urbanisation can be reduced.

Deforestation – the rapid destruction of woodland

Reduction in soil fertility
- Deciduous trees may contain 90% of the nutrients in a forest ecosystem. These nutrients are removed if the trees are cut down and taken away.
- Soil erosion may be rapid in the absence of trees because wind and direct rain may remove the soil, and soil structure is no longer stabilised by tree root systems.
- The soil below coniferous forests is often of poor quality for agriculture because the shed pine needles contain toxic compounds that inhibit germination and growth.

Flooding and landslips
Normally in a woodland, 25% of rainfall is absorbed by foliage or evaporates and 50% is absorbed by root systems. After deforestation water may accumulate rapidly in river valleys, often causing landslips from steep hillsides.

Changes in recycling of materials – fewer trees means:
- atmospheric CO_2 concentration may rise as less CO_2 is removed for photosynthesis
- atmospheric O_2 – vital for aerobic respiration – is diminished as less is produced by photosynthesis
- the atmosphere may become drier and the soil wetter as evaporation (from soil) is slower than transpiration (from trees).

Climatic changes
- Reduced transpiration rates and drier atmosphere affect the water cycle and reduce rainfall.
- Rapid heat absorption by bare soil raises the temperature of the lower atmosphere in some areas, causing thermal gradients which result in more frequent and intense winds.

Species extinction Many species are dependent on forest conditions:
- mountain gorillas depend on cloud forest of central Africa
- golden lion tamarins depend on coastal rainforest of Brazil
- ospreys depend on mature pine forests in northern Europe.

It is estimated that one plant and one animal species become extinct every 30 minutes due to deforestation.

Many plant species may have medicinal properties, e.g. as tranquillisers, reproductive hormones, anticoagulants, pain-killers and antibiotics.
The Madagascan periwinkle, for example, yields a potent drug used to treat leukaemia.

4.15 Disifference of solid waste

4.15 Disposal of solid waste

Objectives

- To recall that humans produce many waste materials
- To understand that human wastes may become food for disease vectors
- To appreciate that there are different ways of disposal of human refuse
- To understand the benefits of recycling

Human refuse contains such items as metals, plastic bags, glass, remains of food and ash. This refuse must not be allowed to accumulate because:

- It is inconvenient, and gets in the way of people, their vehicles and their animals.
- It is unpleasant to look at.
- It could act as breeding ground for organisms which transmit disease.

To prevent refuse (rubbish) from building up it can be delivered to refuse tips, landfill sites or incinerators. It may be taken away by individuals, or communities may arrange collection in refuse collection vehicles. These vehicles often have a mechanical ram to compress the refuse so that more can be collected in one vehicle. The refuse disposal sites are normally sited away from residential areas, and surrounded by fences to stop rubbish blowing away and prevent children from playing in them. Two alternative ways of disposing of the refuse – **incineration** and **landfill** – are described on the page opposite.

Recycling

Recycling involves reusing waste products or materials which would otherwise be thrown away. This includes reusing items in their original form and sending materials away to special centres where they can be melted down or pulped to act as raw materials in industry.

Items that can be reused include:

- glass milk or soft drink bottles
- plastic shopping bags
- paper that has only been written on one side
- clothes

. . . . and materials that can be pulped or melted down include:

- glass bottles
- aluminium cans
- plastic bottles
- paper
- scrap metal.

Plastic bottles can be molten and reused in clothing, for example!

Recycling can make scarce resources last for longer, and can reduce the energy requirements of industry. It takes only 5% of the energy to make an aluminium can from recycled aluminium than from aluminium ore. People and companies will only recycle, however, if:

- their products are cheaper than if they don't use recycling
- governments give subsidies for manufacturing products from recycled materials.

Waste can be dangerous!

Three groups of products are causing concern to environmentalists: refrigerators and air conditioners, discarded rechargeable batteries and used motor products.

Most older **refrigeration equipment** contains freon, a chemical know as a chlorinated fluorocarbon or CFC. Each molecule of a CFC can destroy over 100 000 molecules of the Earth's protective ozone coating, leading to increased risk of sunburn, cataracts and skin cancer.

Rechargeable batteries contain cadmium, which poses little hazard in use (the cadmium is in a stable form) but is a danger in landfills.

Used motor oil contains heavy metals and other toxic substances that are hazardous. Used motor oil can cause skin cancers. Motor oil should never be dumped into drains. **Dumped tyres** tend to breed mosquitoes (see page 274) and may transmit disease. If they are burned they produce very toxic smoke.

Governments are trying to bring in laws to make manufacturers responsible for the recycling of these dangerous wastes.

Refuse disposal in landfill sites

Advantages
- Can help **land reclamation** e.g. in filling old quarry workings.
- Can be made economical in terms of space:
  - lorries use rams to compress rubbish
  - very deep pits can be used.
- Can be situated well away from residential areas, reducing impact of smells and unsightly rubbish.

Disadvantages
- Sites can attract **pests**, such as flies, rats and gulls. These might spread disease (e.g. flies contaminate food) or leave a mess (e.g. gulls leave droppings).
- Ecologically important areas such as marshes and heathland may be used as dumps.

Refuse may be buried under 0.5m of soil. This
- reduces access to pests
- allows bacteria and fungi to decompose organic compounds
- generates **biogas** which can be used to fuel machinery.

Refuse that can be decomposed by microbes is **biodegradable**. Non-biodegradable materials are **inert** (like plastic and glass) or **inhibit decomposition** (like acidic peel from oranges and lemons).

Refuse disposal by incineration

Advantages
- Incineration plant is quite small, so valuable land not used.
- No attraction to pests, so less risk of disease.
- Heat generated can be used – incinerators built as part of housing projects can save energy.

Disadvantages
- May generate toxic fumes (especially from burning plastics).
- Can be very expensive to build.
- Seepage of wastes may pollute groundwater.
- Fuel is consumed to begin the combustion process.

1 Why is a supply of water essential to humans? What dangers might be present in a water supply?

2 How does the treatment of sewage benefit both humans and the environment?

3 Name two waterborne diseases. Why are these diseases common in poor rural areas of developing countries, and in cities following very heavy rainfall?

4 a 'Sewage treatment involves both physical and biological processes'. Explain this statement.

b The supply of safe water also involves some chemical treatment. Why would a Health Authority insist on the addition of:
i chlorine and   ii fluoride to water supplies?

4·16 Humans may have a positive effect on the environment: conservation

Humans do not always damage the environment – growing numbers of **conservationists** try to balance the human demands on the environment with the need to maintain wildlife habitat. They will try to assess the likely effects of any human activity by producing an **Environmental Impact Statement**.

Forest management

Humans have been responsible for deforestation of much of the Earth's surface. Humans have also set up schemes for the large-scale planting of trees – in areas that have been cleared (**reforestation**) or in a new site (**afforestation**). There are a number of reasons for planting trees:

- as a cash crop, providing timber for building (coniferous plantations in the UK) or for fuel (quick-growing eucalyptus trees are widely planted in central Africa)
- to reverse soil erosion, particularly valuable in areas that have become deserts
- to provide valuable wildlife habitats – for example, Scots pine plantations are important habitats for red squirrels
- as recreational areas, providing leisure activities such as camping and mountain-biking.

A well managed forest can combine all of these functions. The Forestry Commission in the UK applies biological knowledge to the management of forests, as illustrated in the programme for conservation of red squirrels outlined opposite.

Endangered species

Competition between humans and other living organisms means that many species have disappeared or declined in number. The reasons for this are not always understood, but the following may be to blame:

- **Pest control** – the term pest includes any species that causes inconvenience to humans. Many species have been hunted ruthlessly, such as red deer (which damage trees), and also predators such as pine martens and red kites.
- **Commercial exploitation** – species of value to humans have been exploited, such as the beaver which was hunted and trapped to extinction for fur in the sixteenth century.
- **Loss of habitat** – more land is being used for agriculture, including previously unusable land that has been drained. This removes habitats for many species, such as cranes in East Anglia.

Conservationists work to slow down or stop the decline in **biodiversity** (the number of different species), and also to raise public awareness of the need to maintain species and their habitats. The number of different species in a community of living organisms can be described by a formula called the **Species Diversity Index**.

Conservation strategies

Conservation involves management of an area, and may include a number of strategies:

- **preservation** – keeping some part of the environment unchanged. This might be possible in Antarctica, but is less significant in a densely populated area like Britain than ...
- **reclamation** – the restoration of damaged habitats such as replacing hedgerows or recovering former industrial sites, and ...
- **creation** – producing new habitats, for example by digging a garden pond, or planting a forest.

A **conservation plan** involves several stages:

- **sampling** to assess the number of organisms
- **devising a management plan** – for example, trying to increase a species' population based on knowledge of its breeding requirements
- **carrying out the plan**
- **re-sampling** to assess the number of the 'conserved' species once more, and find out whether the conservation plan has worked.

The red squirrel in Britain

The red squirrel (*Sciurus vulgaris*) used to be widespread in Britain, but in most areas it has now been replaced by the larger grey squirrel (*Sciurus carolinensis*) which was introduced into Britain from North America. There are a number of possible reasons for the decline of the red squirrel:

- **Competition with the grey squirrel** – the red squirrel feeds mainly on seeds from pine cones. The grey squirrel eats a wider range of foods.

- **Disease** – the grey squirrel may carry a virus which harms red squirrels.

- **Habitat loss** – many recent forest plantings have been composed of trees all of the same age, and have often been of sitka spruce, which produces small seeds and sheds them early in the year, leaving little food for red squirrels in the winter.

Conservation plans to support red squirrel numbers are shown in the diagram below. Introducing a species from another country often causes problems for native wildlife.

1. Briefly describe why red squirrels are endangered in Britain. Outline a conservation strategy which might help to guarantee their survival.

2. What is meant by the term conservation? Why is conservation necessary?

3. It is sometimes stated that 'Conservation is a compromise'. Explain whether you think that this statement is a valid one. Use examples to illustrate your answer.

Tree species chosen to provide a food source that favours red squirrels, such as broad-leaved species that produce small seeds and are less attractive to the grey squirrels. Species favoured by the grey squirrels may be removed. Coniferous species might include Norway spruce and Scots pine, both of which shed their seeds late and thus provide a year-round supply of food for the red squirrels.

Competitor grey squirrels can be poisoned using warfarin-baited food in a 'grey-squirrel-selective' hopper. This strategy is restricted by legislation, but many landowners favour it because of damage to trees by grey squirrels.

Immunosterilisation – a vaccine could sterilise both male and female grey squirrels whilst leaving red squirrels unaffected. This could reduce the grey squirrel population in a humane way because it has little effect on the squirrels other than to make them sterile.

Supplementary feeding using hoppers that only allow access to red squirrels. These are placed in clusters of two or three about 20–30 m apart, and filled with a mixture of yellow maize, wheat, peanuts and sunflower seeds. They must be inspected and filled frequently.

Reintroduction of red squirrels – survival and behaviour of the introduced red squirrels must be carefully monitored by radio tracking and field observation.

Habitat management – red-squirrel reserves should be surrounded by at least 3 km of conifer forest or open land to act as a buffer against the entry of grey squirrels.

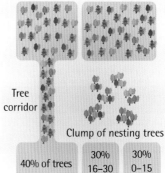

Seed-producing areas

Tree corridor

Clump of nesting trees

40% of trees > 30 years old	30% 16–30 years old	30% 0–15 years old

Clear felled area

Forest management to provide both food and shelter. When clear felling, some single seed-producing trees should be left, and some small groups as nesting sites. Seed-producing areas should be connected by corridors of trees to prevent isolation and allow movement between one area and the next.

Conservation plans to support red squirrel populations involve habitat management for food provision.

4.17 Human management of ecosystems: fish farming and horticulture

Objectives
- To understand how humans can control environmental resistance
- To describe examples of maximising yields in the commercial management of ecosystems

Humans exploit many other organisms, often as sources of food. Our understanding of population growth and the effect of environmental resistance allows us to maximise yields of 'food' populations by minimising environmental resistance. Two examples of the use of biological principles in the management of food-producing ecosystems are described here – greenhouse and fish farming.

Greenhouse management involves an understanding of the limiting factors that control photosynthesis (see page 67). Maximum photosynthesis means maximum plant growth.

Carbon dioxide concentration is a major limiting factor in photosynthesis. In a greenhouse plants may photosynthesise very quickly and CO_2 is rapidly used up. The CO_2 level is usually raised to about 0.1% of the atmosphere (about three times higher than in normal air). This gives an increase in yield of about 50%. The extra CO_2 can be provided by burning paraffin (which also raises the temperature) or by releasing it from a cylinder.

Computer control is widely used in large commercial greenhouses. Sensors provide information about air temperature, CO_2 concentration, water available to roots, humidity and mineral concentration, and the control centre ensures that any changes are corrected.

Temperature sensor → [computer] → Heater

High-yielding strains of crop are used. Selective breeding and/or genetic engineering can develop crop strains which:
- give a high yield
- produce fruit of a desirable colour/texture/size
- produce fruit at the same time
- may have genetic pest resistance.

Temperature affects plant growth because of its effect on the enzymes of photosynthesis. High temperatures may also speed up the life cycle of pests. Sunlight provides some heat (shading may be necessary in summer) but thermostatically regulated heaters provide greater control.

Illumination – it is important to control:
- **intensity** – Higher light intensity → more photosynthesis until some other limiting factor intervenes.
- **quality** – photosynthesis is most efficient at red and blue wavelengths; white light contains some wavelengths (green) which are not useful.
- **duration** – if fruit is the desired product, the plant must flower. Flowering is controlled by day length (the duration of light in a 24-hour period).

Sunlight provides some illumination but artificial lighting systems are more controllable (though more expensive).

Pest control is particularly important – pest species can quickly spread through a greenhouse containing only a single crop.

---

1 Study the diagram on the opposite page and answer the following questions.

a Suggest three biotic and two abiotic factors which might affect the productivity of the fish farm.

b Why are salmon and trout the most widely farmed fish in the UK?

c Suggest three ways in which biological knowledge is used to maximise the profits from the fish farm.

d Some fish farmers put air bubblers in their enclosures. Why might this be necessary?

e Why would doctors be anxious if growth hormones and antibiotics were added to the water in the enclosures?

f Suggest one advantage and one disadvantage of feeding protein pellets instead of live food to the fish in the farm.

Managing ecosystems

Fish farming maximises profit by minimising environmental resistance.

Suspended net keeps out aerial predators such as cormorant, heron and osprey.

Prepared food fed to the fish
- Pellets are easily transported and easily measured out.
- Usually made from fish caught in nets but not used for human consumption – **very high in protein** (gives rapid growth) but very expensive.
- May include **colouring agent** (turns fish pink – favoured by consumers) and **antibiotic** (disease control).

GRO-A-LOT PELLETS

Hanging net
- Keeps out **aquatic predators** such as otter and pike.
- Keeps out other fish and so **reduces competition** for the pelleted food.

Species – the 'farmed' species must:
- grow well under captive conditions
- accept prepared (non-living) food
- have a high **conversion ratio** i.e. convert food ➞ flesh efficiently
- ideally be able to breed under captive conditions
- not be particularly susceptible to disease.

It is usually **expensive** to farm fish so the product should command a **high price**. For this reason the main farmed species in Britain are members of the salmon family.

Fry production
- Fish are often spawned in aquaria using added reproductive hormones.
- Temperature is controlled while fry are 'grown on' (higher temperature gives rapid growth). Oxygen levels are kept high with aerators. Growth hormones may be added to water.
- Fry of **uniform size** are released into the farming pens. This reduces the chance of the fish eating each other!

Disease control – close confinement makes diseases more likely to spread. Pesticides are added to water to control fish lice and fungal infections, and antibiotics are added to food.

Problems
- Very high food costs.
- Poor control of temperature and oxygen availability in large outdoor farming pens.
- Much more research necessary to obtain highest yields – **selective breeding** programmes to develop new fish varieties with improved growth rates and conversion ratios.

Environmental concerns
- Pollution by pesticides which may kill organisms that are foods for wild species.
- Excess food and fish faeces create nutrient-rich environment below netted area ➞ growth of bacterial population ➞ increased **biological oxygen demand.**

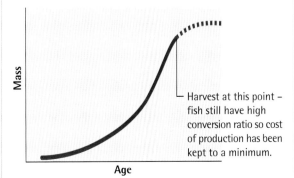

Age for harvesting

(graph: Mass on y-axis, Age on x-axis, showing a sigmoid curve)

Harvest at this point – fish still have high conversion ratio so cost of production has been kept to a minimum.

4.18 Helping the environment: fuel from fermentation

Objectives

▶ To recall that microbes carry out fermentation reactions

▶ To appreciate that fermentation products may be used as fuel rather than as food

▶ To list examples of fuels generated by microbial fermentation reactions

Fermentations make products which can be used as **fuel. Biomass fuels** use raw materials produced by photosynthesis. These materials are from plants and can therefore be regenerated. Biomass fuels include:

▶ **solid fuels** – wood, charcoal and vegetable waste

▶ **liquid fuels** – alcohol and vegetable oil

▶ **gaseous fuel** – biogas (a methane/carbon dioxide mixture).

The production of these biomass fuels is described in the following diagrams.

Solid fuel using natural woodland causes environmental problems but there are alternatives.

Natural woodland – live cutting: see **deforestation** (page 262)

Fallen, dead wood: lesser environmental problem, but still loss of habitat and nutrients

Cut wood: may have to be carried long distances. Heavy because of water content – much time/energy spent in wood-gathering.

---

1. What is a biomass fuel? What advantages might the use of biomass fuels offer?

2. What are the environmental benefits of quick-growing species of tree?

3. Look at the diagram opposite.
   a Suggest three products which could be sold, apart from the alcohol produced.
   b Both amylase and cellulase are involved in the preparation of the glucose feedstock for a gasohol generator. Suggest the exact function of these enzymes.
   c How has genetic engineering helped the gasohol industry?
   d A typical American car travels 10 000 miles a year at 15 m.p.g. This consumes the alcohol generated by the fermentation of 5000 kg of grain. A human on a subsistence diet consumes about 200 kg of grain per year. Comment on these figures.

4. Give two benefits that biogas generators offer to rural communities in poor countries.

5. Why are biogas generators built underground?

6. Why would it be inefficient to add disinfected household waste to the biogas generator?

Heating wood without air present produces almost pure carbon, called **charcoal**.
This fuel:
- burns slowly, releasing much heat
- causes very little pollution.

Producing charcoal

Wood slowly burning   Turf covering wood to keep out air

Quick-growing tree species may provide renewable fuel
e.g. eucalyptus in Zaire ...

WoW!

Erect, regular growth habit means easy cutting and storing.
Rapid growth – 8 m in 3 years.
High resin/oil content means it is clean burning, giving out much heat.

... and **sweet chestnut** from coppices in Kent may fuel local power stations.

Liquid fuel – ethanol
The raw material is called feedstock

Fermentation and distillation stages are energy demanding*

USA uses **Corn**

Soak (then use the liquid as **cattle feed**)
↓
Seed
Grind – separates germ, producing **corn oil**
↓
Starch
Enzymatic hydrolysis uses amylase

Brazil uses **Sugar cane**

Wash and crush
↓
Cane pulp
Enzymes amylases and cellulases   **Separation** – waste is **bagasse**. This is burned, giving energy for distillation*
↓
Syrup
Purification – impure sucrose solution (molasses) → **cattle feed**

Bubble CO₂ to encourage **anaerobic conditions**

Sugar →
Other nutrients →

Dried yeast → vitamins 'Marmite®'

Alcohol solution (15–20%)

Pure ethanol

$$C_6H_{12}O_6 \xrightarrow{\text{Fermentation}} 2C_2H_5OH + 2CO_2$$
(Glucose) → **(Alcohol)**

Fermentation agent
the yeast *Saccharomyces*.
Useful mutants/engineered strains can:
- cope with high temperatures generated during fermentation
- survive at higher alcohol concentrations (up to 15%, compared with 8–9% for 'normal' strains)
- respire anaerobically even when O_2 is present.

Fuel value of gasohol
- Start engine on high petrol/alcohol mixture
- Once warm, engine runs well on alcohol alone.

Environmental impact
- Alcohol fuels do not require 'anti-knock' additives
- Alcohol fuels produce fewer emissions such as CO, SO_2 and NO
- Process does not increase CO_2 in atmosphere (photosynthesis of feedstock removes the CO_2 which is generated by combustion)

Benefits of biogas
- **Cheap** – using surplus materials
- **Disposes** of human waste
- **Reduces** landfill problems
- **Reduces** use of other sources of power.

What are ideal conditions?
- Temperature of 20–30 °C: fermentation rate doubles per 10 °C rise
- Anaerobic conditions: oxygen is toxic to methanogenic bacteria
- Underground position → low O₂/stable temperature

Gas supply to home

Inlet   Strengthening   Outlet   **Discharged slurry used as manure**

Ground level
Concrete inlet pipe
Input contains large molecules from plant and animal waste.
Plaster

3 m
2.70 m
Soil

Fermentation by microbes

Protein → Amino acids → Ammonium salts → **Methanogenic bacteria** → Methane + carbon dioxide ⎤ **Biogas**

Fats → Fatty acids and glycerol

Carbohydrates → Glucose → Anaerobic bacteria → Ethanoic acid

If oxygen present → Carbon dioxide + water

Natural antibiotics: penicillin

A fungus such as *Penicillium* absorbs food molecules from its environment, and then uses these molecules for its own metabolism. Sometimes a *Penicillium* mould will make substances that it secretes into its environment to kill off any disease-causing or competitive microorganisms. A product made by one microorganism to kill off another microorganism is called an **antibiotic**.

The first antibiotic to be discovered was called **penicillin** after the organism *Penicillium* that produced it. Antibiotics used in medicine work in various ways to inhibit the development of bacterial infections, without harming human cells. Penicillin prevents the bacterial cell walls forming (human cells do not have cell walls). Antibiotics only affect bacterial cells – there is no benefit in taking antibiotics to treat viral or fungal diseases.

Production of penicillin

The large-scale production of penicillin takes place in industrial fermenters. Penicillin is a **secondary metabolic product** – it is made when growth of the producer organism is slowing down rather than when it is at its maximum, as shown in the diagram below.

Antibiotics do not always kill bacteria

Bactericidal antibiotics kill the pathogen directly, whereas **bacteriostatic** ones prevent it reproducing, leaving the host's defences to kill the existing pathogens. The diagram opposite illustrates the different effects of a bactericidal agent and a bacteriostatic agent.

Antibiotic resistance

As the use of antibiotics increases, strains of bacteria that are **resistant** to the antibodies are developing, as shown opposite.

Population of *Penicillium* grows rapidly, provided with:
- food for energy and protein synthesis
- oxygen for aerobic respiration
- correct temperature (24 °C) and pH (7.5)

Keep sterile!
- no microbes to compete for nutrients
- no danger of toxic chemicals being produced

Penicillin

Optimum time to collect penicillin – always produced **after** main growth of the mould fungus.

Collect batch and filter to remove fungus.

Filtered liquid contains penicillin.

Penicillin

Penicillin extracted and crystallised, then put into capsules.

Concentration of fungus or antibiotic

Time/days

Penicillin is produced by batch fermentation (see page 35).

Antiseptics are not the same as antibiotics

An **antibiotic** is used to **treat** a bacterial infection. An **antiseptic** can be used to **prevent** infection ('anti' = prevent, 'sepsis' = infection). Antiseptics are chemicals applied to the outside of the body, such as the skin, to kill microbes.

Disinfectants are also chemicals that kill microbes, but they are more powerful and are generally used on worksurfaces or lavatory bowls, where potentially harmful bacteria may be growing.

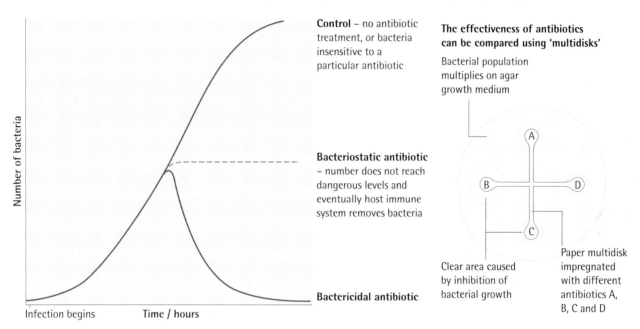

Control – no antibiotic treatment, or bacteria insensitive to a particular antibiotic

Bacteriostatic antibiotic – number does not reach dangerous levels and eventually host immune system removes bacteria

Bactericidal antibiotic

The effectiveness of antibiotics can be compared using 'multidisks'

Bacterial population multiplies on agar growth medium

Clear area caused by inhibition of bacterial growth

Paper multidisk impregnated with different antibiotics A, B, C and D

Penicillin is bactericidal at high concentrations, but these may have some side-effects in humans (and may lead to **resistance** – see below) so penicillin is usually given at bacteriostatic doses.

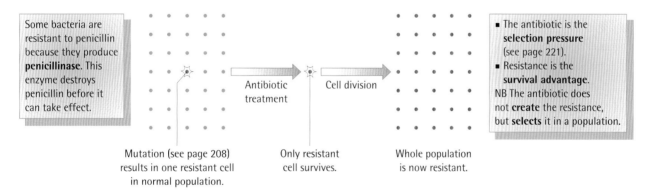

Some bacteria are resistant to penicillin because they produce **penicillinase**. This enzyme destroys penicillin before it can take effect.

Antibiotic treatment

Cell division

Mutation (see page 208) results in one resistant cell in normal population.

Only resistant cell survives.

Whole population is now resistant.

- The antibiotic is the **selection pressure** (see page 221).
- Resistance is the **survival advantage**. NB The antibiotic does not **create** the resistance, but **selects** it in a population.

Antibiotic-resistant strains of bacteria are formed by artificial selection. This is more likely to happen if antibiotics are used unnecessarily, or if people do not finish a course of prescribed antibiotics. This allows some of the bacterial population to recover, and possibly develop strains that are resistant to the antibiotic.

1 Distinguish clearly between the following pairs of terms:
a antiseptic and antibiotic
b antibiotic and antibody
c resistance and immunity.

2 Purified penicillin is normally taken orally (by mouth). The crystals of the drug are enclosed in a capsule for distribution. Suggest three important properties of the material used to make the capsules.

4.20 Controlling disease by understanding vectors

Objective
- To understand how study of an organism's life cycle can offer effective methods of disease control

Vectors and human health
Many small animals, particularly insects, cause a **nuisance** to humans because they bite or because they make food less palatable. More significant than their nuisance value, however, is the fact that they may transmit diseases to humans. Some of the diseases which can be passed from human to human in this way can be fatal.

Vectors and disease
An animal that transmits a pathogen (disease-causing organism) from one host to another is called a **vector**. The vector may transmit the pathogen either by carrying it on its body or by swallowing infected material. In the case of swallowed material – often blood – the pathogen survives and can multiply inside the gut of the vector.

Some important communicable human diseases in which vectors play a part are listed in the table below.

Protoctistans
Protoctistans are single-celled organisms, sometimes large enough to be seen with the naked eye. They cause some devastating diseases in humans. The diagram on the opposite page describes how the disease **malaria** (so called because it was once believed to be caused by 'bad air') is caused by infection with a protoctistan called *Plasmodium*. Understanding the life cycle of *Plasmodium* offers methods of controlling the spread of malaria.

Malaria has killed more humans than any other disease. The mosquito carries the protoctistan – it is the vector. The mosquito does not itself cause the disease.

Vectors and disease

Name of disease	Pathogen	Vector and method of transmission
Rabies	Virus	Mammals, including bats, rats and dogs. Passed on in saliva e.g. from bite of an infected animal
Leptospirosis	Bacterium	Mammals – passed on in urine to bodies of water such as ponds or rivers. Humans wash or bathe in infected water
Dengue fever	Virus	Mosquito (*Aedes aegypti*) which bites and drinks the blood of an infected person and then passes on the virus in its saliva
Malaria	Protoctistan	Mosquito (*Anopheles* species) which bites and drinks the blood of an infected person and then passes on the protoctistan in its saliva
Gastroenteritis	Bacterium of the Salmonella group	Housefly picks up infected material from food or from faeces, and then passes it onto human food as it feeds

Don't forget – the vector does not *cause* the disease, but *passes on* the pathogen from one human host to another!

Control of vector-borne diseases
The fact that the pathogen uses another organism to move from one host to another is a weakness. Doctors and scientists have used this weakness to work out ways of **controlling the transmission** of these diseases, usually by either:

- destroying the breeding grounds of the vectors, such as swamps and marshlands where mosquitoes lay their eggs; or

- reducing the feeding opportunities for the vectors, such as by covering food from houseflies and burning refuse to discourage rats.

Once a human is infected by one of these pathogens it may be necessary to work out some suitable **treatment**. This may involve no more than a period of rest (as in the first case of dengue fever), the administration of drugs (such as antibiotics for Leptospirosis) or immunisation with a powerful vaccine (as with rabies).

The diagrams which follow illustrate the life cycles of some vectors, and show some of the methods used to control the diseases which they may transmit.

Mosquitoes and dengue fever

Dengue fever is an infectious disease carried by mosquitoes, including *Aedes aegypti,* and caused by a virus. The disease is found mostly during and shortly after the rainy season in tropical and subtropical areas of the world. Dengue is *not* contagious from person to person.

Signs and symptoms

Symptoms of typical uncomplicated (classic) dengue usually start with a fever within 5 or 6 days after being bitten by an infected mosquito, and might include:

- severe joint and muscle pain
- pain behind the eyes
- severe headache
- nausea and vomiting.

A common sign of typical dengue fever is a rash which appears over most of the body 3 to 4 days after the fever begins.

Treatment

There is no specific treatment for classic dengue fever, and most people recover completely within 15 days. Doctors recommend plenty of rest, and the drinking of large volumes of fluids. Medicine can be taken to reduce the fever, but painkillers should *not* include aspirin.

The life cycle of *Aedes aegypti*, and some suggestions for control, are shown below.

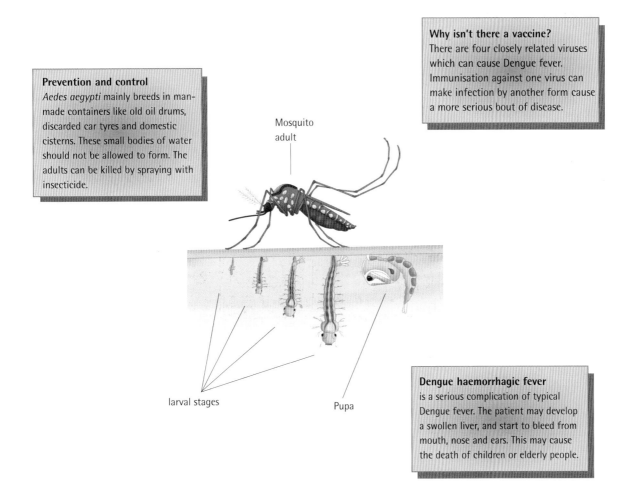

Prevention and control
Aedes aegypti mainly breeds in man-made containers like old oil drums, discarded car tyres and domestic cisterns. These small bodies of water should not be allowed to form. The adults can be killed by spraying with insecticide.

Why isn't there a vaccine?
There are four closely related viruses which can cause Dengue fever. Immunisation against one virus can make infection by another form cause a more serious bout of disease.

Mosquito adult

larval stages

Pupa

Dengue haemorrhagic fever
is a serious complication of typical Dengue fever. The patient may develop a swollen liver, and start to bleed from mouth, nose and ears. This may cause the death of children or elderly people.

Life cycle of *Aedes aegypti*

Houseflies as vectors

The mouthparts of a housefly consist of a long, grooved tongue which contains two channels – one channel releases saliva and the other channel sucks up digested foodstuffs.

As a fly feeds it squirts saliva containing digestive enzymes onto its food. The enzymes partly digest the food (see page 78) and the resulting liquid is sucked up into the fly's intestine where digestion is completed. The decaying remains of dead animals, dung and the remains of food on rubbish tips on which the houseflies feed can contain the microbes which cause typhoid, typhus, cholera, dysentery, tuberculosis and gastroenteritis, together with some tapeworm and threadworm eggs. These microbes and eggs can stick to the housefly's feet, mouthparts and body. If the fly is allowed to settle on uncovered human food and drinks containing sugar the microbes and eggs can be spread to the food as the flies walk over the food and as they release saliva and faeces onto it.

The figure below shows the life cycle of a housefly, and suggests some ways of controlling these animals to limit the diseases they spread.

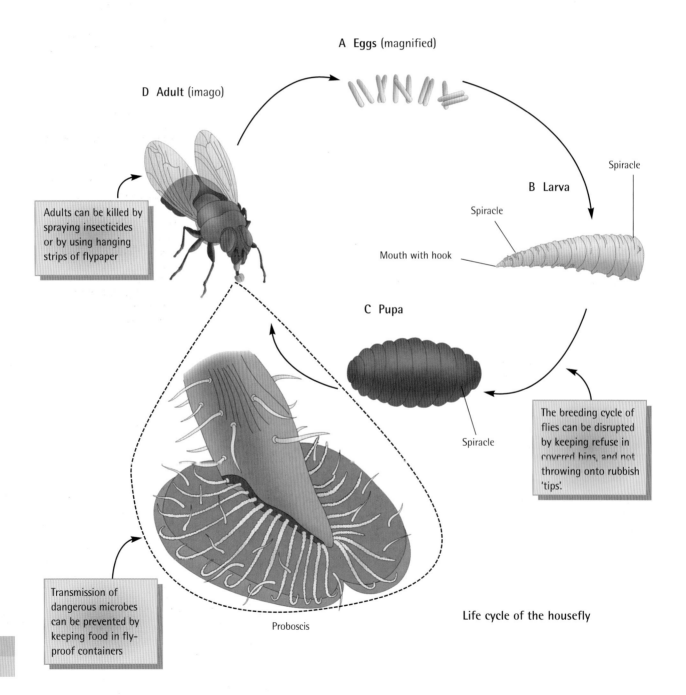

A Eggs (magnified)

D Adult (imago)

Adults can be killed by spraying insecticides or by using hanging strips of flypaper

B Larva

Spiracle

Spiracle

Mouth with hook

C Pupa

Spiracle

The breeding cycle of flies can be disrupted by keeping refuse in covered bins, and not throwing onto rubbish 'tips'.

Transmission of dangerous microbes can be prevented by keeping food in fly-proof containers

Proboscis

Life cycle of the housefly

The life cycle of *Plasmodium*

The *Anopheles* mosquito is the **vector** for the pathogen *Plasmodium*. *Plasmodium* multiplies in the stomach wall of the mosquito, then migrates to the salivary glands.

Adult mosquitoes can be controlled by insecticides, such as DDT, sprayed onto their resting places.

Plasmodium is the protoctist that causes malaria.

It can reproduce sexually inside the mosquito, and the resulting variation (see page 208) makes the production of successful vaccines very difficult.

1
An infected mosquito passes on parasites to an uninfected human. *Plasmodium* passes down the piercing mouthparts from the mosquito's salivary glands.

☐ = point of control

Control methods include:
- sleeping under mosquito nets to prevent biting
- spraying of insect-repellent chemicals onto the skin
- wearing long-sleeved clothes during the evening (time when most likely to be bitten).

4
An uninfected mosquito picks up parasites from the blood of an infected person.

Plasmodium

Liver

3
Parasites released from the liver invade red blood cells where they feed on haemoglobin and divide by **multiple fission**. The red blood cells filled with parasites burst and release the parasites into the blood.

Effects on the red blood cells cause many of the symptoms of malaria:
- tiredness, since fewer red blood cells means less oxygen is transported
- fever, as the red blood cells burst.

2
Parasites multiply rapidly in the human's liver, and are then released into the blood.

Drugs such as Paludrin and Larium control the disease by limiting entry of *Plasmodium* to the liver and reducing multiplication of the parasite.

Mosquitoes breed in bodies of still water, such as lakes and ponds. Rafts of eggs are laid which hatch into larvae, then pupae, which hang just below the water's surface to obtain oxygen through a short air tube.

This is a weak point in the vector's life cycle, and control methods include:
- spraying oil on the surface of the water, to block the breathing tubes
- draining marshes and swamps
- introducing small fish, called mosquito fish, which feed on larvae and pupae

Tonic water contains **quinine**, an anti-malarial drug. Early colonists of malarial areas could justify drinking gin and tonic!

People with sickle cell anaemia are protected from malaria. The parasite cannot feed so well inside 'sickle' cells (see page 214).

Organisms and their environment

Questions on human impacts on environment

1 The diagram on page 259 shows the layout of one type of sewage treatment works.

  a Describe the part played by aerobic bacteria in this type of sewage treatment works.
  b Name the useful gas produced by the anaerobic digester.
  c Why is this gas useful?
  d This gas can also be a pollutant - explain why.
  e Explain what might happen if the treatment failed, and sewage was allowed to enter the river.
  f Explain the function of the chlorination tank.

2 Two of the symptoms of malaria are fever and fatigue. What causes these symptoms?

3 **a** The diseases AIDS, hookworm, athlete's foot and malaria are caused by a number of different organisms. Match up each of these diseases with the type of organism which causes it.

A	AIDS	1	nematode
B	hookworm	2	protoctistan
C	athlete's foot	3	virus
D	malaria	4	fungus

  b Give *one* way in which each of the diseases is spread.

4 Malaria is a disease which is common in many tropical countries.

  a Complete the paragraphs describing some aspects of this disease, using terms from the following list. You may use each term once, more than once or not at all.

  liver, red blood cells, fever, vector, parasite, mosquito, plasmodium, anopheles, white blood cells, muscles, brain damage, anticoagulant, water, kidney

  Malaria is caused by a protoctistan called _____, which is a _____ on humans. The disease-causing organism is carried from one human to another by a _____ of the genus _____ – this second organism is therefore a _____ for the disease.

  The parasite breeds inside the _____ and the _____ of the human. It is able to enter the blood since the biting insect includes an _____ in its saliva and so the human blood does not clot quickly enough to act as a barrier. An infected human will soon suffer from _____, and many people die each year from the effects of this disease.

  b Describe *three* ways in which malaria may be controlled. Explain why each method has had some success.

  c Explain why it is very difficult to develop a vaccine to malaria.

Index